Contract Cheating in Higher Education

"Contract cheating represents a looming disaster for post-secondary education, and this collection provides coverage of basic concepts, advanced theory, and practical solutions that are suitable for teaching faculty, policymakers, and scholars alike. The editors and contributors represent the most sophisticated thinkers on this topic and a wide range of perspectives that will set the agenda for the study and prevention of contract cheating. This volume is an invaluable contribution to the field."

—David Rettinger, President Emeritus, *International Center for Academic Integrity*, USA

"This is a timely book, global and multi-disciplinary in scope, that will serve to establish a coherent body of knowledge on the problem of contract cheating from some of the world's leading academic integrity researchers. It should be added to the library collections of higher education providers worldwide."

—Rowena Harper, Director, *Centre for Learning and Teaching, Edith Cowan University*, Australia

"Contract cheating is a virus infecting quality teaching and learning around the world, supported in part by unwitting educators and educational leaders who create the conditions under which this virus thrives and spreads. This first edited book on contract cheating provides the life-saving vaccine as long as educators, educational leaders, quality assurance agencies, and world leaders choose to apply its lessons towards the goal of eradicating this virus and saving our global education system."

—Tricia Bertram Gallant, Director, *Office of Academic Integrity, UC San Diego*, USA

"This book is both timely and invaluable. It addresses the growing challenge of contract cheating to the standards and the reputation of higher education from a rich diversity of perspectives. It is sometimes difficult to see beyond the boundaries of the University when addressing these issues, but through the expertise of these authors, we see how contract cheating is a global industry and equally how we all have agency in tackling it."

—David Sadler, Chair, *Universities Australia Academic Integrity Working Group*

Sarah Elaine Eaton
Guy J. Curtis
Brenda M. Stoesz • Joseph Clare
Kiata Rundle • Josh Seeland
Editors

Contract Cheating in Higher Education

Global Perspectives on Theory, Practice, and Policy

Editors
Sarah Elaine Eaton
Werklund School of Education
University of Calgary
Calgary, AB, Canada

Brenda M. Stoesz
The Centre for the Advancement
of Teaching and Learning
University of Manitoba
Winnipeg, MB, Canada

Kiata Rundle
Discipline of Psychology and
School of Law
Murdoch University
Murdoch, WA, Australia

Guy J. Curtis
School of Psychological Science
University of Western Australia
Perth, WA, Australia

Joseph Clare
Law School
University of Western Australia
Perth, WA, Australia

Josh Seeland
Academic Integrity & Copyright
Assiniboine Community College
Brandon, MB, Canada

ISBN 978-3-031-12679-6   ISBN 978-3-031-12680-2 (eBook)
https://doi.org/10.1007/978-3-031-12680-2

© The Editor(s) (if applicable) and The Author(s), under exclusive licence to Springer Nature Switzerland AG 2022
This work is subject to copyright. All rights are solely and exclusively licensed by the Publisher, whether the whole or part of the material is concerned, specifically the rights of translation, reprinting, reuse of illustrations, recitation, broadcasting, reproduction on microfilms or in any other physical way, and transmission or information storage and retrieval, electronic adaptation, computer software, or by similar or dissimilar methodology now known or hereafter developed.
The use of general descriptive names, registered names, trademarks, service marks, etc. in this publication does not imply, even in the absence of a specific statement, that such names are exempt from the relevant protective laws and regulations and therefore free for general use.
The publisher, the authors, and the editors are safe to assume that the advice and information in this book are believed to be true and accurate at the date of publication. Neither the publisher nor the authors or the editors give a warranty, expressed or implied, with respect to the material contained herein or for any errors or omissions that may have been made. The publisher remains neutral with regard to jurisdictional claims in published maps and institutional affiliations.

This Palgrave Macmillan imprint is published by the registered company Springer Nature Switzerland AG.
The registered company address is: Gewerbestrasse 11, 6330 Cham, Switzerland

In the time between this book being an idea and becoming a reality, we lost a giant in the field of academic integrity, contract cheating research, and advocacy—Professor Tracey Bretag. Tracey was a friend, mentor, and colleague whose work on contract cheating has been, and will remain, highly impactful, as can be seen by her name being peppered liberally among the citations in this book. Tracey is sadly missed, and we encourage people to get to know about her lasting influence on our field and our lives through the tributes to her published in the journal she founded: the International Journal for Educational Integrity *(see Eaton et al., 2020).*
It was really Tracey who brought the editorial team and authors of this book all together, however indirectly, through her constant commitment to building a global community for academic integrity. In her final book, A Research Agenda for Academic Integrity *(Bretag, ed., 2020), she laid the groundwork for future research on academic integrity, including contract cheating. Her work continues to inspire many of us all over the world and this book is evidence of her enduring impact on the field.*

REFERENCES

Bretag, T. (Ed.). (2020). A research agenda for academic integrity. Cheltenham, UK: Edward Elgar Publishing.

Eaton, S. E., Titchener, H., Rogerson, A., Mahmud, S., Prentice, F., Curtis, G. et al. (2020). In memory of Tracey Bretag: A collection of tributes. [Editorial]. International Journal for Educational Integrity, 16, 15 https://doi.org/10.1007/s40979-020-00066-2

Preface

Contract cheating is an emerging hot topic in higher education generally and academic integrity specifically. Although the term contract cheating was first published in 2006, more than half of the academic journal articles on contract cheating have been published since just 2019 (Lancaster, 2022). The International Center for Academic Integrity publishes a "Reader" of journal articles so that people new to the field of academic integrity can become familiar with key literature. In the first edition of the Reader in 2012, there were no papers on contract cheating. In the second edition of the Reader in 2022, nearly 30% of the papers listed are on contract cheating (Rogerson et al., 2022). The 2016 *Handbook of Academic Integrity* contained three chapters on contract cheating. The forthcoming second edition of the *Handbook* has a dedicated section on contract cheating containing ten planned chapters. And, here, we have released the first ever book on contract cheating.

According to *The Simpsons*, there are three ways to do something: the right way, the wrong way, and the Homer Simpson way—which is the wrong way, only faster. We can now add a fourth way to this list, the way we produced this book—which is the right way, only slower.

This book started as two projects, with two teams of three editors, each team based on separate continents, with editors living in four cities. The book finished as one project with one team of six editors based on two continents, with editors living in five cities. Even though most of us have barely been allowed to travel in the past two years because of the COVID-19 pandemic, it has been quite a journey.

The story of how this book came together starts with the Australian team (Kiata, Joe, and Guy). In mid-2019, Kiata presented research on "reasoning and individual differences underpinning contract cheating," at the Higher Education Research and Development Society of Australasia's annual conference. This presentation caught the eye of a publishing representative from Palgrave who was aware of the increasing interest in contract cheating as a topic and had noticed a lack of theory-based perspectives on it. The representative contacted Kiata, who was working on her PhD under the supervision of Joe and Guy, to ask whether she would like to consider proposing a book. As a PhD student, writing a whole book looked a little daunting, so Guy suggested an edited book, with separately authored chapters. This seemed like a more manageable idea, especially as Kiata, Guy, and Joe, had just co-written a chapter in another edited book and felt as though they knew how this was done. Leaving Kiata to focus on her PhD, Guy began slowly putting together a book proposal in the first half of 2020, which included contacting prospective chapter authors.

Half a world away in Canada, the team of Sarah, Brenda, and Josh were doing much the same thing. Separated by more than 1100 kilometres, the three of them correspond regularly via email about academic integrity and contract cheating. Sarah proposed that the three of them start working on an edited volume. The book idea started with a series of emails one day when Josh, as he was sitting in on a webinar offered by a commercial file-sharing company, backchannelling to Brenda and Sarah, who were unable to join the virtual event in real time (J. Seeland, personal communication, 10 June 2020). The exchange ended with Sarah suggesting an edited book and the other two agreeing. Sarah's original idea was that the book could be released in 2022, which would recognise the 50th anniversary of the first attempt to legislate against contract cheating in Canada (see Eaton, 2022), catalysing further action towards legislation that exists in countries such as Australia, New Zealand, and Ireland. Within a few weeks, they had a book proposal under development.

As Guy's list of chapters and authors was coming together nicely, in August 2020 he received an email from Phill Dawson letting him know that Sarah was also working on a contract cheating book—Sarah had asked Phill to write a chapter, but Phill declined because he had already committed to write for the Australian team. Phill said that, as far as he knew, Sarah and her team had their book in the proposal stage, just like the book being developed out of Australia. With this new information to hand, Guy emailed Sarah to discuss their separate projects.

Guy and Sarah managed to organise a meeting via a Zoom video call, which felt like a solid first achievement being 14 hours and an international-dateline apart. They discussed various ideas, with two main ones in mind: (1) pushing on with separate, potentially competing books with some overlap and differences in content, or (2) joining forces to make one book and make it the best it can be. You know which one we picked, and that's the way we all became the Brady Bunch.

From this point on, progress on the book was steady and consistent. We got the hang of Zoom calls across anywhere between three and five time zones—depending on the seasons. We contacted authors who had agreed to write two chapters with the good news that they now only had to write one. The proposal took shape, and it got submitted, reviewed, revised, and approved. From there, the writing and editing commenced. What we have now, about three years since Palgrave first suggested that a book on contract cheating would be a good idea, is a book on contract cheating.

We began as an editorial team who had never met in person and knew one another only from reading each other's published works. Even if we had wanted to meet up in person during the project, travel restrictions resulting from COVID-19 prevented that. So, we committed to the book and to each other and we got on realising our shared vision. At the conclusion of the project, we still have yet to all meet face-to-face, but through regular synchronous virtual meetings, email, and asynchronous work, we have developed friendships that transcend geographical distance and a new appreciation for the need to address contract cheating at a global level.

Calgary, Canada	Sarah Elaine Eaton
Perth, Australia	Guy J. Curtis
Winnipeg, Canada	Brenda M. Stoesz
Perth, Australia	Kiata Rundle
Murdoch, Australia	Joseph Clare
Brandon, Canada	Josh Seeland

References

Eaton, S. E. (2022). Contract cheating in Canada: A comprehensive overview. In S. E. Eaton & J. Christensen Hughes (Eds.), *Academic integrity in Canada: An enduring and essential challenge* (pp. 165–187). Springer.

Lancaster, T. (2022). The past and future of contract cheating. In D. A. Rettinger & T. Bertram Gallant. *Cheating academic integrity: Lessons from 30 years of research* (pp. 45–63). Jossey-Bass.

Rogerson, A., Bertram Gallant, T., Cullen, C., & Ives, R. T. (2022). Celebrating 30 years of research on academic integrity: A review of the most influential pieces. In D. A. Rettinger & T. Bertram Gallant. *Cheating academic integrity: Lessons from 30 years of research* (pp. 201–231). Jossey-Bass.

Acknowledgements

Although a six-person editorial team is rather a lot for one book, we, and the chapter authors, are not the only people who have contributed to it. We would like to thank the anonymous reviewers of our book proposal, who provided helpful feedback on the initially devised content and structure. We would also like to thank the helpful team from Palgrave, who were quick to answer our questions and were on-the-ball with reminders about our deadlines.

There are many more people for us to thank, including our partners and families, who put up with us working extra-long days and nights to make this book a reality. To our families and close friends and colleagues who support us, we are forever grateful for you.

Contents

1 Contract Cheating: An Introduction to the Problem   1
Guy J. Curtis, Joseph Clare, Kiata Rundle, Sarah Elaine Eaton, Brenda M. Stoesz, and Josh Seeland

2 What Can We Learn from Measuring Crime When Looking to Quantify the Prevalence and Incidence of Contract Cheating?   15
Joseph Clare and Kiata Rundle

3 Limitations of Contract Cheating Research   29
Veronika Krásničan, Tomáš Foltýnek, and Dita Henek Dlabolová

4 Essay Mills and Contract Cheating from a Legal Point of View   43
Michael Draper

5 Leveraging College Copyright Ownership Against File-Sharing and Contract Cheating Websites   61
Josh Seeland, Sarah Elaine Eaton, and Brenda M. Stoesz

6 The Encouragement of File Sharing Behaviours Through Technology and Social Media: Impacts on Student Cheating Behaviours and Academic Piracy 77
Ann M. Rogerson

7 Higher Education Assessment Design 91
Wendy Sutherland-Smith and Phillip Dawson

8 Critical Thinking as an Antidote to Contract Cheating 107
Brenda M. Stoesz, Sarah Elaine Eaton, and Josh Seeland

9 Contract Cheating and the Dark Triad Traits 123
Lidia Baran and Peter K. Jonason

10 Contract Cheating: The Influence of Attitudes and Emotions 139
Guy J. Curtis and Isabeau K. Tindall

11 Applying Situational Crime Prevention Techniques to Contract Cheating 153
Joseph Clare

12 Presentation, Properties and Provenance: The Three Ps of Identifying Evidence of Contract Cheating in Student Assignments 169
Robin Crockett

13 "(Im)possible to Prove": Formalising Academic Judgement Evidence in Contract Cheating Cases Using Bibliographic Forensics 185
Cath Ellis, Ann M. Rogerson, David House, and Kane Murdoch

14 Aligning Academic Quality and Standards with Academic Integrity 199
Irene Glendinning

15	Addressing Contract Cheating Through Staff-Student Partnerships Thomas Lancaster	219
16	The Extortionate Cost of Contract Cheating Terisha Veeran-Colton, Lesley Sefcik, and Jonathan Yorke	233
17	The Rise of Contract Cheating in Graduate Education Ceceilia Parnther	251
18	Listening to Ghosts: A Qualitative Study of Narratives from Contract Cheating Writers from the 1930s Onwards Sarah Elaine Eaton, Brenda M. Stoesz, and Josh Seeland	271
19	Assessment Brokering and Collaboration: Ghostwriter and Student Academic Literacies Emma J. Thacker	287
20	Contract Cheating: A Summative Look Back and a Path Forward Sarah Elaine Eaton, Brenda M. Stoesz, Josh Seeland, Guy J. Curtis, Joseph Clare, and Kiata Rundle	303
Index		313

Notes on Contributors

Lidia Baran is an Assistant Professor at the Institute of Psychology, the University of Silesia in Katowice, Poland. She is an academic dishonesty and honesty researcher and a psychologists' professional ethics educator.

Joseph Clare is Associate Professor of Criminology in the Law School at the University of Western Australia. He is an author of over 45 journal articles and book chapters and is a multi-award-winning teacher and researcher. His research focuses on policing, applied evaluation, and academic integrity.

Robin Crockett is University Academic Integrity Officer at the University of Northampton, UK, and Academic Visitor at Loughborough University, UK. He has an extensive publication record in time-series and Fourier analysis and is now extending aspects of that research for authorship attribution in contract cheating.

Guy J. Curtis is a Senior Lecturer in the School of Psychological Science at The University of Western Australia. He conducts research on academic integrity and applied psychology. He is an author of over 50 journal articles and book chapters and is a multi-award-winning university teacher.

Phillip Dawson is Professor of Higher Education Learning and Teaching, and Associate Director of the Centre for Research in Assessment and Digital Learning (CRADLE) at Deakin University, Melbourne, Australia. He researches assessment, feedback, and cheating. His most recent book is *Defending Assessment Security in a Digital World* (2021).

Dita Henek Dlabolová is an Executive Manager of the European Network for Academic Integrity. She has been involved in several international academic integrity projects, and she is a teacher and trainer in the field of academic integrity with the main focus on plagiarism prevention.

Michael Draper is Deputy Pro Vice Chancellor for Education at Swansea University, UK, Co-chair of the Welsh Integrity and Assessment Network, and a member of the UK Quality Assurance Agency Advisory Group on Academic Integrity.

Sarah Elaine Eaton is an Associate Professor in the Werklund School of Education at the University of Calgary, Canada. She is a nationally and internationally awarded scholar for her research on academic integrity.

Cath Ellis is a Professor in the School of the Arts and Media, in the Faculty of Arts, Design, and Architecture at UNSW Australia. Her research and advocacy on the problem of contract cheating was recognised by *Times Higher Education*, naming her as one of 2019 'People of the Year'.

Tomáš Foltýnek is a Lecturer at the Faculty of Informatics, Masaryk University, Czechia. He is President of the Board of the European Network for Academic Integrity. Since 2008, he has been involved in and has led several projects on plagiarism and academic integrity; since 2013, he has been organising conferences on this topic.

Irene Glendinning is an Associate Professor at Coventry University, UK. Her current role is institutional lead on academic integrity. Her research interests include academic integrity policies, quality assurance, pedagogy, and student experience.

David House holds an LLB from the University of Technology Sydney and has worked for nearly a decade in the tertiary education sector as a misconduct investigator and ombudsman. His focus is on digital-forensic detection methods and best practices for collaboration among academic and professional staff to stop contract cheating.

Peter K. Jonason is an Associate Professor at the University of Padua (IT) and University of Cardinal Stefan Wyszyński (POL). He is a world leading expert in research on the dark side of personality from an evolutionary perspective. He holds a PhD (2009) from the New Mexico State University.

Veronika Krásničan is a PhD student in the Department of Law and Social Sciences at the Faculty of Business and Economics, Mendel

University in Brno. She is a leading expert on contract cheating in the Czech Republic and in 2021 she received The ENAI Outstanding Student Award.

Thomas Lancaster is Senior Teaching Fellow in Computing at Imperial College London, UK. Along with Robert Clarke, he coined the term contract cheating and is in-demand international speaker on topics relating to academic integrity.

Kane Murdoch is the Manager of Complaints, Appeals, and Misconduct at Macquarie University, Australia. He is an award-winning misconduct investigator, with particular expertise in the detection of contract cheating.

Ceceilia Parnther is an Assistant Professor and doctoral programme coordinator in the Department of Administrative and Instructional Leadership in the School of Education at St. John's University. She researches equity in higher education, specifically, the role of leadership, policy, and practice on student success and academic integrity.

Ann M. Rogerson is Professor of Higher Education and Associate Dean (Education) for the Faculty of Business and Law at the University of Wollongong (Australia). She is nationally and internationally recognised for her work on textual patterns to detect breaches of academic integrity and areas of file-sharing and paraphrasing tool use.

Kiata Rundle is a PhD candidate in Psychology and Criminology at Murdoch University, in Western Australia. Her research examines contract cheating through psychological and criminological perspectives. She has several published journal articles and book chapters.

Josh Seeland is the Manager of library services at Assiniboine Community College (ACC) in Brandon, Manitoba, Canada, where his portfolio items include academic integrity and copyright. He is a member of the Manitoba Academic Integrity Network (MAIN) and chairs ACC's Academic Integrity Advisory Committee.

Lesley Sefcik is a Senior Lecturer and academic integrity advisor at Curtin University, Australia. She provides university-wide teaching, advice, and research related to academic integrity. She is known for her work on remote invigilation of online assessment and extortion related to contract cheating.

Brenda M. Stoesz is a Senior Faculty Specialist at The Centre for the Advancement of Teaching and Learning, University of Manitoba, Winnipeg, Manitoba, Canada, where she develops educational resources and professional development opportunities for post-secondary academic staff and conducts research on academic integrity.

Wendy Sutherland-Smith has been researching academic integrity for 30 years. She has published on multiple aspects of academic integrity, including plagiarism, collusion, contract cheating, and ethics. She is an Adjunct Associate Professor at the Centre for Research in Assessment and Digital Learning (CRADLE) in Deakin University, Australia.

Emma J. Thacker is an administrator at the University of Toronto, specialising in governance, policy, and ombuds work. She has held several positions to support institutional quality assurance, academic integrity, and quasi-judicial affairs. She has research interests in higher education policy and academic integrity.

Isabeau K. Tindall is a research associate at the Future of Work Institute, Curtin University. She has conducted research on the relationship between negative emotionality and areas such as plagiarism and need satisfaction. Recently, her research focuses on work design and how to ensure good work design practices.

Terisha Veeran-Colton is an Adjunct with the Office of the Academic Registrar at Curtin University in Western Australia. She holds a PhD from The University of Melbourne. Her research interests include geography, environmental psychology, and drowning prevention. More recently, she has published in the field of academic integrity.

Jonathan Yorke is the Interim Deputy Vice-Chancellor, Academic, at Curtin University, responsible for the strategic leadership of learning, teaching, and the student experience. He has a particular interest in assessment and the promotion of academic integrity.

List of Figures

Fig. 10.1	The theory of planned behaviour (TPB) applied to contract cheating (white filled boxes) and extended to include current and anticipated affective states (black filled boxes)	144
Fig. 12.1	The zipped file folder structures for DOCX (left) and ODT (right). Folder names are in bold and folder contents are indented (↳)	178
Fig. 14.1	CIQG project—Concerns from AQABs about corruption in student assessment, n = 69 (Glendinning, I., Orim, S., & King, A. (2019). Policies and Actions of Accreditation and Quality Assurance Bodies to Counter Corruption in Higher Education, published by CHEA/CIQG, 2019, p. 18: https://www.chea.org/quality-assurance-combatting-academic-corruption-resources)	201
Fig. 14.2	Aligning institutional academic integrity strategy with quality and standards	208
Fig. 16.1	Graphical representation of the contract cheating scenario	235
Fig. 16.2	Consequences of contract cheating broken down into sub-themes	236
Fig. 19.1	Contract cheating literacies spaces, a fourth space	296

LIST OF TABLES

Table 2.1	Comparing and classifying the various approaches to measuring crime and contract cheating	24
Table 3.1	Summary of limitations within the reviewed papers	36
Table 4.1	Relevant section of the New Zealand Education Act 1989	47
Table 4.2	Key statements made in the House of Representatives throughout the TEQSA Amendment (Prohibiting Academic Cheating Services) Bill debate in 2020	51
Table 11.1	The 25 techniques of situational crime prevention, with crime prevention examples of each technique (from Clarke, 2017)	158
Table 11.2	Placing a range of proposed interventions within the framework of the 25 techniques of SCP (adapted from Clarke, 2017)	163
Table 13.1	Bibliographic categories, explanations and examples with exemplar rationale	190
Table 15.1	The categorised impact of contract cheating as a social issue (Khan et al., 2020)	222
Table 16.1	Consequences of plagiarism in relation to age, reproduced from Gilmore (2009)	238
Table 18.1	Overview of sources	276

CHAPTER 1

Contract Cheating: An Introduction to the Problem

Guy J. Curtis, Joseph Clare, Kiata Rundle,
Sarah Elaine Eaton, Brenda M. Stoesz, and Josh Seeland

Contract cheating is the outsourcing of students' assessment work in an educational context. We have a bit more to say about the definition of the term contract cheating later, but this will do for now. Although the term contract cheating is relatively recent, students outsourcing assessment work in higher education is not. For example, as a college student in the 1960s, the 45th President of the United States is reported to have outsourced both his exams and his homework. As his niece, Mary Trump, explains:

G. J. Curtis (✉)
School of Psychological Science, University of Western Australia, Crawley, WA, Australia
e-mail: guy.curtis@uwa.edu.au

J. Clare
School of Law, University of Western Australia, Crawley, WA, Australia
e-mail: joe.clare@uwa.edu.au

K. Rundle
Murdoch University, Murdoch, WA, Australia
e-mail: Kiata.Rundle@murdoch.edu.au

© The Author(s), under exclusive license to Springer Nature Switzerland AG 2022
S. E. Eaton et al. (eds.), *Contract Cheating in Higher Education*, https://doi.org/10.1007/978-3-031-12680-2_1

Aware of the Wharton [Business] School's reputation, Donald set his sights on the University of Pennsylvania. Unfortunately, even though [his sister] Maryanne had been doing his homework for him, she couldn't take his tests, and Donald worried that his grade point average, which put him far from the top of his class, would scuttle his efforts to get accepted. To hedge his bets he enlisted Joe Shapiro, a smart kid with a reputation for being a good test taker, to take his SATs for him. That was much easier to pull off in the days before photo IDs and computerized records. (Trump, 2020, p. 72)

Outsourced cheating for payment has appeared in the storylines of recent popular television shows. For instance, in the series *Sex Education*, a school student character, Maeve, supports herself financially in the absence of her parents by charging other students to do their homework. This scheme ultimately leads to blackmail when the headmaster's son, Adam, wins an essay prize for a piece that he had paid Maeve to write. Maeve threatens to reveal this fact and embarrass the headmaster in order to save herself from expulsion. In the crime drama *Ozark*, the precocious teenager Jonah Byrde runs a profitable "homework service", which, in one episode, he uses to launder $5000 in drug money.

Back to reality, instances of contract cheating have been exposed widely in the media in recent years. A cheating service called EduBirdie paid hundreds of highly followed YouTubers to promote their website (Bretag, 2019). The *New York Times* reported the existence of a Facebook group of over 50,000 people who are paid to write students' assignments (Stockman & Mureithi, 2019). *Forbes* magazine interviewed 52 students who use the services of a multi-billion-dollar "study help" company—48 of these students (over 92%) used the site for cheating (Adams, 2021). In 2021, the Tertiary Education and Quality and Standards Agency in Australia sent 34 universities over 2600 cases of suspected contract cheating that had been identified by researchers (Matchett, 2021).

S. E. Eaton
University of Calgary, Calgary, AB, Canada
e-mail: seaton@ucalgary.ca

B. M. Stoesz
University of Manitoba, Winnipeg, MB, Canada
e-mail: Brenda.Stoesz@umanitoba.ca

J. Seeland
Assiniboine Community College, Brandon, MB, Canada
e-mail: seelandjl@Assiniboine.net

As the example of Donald Trump's SAT exam impersonator illustrates, the problem of contract cheating is not limited to written assignments. Research indicates that all kinds of assessments are vulnerable to contract cheating (Bretag et al., 2019b). In fact, students who outsource exams are caught relatively less frequently than students who outsource written work (Harper et al., 2021). Contract cheating services can provide students with answers to tests or dissertation proposals, pre-prepared presentations and speeches, or mathematics and statistics calculations, computer code, multiple-choice test completion, and annotated bibliographies—just to name a few of the options for sale in the market (Rowland et al., 2018). Intuitive wisdom among higher education teachers is that authentic assessments (those which more resemble real life and specific local knowledge) should be hard to outsource, yet contract cheating providers readily provide ghostwritten responses to authentic assessments (Ellis et al., 2020). Even an oral defense of submitted written work, often called a *viva*, can be outsourced (Bretag et al., 2019b).

But, just because contract cheating is happening, why should those who work in educational contexts care? Is contract cheating just a peccadillo that peeves persnickety pedants or is it catastrophic clandestine criminality? Alliteration aside, for our part, we think it is acutely serious. When a student engages in contract cheating their education assessment work is substantially, if not wholly, completed by another person. If the outsourced assessment is not detected as being outsourced, the student receives academic credit toward their qualification that may not reflect their own knowledge, skills, and abilities. Moreover, outsourced work means that the student did not engage in the study and the learning that the assessment task was designed to promote. The gravity of this situation is best illustrated with a literal concrete example involving gravity. Imagine an engineering student who pays another person to complete their major assignments on how to design sturdy and resilient physical structures. This student is awarded their degree, obtains a job in construction engineering, and designs a bridge that will not bear the weight of the traffic that passes over it. The bridge turns to rubble shortly after construction with some drivers plunging to their deaths while others are crushed in their cars below.

Aside from raising serious questions about the integrity of credentials in higher education, contract cheating poses a diabolical problem for higher education institutions and markers to detect outsourced student assessments. Worldwide, higher education has become increasingly "massified" in the past three decades (Bretag et al., 2019a). Massification means that higher education is delivered to many more students than in the past, without resources increasing at the same rate as student numbers. This mismatch between student numbers and resources has led to larger classes and less personalized relationships between teachers and students. In an early twentieth-century model of higher education, where a single academic staff member tutored a handful of students, it may have been relatively easy for the educator to recognize assessment work that was different from what the student typically produced and thus suspect that the work was written by someone else. However, in contemporary classes, where student enrolments can number in the thousands and marking of assessments may be undertaken by low-paid time-poor precariously-employed adjunct teachers, it is unlikely that those grading students' work will know their students well enough to detect inconsistencies in writing quality and style.

A technological solution that has been widely adopted in higher education to help ensure academic integrity is text-matching software. Text-matching software compares the text of students' assessments to databases of academic journal articles, books, websites, and previous students' papers (Davis & Carroll, 2009). The software conveniently highlights matching text that allows markers to assess whether uncited or improperly cited text may constitute plagiarism. Such plagiarism often involves a lack of awareness of rules for citation and referencing on the part of the student, and detection of matched text can provide opportunities for education professionals to assist students to learn these sometimes-arcane conventions. Indeed, evidence from the past 30 years suggests that the implementation of text-matching software has aided students' understanding of referencing and corresponded with a decline in rates of copy-paste plagiarism (Curtis, 2022). However, although text-matching software may help to detect plagiarism by students bamboozled by referencing rules, students who engage in skullduggery by coopting another person to produce a freshly written assignment may evade detection by text-matching software. Indeed, evidence from numerous sources suggests that outsourced assessments commonly go undetected (Ahsan et al., 2021; Awdry et al., 2021; Bretag et al., 2019b, 2019a).

Defining Contract Cheating

Various authors have used definitions of contract cheating that include and exclude certain behaviors, actors, and contingencies from the definition. For example, it is an ongoing question whether contract cheating is limited to assessment outsourcing that is done for payment by a third party who is a stranger to the student, whether this term also applies to assessments that are freely completed by a student's family member, and whether the term applies to both bespoke and pre-written assessments.

Clarke and Lancaster (2006) were the first authors to publish the term contract cheating, where they used it to describe "the submission of work by students for academic credit which the students have paid contractors to write for them" (p. 1), and also "the process of offering the process of completing an assignment for a student out to tender" (p. 2). This definition drew from their work examining the outsourcing of students' assessments in computer coding via an internet-mediated site where coders bid for jobs. The specific use of the word "contracting" implies an agreement between a buyer and a seller to undertake commissioned work.

The influential work of Walker and Townley (2012) expanded upon Clarke and Lancaster's (2006) definition by removing the necessity for a tender process. Walker and Townley described contract cheating as "a form of academic dishonesty, where students contract out their coursework to writers or workers, usually found via the internet, in order to submit the purchased assignments as their own work" (p. 27). Nonetheless, the definition retained the concept that contract cheating is the provision of made-to-order assessments for payment.

The definition of contract cheating was broadened substantially by Bretag et al. (2019a), who conducted the largest survey to date of student assessment outsourcing. They suggested that the term "encompass[es] a cluster of practices relating to the outsourcing of students' assessment to third parties, whether or not these entities are commercial providers" (Bretag et al., 2019a, p. 1838). Specifically, they defined contract cheating as:

> ...*where a student gets someone – a third party – to complete an assignment or an exam for them. This third party might be a friend, family member, fellow student or staff member who assists the student as a favour. It might be a pre-written assignment which has been obtained from an assignment 'mill'. The third party may also be a paid service, advertised locally or online.* (Bretag et al., 2019a, p. 1838)

Bretag et al.'s (2019a) definition explicitly adds examinations as an assessment that can be outsourced, not limiting contract cheating to pre-done assessments. Additionally, their definition captures pre-written work in addition to newly written assessments. Moreover, the definition removes the need for outsourcing to be paid to be considered contract cheating. In contrast, some authors have taken to using the term "commercial contract cheating" (e.g., Newton, 2018; Curtis et al., 2021) to distinguish contract cheating that necessarily involves an exchange or payment for a commercial purpose, from outsourcing that may be unpaid. From the development of definitions, and the recency of both broad and specific definitions, we can see that agreeing on a settled definition is still a work in progress.

Another question to consider in the definition of contract cheating is whether it falls within the broader concept of plagiarism. Plagiarism itself is a word with "no singular or absolute definition" (Eaton, 2021, p. 1), but is generally taken to mean the use of others' words, work, or ideas without proper attribution. Within this general definition, then, students submitting assessment work completed by someone else in order to obtain academic credit for themselves fits the definition of plagiarism (Eaton, 2021). Before the term contract cheating was first published, Walker (1998) defined seven forms of plagiarism in higher education. According to Walker (1998), plagiarism in the form of *ghostwriting* is defined as "assignment written by third party and represented as own work" (p. 103). Defined in this way, ghostwriting as a form of plagiarism involves the outsourcing of assessment work by the student to another person, whether paid or unpaid, and therefore aligns with Bretag et al.'s (2019a) definition of contract cheating. Indeed, it is common to see authors on contract cheating refer to the suppliers of outsourced assignments as ghostwriters. Still, who or what constitutes a ghostwriter is itself a contested definition (Eaton, 2021).

In this book, authors have used, either implicitly or explicitly, various definitions of contract cheating—and related terminologies such as ghostwriters, essay/paper mills, and plagiarism. To reflect the evolving nature of the term contract cheating, as Editors, we have taken a neutral position on the definition, and not imposed a single definition within the book.

An Overview of the Book

Contract cheating is a problem with many moving parts. To tackle contract cheating successfully, there must be barriers against it at the societal, institutional, and individual levels (Rundle et al., 2020). To understand how best to construct these barriers, we must also know how much cheating happens, how contract cheating businesses work, why students cheat, and what actions against cheating are effective. To do all of these things, we can draw on basic theoretical, translational, and applied research from numerous fields of study to inform best practices in reducing contract cheating.

This book contains chapters by expert authors and leading researchers in academic integrity and contract cheating who come from a diverse range of academic backgrounds including education, faculty development, psychology, library sciences, law, criminology, computer science, and business. The chapters present a diversity of perspectives covering the what, why, where, and how questions about contract cheating from complimentary perspectives. The book brings together the latest research in a series of chapters that, taken together, provide a broad and deep overview of the problem of contract cheating in higher education. A starting point for the book is the question: How many students engage in contract cheating and how often do they do it?

Various studies have attempted to estimate what proportion of students engage in contract cheating (i.e., the prevalence of contract cheating) and how often they do it (i.e., the incidence of contract cheating). Some of these studies have made dramatic media headlines, for example, "Contract cheating 'ripe to explode'" (Ross, 2018 reporting on Bretag et al., 2019a) and "Are you part of the 11 per cent who have cheated at University?" (Karvelas, 2021 reporting on Curtis et al., 2021). However, the academic studies these media stories report differ in their definitions of contract cheating and their methods and sources of data collection. As a consequence, the prevalence of contract cheating has been estimated in various studies as anywhere between about 0.3% and 45% of students (Newton, 2018).

In truth, we do not know what proportion of students engage in contract cheating or how often they do it. Still, this does not mean that we cannot make some educated guesses and consider what we would need to know to make our estimates more accurate. Two chapters in this book consider the question of how to estimate the prevalence and incidence of contact cheating (Clare & Rundle, 2022; Krásničan et al., 2022). Krásničan et al. reviewed the methodology of studies that have used self-report surveys to estimate the prevalence of contract cheating and provided guidance for future researchers on how to increase the validity of such work. Drawing on criminology methods, Clare and Rundle

(2022) discuss the many sources of information that can potentially be triangulated to estimate the extent of contract cheating in higher education.

Contract cheating occurs within wider societal, legal, commercial, educational, and administrative environments. Draper's chapter outlines legal responses to contract cheating, including moves to outlaw academic cheating services in various jurisdictions. Rogerson's (2022) chapter positions academic file-sharing in the larger context of the sharing culture promoted by social media. She explains how file-sharing can underlie contract cheating and how students may be unaware of the ethics and consequences of file-sharing. The chapter by Seeland et al. explains how existing copyright laws may be employed to counteract academic file-sharing.

Why do students engage in contract cheating? A neat and plausible answer is that it is easier for someone else to do a student's assessment work for them than for them to do it for themselves. However, as H. L. Mencken (1920) said, for every question there is an answer that is "neat, plausible, and wrong" (p. 158). As noted above, contract cheating suppliers are easily accessible and contract cheaters may be rarely caught, yet the varied estimates of contract cheating's prevalence always suggest that it is something only a minority of students do. Thus, researchers have asked not only why students engage in contract cheating, but also why they do not (e.g., Rundle et al., 2019).

In this book, several chapters provide theory-based discussions of why students do, and do not, engage in contract cheating. Citing evidence that students who are dissatisfied with the educational environment engage in more contract cheating (Bretag et al., 2019a), Sutherland-Smith and Dawson (2022) explain how principles of Self-Determination Theory may be applied to assessment design to make completing assessments more satisfying for students. By extension, more satisfied students should be less inclined to engage in contract cheating. Stoesz et al.'s (2022) chapter provides an alternative assessment-and-teaching-based strategy, explaining how developing students' critical thinking skills may reduce contract cheating.

According to singer Hank Williams, the pangs of conscience experienced after infidelity mean that eventually: "your cheating heart will tell on you." This idea that a cheating heart will experience remorse, possibly leading to a confession of wrongdoing, assumes that bad actors will feel guilt-ridden. Thus, students who cheat and feel guilty may own up to their actions, but what of students who do not tend to feel guilty? Baran and Jonason's chapter considers "dark" personality traits (narcissism, Machiavellianism, and psychopathy) in students that may be associated with contract cheating and academic misconduct, and how personality predispositions to cheating may be attenuated. Their chapter may also help us understand the contract cheating by the famously narcissistic Donald Trump that we mentioned earlier. Similarly, Curtis and Tindall's (2022) chapter considers students' attitudes, current emotions, and anticipated emotions as potential psychological drivers of contract cheating behavior. In contrast, Clare's (2022) chapter outlines deterrence strategies for contract cheating based on situational crime prevention theories. This chapter's contentions inherently assume that contract cheating is less likely to occur the more difficult the situation makes its occurrence, without regard to the psychological predispositions of students.

In whatever way educators and administrators in higher education deal with the problem of contract cheating, it must be a multi-faceted approach (Rundle et al., 2020). Chapters by Crockett (2022) and Ellis et al. (2022) provide concrete practical advice for higher education professionals on how to detect contract cheating by students, with an aim of making markers and investigators the nemesis of nefarious cheating service providers. Glendinning's (2022) chapter focuses on policy design to counteract contract cheating within wider quality assurance frameworks. Considering engagement with, and contributions from students in counteracting contract cheating, Lancaster's (2022) chapter outlines successful collaborations between students and academic staff that promote academic integrity and seek to reduce contract cheating. Veeran-Colton et al.'s (2022) chapter discusses the inherent risk to students of placing themselves in a position where someone (i.e., the ghostwriter) knows that they have cheated. Importantly, they outline research which shows that alerting students to the risks of being exposed as a cheat reduces students' willingness to engage in contract cheating.

Several chapters in this book also consider the methods of contract cheating businesses and writers. Parnther's (2022) chapter outlines original research that investigates how contract cheating businesses market their services to postgraduate students. Eaton et al.'s (2022) chapter examines ghostwriters' own accounts of their experiences in the contract cheating industry and elucidates common themes among the narratives of ghostwriters who worked across a span of time, academic disciplines, and geographical locations. A new perspective on the collaboration between contracted writers and their student customers is outlined in Thacker's (2022) chapter. Thacker (2022) describes situations ranging from guided collaboration to co-authoring of papers between students and ghostwriters, which highlights that contract cheating is not universally a case of hands-off outsourcing.

In sum, this book is the most comprehensive work on contract cheating assembled to date. Our hope, as an editorial team, is that the book will provide a go-to reference for educators, researchers, and administrators who are attempting to deal with the problem of contract cheating.

REFERENCES

Adams, S. (2021, March 31). This $12 billion company is getting rich off students cheating their way through Covid. *Forbes*. https://www.forbes.com/sites/susanadams/2021/01/28/this-12-billion-company-is-getting-rich-off-students-cheating-their-way-through-covid/?sh=346bb1a4363f

Ahsan, K., Akbar, S., & Kam, B. (2021). Contract cheating in higher education: A systematic literature review and future research agenda. *Assessment & Evaluation in Higher Education*, 1–17. https://doi.org/10.1080/02602938.2021.1931660.

Awdry, R., Dawson, P., & Sutherland-Smith, W. (2021). Contract cheating: To legislate or not to legislate-is that the question? *Assessment & Evaluation in Higher Education*, 1–15. https://doi.org/10.1080/02602938.2021.1957773.

Bretag, T. (2019). Contract cheating will erode trust in science. *Nature, 574*, 599. https://doi.org/10.1038/d41586-019-03265-1

Bretag, T., Harper, R., Burton, M., Ellis, C., Newton, P., Rozenberg, P., Saddiqui, S., & van Haeringen, K. (2019a). Contract cheating: A survey of Australian university students. *Studies in Higher Education, 44*(11), 1837–1856. https://doi.org/10.1080/03075079.2018.1462788

Bretag, T., Harper, R., Burton, M., Ellis, C., Newton, P., van Haeringen, K., Saddiqui, S., & Rozenberg, P. (2019b). Contract cheating and assessment design: Exploring the relationship. *Assessment & Evaluation in Higher Education, 44*(5), 676–691. https://doi.org/10.1080/02602938.2018.1527892

Clare, J. (2022). Applying situational crime prevention techniques to contract cheating. In S. E. Eaton, G. Curtis, B. M. Stoesz, K. Rundle, J. Clare, & J. Seeland (Eds.), *Contract cheating in higher education: Global perspectives on theory, practice, and policy*. Palgrave Macmillan.

Clare, J., & Rundle, K. (2022). What can we learn from measuring crime when looking to quantify the prevalence and incidence of contract cheating? In S. E. Eaton, G. Curtis, B. M. Stoesz, K. Rundle, J. Clare, & J. Seeland (Eds.), *Contract cheating in higher education: Global perspectives on theory, practice, and policy*. Palgrave Macmillan.

Crockett, R. (2022). Presentation, properties and provenance: the three Ps of identifying evidence of contract-cheating in student assignments. In S. E. Eaton, G. Curtis, B. M. Stoesz, K. Rundle, J. Clare, & J. Seeland (Eds.), *Contract cheating in higher education: Global perspectives on theory, practice, and policy*. Palgrave Macmillan.

Clarke, R., & Lancaster, T. (2006, June). Eliminating the successor to plagiarism? Identifying the usage of contract cheating sites. In *Proceedings of 2nd International Plagiarism Conference* (pp. 19–21). Newcastle, United Kingdom.

Curtis, G. J. (2022). Trends in plagiarism and cheating prevalence: 1990–2020 and beyond (pp. 11–44). In D. Rettinger & T. Bertram Gallant (Eds.), *Cheating academic integrity: Lessons from 30 years of research*. Jossey-Bass/Wiley.

Curtis, G. J., McNeill, M., Slade, C., Tremayne, K., Harper, R., Rundle, K., & Greenaway, R. (2022). Moving beyond self-reports to estimate the prevalence of commercial contract cheating: An Australian study. *Studies in Higher Education*, 47(9), 1844-1856. https://doi.org/10.1080/03075079.2021.1972093

Davis, M., & Carroll, J. (2009). Formative feedback within plagiarism education: Is there a role for text-matching software? *International Journal for Educational Integrity*, 5(2), 58–70. https://doi.org/10.21913/IJEI.v5i2.614

Eaton, S. E. (2021). *Plagiarism in higher education: Tackling tough topics in academic integrity*. ABC-CLIO.

Eaton, S. E., Stoesz, B. M., & Seeland, J. (2022). Listening to ghosts: A qualitative study of narratives from contract cheating writers from the 1930s onwards. In S. E. Eaton, G. Curtis, B. M. Stoesz, K. Rundle, J. Clare, & J. Seeland (Eds.), *Contract cheating in higher education: Global perspectives on theory, practice, and policy*. Palgrave Macmillan.

Ellis, C., Rogerson, A. M., House, D., & Murdoch, K. (2022). "(Im)possible to prove": Formalising academic judgement evidence in contract cheating cases using bibliographic forensics. In S. E. Eaton, G. Curtis, B. M. Stoesz, K. Rundle, J. Clare, & J. Seeland (Eds.), *Contract cheating in higher education: Global perspectives on theory, practice, and policy*. Palgrave Macmillan.

Ellis, C., van Haeringen, K., Harper, R., Bretag, T., Zucker, I., McBride, S., Rozenberg, P., Newton, P., & Saddiqui, S. (2020). Does authentic assessment assure academic integrity? Evidence from contract cheating data. *Higher Education Research & Development*, 39(3), 454–469. https://doi.org/10.1080/07294360.2019.1680956

Glendinning, I. (2022). Aligning academic quality and standards with academic integrity. In S. E. Eaton, G. Curtis, B. M. Stoesz, K. Rundle, J. Clare, & J. Seeland (Eds.), *Contract cheating in higher education: Global perspectives on theory, practice, and policy*. Palgrave Macmillan.

Harper, R., Bretag, T., & Rundle, K. (2021). Detecting contract cheating: Examining the role of assessment type. *Higher Education Research & Development*, 40(2), 263–278. https://doi.org/10.1080/07294360.2020.1724899

Karvelas, P. (2021, August 31). *Are you part of the 11 per cent who have cheated at University?* Australian Broadcasting Corporation. https://www.abc.net.au/radionational/programs/drive/are-you-part-of-the-11-per-cent-who-have-cheated-at-university/13521764

Krásničan, V., Foltýnek, T., & Dlabolová, D. H. (2022). Limitations of contract cheating research. In S. E. Eaton, G. Curtis, B. M. Stoesz, K. Rundle, J. Clare, & J. Seeland (Eds.), *Contract cheating in higher education: Global perspectives on theory, practice, and policy*. Palgrave Macmillan.

Lancaster, T. (2022). Addressing contract cheating through staff-student partnerships. In S. E. Eaton, G. Curtis, B. M. Stoesz, K. Rundle, J. Clare, & J. Seeland (Eds.), *Contract cheating in higher education: Global perspectives on theory, practice, and policy*. Palgrave Macmillan.

Matchett, S. (2021, May 10). *TEQSA gets down to cases on cheating.* Campus Morning Mail. https://campusmorningmail.com.au/news/teqsa-gets-down-to-cases-on-cheating/

Mencken, H. L. (1920). *Prejudices: second series*. Knopf.

Newton, P. M. (2018). How common is commercial contract cheating in higher education and is it increasing? A systematic review. *Frontiers in Education, 3*(67). https://doi.org/10.3389/feduc.2018.00067

Parnther, C. (2022). The rise of contract cheating in graduate education. In S. E. Eaton, G. Curtis, B. M. Stoesz, K. Rundle, J. Clare, & J. Seeland (Eds.), *Contract cheating in higher education: Global perspectives on theory, practice, and policy*. Palgrave Macmillan.

Rogerson, A. M. (2022). The encouragement of file sharing behaviours through technology and social media: Impacts on student cheating behaviours and academic piracy. In S. E. Eaton, G. Curtis, B. M. Stoesz, K. Rundle, J. Clare, & J. Seeland (Eds.), *Contract cheating in higher education: Global perspectives on theory, practice, and policy*. Palgrave Macmillan.

Ross, J. (2018, April 23). Contract cheating 'ripe to explode'. *Times Higher Education*, https://www.timeshighereducation.com/news/contract-cheating-ripe-explode

Rowland, S., Slade, C., Wong, K. S., & Whiting, B. (2018). 'Just turn to us': The persuasive features of contract cheating websites. *Assessment & Evaluation in Higher Education, 43*(4), 652–665. https://doi.org/10.1080/02602938.2017.1391948

Rundle, K., Curtis, G. J., & Clare, J. (2019). Why students do not engage in contract cheating. *Frontiers in Psychology, 10*, 2229. https://doi.org/10.3389/fpsyg.2019.02229

Rundle, K., Curtis, G. J., & Clare, J. (2020). Why students choose not to cheat. In T. Bretag (Ed.), *A research agenda for academic integrity* (pp. 100–111). Edward Elgar. https://doi.org/10.4337/9781789903775.00014

Stockman, F., & Mureithi, C. (2019, Sept 7). Cheating, Inc.: How writing papers for American college students has become a lucrative profession overseas. *The New York Times.* https://www.nytimes.com/2019/09/07/us/college-cheating-papers.html

Stoesz, B. M., Eaton, S. E., & Seeland, J. (2022). Critical thinking as an antidote to contract cheating. In S. E. Eaton, G. Curtis, B. M. Stoesz, K. Rundle, J. Clare, & J. Seeland (Eds.), *Contract cheating in higher education: Global perspectives on theory, practice, and policy.* Palgrave Macmillan.

Sutherland-Smith, W., & Dawson, P. (2022). Higher education assessment design. In S. E. Eaton, G. Curtis, B. M. Stoesz, K. Rundle, J. Clare, & J. Seeland (Eds.), *Contract cheating in higher education: Global perspectives on theory, practice, and policy.* Palgrave Macmillan.

Trump, M. (2020). *Too much and never enough: How my family created the world's most dangerous man.* Simon & Schuster.

Veeran-Colton, T., Sefcik, L., & Yorke, J. (2022). The extortionate cost of contract cheating. In S. E. Eaton, G. Curtis, B. M. Stoesz, K. Rundle, J. Clare, & J. Seeland (Eds.), *Contract cheating in higher education: Global perspectives on theory, practice, and policy.* Palgrave Macmillan.

Walker, J. (1998). Student plagiarism in universities: What are we doing about it? *Higher Education Research and Development, 17*(1), 89–106. https://doi.org/10.1080/0729436980170105

Walker, M., & Townley, C. (2012). Contract cheating: A new challenge for academic honesty? *Journal of Academic Ethics, 10*(1), 27–44. https://doi.org/10.1007/s10805-012-9150-y

Thacker, E. J. (2022). Collaboration and collusion between ghostwriters and students. In S. E. Eaton, G. Curtis, B. M. Stoesz, K. Rundle, J. Clare, & J. Seeland (Eds.), *Contract cheating in higher education: Global perspectives on theory, practice, and policy.* Palgrave Macmillan.

CHAPTER 2

What Can We Learn from Measuring Crime When Looking to Quantify the Prevalence and Incidence of Contract Cheating?

Joseph Clare and Kiata Rundle

This chapter examines the importance of decisions about how we measure contract cheating frequency for attempts to reduce the opportunity for this behaviour. After outlining the range of approaches that have been taken to measure this academic integrity issue so far, we provide a summary of the various imperfect ways that criminologists have been measuring crime (a related type of deviant behaviour). We discuss the relevance of the lessons learned from criminology and emphasise the importance of triangulating multiple approaches to measuring contract cheating moving forward, to assist the development and evaluation of detection and prevention strategies.

J. Clare (✉)
School of Law, Universty of Western Australia, Crawley, WA, Australia
e-mail: joe.clare@uwa.edu.au

K. Rundle
Murdoch University, Murdoch, WA, Australia

The Variety of Measurement Approaches Influence Contract Cheating Estimates

The definition that is used across contract cheating research has a direct impact on the research findings. For example, one major variable issue is whether payment is a necessary component of a contract cheating transaction: 'commercial' contract cheating (e.g., Newton, 2018, estimated a historic average of 3.5% of students) versus broader definitions involving sharing and help (e.g., Bretag et al., 2019, estimated 15.3% of students bought/traded/sold notes and 27.2% shared completed assignments). Estimates are also affected by the scope of behaviours that are included in the 'contract cheating' category label. For example, Bretag et al. (2019) examined a spectrum of seven outsourcing behaviours, ranging from buying/trading notes and sharing assignments to paying a third party to take an exam, with the latter having an estimated prevalence of 0.2%. While there is no 'right' approach to resolving these issues, and there are good reasons for looking at this problem from varying perspectives, all definitional decisions have a direct influence on any attempts to quantify contract cheating prevalence and incidence.

On a less overt level, once a definition has been settled on, the way that contract cheating is measured also has a substantial impact on the prevalence and incidence estimates that are produced. Moving beyond definitions, the remainder of the first part of this chapter will examine the various estimates that have been produced across the main methodological categories used to date. In broad terms, we examine the role of survey estimates, demand for contract cheating services, what we know about people getting caught for this form of academic misconduct, and other approaches to gaining insight into how frequent this issue is.

What Do 'Offenders' Say? Self-Report Surveys

To date, the literature on contract cheating has relied heavily on self-report methods involving surveys of 'offenders', which also typically produce the highest prevalence estimates of this behaviour (Curtis et al., 2021). Curtis and Clare (2017) aggregated data on 'commercial' contract cheating from five studies and found a prevalence rate of 3.5% of students engage in contract cheating, with 62.5% doing so on more than one occasion (incidence estimates). They note, however, that this estimate was skewed by the data from one of the studies (see Zafarghandi et al., 2012) which had a rate of engagement of 7.9%. By removing this data, prevalence dropped to 2.1%. Producing comparable estimates, Newton (2018) completed a systematic review of the commercial contract cheating literature from 1978 to 2016 and found a prevalence of 3.5%. However, Newton (2018) also argued that engagement in contract cheating is on the rise, with prevalence rates of over 20% in research almost entirely from 2009 onwards. Highlighting the importance of measurement methodology, it is unclear whether higher rates of reported engagement in contract cheating are a true reflection of an increase in contract cheating behaviour or whether they reflect variations in the methodology of the research being done (e.g., shifts in attitudes towards self-reporting, more encompassing definitions, and better and more varied methodologies of research).

To demonstrate the importance of these methodological factors, we highlight the Bretag et al. (2019) survey that incorporated a broad examination of contract cheating frequency. As explained above, Bretag et al. (2019) counted 'sharing' behaviours (e.g., providing an assignment for any reason or buying/selling notes) in addition to 'cheating' behaviours (e.g., students obtaining a completed assignment to submit as their own). They included within their definition of 'cheating' behaviours incidences where the student obtained an assignment, but no financial transaction was involved. Looking across these different behaviours, the prevalence rate of students who reported obtaining an assignment to submit was 2.2%, whereas 27.2% of students reported providing an assignment for any reason (Bretag et al., 2019). Bretag et al. (2019) noted that students who engaged in cheating behaviours were more likely to also engage in sharing behaviours and were twice as likely to provide another student with a copy of an assignment. Bretag et al. (2019) found that 37% of students in the cheating group had obtained an assignment, 68.5% of whom had submitted the work as their own. Again, when examining the incidence of obtaining an assignment to submit, 79.4% did so once or twice, while 20.6% did so three-or-more times (Bretag et al., 2019). This survey also found that 13.3% of the cheating group exchanged money to obtain an assignment, but it is unclear how often this translated into submitting the purchased work for assessment (Bretag et al., 2019).

To further complicate the interpretation of survey results, research by Curtis et al. (2021) incorporated an innovative method of estimation of contract cheating prevalence by incentivising truth-telling, using a Bayesian Truth Serum methodology as per John et al. (2012). This method triangulated prevalence estimates that participants produced with respect to peer prevalence, peer admission, and personal admission (relating to their lifetime and during the most recent year). Using this method, Curtis et al. (2021) produced estimates that were three to four times higher than those derived from admission rates in other self-report studies (as discussed above): 7.9% of students having ever bought and submitted assignments from commercial contract cheating sites and 11.4% having ever submitted work from commercial file-sharing sites. These findings clearly emphasise the importance of methodology when estimating the frequency of this problem behaviour.

A range of other methodological factors also influence frequency estimates. First, the country of origin of research participants impacts measurements, with Australian work indicating 2.2% of students submitted assignments completed by a third party (Bretag et al., 2019) compared to Czech work estimating a prevalence of 7.6% (Foltýnek & Králíková, 2018). Second, the prevalence time periods of interest matter. Most of these surveys have focused on prevalence ('have you ever?' questions) compared to incidence ('how often have you?'). For example, Curtis et al. (2021) estimated a lifetime contract cheating prevalence of 1.8% versus a one-year estimate of 0.7%. Finally, there is a clear indication that students at English-speaking universities whose first language is not English are more likely to engage in contract cheating, relative to native English speakers (Bretag et al., 2019; Curtis et al., 2021). This means that, in addition to how contract cheating is defined, survey estimates will be influenced by who chooses to respond, where the research is conducted, how far back participants are asked to report (lifetime vs previous year), and whether respondents are incentivised to tell the truth about their past behaviour.

Can We Measure the Demand for Cheating Services?

Looking to alternative approaches, this section considers work that has attempted to measure the demand for contract cheating services, as an alternative measure of the extent of this problem. To this end, Amigud and Lancaster (2020) examined how social media, specifically Twitter, facilitates contract cheating through enabling cheat-curious students and contract cheating services to find each other. Amigud and Lancaster (2020) analysed 1579 tweets and demonstrated that at least some of the demand for contract cheating is publicly available. Looking at this issue from a different perspective, Bretag et al. (2019) estimated the attrition between procurement and submission of purchased assignments, finding that only 68.5% of students reported submitting an assignment they obtained from a third party. Finally, others have reviewed public data from providers of contract cheating services to explore how these services advertise and operate (e.g., Lancaster, 2019).

Administrative Data: Who Gets Caught Contract Cheating?

Although the detection rates for contract cheating are imperfect and likely to be low, another way to estimate the size of this issue is through administrative data relating to who gets caught for contract cheating. The 2014 *MyMaster* scandal in Australia highlighted the issue of contract cheating at 16 universities through a single site (Visentin, 2015), which had targeted Australian-based international students with contract cheating services focused on writing assignments and completing online tests (McNeilage & Visentin, 2014). The journalists exposed 700 receipts of payment to the contract cheating provider, with the purchasers coming from several Australian universities and across a range of courses. As a fall-out, one university indicated that 24 students (across 51 units) received a failing grade for courses completed in 2014 with another university indicating 43 students (who had logged 128 requests) had been subject to disciplinary hearings relating to the use of this service. In a different context, Baird and Clare (2017) also incorporated measures of detection (and whistle-blowing) when evaluating the effectiveness of a targeted contract cheating prevention intervention focused on a business capstone unit.

Another way students may be caught engaging in contract cheating is if the contract cheating service reports them. Yorke et al. (2020) examined students' willingness to engage in contract cheating when presented with the risk of being blackmailed by the service. Of their sample of 587 students, 14 were willing to cheat when not faced with a risk of being blackmailed (scenario 1). However, when presented with scenario 2, which included a risk of blackmail, only 7 of the 14 students were still willing to cheat. The remaining respondents were not willing to cheat in either scenario.

Has Anyone Tried Anything Else?

Looking beyond surveys, service demand, and administrative data about who gets caught, other relevant studies have used different methods to estimate aspects of the contract cheating problem. For example, Clare et al. (2017) examined differences between students' performances on supervised and unsupervised assessment items within units, to identify rule-based, unusually big differences suggesting that students did much better than expected when they were not supervised. This study found unusual patterns in 2.1% of the marks examined (a frequency remarkably like prevalence estimates for contract cheating from several of the surveys discussed, above). Although this was not a confirmation of contract cheating engagement, it was a useful demonstration of the potential value of analysing existing administrative data to expose non-random, unusual patterns indicative of a student doing much better on assessments that were not supervised.

Using a different approach, Rigby et al. (2015) measured students' hypothetical willingness to engage in contract cheating (i.e., buy an essay), based on the cost of the essay, the risk of being caught, the potential penalty if caught, and the grade they would receive on the purchased essay. Students were presented with eight scenarios, where they could choose to buy an essay from one of three options, based on the variables listed above, or to buy none. Rigby et al. (2015) also measured students' risk aversion with a gambling task. Rigby et al. (2015) found that 7 students, from a sample of 90, were willing to cheat in all 8 scenarios presented to them, whilst 50% of their sample were unwilling in any circumstance to hypothetically purchase an essay. Willingness to purchase an assignment was influenced by students' risk aversion and whether English was their first language, with those who were less risk averse and had English as an additional language more likely to choose to buy an essay.

A further study that demonstrates the significance of methodology and the fallibility of self-report is the work of Kolb et al. (2015), who conducted interviews to ask students about cheating opportunities, with a specific focus on why they do not cheat. Kolb et al. (2015) emphasised cheating as a 'conscious deception' and conducted interviews at the start and end of a seminar. They found that 5.9% of their sample reported having engaged in a cheating behaviour in their first interview, but only 2.9% of the sample reported cheating during their second interview. The reasons for these differences were not fully explored by Kolb et al. (2015), but it is possible they relate to the time period issue discussed above, with follow-up interviews conducted at the end of semester and a research emphasis on 'recent' scenarios where students may have had the temptation to cheat.

Clearly, therefore, how much contract cheating we think is occurring is influenced by (a) the definition, (b) where and when the sample is taken from, (c) the estimation method that is used, (d) the attrition between procuring work and submitting work, and (e) the contextual 'risk' involved with the actual (and hypothetical) situation. Moving on, we demonstrate the similarity of the importance of these methodological factors for measurement of a different type of deviance: the measurement of crime.

How Does Criminology Measure Deviance?

At a high level, 'crime' is a form of deviance that shares a lot of common measurement issues with attempts to quantify contract cheating. As with the various measures discussed above, there is no 'right' way to measure crime. This section describes the main methods that have been used, along with their respective strengths and limitations. We demonstrate how the approaches to measuring contract cheating can map cleanly into the same categories used to quantify crime: catching offenders, resource use, crime that happens but does not come to the attention of authorities (the 'dark figure'), and non-crime proxies that are used to quantify problems. The absence of a correct measure and the development of related, flawed measures has required criminology to adopt a triangulation approach to measurement, whereby the best-available data is considered in parallel to give insight into the prevalence and incidence of crime.

Catching Offenders: The Role of Administrative Data

One of the original ways to measure crime depended on counting the things the criminal justice system knew about: what gets reported to police, what police record, who gets apprehended, what happens in court, and who gets sentenced. Police recorded crime statistics were first published in the UK from the mid-nineteenth century, the US from 1930, and Australia from 1964 (Morgan & Clare, 2021). There are strengths associated with these measures, in that they capture a lot of detail about the records that are made (offender/victim information, context information about where and when things occur) and they are embedded in a legislative and policy framework. However, these measures are imperfect. Different policing jurisdictions have different laws (and different interpretation of laws); there can be longitudinal variations within agencies that mean recording practices change (making crime appear to go up or down, when really nothing is 'different'), and police have discretion that influences the recording of reported events (how and if reported events are entered into police records—for a detailed discussion on 'attrition' see Tilley & Burrows, 2005). It is also the case that not all crime events are reported to police (estimated to be 42% overall, Flatley et al., 2010); there is wide variation in the rate at which specific types of crime are reported (with the most highly reported crimes, such as burglary and car theft, strongly influenced by insurance requirements, e.g., Australian Bureau of Statistics, 2021), and that event seriousness, individual victim characteristics, and victim-offender characteristics influence the likelihood of reporting (see Tarling & Morris, 2010, for a discussion of these factors).

Accessing the Dark Figure of Crime Through Victim/ Offender Surveys

To address these (and other) measurement limitations with official crime statistics, commencing in the 1960s, criminologists started using surveys to tap into the 'dark figure of crime' (see Morgan & Clare, 2021, for a discussion). Most surveys have focused on victimisation, randomly selecting a representative sample of the population, and using common language ('hit' instead of 'assault') to ask people about a specific period of time (i.e., the last 12 months) to expose crime that never comes to the attention of the criminal justice system. Self-report offending surveys have also been undertaken (although less frequently and systematically, e.g., Budd et al., 2005) to uncover more about the prevalence and incidence of offending behaviour, irrespective of whether it has come to the attention of authorities. Operating in a similar way to victimisation surveys, random samples of the population are asked questions about things they have done that would constitute crime. A common finding across these exercises is the non-randomness of these patterns, with very small subsets of victims and offenders accounting for a very large amount of the crime that is captured by the surveys (e.g., Hales et al., 2009). Strengths of this approach to measurement include (a) results are independent of issues relating to reporting, recording, and discretion, (b) the information is taken directly from the victim/offender source, (c) there is limited influence of politics and managerial pressures from within the justice system, and (d) they can reveal meaningful longitudinal patterns that can demonstrate changes in victimisation and offending (Morgan & Clare, 2021).

Despite these strengths, just as with the administrative approaches to measuring crime, there are also limitations with surveys. The estimates that are produced are influenced by methodological decisions including questionnaire length, the order of questions, how the survey is conducted (e.g., in-person vs online), and the time period in question (12 months vs 5 years vs lifetime). Individual respondents can also forget, confabulate, and/or lie, resulting in verifiable inconsistencies between survey-based accounts and police records (e.g., Averdijk & Elffers, 2012), or respondents can choose to under-report their own criminal behaviour (Bernasco et al., 2020).

Indirect and Novel Measures into Specific Crime Issues

Another window into the volume of crime is provided by police calls for service. In addition to demonstrating variations in demand for police services over time, these data, which are collected based on police activity but not influenced by discretion and recording decisions, can give meaningful insight into temporal and geographic crime patterns. Recent examples have used this measure to look at time/space service overlap from police, fire, and ambulance workload (Clare et al., 2019), and to monitor the impact of COVID-19 lockdowns on crime and disorder during the early months of the pandemic (Ashby, 2021). It is important to note that calls for service do not equal crime, as police attend a lot of non-crime calls, so this measure has the potential to over-count crime-related activity.

It is also worth briefly considering some alternative approaches to measuring aspects of crime. Drug test data is frequently used to monitor trends in drink/drug driving (e.g., Midgette et al., 2021) or prevalence of drug use in offender populations (e.g., Doherty & Sullivan, 2020). Emergency room data and hospital admissions provide another window into certain types of violent crime, such as intimate partner violence, alcohol-related violence, or violence against vulnerable groups in society (e.g., Macdonald et al., 2005). The common themes across these approaches are that they focus on relatively specific types of crime and provide a non-random estimate of the prevalence and incidence of the crime they relate to. Finally, social media is emerging as an alternative way to measure crime, with studies demonstrating the relevance and utility of Twitter for monitoring low-level crime and disorder in micro-geographic areas (Williams et al., 2016). Facebook is also being used to help monitor cybercrime victimisation (Aliyu et al., 2020).

Lessons for Measuring Contract Cheating: Triangulation Is the Key

As with approaches to measuring contract cheating, there is no single, correct way to measure crime. In both cases, 'problem' estimates are influenced by the way the data are collected and the context within which collection occurs. To emphasise the commonalities of the approaches adopted in these two contexts, Table 2.1 uses the varying focuses on administrative data, surveys, resource use, and indirect/novel measures to align the major measurement approaches used so far for contract cheating and those developed over a much longer period in criminology focused on measuring crime. The consistency is useful, as it can be used as a platform to encourage contract cheating researchers to embrace the imperfect nature of measurement in this area. Rather than seeking to find the single, right measure of how much contract cheating is occurring, adopting a triangulation approach to measuring the issue moving forward will be the most useful for assisting the development and evaluation of detection and prevention strategies.

As discussed above, surveys are limited as they are influenced by factors such as who is asked, what time period is covered, how the behaviour is defined, prevalence and incidence, and memory errors of respondents. Resource use is also imperfect because engaging with a provider does not

Table 2.1 Comparing and classifying the various approaches to measuring crime and contract cheating

Data focus	Crime	Contract cheating
Administrative data	Police data	Academic integrity reports
	Sentencing data	Academic integrity guilty findings
Surveys	Victimisation surveys	Self-report offending surveys
	Self-report offending surveys	Hypothetical offending experiments
Resource use	Police calls for service	Twitter requests
		Contract cheating website usage
		Search engine trends
		Uploading to file-sharing sites
Indirect/novel measures	Hospital admissions	Blackmail
	Offender drug use audits	Third-party reporting
	Twitter/social media more broadly	Unusual difference scores

mean people submit the work and there are grey areas around file sharing. Furthermore, the utility of administrative data is also limited, influenced by who is caught, variations in policy and practice over time and across institutions, and the threshold of proof involved (suspected vs proved). Triangulating these imperfect estimates whenever possible will help give the best representation of the current state of the problem. In a crime context, an increase in police recorded crime could represent an increase in real crime or it could reflect an increased willingness to report crime events to police. Without surveys against which to compare victimisation (with the closest potential survey represented in the work by Harper et al., 2019), it is very difficult to know which of these was driving the increase in official statistics. For the same reasons, a triangulation approach could help address the concerns raised from Newton's work as to whether the recent increase in prevalence estimates represents an actual increase in contract cheating, a shift in methodology/measurement, changes to definitions, a combination of these factors, or something else entirely. Furthermore, relying on multiple measurement strategies may well mean researchers and policy makers are staying alert to emerging problems (such as cyber fraud, in a crime context, which traditional victimisation surveys and police records do not capture well). This type of issue is of particular concern when it comes to the dark figure of contract cheating and the impact of COVID-19, as we did not know what the prevalence and incidence of this misconduct were before the pandemic, but we can reasonably assume it will have increased as a result of the rapid changes to assessment structures and opportunities.

In conclusion, we urge contract cheating researchers to be cognisant of the measurement issues in this research area, learn from the developments in a related, fuzzy measurement space provided by criminological research, and commit to increased use of mixed-methods and data triangulation in contract cheating research. As has been seen within criminal justice research, this will assist the development and evaluation of contract cheating detection and prevention strategies.

References

Aliyu, N. I., Abdulrahaman, M. D., Ajibade, F. O., & Abdurauf, T. (2020). Analysis of cyber bullying on Facebook using text mining. *Journal of Applied Artificial Intelligence, 1*(1), 1–12. https://doi.org/10.48185/jaai.v1i1.30

Amigud, A., & Lancaster, T. (2020). I will pay someone to do my assignment: an analysis of market demand for contract cheating services on Twitter. *Assessment & Evaluation in Higher Education, 45*(4), 541–553. https://doi.org/10.1080/02602938.2019.1670780

Ashby, M. P. J. (2021). Changes in Police Calls for Service During the Early Months of the 2020 Coronavirus Pandemic. *Policing: A Journal of Policy and Practice, 14*(4), 1054–1072. https://doi.org/10.1093/police/paaa037

Australian Bureau of Statistics. (2021). *Crime Victimisation, Australia, 2019-20*. Australian Bureau of Statistics. https://www.abs.gov.au/statistics/people/crime-and-justice/crime-victimisation-australia/2019-20#key-statistics

Averdijk, M., & Elffers, H. (2012). The discrepancy between survey-based victim accounts and police reports revisited. *International Review of Victimology, 18*(2), 91–107. https://doi.org/10.1177/0269758011432955

Baird, M., & Clare, J. (2017). Removing the opportunity for contract cheating in business capstones: a crime prevention case study. *International Journal for Educational Integrity, 13*(6), 1–15. https://doi.org/10.1007/s40979-017-0018-1

Bernasco, W., Lammers, M., Menting, B., & Ruiter, S. (2020). Are frequent offenders more difficult to find and less willing to participate? An analysis of unit non-response in an online survey among offenders. *European Journal of Criminology*. https://doi.org/10.1177/1477370820941422

Bretag, T., Harper, R., Burton, M., Ellis, C., Newton, P., Rozenberg, P., Saddiqui, S., & Van Haeringen, K. (2019). Contract cheating: A survey of Australian university students. *Studies in Higher Education, 44*(11), 1837–1856. https://doi.org/10.1080/03075079.2018.1462788

Budd, T., Sharp, C., & Mayhew, P. (2005). *Offending in England and Wales: First results from the 2003 Crime and Justice Survey - Home Office Research Study 275*. https://www.politieacademie.nl/kennisenonderzoek/kennis/mediatheek/PDF/45315.pdf

Clare, J., Townsley, M., Birks, D. J., & Garis, L. (2019). Patterns of police, fire, and ambulance calls-for-service: Scanning the spatio-temporal intersection of emergency service problems. *Policing: A Journal of Policy and Practice*. https://doi.org/10.1093/police/pax038

Clare, J., Walker, S., & Hobson, J. (2017). Can we detect contract cheating using existing assessment data? Applying crime prevention theory to an academic integrity issue. *International Journal for Educational Integrity, 13*(4), 1–15. https://doi.org/10.1007/s40979-017-0015-4

Curtis, G. J., & Clare, J. (2017). How prevalent is contract cheating and to what extent are students repeat offenders? *Journal of Academic Ethics, 15*(2), 115–124. https://doi.org/10.1007/s10805-017-9278-x

Curtis, G. J., McNeill, M., Slade, C., Tremayne, K., Harper, R., Rundle, K., & Greenaway, R. (2022). Moving beyond self-reports to estimate the prevalence of commercial contract cheating: An Australian study. *Studies in Higher Education*, 47(9), 1844–1856. https://doi.org/10.1080/03075079.2021.1972093

Doherty, L., & Sullivan, T. (2020). *Drug use monitoring in Australia: Drug use among police detainees, 2019*. Statistical Report no. 30. Canberra: Australian Institute of Criminology. https://doi.org/10.52922/sr04695.

Flatley, J., Kershaw, C., Smith, K., Chaplin, R., & Moon, D. (2010). *Crime in England and Wales, 2009–10*. https://assets.publishing.service.gov.uk/government/uploads/system/uploads/attachment_data/file/116347/hosb1210.pdf

Foltýnek, T., & Králíková, V. (2018). Analysis of the contract cheating market in Czechia. *International Journal for Educational Integrity*, 14(4), 1–15. https://doi.org/10.1007/s40979-018-0027-8

Hales, J., Nevill, C., Pudney, S., & Tipping, S. (2009). *Longitudinal analysis of the offending, crime and justice survey 2003–2006*. https://assets.publishing.service.gov.uk/government/uploads/system/uploads/attachment_data/file/116611/horr19-report.pdf

Harper, R., Bretag, T., Ellis, C., Newton, P., Rozenberg, P., Saddiqui, S., & van Haeringen, K. (2019). Contract cheating: a survey of Australian university staff. *Studies in Higher Education*, 44(11), 1857–1873.

John, L. K., Loewenstein, G., & Prelec, D. (2012). Measuring the prevalence of questionable research practices with incentives for truth telling. *Psychological Science*, 23(5), 524–532. https://doi.org/10.1177/0956797611430953

Kolb, K., Longest, K., & Singer, A. (2015). Choosing not to cheat: A framework to assess students' rationales for abiding by academic integrity policies. *Journal for the Scholarship of Teaching and Learning*, 9(1), 10.20429/ijsotl.2015.090109.

Lancaster, T. (2019). Profiling the international academic ghost writers who are providing low-cost essays and assignments for the contract cheating industry. *Journal of Information, Communication & Ethics in Society*, 17(1), 72–86. https://doi.org/10.1108/JICES-04-2018-0040

Macdonald, S., Cherpitel, C. J., Borges, G., DeSouza, A., Giesbrecht, N., & Stockwell, T. (2005). The criteria for causation of alcohol in violent injuries based on emergency room data from six countries. *Addictive Behaviors*, 30, 103–113. https://doi.org/10.1016/j.addbeh.2004.04.016

McNeilage, A., & Visentin, L. (2014). Yingying Dou: The mastermind behind the university essay writing machine. *Sydney Morning Herald*. https://www.smh.com.au/education/yingying-dou-the-mastermind-behind-the-university-essay-writing-machine-20141111-11kk50.html

Midgette, G., Kilmer, B., Nicosia, N., & Heaton, P. (2021). A natural experiment to test the effect of sanction certainty and celerity on substance-impaired driving: North Dakota's 24/7 Sobriety Program. *Journal of Quantitative Criminology*, 37(3), 647–670. https://doi.org/10.1007/s10940-020-09458-6

Morgan, F., & Clare, J. (2021). The distribution of crime over populations, space and time. In D. Dalton, W. De Lint, & D. Palmer (Eds.), *Crime and Justice: A Guide to Criminology* (6th ed.). Thomson Reuters Lawbook Co..

Newton, P. M. (2018). How common is commercial contract cheating in higher education and is it increasing? A systematic review. *Frontiers in Education, 3*(67). https://doi.org/10.3389/feduc.2018.00067/full

Rigby, D., Burton, M., Balcombe, K., Bateman, I., & Mulatu, A. (2015). Contract cheating and the market in essays. *Journal of Economic Behavior and Organization, 111*, 23–37. https://doi.org/10.1016/j.jebo.2014.12.019

Tarling, R., & Morris, K. (2010). Reporting crime to the police. *British Journal of Criminology, 50*(3), 474–490. https://doi.org/10.1093/bjc/azq011

Tilley, N., & Burrows, J. (2005). *An overview of attrition patterns* (Online Report No. 45/05). Home Office. https://webarchive.nationalarchives.gov.uk/ukgwa/20130128103514/http://www.homeoffice.gov.uk/rds/pdfs05/rdsolr4505.pdf

Visentin, L. (2015). MyMaster essay cheating scandal: More than 70 university students face suspension. *Sydney Morning Herald*. https://www.smh.com.au/national/nsw/mymaster-essay-cheating-scandal-more-than-70-university-students-face-suspension-20150312-1425oe.html

Williams, M. L., Burnap, P., & Sloan, L. (2016). Crime sensing with big data: The affordances and limitations of using open source communications to estimate crime patterns. *British Journal of Criminology*, azw031. https://doi.org/10.1093/bjc/azw031.

Yorke, J., Sefcik, L., & Veeran-Colton, T. (2020). Contract cheating and blackmail: A risky business? *Studies in Higher Education*. https://doi.org/10.1080/03075079.2020.1730313

Zafarghandi, A. M., Khoshroo, F., & Barkat, B. (2012). An investigation of Iranian EFL Masters students' perceptions of plagiarism. *International Journal for Educational Integrity, 8*, 69–85. https://doi.org/10.21913/IJEI.v8i2.811

CHAPTER 3

Limitations of Contract Cheating Research

*Veronika Krásničan, Tomáš Foltýnek,
and Dita Henek Dlabolová*

Once upon a time, a diligent PhD student was engaged in research in the field of academic integrity at a faculty of economics. She wanted to continue the research she started during her master's studies and to further analyse the contract cheating market. During her studies, she had to pass an exam adjudicated by a commission composed of experts in economics, statistics, and management. She prepared all the documents for this exam. It took her a whole year of thorough effort to collect data on contract cheating using a self-reporting questionnaire. She presented her results confidently because she did her best to follow the methodology taken

V. Krásničan (✉)
Mendel University in Brno, Brno, Czechia
e-mail: veronika.krasnican@mendelu.cz

T. Foltýnek
Masaryk University, Brno, Czechia
e-mail: foltynek@fi.muni.cz

D. Henek Dlabolová
European Network for Academic Integrity, Brno, Czechia
e-mail: dita.dlabolova@academicintegrity.eu

© The Author(s), under exclusive license to Springer Nature
Switzerland AG 2022
S. E. Eaton et al. (eds.), *Contract Cheating in Higher Education*,
https://doi.org/10.1007/978-3-031-12680-2_3

from experts in academic integrity, big names like Donald McCabe (2005) and Tracey Bretag (2019). But what followed drove her crazy.

The members of the examination commission mercilessly questioned crucial parts of the methodology, in which they saw enormous shortcomings. They criticised the form of the questionnaire and the unbalanced distribution of respondents; they pointed out the absence of data necessary for statistical evaluation and for assessing the relevance of the results. The student was desperate. Were the academic integrity experts wrong, or did she not follow them appropriately? Where was the mistake? What should she do?

This story is not a fairy tale. It is a real experience of the first author and the project in question was the Global Essay Mills Survey (GEMS). The data from this project appear, for instance, in the studies by Králíková et al. (2019) and Awdry and Ives (2020). The observations of colleagues and experts, who deal with completely different fields than academic integrity, served as an eye-opener, which showed us the shortcomings in the research we had done before. And, the overall experience from this project showed us mistakes that we did not perceive as a problem at all at some point, but later it cost us a lot of unnecessary effort and time to address these problems while writing the papers stemming from this project. Since then, we have been thinking of the drawbacks and limitations of contract cheating research. While reading the studies about contract cheating, we came across numerous problems. In some studies, researchers apparently do their best to mitigate, address, and acknowledge the limitations. However, it is not always the case. Some studies do not address the limitations sufficiently; some even do not mention any. The aim of this chapter is to point out the possible limitations of the current contract cheating research and contribute to improvements in its quality.

The term "contract cheating research" includes various types of studies that focus on different aspects of the issue, on different stakeholders, use different methods or ask varied research questions. Clarke and Lancaster (2006) in their seminal study about contract cheating examined a website where students can hire a programmer. A similar approach was used also in Lancaster's (2020) study about micro-outsourcing websites. Wallace and Newton (2014) examined the turnaround time of contract cheating suppliers and revealed the excess of supply over demand, while Comas-Forgas et al. (2021) estimated the extent of contract cheating by analysis of internet search activity. Other studies focus on qualitative information obtained from interviews with academics (Eaton et al., 2019) or the relationship between contract cheating and assessment design (Bretag et al., 2019a, 2019b; Ellis et al., 2020). A separate perspective is a legal approach against contract cheating. Such studies might discuss methods concerning how countries address this issue in the national laws (Draper & Newton 2017).

Our chapter focuses on one particular type of contract cheating research—on the studies aiming to find out how many students are involved in such behaviour using self-reported data collected via questionnaires or qualitative interviews. We focused on this particular type of research not only because of our personal experience described in the introduction. There are numerous drawbacks to this method, like self-selection bias, confirmation bias, and many others (Mahmud & Bretag, 2013). Results from the self-reported surveys are often cited by the media, as they provide journalists with material to create click-bait headlines. The percentage of cheating students is clearly understandable for the general public, even though narrowing the whole phenomenon to one number is not possible without oversimplification. Also, problems with self-reporting questionnaires as methodological tools have been already pointed out by other authors. For example, Siev and Kliger (2019) and Curtis et al. (2021) recommend that researchers focus on methods beyond these questionnaires.

The aim of this chapter is to increase the quality and credibility of contract cheating research. Based on the analysis of the state-of-the-art research papers, we designed a checklist of measures that researchers should apply to help minimise the limitations and their impact on the results. In this chapter, we want to answer the following research questions: What problems and limitations are frequently present in contract cheating research? To what extent do authors acknowledge the limitations and take them into account when interpreting results?

Methodology

To identify the limitations of contract cheating research, we have combined the following methods:

1. Qualitative research—we conducted an online brainstorming session with experts from the survey working group of the European Network for Academic Integrity (ENAI).
2. A scientific literature review—we have critically evaluated state-of-the-art research papers and identified limitations.

Qualitative Research

As a baseline for the limitations, we used the opinions of experts with experience in research—not only contract cheating research but also with research in other disciplines. We contacted the *Academic Integrity Surveys Working Group* of the ENAI (https://academicintegrity.eu/wp/wg-surveys/). The working group has 15 members (including two of this chapter's authors) from various countries and with various research backgrounds.

An online brainstorming session was organised with the working group, posing the question "What problems do you see in contemporary contract cheating research?" During the discussion, one person took notes and later identified a set of limitations mentioned by the working group members.

Scientific Literature Review

For the scientific literature review we collected studies examining students' experience with contract cheating. We focused only on research methods—self-reporting questionnaires and interviews, which were frequently the second stage of research. As we decided to deal with state-of-the-art research only, we limited the search for studies published from 2017 to August 2021.

With the aim to focus only on research papers and not to deal with "grey" literature, we used two databases as the sources of the papers: Web of Science and Scopus. We were interested only in papers written in English. In both databases, the search terms were: "contract cheating" or "ghost writing" or "ghostwriting". In Web of Science, all fields were searched (topic and title being relevant), and in Scopus the title, abstract, and keywords were searched. The given keywords and the range of the publishing year from 2017 to 2021 provided us with 141 papers from Web of Science and 145 from Scopus, with an overlap of 104 papers.

As our methodology for the review was inspired by Newton's (2018) systematic review on how common is commercial contract cheating in higher education, we performed a second search using the same 67 keywords and key phrases that he used. This added 19 new papers from the Web of Science, and 2 new papers from Scopus. From this search, we obtained 205 papers on the topic of contract cheating or ghost writing from 2017 to 2021, inclusive. Obviously, this collection involved studies that were out of the scope of our interest, so the next step was the manual exclusion of the papers to reach the final collection of the studies on student contract cheating, asking students whether they were involved in such behaviour, and using self-reported questionnaires as the data collection methods. The first round of excluding unsuitable papers was based on their title, and/or abstract, where the title was ambiguous. Further examination of the abstract or texts of the remaining papers led to exclusion of a few more studies. The final collection of papers that was thoroughly examined included 18 articles.

Identification of Limitations

When selecting individual papers, we carefully read all of them (especially the methodology, results, limitations, and conclusion). Thanks to the results of brainstorming and our own experience, we critically evaluated the possible limitations of the methodology, data collection, respondent selection, questionnaire design, or interpretation of results, whether or not they were directly mentioned.

In this way, we identified seven limitations, which we encoded. Subsequently, we re-read the selected 18 papers that met the requirements of our methodology. While reading, we noted all the limitations that we were able to identify in the papers, using the created codes. Based on the results we created a table that represents the absolute frequency of occurrence of selected limitations.

PROBLEMS OF CONTEMPORARY RESEARCH

Based on the literature review and the brainstorming with the ENAI survey group, we identified the following limitations of questionnaires used to collect self-reported data about student cheating.

Unclear terminology: Many terms related to contract cheating do not exist in various languages. This is true even for the term "contract cheating", which does not have an equivalent term in most European languages. Thus, translations to local languages often suffer from a lack of clarity for readers. The terminology used in the questionnaire should be made clear to the respondents; this explanation should be as specific as possible. If students are the target group of the survey, the language should be understandable by all students. However, it is better not to use potentially unclear terms at all, and to provide respondents with terminology understandable to anyone.

Unspecific terminology: In different languages, the terms might have different connotations or different implicit contexts. For example, the term "cheating" is limited to "exam cheating" in some languages. In some cultural contexts, sharing exam answers is considered cheating, whereas in others it is not. Thus, the term "cheating" might be unclear. It is necessary to be very specific not only about the meaning of particular terms but also about the cultural context.

Loaded language: The social desirability bias is sometimes fuelled by loaded language that clearly indicates the immorality of a particular behaviour. For example, using the term "cheating" may dissuade respondents from admitting such behaviour. We opted to use neutral language and based the questionnaire on scenarios rather than use loaded language. It is also useful to provide a neutral context and ask what other people do rather than what the respondent does. An example of such wording might be, "Some people do something because… Do you…?"

Indicators language: The concept that is actually being examined should not appear in the survey. There should be a list of actions, which are considered contract cheating, but the respondents should not encounter the term "contract cheating" in the survey at all.

Language issues: We were unable to determine if respondents filled out the questionnaire in their first or second language. In the case of the latter, can the researchers be sure that respondents understand all terms used in the survey? And was respondents' understanding the same as the understanding of researchers? Obviously, it is hardly possible to translate the surveys into all languages. The language issues should be taken into account when interpreting the results.

Using multiple-choice questions with a given set of options: This might be a problem, for example, when asking for reasons that led students to cheat. In order to facilitate the analysis, the reasons for student cheating were usually presented as a closed set to choose from. Respondents' answers may therefore have been influenced by the order of items. Even though an option "Other" is usually provided, very few respondents selected it. Thus, drawing conclusions about the most frequent reasons might be problematic. The respondents should be given a blank text field to provide an uninfluenced answer. The answers might later be automatically grouped.

Unfinished surveys: Some surveys suffer from very high percentages of the respondents who dropped out. This was particularly a problem in the GEMS survey (Awdry & Ives, 2020; Awdry et al., 2021). If the section collecting demographic data is placed at the end of the survey, it is not possible to figure out who dropped out and why. In fact, this might be very important information. Therefore, the section about the demographic data should be placed at the beginning, which allows researchers to trace the behaviour of particular demographic groups.

Target group bias: Most surveys are designed for students. However, researchers agree that contract cheating is a systemic problem involving educators, as well as higher education administrators. Moreover, interesting information may be supplied also by contractors, parents, and so on.

Gender equity: It is common for women to complete surveys significantly more often than men. However, male respondents admit having cheated significantly more frequently than female respondents. Unfortunately, this apparent discrepancy is usually not taken into account when calculating an overall percentage of cheating students. Let us take the analysis of contract cheating in Czechia (Foltýnek & Králíková, 2018) as an example. Out of 1016 respondents, 77 reported contract cheating, which is 7.6%. Nonetheless, the percentage of cheating among men was 14.6% (28/199), compared to 5.9% (48/817) for women. Presuming gender balance in the overall student population and honesty of responses for both men and women, the total percentage of cheating students should be obtained as an average of 14.6 and 5.9, which is 10.25—a significantly different number from 7.6. Therefore, a weighted average should have been used in this and similar cases. Research should also consider including an "other gender" or a "non-binary" option.

Social desirability bias: Self-reported data are not objective due to social desirability bias (Rundle et al., 2019). People tend not to admit behaviour that is considered immoral. Another form of social desirability bias is the tendency to provide answers that researchers are expected to want. If the respondents get the impression that researchers want to describe the situation as "everybody is cheating", they may exaggerate the reality.

Voluntary participation: Were the respondents assured that participation was voluntary and anonymous? Do the respondents trust anonymity? If not, the honesty of responses may be influenced.

The limitations can also appear after conducting the survey itself. In the later phases of the research, we identified the following limitations.

Interpretation bias: Researchers should pay special attention to how the results are presented with respect to possible misinterpretations. For example, a study showing that management students have the highest percentage of contract cheaters can be presented by the media as if to say that only students of management are cheating and create a false impression that cheating does not happen in other fields of study.

Insufficient statistics: Statistical checks on reliability, validity, and consistency of questions are usually missing. For example, Cronbach's alpha, which checks inter-item consistency, might be useful to measure the reliability of the survey. Another issue is connected to validity, which may be established via exploratory factor analysis.

LIMITATIONS IDENTIFIED DURING THE SCIENTIFIC LITERATURE REVIEW

We identified a sample of 18 papers that used self-reported questionnaires or interviews that focused on students and their attitude to contract cheating (Awdry, 2021; Awdry et al., 2021; Awdry & Ives, 2020; Bielska & Rutkowski, 2021; Bretag et al., 2019a, 2019c; Curtis & Clare, 2017; Curtis et al., 2021; Foltýnek & Králíková, 2018; Harrison et al., 2020; Králíková et al., 2019; Nguyen, 2021; Peytcheva-Forsyth et al., 2018; Pitt et al., 2020; Rozenberg et al., 2019; Shala et al., 2020; Wang & Xu, 2021; Yorke et al., 2020). Based on the identified limitations, a table was created with the frequencies of their occurrence (Table 3.1).

It should be noted that we were not able to identify all the limitations in selected papers, due to missing information in some of them. But, from our point of view, even this minimal information was generally able to be analysed for the purpose of our review.

The state-of-the-art contract cheating research that uses self-reporting questionnaires and interviews focused on students has several limitations, which should be noted. First of all, it is the *dominance of female respondents in the sample*. Second, it is an *unbalanced age distribution of respondents in the sample*. The predominance of younger students over older

Table 3.1 Summary of limitations within the reviewed papers

Limitations	Number of articles	%
Dominance of female respondents in sample	12	67
Unbalanced age distribution of respondents	10	56
Small sample of respondents	7	39
Results from a single university	5	28
Mix of respondents from different cultural backgrounds	3	17
No limitations mentioned	3	17
Missing information about respondents	2	11

ones may be natural, however, the actual age distribution at the university or in the country being studied should be mentioned. This important information will help to assess whether the sample of respondents is representative or not. The next limitation we call *Results from the single university*, which on one hand, does not have to be a problem at all. On the other hand, if this limitation is not clearly stated in the abstract and also the paper itself, it could cause misinterpretation of the results and there is also the possibility of incorrect generalisation not only by the researcher but by the media.

Working with students across different countries may also be very problematic. It is necessary to work very carefully with this issue, as different countries have their own *cultural specifics*. These specifics may mean that the combination of these respondents could be the limitation of the research. It is always necessary to consider whether it is appropriate to include all respondents from different countries in the overall results or to present them separately.

Furthermore, we would like to draw attention to the *missing information* in the papers themselves, which we came across during our search. If researchers are talking about the respondents as such, they should certainly mention all the relevant information that could have influenced the results. Even if some biographical information is not collected, it should be mentioned and justified.

During the scientific literature review, we were able to identify papers that do not mention any limitations at all, even though these limitations were obvious from the text. We did not include papers in our table that had a separate chapter on limitations or at least mentioned them in another chapter. Even so, we believe that not all of the potential limitations that may have occurred have been mentioned.

As a few "best practice" examples, we can name three studies where researchers were aware of all potential limitations, mentioned or justified them, acquainted the reader with all information about the respondents, and described in detail the research methodology: Rundle et al. (2019), Curtis et al. (2021), and Bretag et al. (2019c).

CHECKLIST

Based on the brainstorming, systematic literature review, and general guidelines for survey research described by Rossi et al. (2013), we propose the following checklist for the researchers using self-reporting questionnaires about contract cheating.

- Is a questionnaire the best way to collect data?
- Besides a questionnaire, is there at least one more method used?
- Does the questionnaire contain explanations of all terms?
- Does the survey combine respondents answering in their first language and respondents answering in a second language? If yes, are the differences addressed?
- Does the survey provide text fields rather than multiple-choice options whenever possible?
- Does the survey tool allow the researchers to trace the drop-outs? Are the drop-outs sufficiently discussed?
- Are the target groups of the survey appropriate? If excluding some target groups, does the research still cover all important aspects?
- Does the gender distribution of respondents correspond to the gender distribution of the examined population?
- In general, does the demographic distribution of respondents correspond to the demographic distribution of the examined population?
- Is the risk of social desirability bias appropriately minimised?
- Does the survey avoid loaded language?
- Does the survey use indicators language rather than direct terms naming specific phenomena?
- Is the participation voluntary and anonymous? And are the participants properly and sufficiently assured about it? Is the informed consent included?
- Did the researchers perform statistical checks on the reliability, validity, and consistency of questions?
- Did the researchers describe clearly all possible limitations of their research?

Limitations of This Study

As this chapter deals with the limitations of other studies, it is fair to elaborate on the limitations of this particular study. The biggest limitation is undoubtedly the subjectivity of authors. Even though we have long-term experience with projects related to academic integrity, we might still be unaware of some problems. To mitigate this limitation, we included the ENAI survey working group members in the process of creating the list of limitations. However, this does not ensure a perfect list either. Even experts working in their own areas may miss some issues. Moreover, group brainstorming is prone to expanding mostly on what has already been mentioned rather than coming up with new ideas. However, we hope that the combined expertise of all of the people involved resulted in a set of limitations that is as complete as possible.

Some limitations cannot be revealed from the papers. If the survey instrument was not attached (which was the case of most studies), we were unable to judge all of the limitations. Therefore, the limitations included in the overview table are more minimal than exhaustive. We were also unable to judge the language issues if the survey instrument was in a language we do not speak or read. And, further to languages, this study covers only papers written in English. There might be studies published in other languages (e.g. theses), which we did not take into account. We might also have omitted some research by focusing only on papers indexed in Web of Science and Scopus. Having said that, our aim was to collect the limitations from research papers only.

Thus, it is again necessary to bear in mind the aim of this study—to point out the limitations we consider frequent and important. We are confident that even an incomplete set of limitations will be useful for researchers in the area and contributes to the quality of research.

Conclusion

We appreciate the work performed by other researchers and their results, and this chapter does not aim to degrade them when pointing out the limitations. The aim of this chapter was to point out the possible limitations which, according to our research, are inadequately addressed in most papers. Thus, we want to inspire other researchers in this area so they are aware of the possible issues and they can pay special attention to them. Admitting research limitations is not a shame, it is a good research practice that is in harmony with academic and research integrity.

All researchers should bear in mind possible problems in all parts of the research and do their best to mitigate them. One part involves research methodology, the creation of the survey, its distribution, and the contacting respondents. The next part is data processing and presentation of the results in papers. We hope this chapter contributes to increasing the quality of all parts of the research about contract cheating.

References

Awdry, R. (2021). Assignment outsourcing: Moving beyond contract cheating. *Assessment & Evaluation in Higher Education, 46*(2), 220–235. https://doi.org/10.1080/02602938.2020.1765311

Awdry, R., Dawson, P., & Sutherland-Smith, W. (2021). Contract cheating: To legislate or not to legislate-is that the question? *Assessment & Evaluation in Higher Education, 47*(5), 712–726. https://doi.org/10.1080/02602938.2021.1957773

Awdry, R., & Ives, B. (2020). Students cheat more often from those known to them: Situation matters more than the individual. *Assessment & Evaluation in Higher Education, 46*(8), 1254–1268. https://doi.org/10.1080/02602938.2020.1851651

Bielska, B., & Rutkowski, M. (2021). "There must be someone's name under every bit of text, even if it is unimportant or incorrect": Plagiarism as a learning strategy. *Journal of Academic Ethics*, 1–20. https://doi.org/10.1007/s10805-021-09419-z

Bretag, T. (2019). From 'perplexities of plagiarism' to 'building cultures of integrity': A reflection on fifteen years of academic integrity research, 2003–2018. *HERDSA Review of Higher Education, 6*, 5–35.

Bretag, T., Harper, R., Burton, M., Ellis, C., Newton, P., Rozenberg, P., et al. (2019a). Contract cheating: A survey of Australian university students. *Studies in Higher Education, 44*(11), 1837–1856. https://doi.org/10.1080/03075079.2018.1462788

Bretag, T., Harper, R., Burton, M., Ellis, C., Newton, P., van Haeringen, K., Saddiqui, S., & Rozenberg, P. (2019b). Contract cheating and assessment design: Exploring the relationship. *Assessment & Evaluation in Higher Education, 44*(5), 676–691. https://doi.org/10.1080/02602938.2018.1527892

Bretag, T., Harper, R., Rundle, K., Newton, P. M., Ellis, C., Saddiqui, S., & van Haeringen, K. (2019c). Contract cheating in Australian higher education: A comparison of non-university higher education providers and universities. *Assessment & Evaluation in Higher Education*. https://doi.org/10.1080/02602938.2019.1614146

Clarke, R., & Lancaster, T. (2006). Eliminating the successor to plagiarism? Identifying the usage of contract cheating sites. In *Proceedings of the 2nd International Plagiarism Conference*, Gateshead, UK.

Comas-Forgas, R., Lancaster, T., Calvo-Sastre, A., & Sureda-Negre, J. (2021). Exam cheating and academic integrity breaches during the COVID-19 pandemic: An analysis of internet search activity in Spain. *Heliyon, 7*(10), e08233. https://doi.org/10.1016/J.HELIYON.2021.E08233

Curtis, G. J., & Clare, J. (2017). How prevalent is contract cheating and to what extent are students repeat offenders? *Journal of Academic Ethics*, *15*(2), 115–124. https://doi.org/10.1007/s10805-017-9278-x

Curtis, G. J., McNeill, M., Slade, C., Tremayne, K., Harper, R., Rundle, K., & Greenaway, R. (2022). Moving beyond self-reports to estimate the prevalence of commercial contract cheating: An Australian study. *Studies in Higher Education*, *47*(9), 1844–1856. https://doi.org/10.1080/03075079.2021.1972093

Draper, M. J., & Newton, P. M. (2017). A legal approach to tackling contract cheating? *International Journal for Educational Integrity*, *13*(11), 1–26. https://doi.org/10.1007/s40979-017-0022-5

Eaton, S. E., Chibry, N., Toye, M. A., & Rossi, S. (2019). Interinstitutional perspectives on contract cheating: A qualitative narrative exploration from Canada. *International Journal for Educational Integrity*, *15*(1), 9. https://doi.org/10.1007/s40979-019-0046-0

Ellis, C., van Haeringen, K., Harper, R., Bretag, T., Zucker, I., McBride, S., Rozenberg, P., Newton, P., & Saddqui, S. (2020). Does authentic assessment assure academic integrity? Evidence from contract cheating data. *Higher Education Research & Development*, *39*(3), 454–469. https://doi.org/10.1080/07294360.2019.1680956

Foltýnek, T., & Králíková, V. (2018). Analysis of the contract cheating market in Czechia. *International Journal for Educational Integrity*, *14*(1), 1–15. https://doi.org/10.1007/s40979-018-0027-8

Harrison, D., Patch, A., McNally, D., & Harris, L. (2020). Student and faculty perceptions of study helper websites: A new practice in collaborative cheating. *Journal of Academic Ethics*, *19*, 483–500. https://doi.org/10.1007/s10805-020-09373-2

Králíková, V., Vajdíková, R., & Foltýnek, T. (2019). Global Essay Mills Survey: Is student cheating related to the national economy? *Ethical Perspectives*, *26*(1), 91–118. https://doi.org/10.2143/EP.26.1.3286290

Lancaster, T. (2020). Commercial contract cheating provision through micro-outsourcing web sites. *International Journal for Educational Integrity*, *16*(4). https://doi.org/10.1007/s40979-020-00053-7

Mahmud, S., & Bretag, T. (2013). Postgraduate research students and academic integrity: 'It's about good research training'. *Journal of Higher Education Policy and Management*, *35*(4), 432–443. https://doi.org/10.1080/1360080X.2013.812178

McCabe, D. L. (2005). Cheating among college and university students: A North American perspective. *International Journal of Educational Integrity*, *1*(1), 1–11. https://doi.org/10.21913/IJEI.V1I1.14

Newton, P. M. (2018). How common is commercial contract cheating in higher education and is it increasing? A systematic review. *Frontiers in Education*, *3*(00067), 2504–284X. https://doi.org/10.3389/feduc.2018.00067

Nguyen, D. T. T. (2021). University students' understandings, attitudes and experiences on plagiarism. *Cypriot Journal of Educational Sciences*, *16*(4), 1471–1478. https://doi.org/10.18844/cjes.v16i4.6001

Peytcheva-Forsyth, R., Aleksieva, L., & Yovkova, B. (2018). The impact of prior experience of e-learning and e-assessment on students' and teachers' approaches to the use of a student authentication and authorship checking system. In *Proceedings from 10th Annual International Conference on Education and New Learning Technologies, Palma de Mallorca, Spain* (pp. 2–4).

Pitt, P., Dullaghan, K., & Sutherland-Smith, W. (2020). 'Mess, stress and trauma': Students' experiences of formal contract cheating processes. *Assessment & Evaluation in Higher Education*, *46*(4), 659-672. https://doi.org/10.1080/02602938.2020.1787332

Rossi, P. H., Wright, J. D., & Anderson, A. B. (Eds.). (2013). *Handbook of survey research*. Academic Press.

Rozenberg, P., Newton, P., & Saddiqui, S. (2019). Does authentic assessment assure academic integrity? Evidence from contract cheating data. *Higher Education Research & Development*, *39*(3), 1–16. https://doi.org/10.1080/07294360.2019.1680956

Rundle, K., Curtis, G. J., & Clare, J. (2019). Why students do not engage in contract cheating. *Frontiers in Psychology*, *10*(02229), 1664–1078. https://doi.org/10.3389/fpsyg.2019.02229

Shala, S., Hyseni-Spahiu, M., & Selimaj, A. (2020). Addressing contract cheating in Kosovo and international practices. *International Journal for Educational Integrity*, *16*(1), 1–17. https://doi.org/10.1007/s40979-020-00061-7

Siev, S., & Kliger, D. (2019). Cheating in academic exams: A field study. In A. Bucciol & N. Montinari (Eds.), *Dishonesty in behavioral economics* (pp. 111–140). Academic Press. https://doi.org/10.1016/B978-0-12-815857-9.00008-X

Wallace, M. J., & Newton, P. M. (2014). Turnaround time and market capacity in contract cheating. *Educational Studies*, *40*(2), 233–236. https://doi.org/10.1080/03055698.2014.889597

Wang, Y., & Xu, Z. (2021). Statistical analysis for contract cheating in Chinese universities. *Mathematics*, *9*(14), 1684. https://doi.org/10.3390/math9141684

Yorke, J., Sefcik, L., & Veeran-Colton, T. (2020). Contract cheating and blackmail: A risky business? *Studies in Higher Education*, *47*(1), 53–66. https://doi.org/10.1080/03075079.2020.1730313

CHAPTER 4

Essay Mills and Contract Cheating from a Legal Point of View

Michael Draper

ESSAY MILLS AND CONTRACT CHEATING FROM A LEGAL POINT OF VIEW

Essay mills—those individuals or organisations producing work to order and often to a precise specification for commercial gain—may take the form of an individual creating such work either alone or in partnership with others. Essay mills usually function as a writing collective or through a corporate structure (Ellis et al., 2018). There are no formalities for a sole trader or indeed a partnership to commence trading through such a structure in the United Kingdom (UK). A company, however, will usually require incorporation through a formal process, which in the UK is recognised by and enforced through the *Companies Act 2006*. The formality of incorporation is a common feature globally (DLA Piper, 2021).

A company may not be incorporated for a purpose that is unlawful within the incorporating jurisdiction. This of course raises the question as

M. Draper (✉)
Hillary Rodham Clinton School of Law, University of Swansea, Swansea, Wales, UK
e-mail: m.j.draper@swansea.ac.uk

© The Author(s), under exclusive license to Springer Nature Switzerland AG 2022
S. E. Eaton et al. (eds.), *Contract Cheating in Higher Education*, https://doi.org/10.1007/978-3-031-12680-2_4

to whether those wishing to incorporate an essay mill within a particular jurisdiction will be permitted to do so. In the UK, the uncomfortable answer is that there is very likely no impediment to incorporation on this ground of illegality or unlawfulness. The reason is that a company is often incorporated with a general commercial purpose (the objects clause) as opposed to a narrow objects clause —such as the commercial sale of bespoke essays or other written work. In the UK, the sale of such bespoke essays is not, at the time of writing, unlawful.

The sale of bespoke work to an order based on an assessment question is not illegal as a form of fraud. The criminal elements of fraud normally involve some form of dishonesty with a view to commercial gain. Draper et al. (2017) demonstrated the difficulties of using Section "Rationale for Criminal Legal Intervention Against Essay Mills" of the *Fraud Act 2006* to penalise such services and act against essay mills. In essence, this section makes it an offence to commit fraud by false representation intending to make a gain. It is difficult to apply Section "Rationale for Criminal Legal Intervention Against Essay Mills" because of the terms and conditions used by these organisations, as well as the impact of those terms and conditions on the tests for dishonesty, intention, and knowledge. Ultimately, these tests are necessary to establish criminal liability under the Act.

Essay mills typically use disclaimers stating that the work they provide should not be submitted for academic credit as the students' own work. A typical example takes the form of:

> *The work we provide to you is a perfect model answer to help you to complete your own work. You should **not** submit it directly.*

The argument is that such disclaimers utilised by essay mills negate dishonest intent and serve to establish their innocence. Both knowledge and intention present potential issues in application. Knowledge in criminal law is a complex concept, entangled by factors such as 'wilful blindness', essentially shutting one's eyes to the obvious. It is unclear what level of knowledge would be required to establish criminal liability, and whether the application of wilful blindness would be relevant. In practice, any prosecution would turn on its facts and the interaction between an essay mill and its client.

Similar uncertainty arises concerning the question of intention. Intention means acting to bring about a particular result or acting in the face of virtual certainty that the result would come about. Once again, essay mills would refer to their disclaimers, and much would depend on the interaction between the essay mill and its client.

Additional factors mitigating against prosecution include concerns of public interest and societal need. For any prosecution to take place, a prosecuting authority must be satisfied both that there is a reasonable prospect of conviction and that it is in the public interest to bring the case. There is little public appetite though for the criminalisation of students regarding academic matters although exceptions have been made for assessment impersonation.

Rationale for Criminal Legal Intervention Against Essay Mills

The criminal law prohibits conduct that causes or threatens the public interest. Typically, a new criminal offence would only be considered when necessary to prevent or restrict an activity that endangers public safety or property, or the welfare or health of individuals.

Academic misconduct or cheating poses a threat to the academic standards of higher education (HE) institutions, and by extension to the reputation of the entire HE system. It calls into doubt the integrity of qualifications awarded to students who achieve their degrees and certifications through their independent learning and effort. Are these sufficient public interest reasons to justify the introduction of a criminal offence concerning essay mills and their activity of supply?

The UK government did not think so in 2017:

> ...although we share the general intent, we are keen to ensure that non-legislative methods have been as effective as they can be before resorting to creating new criminal offences. If legislation does become necessary, we will need to take care to get it right. We have to be absolutely clear about what activity should be criminalised and what activity should remain legitimate. That requires evidence, discussion[,] and consensus. We do not yet have that... The effectiveness of a legislative offence operating as a deterrent will depend on our ability to execute successful prosecutions, and as such, we will need to be confident about these principles, as well as about who has the power to prosecute and how they will capture sufficient evidence. (Baroness Goldie, 2017, as cited in Hansard - UK Parliament, 2017)

Some of the arguments against the introduction of a new criminal offence against essay mills are alluded to in the quotation above. Reasonings include the proliferation of unnecessary new offences, ensuring that any new offence is fit for purpose, and guaranteeing that the impacts and cost to the criminal justice system are taken into account (UK Ministry of Justice Cabinet Office, 2015).

The prosecution of general offences of fraud involves establishing dishonesty on the part of the perpetrator and it may result in prosecutions in which students are either involved as witnesses or as defendants. Students knowingly and intentionally submit work by a third party for academic credit leading to a commercial gain (i.e., employment with students in some cases graduating directly into a profession, such as medicine). Objectively, this looks like dishonest behaviour, and this uncomfortable conclusion has led to the argument that a new offence has the advantage of simply targeting the supply rather than the demand side of essay mills.

This is achieved by creating an offence of strict liability removing the problems and costs associated with finding evidence of intention, as well as the knowledge at the required standard of proof in criminal prosecutions. In the UK, this required standard is for the prosecuting authority to establish that it is beyond reasonable doubt that an offence has been committed (The Crown Prosecution Service [CPS], 2018).[1] As recognised in common law jurisdictions, an individual or company should not normally be found guilty of a criminal offence without a 'guilty mind' establishing by facts indicating knowledge, intent, or recklessness as to an outcome. However, offences may be committed without requiring proof of fault. These offences are known as strict liability offences and are usually accompanied by a defence of due diligence or honest and a reasonable mistake (Australian Law Reform Commission, 2015).

All that a prosecuting authority needs to establish is that the facts fit the offence. For example, advertising or providing an essay mill service rather than establishing that an essay mill knew or intended that a student would submit the supplied work as their own, or where reckless as to that possible outcome.

---

[1] "When deciding whether there is enough evidence to charge, Crown Prosecutors must consider whether evidence can be used in court and is reliable and credible, and there is no other material that might affect the sufficiency of [the] evidence. Crown Prosecutors must be satisfied there is enough evidence to provide a 'realistic prospect of conviction' against each defendant" (The Crown Prosecution Service, 2018).

The difficulties around establishing knowledge or intent in the face of disclaimers used by essay mills are illustrated by the fact that despite the increased global activity of mills, there has only been one public prosecution under the specific law established in New Zealand which utilises the concepts of knowledge and intent as part of the relevant offences: s.292E of the *New Zealand Education Act 1989* (Table 4.1).

Responding to a request for information in 2019, the New Zealand Qualifications Authority confirmed that there has been one section 292E-related proceeding (Bean, 2019). However, the existence of the offence does act as a statement that regulators take the issue seriously and acts as a deterrent.

The Rationale for Legislation in the Republic of Ireland (Ireland)

The relevant legislation was enacted on 23rd July 2019 in Ireland. The offence, contained in the *Qualifications and Quality Assurance (Education and Training) (Amendment) Act 2019*, is modelled on the New Zealand legislation. It provides the Quality and Qualifications Ireland (QQI)[2] with powers to prosecute a person who provides cheating services as set out in s.43A of the *Qualifications and Quality Assurance (Education and Training) (Amendment) Act 2019* (eISB):

Table 4.1 Relevant section of the New Zealand Education Act 1989

292E offence to provide or advertise cheating services
*(1) A person commits an offence if the person provides any service specified in subsection (4) with the **intention** of giving a student an unfair advantage over other students.*
*(2) A person commits an offence if the person advertises any service described in subsection (4) **knowing** that the service has or would have the effect of giving a student an unfair advantage over other students.*

Note. Adapted to present legislation taken from *New Zealand Education Act* 2020 s. 393. E. (NZ)

---

[2] The QQI "is an independent State agency responsible for promoting quality and accountability in education and training services in Ireland. It was established in 2012 by the Qualifications and Quality Assurance (Education and Training) Act 2012" (QQI, 2018).

(3) A person who does either of the acts specified in subsection (4) with **the intention** of giving an enrolled learner an unfair advantage over other similarly enrolled learners commits an offence.

(5) A person commits an offence if the person advertises that the person will perform…

(6) A person commits an offence who publishes…(a) and advertisement of any service…

The numbers involved in 'contract cheating' in Ireland by buying work from essay mills before adopting this new law were challenging to determine. The Irish Ministry of Education revealed at the time that:

> It was very difficult to get statistical information on [the] prevalence of usage as 'it is a form of cheating given that those offering the *service* will not disclose it, those buying it will not, and there is no system-wide recording of detected instances of this or any other form of plagiarism'. (Bruton, 2017, as cited in O'Brien, 2017)

Quality and standards played a significant part in the argument for the creation of new criminal offences. The then Minister for Education and Skills, Richard Bruton, recognised that steps had to be taken to stamp out cheating in the education system, to also strengthen Ireland's international reputation. Bruton also claimed that the Bill was part of the government's plan to develop and expand Ireland's education system to become a business worth €2.1 billion. This was part of a wider plan to strengthen education and training services in the hope that within a decade it would become the best in Europe. Bruton considered that standards and reputation were vital in achieving this (Raidió Teilifís Éireann, 2017).

The QQI is the national agency with responsibility for external quality assurance and qualifications across further and HE sectors (Department of Education and Skills, 2017). Provided the QQI's role, this agency recognised the facilitation of cheating by essay mills as a growing threat to the integrity of Irish education (eolas Magazine, 2019). While pointing to several recent exposures in other jurisdictions, the QQI viewed the creation of the new offences as a bolster to the reputation of the Irish education system. The chief executive officer of the QQI at the time noted:

> This is a global problem from which no institution is immune, and QQI will work closely with international counterparts, in countries such as the UK and Australia, in sharing information and best practice to achieve the best

outcomes for the reputation of Irish education and training. (Walsh 2019, as cited in eolas Magazine, 2019)

Dr Deirde Stritch, Manager at QQI, in 2019 stated:

The Bill as currently proposed does not set out these offences as strict liability offences and I think the rationale behind that is that the legislation, as currently formulated, [does not] address essay mills or that type of entity exclusively. It is possible, and likely, that those committing these types of offences in many instances will be other learners, and/or their family and friends and other people who may be assisting, as they view it, a learner and so unintentionally landing themselves in this sort of territory. (Stritch, 2019, pp. 47–48)

Ireland, therefore, declined the opportunity to adopt the principle of strict liability in relation to the offences. This was because of concerns relating to the criminalisation of behaviour of those engaged in aiding students in assessed work beyond simply those engaged commercially in this activity (i.e. essay mills).

A criticism of this approach is that such frameworks may lead to a lack of successful prosecutions against essay mills, and thus lessen the impact of the offences. However, the value of such offences is that it changes the conversation that educational institutions have with their students. For instance, purchasing an essay is no longer simply a matter of academic integrity but involves the commission of an offence by the essay mill. It also changes the conversation with those that advertise or support the marketing of essay mills.

At the time of writing, no prosecutions against an essay mill have been brought by the QQI. Nonetheless, there has been considerable success in cutting off the oxygen of supply through advertising via social media and other platforms of essay mill services in Ireland (Stritch, 2021).

What is of interest is the express desire on record of developing education and training services to a best in Europe standard and using a framework that includes offences against essay mills as means of achieving such an objective. In Australia, however, legislation against essay mills was seen as a way of protecting the reputation of an already established global HE industry.

The Rationale for Legislation Against Essay Mills in Australia

The Bills Digest noted that the catalyst for action was the following:

> The issue of commercial cheating services (often referred to as 'contract cheating') came to the attention of the Australian Government in November 2014. This occurred in the wake of media reports about widespread use by students of the commercial cheating site 'MyMaster'. (Ferguson, 2020, p. 3)

The Higher Education Standards Panel (HESP) in Australia subsequently made three recommendations including that the government should consider introducing legislation modelled on *292E of New Zealand Education Act 1989* (Ferguson, 2020).

The Australian government accepted the recommendations and introduced the *Tertiary Education Quality and Standards Agency (TEQSA) Amendment (Prohibiting Academic Cheating Services) Bill*. As this Bill made its way in the Parliament, the debate was recorded through the official Hansard record of the House of Representatives. Reasons given for the need for legislation included:

- Protecting the international reputation of the HE sector;
- Protecting access to HE;
- Maintaining the attractiveness of graduates to employers across disciplines and sectors;
- Barriers to enforcement using existing laws;
- Targeting the supply of cheating services;
- Maintaining the credibility of qualifications and international mobility of students;
- Strong penalties acting as a deterrence;
- The capacity to block cheating websites making it harder for students in Australia to access these services; and
- Ensuring public confidence in the quality of graduates from HE institutions and stopping unscrupulous cheating services preying on vulnerable students.

Table 4.2 highlights key statements that were selected based on the debate in which the *TEQSA Amendment (Prohibiting Academic Cheating Services) Bill* was discussed. The table includes the names of the

Table 4.2 Key statements made in the House of Representatives throughout the TEQSA Amendment (Prohibiting Academic Cheating Services) Bill debate in 2020

Representative	Statement
Dr Katrina Jane Allen (Higgins, VIC, of the Liberal Party of Australia [LP] Party 12:24)	Economically, the provision of education to overseas students amounts to $32 billion as an industry. **From 2011 until 2015, domestic enrolments from regional locations increased by 17 per cent—this is very pleasing—and Indigenous enrolments increased by 38 per cent. One in four Australian students are now completing university units online** (2020, p. 4099).
Dr Katrina Jane Allen (Higgins, VIC, of the LP Party 12:24)	As our fourth-biggest export, it is crucial that we endeavour to maintain confidence and integrity in the higher education sector. However, **the growth of our education sector and the development of technology have also coincided with the development of third-party academic cheating services. Companies such as MyMaster and EssayMill reaped $160,000 in 2014, before being investigated** (pp. 4099–4100).
Dr Katrina Jane Allen (Higgins, VIC, of the LP Party 12:24)	The value of our higher education sector relies on us protecting its integrity. It will ensure that universities remain competitive on a global scale and an attractive destination for students and will also make our graduates more attractive to our employers (p. 4100).
Ms Celia Monica Hammond (Curtin, WA, of the LP 12:45)	…., this legislation is aimed at those who provide cheating services and not at the students who might use such services (p. 4104).
Ms Celia Monica Hammond (Curtin, WA, of the LP, 12:45)	**Ensuring academic integrity in our higher education system is of vital importance.** The consequences of not having a robust and multifaceted approach to ensuring academic integrity can result in great damage to the domestic and international reputation of Australian higher education. It's also a risk to employers. How do you know that the person that you're employing actually did all of the work that led to their qualification? **It is a risk to student mobility.** Once our border restrictions are lifted and our students are able to travel internationally to undertake further studies, if the academic integrity of our system has been put under attack and is in question then the mobility of our students, either as students or as graduates, will be greatly harmed. It also undermines the integrity of all of the certifications (p. 4105).

(continued)

Table 4.2 (continued)

Representative	Statement
Hon. Kevin John Hogan (page, NSW, of the National Party of Australia [NATS]—assistant minister to the deputy prime minister, 13:08)	The strong penalties in this bill will significantly deter the provision and advertising of academic cheating services. **The capacity to block cheating websites will make it harder for students in Australia to access these services** (pp. 4108–4109).

Note. Adapted to include statements taken from House of Representatives—Commonwealth of Australia (2020, June 12). *TEQSA Amendment (Prohibiting Academic Cheating Services) Bill 2019*

representatives that made each statement, and the relevant arguments were bolded for further reference. Statements are cited verbatim as per the available transcription online.

The *Prohibiting Academic Cheating Services Bill 2019* (the Bill) amended the *TEQSA Act 2011* and was passed by Parliament on 26 August 2020. It formally became law on 3 September 2020. A key definition of an academic **cheating service** is that it:

> Means the provision of work to or the undertaking of work for students, in circumstances where the work:
>
> (a) Is, or forms a substantial part of, an assessment task that students are required to personally undertake; or
> (b) Could reasonably be regarded as being, or forming a substantial part of, an assessment task that students are required to personally undertake. (The Parliament of the Commonwealth of Australia House of Representatives, 2019a, p. 3)

According to the Parliament of the Commonwealth of Australia House of Representatives (2019), its explanatory memorandum states that:

> The definition of ***academic cheating service*** limits the types of assistance that are prohibited by the Bill to cases where all or a substantial part of an assessment task is offered or provided by the service. In practice, this means that incidental or inconsequential assistance, advice or example answers that might be offered to a student are not at risk of being captured by the new offence provisions. Any assistance that did not change the intent or meaning

of the student's work would not be prohibited by the Bill. (The Parliament of the Commonwealth of Australia House of Representatives, 2019b, p. 11)

As an example, the document suggests that "while editing of a student's work by a third party might be prohibited by institutional policy, it would not be prohibited by the Bill so long as it [did not] represent a substantial part of the work" (The Parliament of the Commonwealth of Australia House of Representatives, 2019b, p. 11).

The explanatory memorandum further notes the following in relation to the definition of **academic cheating**:

> […This definition] limits the types of assistance that are prohibited by the Bill to cases where all, or a substantial part, of an assessment task that a student is required to personally undertake is offered or provided by the service. Because of this, no specific exemptions for types of assistance are considered necessary to include in the Bill. (The Parliament of the Commonwealth of Australia House of Representatives, 2019b, p. 15)

Unlike New Zealand and Ireland, strict liability in Australia applies to the commission of an offence of providing an academic cheating service. Additionally, a prosecuting authority does not need to establish the provision of a cheating service to a particular student. Hence, the prosecuting authority simply must establish the facts fitting the offence without reference to a need to prove intention or knowledge, or that a cheating service has been offered or provided to a particular student. Namely, the prosecuting authority does not need to establish fault for the elements of the relevant offence.

The prosecuting would simply need to prove that the person intended to provide, offer to provide, or arranged an academic cheating service and that they were reckless as to whether it was provided for a commercial purpose. These are important provisions because prosecution would not necessarily result in an HE institution becoming a 'crime scene' with the necessity of a student being a key witness to an offence. At the time of writing no prosecutions have been undertaken; although like Ireland, additional relevant actions have been taken against online services.

For example, a news article in *The Guardian* published on 7 July 2021 reported that "in the first court case of its kind under new laws passed in 2020, the Tertiary Education Quality and Standards Agency (TEQSA) is seeking to force 51 internet service providers in Australia to block access to Assignmenthelp4you.com" (Taylor, 2021). This news article explains that this website not only offers online tutoring and exam prep services, but it also provides assignment writing (Taylor, 2021). In October 2021 TEQSA obtained a federal court order under section 127A of the TEQSA Act that required 51 carriage service providers to block access to the website Assignmenthelp4you.com. A key takeaway from this decision is that HE institutions and internet service providers should act when they are made aware that academic cheating services exist.

The Rationale for Legislation Against Essay Mills in the United Kingdom

As noted above, the UK government in 2017 did not support the introduction of legislation for the reasons identified, choosing to focus on sector-led non-legislative initiatives. However, the case for specific legislation in the UK to establish bespoke strict liability offences in relation to essay mills has been made consistently by scholars in the field (Draper & Reid-Hutchings, 2019; Draper et al., 2017; Draper & Newton, 2017).

In June 2020, the Parliamentary Under Secretary of State at the Department for Education noted the introduction of legislation in several countries. Baroness Berridge (2020) added:

> We would be willing to consider supporting any legislation, including a private member's bill, that is workable and that contains measures that would eliminate essay mills in ways that cannot be delivered through other means, provided that the parliamentary time permitted. (as cited in UK Parliament, 2020)

Subsequently in early 2021 Chris Skidmore, former Universities Minister, brought a motion for leave to bring in a Parliamentary Bill to prohibit the operation and advertising of essay mill services, noting that:

> ...46 vice-chancellors wrote a joint letter calling for these websites to banned. This call is now supported by Universities UK, the Russell Group, GuildHE, the Quality Assurance Agency for Higher Education and indeed most, if not all, of the higher education institutions and organisations that I have had the privilege of working with both as Universities Minister, and now as co-chair of the all-party university group. For me, the most passionate advocates of ending essay mills have been the students themselves and student unions, which have campaigned determinedly against their operation. (Skidmore, 2021, as cited in UK Parliament—Hansard, 2021)

Skidmore also included a reference to the website www.uktopwriters.com, and spoke about the following findings:

> The QAA has revealed today that there are at least 932 sites in operation in the UK, up from 904 in December 2020, 881 in October 2020 and 635 back in June 2018. Their increased presence is even boasted of on a website, www.uktopwriters.com, which provides a 'compare the market' service. (Skidmore, 2021, as cited in UK Parliament—Hansard, 2021)[3]

The argument for the bespoke legislation was thus framed in the context of strong student support for a ban, the development of a consumer style market for essay mills and their services, and the initial success of legislation in Ireland and Australia.

The continued growth of essay mill services highlighted by the QAA served to demonstrate that the 2017 government preferred approach had not worked despite strong sector-led initiatives to combat contract cheating.

Consequently, on 16 June 2021, Lord Storey, acknowledging student concerns in this area, introduced the Higher Education Cheating Services Bill into the House of Lords with cross-party support (as cited in Brown, 2021).

The Bill takes a similar approach to that taken in Australia with the introduction of a strict liability offence but subject to a defence of due diligence as advocated by Draper et al. (2017). A person would commit an offence if they both provide and receive, or reasonably expect to receive, a payment, financial reward, or other financial benefit for providing an HE 'cheating' service. A person would also commit an offence if they advertised or published, without reasonable excuse, an advertisement for such a service. Nonetheless, they would not be guilty of an offence for doing any of the above if they could demonstrate they would not be able to know the work could be used in such a way.

---

[3] Further statements suggested that "Australia, New Zealand, South Africa and, most recently, Ireland have already taken action to make essay mills illegal in their countries, and the Quality Assurance Agency has been in close contact with the countries that have banned essay mills to monitor the effect of the ban. The ban is already making a difference. In Australia, following legislation, the Edubirdie, EssayShark, and Custom Writings websites, for instance, now all state 'Our service is not available in your region;' yet, in contrast, they all still thrive in the UK" (Skidmore, 2021, as cited in UK Parliament—Hansard, 2021).

Enforcement of Cross-Border Co-operation and Jurisdictional Issues

Essay mills operate globally and through the internet without reference to national borders and threaten the credibility of education systems around the world (Fogarty, n.d.). Different jurisdictional interests—regulatory and law enforcement—are a factor to be considered in enforcement of offences. Broadly criminal offences apply within national jurisdictions only and offences do not normally have extraterritorial effect although exceptions may apply in relation to tax evasion money laundering and fraud which are serious forms of dishonesty. Generally, therefore an offence will only be trialable in the jurisdiction in which the offence takes place or has a substantial connection to the jurisdiction unless the offence itself enables extraterritorial jurisdiction (CPS, 2021).

The Legislation in the Republic of Ireland, Commonwealth of Australia, and the proposed legislation in the UK do not expressly refer to extraterritorial effect. Given that essay mills operate globally this is a significant barrier to enforcement if the essay mill or individual is a legal entity and legally based (domiciled) in another jurisdiction. For this reason, co-operation between member states and global social media platforms is essential for the successful enforcement of offences.

The QQI has signed a Memorandum of Understanding with its Australian sister agency, TEQSA, to share information and offer professional advice about academic fraud and contract cheating. This type of information-sharing arrangement is of limited use in supporting the successful enforcement of offences across borders because it does not create legally binding relations between the parties or a commitment to assist in prosecutions. Notwithstanding obvious limitations, it serves as a useful marker as a statement of intent of co-ordinated action against essay mills (Walsh & McClaran, 2019). A similar arrangement has been made between the QAA and TEQSA (Blackstock & McClaran, 2019).

Demonstrating the importance of such cross-border co-operation TEQSA warned the QAA in 2021 that essay mills were seeking to hack university websites using malware that directed students to essay mills following similar attempts using malicious code made against HE providers in Australia (McKie, 2021).

The Draft Recommendation of the Committee of Ministers to member states on countering education fraud will contain a provision directed to the member states of the Council of Europe (2021a). This Draft Recommendation encourages international co-operation in the enforcement and prosecution of offences or other forms of legal redress related to Education Fraud even if the provision or contract for such services takes place wholly outside the member state in which the legal entity is domiciled (Council of Europe, 2021b).

However, it is through co-operation—backed by legislation or otherwise—with global online platforms such as Facebook, Google, YouTube, and PayPal that countries seeking to combat essay mills have seen and are likely to see the greatest enforcement success. Action has been taken in Ireland and Australia and similarly in the UK with requests by the QAA to block essay mill providers (QAA, 2018).

REFERENCES

Australian Law Reform Commission (ALRC). (2015). 10. Strict and absolute liability. In ALRC (Ed.), *Traditional rights and freedoms—Encroachments by commonwealth Laws final report* (pp. 285–308). Fineline Print & Copy Service NSW.

Bean, D. (2019, November 7). *Official information act request*. New Zealand Qualifications Authority. https://www.nzqa.govt.nz/assets/About-us/Information-releases/OIA-releases/December-2019/Numbers-charged-under-s292E-of-the-Education-Act-1989-CR19687.pdf.

Blackstock, D., & McClaran, A. (2019, November 4). *Memorandum of co-operation between the QAA, United Kingdom and the TEQSA, Australia*. Australian Government - QAA. https://www.qaa.ac.uk/docs/qaa/international/teqsa-qaa.pdf?sfvrsn=732df381_10

Brown, T. (2021, June 16). *In focus: Higher education cheating services prohibition bill [HL]*. UK Parliament – House of Lords Library. https://lordslibrary.parliament.uk/higher-education-cheating-services-prohibition-bill-hl/

Council of Europe. (2021a). *About ETINED*. https://www.coe.int/en/web/ethics-transparency-integrity-in-education/about-etined.

Council of Europe. (2021b). *2nd ETINED plenary session (2018)*. https://www.coe.int/en/web/ethics-transparency-integrity-in-education/2nd-etined-plenary-session.

Department of Education and Skills. (2017, May 15). *Bruton announces new powers for the higher and further education regulator*. https://merrionstreet.ie/en/category-index/education/bruton_announces_new_powers_for_the_higher_and_further_education_regulator.125846.shortcut.html.

DLA Piper. (2021, July 12). *Corporate: Incorporation process.* https://www.dlapiperintelligence.com/goingglobal/corporate/index.html?t=06-incorporation-process.

Draper, M., Ibezim, V., & Newton, P. (2017). Are essay mills committing fraud? An analysis of their behaviours vs the 2006 fraud act. *International Journal for Educational Integrity, 13*(3), 1–14. https://doi.org/10.1007/s40979-017-0014-5

Draper, M. J., & Newton, P. M. (2017). A legal approach to tackling contract cheating? *International Journal for Educational Integrity, 13*(11), 1–16. https://doi.org/10.1007/s40979-017-0022-5

Draper, M. J., & Reid-Hutchings, C. (2019). Are essay mills committing fraud? A further analysis of their behaviours vs the 2006 fraud act (UK). *International Journal for Educational Integrity, 15*(11), 1–16. https://doi.org/10.1007/s40979-019-0050-4

Ellis, C., Zucker, I. M., & Randall, D. (2018). The infernal business of contract cheating: Understanding the business processes and models of academic custom writing sites. *International Journal of Educational Integrity, 14*(1). https://doi.org/10.1007/s40979-017-0024-3

eolas Magazine. (2019, December). *Clamping down on academic cheating in Ireland.* https://www.eolasmagazine.ie/clamping-down-on-academic-cheating-in-ireland/

Ferguson, H. (2020, February 13). *TEQSA (prohibiting academic cheating services) bill* 2019. Bills digest, 2019–2020 (84), Parliament of Australia, Australia. https://parlinfo.aph.gov.au/parlInfo/download/legislation/billsdgs/7182391/upload_binary/7182391.pdf.

Fogarty, P. (n.d.). *How students turn to 'essay mills' to help them cheat.* BBC. https://www.bbc.com/worklife/article/20190329-the-essay-mills-that-help-students-cheat

Hansard - UK Parliament. (2017, January 25). *Higher education and research bill volume 778: Debated on Wednesday 25* January 2017. https://hansard.parliament.uk/Lords/2017-01-25/debates/B510EEDD-43EC-4FA9-8222-865249D8A3D2/HigherEducationAndResearchBill?highlight=contract%20cheating#contribution-968EC100-680F-438B-B16A-D4A9C7818DE8

House of Representatives - Commonwealth of Australia. (2020, June 12). *Tertiary education quality and standards agency amendment (prohibiting academic cheating services) bill 2019.* https://parlinfo.aph.gov.au/parlInfo/download/chamber/hansardr/5d3da435-cd86-4b4d-ad95-255f2729535d/toc_pdf/House%20of%20Representatives_2020_06_12_7767_Official.pdf;fileType=application%2Fpdf#search=%22chamber/hansardr/5d3da435-cd86-4b4d-ad95-255f2729535d/0043%22.

McKie, A. (2021, April 22). *Australia warns UK over essay mills hacking university websites*. Times Higher Education. https://www.timeshighereducation.com/news/australia-warns-uk-over-essay-mills-hacking-university-websites.

New Zealand Education Act 2020 s. 393. E. (NZ). Retrieved from https://www.legislation.govt.nz/act/public/2020/0038/latest/whole.html#LMS202497

New Zealand Education Act 1989 s. 292. E. (NZ).

O'Brien, C. (2017, May 12). *Plan to prosecute firms who offer paid-for essays to students*. Irish Times. https://www.irishtimes.com/news/education/plan-to-prosecute-firms-who-offer-paid-for-essays-to-students-1.3007509.

QQI. (2018). *About Us*. https://www.qqi.ie/Articles/Pages/About-Us.aspx

Qualifications and Quality Assurance (Education and Training) (Amendment) Act 2019 (eISB) s. 43.A (IE.). Retrieved from http://www.irishstatutebook.ie/eli/2019/act/32/section/15/enacted/en/html#sec15

Raidió Teilifís Éireann (RTE). (2017, May 15). *Bruton outlines bill to tackle cheating in education system*. https://www.rte.ie/news/education/2017/0515/875195-bruton-bill-cheating/

Stritch, D. (2019, May 22). Lessons from abroad on developing effective legislation. Dr Deirdre Stritch, provider approval and monitoring manager, QQI awards, quality and qualifications Ireland. In Westminster Higher Education Forum (Ed.), *Keynote seminar: Contract cheating in higher education - prevention, detection, disruption and legislative options* (pp. 46–49). Westminster Higher Education Forum.

Stritch, D. (2021, March 18). *Supporting academic integrity – A view from Ireland: ENQA: Protecting and promoting academic integrity: How quality assurance agencies can take action*. QQI. https://www.enqa.eu/wp-content/uploads/Academic-Integrity-The-View-From-Ireland-March-2021.pdf

Taylor, J. (2021, July 7). *University regulator tries to block Australian students from using alleged cheating website: [TEQSA] wants 51 internet service providers to block access to Assignmenthelp4you.com*. The Guardian. https://www.theguardian.com/australia-news/2021/jul/07/university-regulator-tries-to-block-australian-students-from-using-alleged-cheating-website-assignmenthelp4you-assignment-help-for-you

The Crown Prosecution Service. (2018, October 26). *The code for crown prosecutors*. https://www.cps.gov.uk/publication/code-crown-prosecutors.

The Crown Prosecution Service. (2021, July 26). *Jurisdiction*. https://www.cps.gov.uk/legal-guidance/jurisdiction.

The Parliament of the Commonwealth of Australia House of Representatives. (2019a). *TEQSA amendment (prohibiting academic cheating services) bill 2019 No. 2019 (Education): A bill for an act to amend the TEQSA Act 2011, and for related purposes*. https://parlinfo.aph.gov.au/parlInfo/download/legislation/bills/r6483_first-reps/toc_pdf/19257b01.pdf;fileType=application%2Fpdf

The Parliament of the Commonwealth of Australia House of Representatives. (2019b). *TEQSA amendment (prohibiting academic cheating service) bill 2019: Explanatory memorandum.* https://parlinfo.aph.gov.au/parlInfo/download/legislation/ems/r6483_ems_d9f89ad0-f957-4e43-873a-bff12b21d878/upload_pdf/723541.pdf;fileType=application%2Fpdf

UK Ministry of Justice Cabinet Office. (2015, December 2). *Advice on introducing or amending criminal offences and estimating and agreeing implications for the criminal justice system.* https://assets.publishing.service.gov.uk/government/uploads/system/uploads/attachment_data/file/481126/creating-new-criminal-offences.pdf.

UK Parliament. (2020, June 4). Students: Plagiarism question for Department of Education. https://questions-statements.parliament.uk/written-questions/detail/2020-06-04/HL5328.

UK Parliament – Hansard. (2021, February). *Essay Mills (prohibition) volume 689: Debated on Wednesday 10 February 2021.* https://hansard.parliament.uk/commons/2021-02-10/debates/5E37B30F-EFD9-40A2-AA28-5D05327A7596/EssayMills(Prohibition)

Walsh, P., & McClaran, A. (2019, November 29). Memorandum of understanding between the TEQSA and the quality and qualifications Ireland (QQI). TEQSA - QQI. https://www.qqi.ie/Downloads/Memorandum%20of%20Understanding%20betwen%20QQI%20and%20TEQSA%20(Australia)%20-%2029%20Nov%202019.pdf

CHAPTER 5

Leveraging College Copyright Ownership Against File-Sharing and Contract Cheating Websites

Josh Seeland, Sarah Elaine Eaton, and Brenda M. Stoesz

ACADEMIC FILE-SHARING (AFS)

Many of us engage in our online habits with little conscious thought. As a whole, file-sharing is one of the main activities of the Internet, brought to the general public's attention with incidents such as those surrounding Napster and the downloading of digital music, which spread the practice of file-sharing even further (Danaher et al., 2014). Academic file-sharing (AFS), on the other hand, is comparatively recent, and lies "in the digital

J. Seeland (✉)
Assiniboine Community College, Brandon, MB, Canada
e-mail: seelandjl@Assiniboine.net

S. E. Eaton
University of Calgary, Calgary, AB, Canada
e-mail: seaton@ucalgary.ca

B. M. Stoesz
University of Manitoba, Winnipeg, MB, Canada
e-mail: Brenda.Stoesz@umanitoba.ca

© The Author(s), under exclusive license to Springer Nature Switzerland AG 2022
S. E. Eaton et al. (eds.), *Contract Cheating in Higher Education*, https://doi.org/10.1007/978-3-031-12680-2_5

nature of the practice" (John, 2014, p. 201). Accessing shared files stored on other authorised computers is quite different from indiscriminate digital "reproduction and distribution of files" (John, 2014, p. 203), and the latter is the type of file-sharing discussed here, perhaps more accurately described as impersonal file transfer. Siegfried (2004) also points out that software piracy pre-dates the introduction of the personal computer.

Academic misconduct involving collusion and other types of unauthorised group efforts is well-documented as being nothing new. Rogerson and Basanta (2016) contrasted the online platforms used by students to trade or otherwise access completed assessments and other academic resources for little to no cost against those commanded by online essay mills, or commercial contract cheating sites (Lancaster, 2020), which create customised assessments for student customers. Students recognise the difference between using these two types of platforms (Harrison et al., 2021), with an estimated average of 8% of students submitting "custom ghost-writing," whereas 11% submit assessments obtained via file-sharing (Curtis et al., 2021). Bretag et al. (2019a) placed these activities on a spectrum of sharing behaviours (i.e., "buying, selling, or trading notes") to cheating behaviours, with "arranging for another to take one's exam" representing the worst of the "unequivocal cheating behaviours" (p. 4). This spectrum suggests differences in intent, severity of misconduct, learning, copyright implications, and many other metrics between AFS and contract cheating.

The fact that file-sharing is a global social norm makes AFS more difficult to address. Because the number of people who participate in file-sharing is high, and its being deemed unethical is not self-evident (Bateman et al., 2013), it is logical to expect that many college and university students comfortably engage in the activity. Thus, careful education and contextualisation of the activity within both copyright and academic integrity are advisable.

Factors Influencing File-Sharing

File-sharing sites, marketing themselves as innocuous student collectives and crowd-sourced platforms, could be contributing to a student attitude of which many may be unaware. Some students may identify with the file-sharing culture, one which is said to grow and find cohesion in attempts to crack down on and level the term "piracy" against it (John, 2014). The Napster debate between music fans and the music industry is said to, at its root, be one of viewing the Internet as either a cultural and public space or as a method of bringing a product to the marketplace, respectively (Sano-Franchini, 2010). Intertwined with the file-sharing culture is the anti-copyright culture, a vocal and global ideology (Martin & Newhall, 2013). Free-sharing and anti-copyright mindsets in some students may have been exacerbated by the hasty move to online learning necessitated by the COVID-19 pandemic, where postsecondary students and learning materials provided by colleges and universities are spread across the globe.

How a person defines themself may apply to their likelihood of engaging in AFS. Membership in, or strong identification with, many types of groups increases the likelihood of academic misconduct (Harrison et al., 2021). This has been well-discussed and researched in the context of academic integrity policies and their application to students from collectivist cultures. Siegfried (2004) also found that the likelihood of engaging in software piracy was positively correlated with one's sense of cultural individualism. Bretag et al. (2019a) found that students who engaged in cheating behaviours were also much more likely to engage in sharing behaviours.

Colleges, universities, and those working in them are often part of academic cultures that lag behind those of their students when it comes to technological issues such as file-sharing. It, after all, is a culture which grew from the digital age (John, 2014), rather than tried to adapt to it like education and the entertainment industry have. This would also seem to apply to related concepts such as "ownership and intellectual property" (Sano-Franchini, 2014, p. 208). In their work on contract cheating, Clarke and Lancaster (2013) point out that university students often possess technical skills ahead of those who teach them. In the context of cultures, this is echoed in Sano-Franchini (2010) citing research about technology in general evolving faster than culture and creating a disequilibrium along the way.

There are many dangers of academic file-sharing. Due to the innocuous or even legitimate image file-sharing sites try to create for themselves, students may be "knowingly or unknowingly breaching institutional academic integrity policies in addition to laws that protect areas such as intellectual property and copyright" (Rogerson & Basanta, 2016, p. 274). Although some file-sharing sites simply provide a platform for file exchange, others provide access to contract cheating services (Lancaster & Cotarlan, 2021). Students who circumvent the learning process through this practice may "find themselves unfit for professional practice and then may be vulnerable to engaging in unethical behaviours in the workplace" (Ellis et al., 2020, p. 465). Unlike possessing entertainment files that were not legally purchased, possessing and submitting the academic work of another student ultimately "undermines public trust in the operation of HEIs [higher education institutions] to graduate students who, having been vetted for, can support the intellectual and workforce health of constituent communities" (Locquiao & Ives, 2020, p. 1). Although the tallying of financial loss through file-sharing is usually reserved for large media industries, Lancaster and Cotarlan (2021) compiled some figures related to universities whose materials had been posted to file-sharing sites. Focusing on financial loss, however, may further the perception of higher education's commercialisation and encourage file-sharing among students who identify with this view.

Despite the risk of academic misconduct, there are also many reasons for using file-sharing sites. Language and communication skills deficiencies, time management problems, personal life challenges, and lack of interest may all contribute to decisions to cheat (Rogerson & Basanta, 2016). Dissatisfaction with the learning environment and ample opportunities are two more reasons why students cheat (Bretag et al., 2019a). Engaging in AFS, specifically, is also strongly influenced by student age and discipline of study (Bretag et al., 2019a). As a result, students might engage in AFS as an act of resistance against their schools or the educational system in general (Eaton, 2021). Siegfried (2004) showed the relationship between ethics and software piracy, which parallels file-sharing and academic integrity. The author found that many students' responses revealed ethical acceptance of actions, including using other students' computer accounts (50%), selling information from university directories (8%), and collusion (57%), which would be deemed academic or non-academic misconduct at many colleges and universities.

The commercialisation of higher education may also come into play here. Kezar and Bernstein-Sierra (2016) summarise this as higher education moving away from a societal public good focus to one of making money; this further ties into a similar student mindset of moving away from seeing learning as transformational to transactional, or one of credentialism. Here, students are simply consumers of the product that schools are perceived as selling, and academic misconduct is justified in order to finish school and make money. File-sharing companies have begun to participate in this process by targeting adjunct faculty, sponsoring student events, and even working with universities. Danaher et al.

(2014) discussed the impact of piracy on the media industries, and in becoming more commercialised, higher education could be viewed by some in the piracy subculture as but another huge industry to undermine through file-sharing, specifically of an academic nature.

Added to this already complex set of factors is the fact that not all uses of file-sharing sites involve breaking copyright law. For example, students may, under the copyright laws of most countries, legally upload their own academic work to file-sharing sites if they own the copyright to it. In some cases, however, this may constitute facilitating academic misconduct in an academic integrity policy as another student could then use it in part or in whole and submit it as their own for grades. The student who uploaded the file may not know, or care, if or how anyone else uses their work. Many academic integrity policies do not deal directly with the complexities of AFS, and students, instructors, and administrators may be required to apply traditional definitions of plagiarism to the file-sharing practice. Again, the recency of AFS technology seems at odds with the slower pace of academic culture.

Academic File-Sharing Prevention

There are many ways to help prevent unauthorised AFS among students. One way is to contextualise copyright within academic integrity, and both concepts in turn within quality assurance frameworks. In this way, academic integrity becomes a regular measurement of quality curriculum (McKenzie, 2019), and is integrated into an institutional procedure. Copyright finds a home here with its legal implications for students who are uploading to file-sharing sites the quality materials provided to them by their educational institution. These contexts then provide further frameworks for educating students on both copyright and academic integrity. The UK's Quality Assurance Agency (QAA) for Higher Education (2020) proposes recommendations that include education, reduction of cheating opportunities, detection of misconduct, and regulations and policies. Within these recommendations lie opportunities for proactive education targeting both students and staff/faculty about academic integrity and copyright, ways to reduce and detect academic misconduct and copyright violations, and alignment with and development of institutional policies.

Many assessment design strategies used to reduce and prevent plagiarism can also work for AFS. Bretag et al. (2019b) include individualising and regularly updating assessments as recommendations. Some have encouraged scaffolding, multiple assessment types, and the enabling of critical thinking in assessments as ways to reduce avenues of academic misconduct (see Velliaris & Pierce, 2019; Stoesz et al., 2022). Bretag et al. (2019a) recommend ensuring that students understand assignment requirements and receive sufficient feedback on them. More importantly, there are also benefits to both teaching and learning in their implementation (Bertram Gallant, 2016). Ellis et al. (2020) showed decreases in academic integrity violations associated with using authentic assessment methods. Yet, no one method can single-handedly eliminate any type of academic misconduct. Rather, educators and their institutions may yield incremental improvements in their academic integrity efforts by implementing assessment design strategies (Dawson, 2021).

Educators can help to control the narrative around AFS by discussing it proactively. Danaher et al. (2014) suggested encouraging file-sharers to share on legal channels, with hallmarks of "timing, convenience, and quality" (p. 56). In higher education, and in accordance with QAA (2020) recommendations, instructors could talk about file-sharing with students, specify what can be shared, where, and with whom, and provide a platform to do so—within a learning management system, for example. Knowing the consequences of AFS and having a viable option may then deter some students from engaging in the practice on illicit platforms (Rogerson & Basanta, 2016).

As copyright is a legal issue, and academic integrity in most cases an ethical one, their intermingling in the context of AFS is here again beneficial to educators wanting to control the narrative within their classrooms. Bateman et al. (2013) suggest tying ethics into the file-sharing debate, citing research about the effectiveness in presenting it as a consensus of being illegal and ethically wrong.

Along with verbal reduction strategies there are physical ones. Blocking access to contract cheating and file-sharing sites through institutional networks is another way to reduce AFS (Seeland et al., 2020; TEQSA, 2021), but there are advantages and disadvantages to this method. Among the advantages are nullifying the marketing and search engine optimisation performed by file-sharing and contract cheating sites that often enable them to elude existing filters by being identified as "education" or "online shopping." Subsequently, the time-consuming manual organisation of URLs requires dedicated and knowledgeable staff, along with cooperation from IT colleagues.

The systematic use of text-matching software may also help prevent AFS. By deploying this software as an educational tool, students would be given a chance to improve on the academic skill of citing before assignment submission. In this way, comparatively minor misconduct such as plagiarism is both contextualised against more serious types of misconduct such as collusion and contract cheating, and the need for detection of plagiarism and the administration of policy may be reduced (Stephens, 2016). At the same time, problems with accessing sources for verification in cases of suspected AFS (Rogerson & Basanta, 2016) may be reduced in having access through the institutional repositories of student assignments built when they are analysed for similarity using text-matching software. This would provide centralised access for all faculty at an institution should an incident of misconduct related to file-sharing arise.

Perhaps most importantly, contextualising copyright within academic integrity can provide institutions with a lever for accessing file-sharing sites. Suspected academic misconduct and its ethical implications are not enough for institutions to be granted access to file-sharing sites. What is effective, however, is requesting the removal of materials based on copyright violations. With multiple files available, and institutions being a searchable parameter on these sites, copyright compliance becomes a matter of hundreds or thousands of files. Thus, Rogerson and Basanta's (2016) concerns about the identity of uploaders, ownership of the material, and access to sources can find in copyright a lever for investigation. Once it is known, both proactively and due to the administration of policy when applicable, that institutions are monitoring and acting upon both their copyrighted material and potential academic misconduct related to AFS sites, some students may avoid engaging in this doubly problematic behaviour.

Copyright Implications

To leverage copyright compliance against file-sharing sites, institutions might begin by asking themselves who retains intellectual property: individual educators or the institution? In the case of Assiniboine Community College (ACC), along with many other colleges in Canada, copyright of materials produced by employees is retained by the institution. Therefore, individual faculty members do not carry the burden of enforcing copyright compliance, and cases of academic misconduct related to AFS were supported by staff with experience in both copyright and academic integrity violations, such as the first author.

In Canada, copyright issues centre on the federal Copyright Act, whereas in the US, the Digital Millennium Copyright Act (DMCA) holds sway. At the time of writing, most major AFS and contract cheating sites were based in the US, and thus respond to copyright takedown notices referencing the DMCA. Some even reference the related requirements when discussing potential copyright violations in the fine print of their websites. Many colleges and universities have takedown request templates for both Canada and the US, which can be found easily through search engines.

An institution's educational efforts about file-sharing for both students and staff can find its footing in copyright. Siegfried (2004) showed a lack of student understanding related to concepts such as public domain, fair use exemptions (similar to Canada's fair dealing exemptions), and the difference between plagiarism and copyright violations. In the case of the final example, there is yet another benefit to contextualising copyright within academic integrity.

Being careful in how an institution labels AFS is also important. John (2014) contrasts this against the term "piracy," which was likely popularised by governments and the entertainment industry. Martin and Newhall (2013) traced the expansion of copyright criminalisation and show how it is tied to the entertainment industry and its ability to lobby governments to protect its goods from piracy. Mehta (2020) highlighted how another large industry, that of academic publishers, seeks to partner with university libraries to use surveillance software to protect their own profits from piracy on platforms such as Sci-Hub. Higher education may do well to be aware of this terminological contrast and larger implications, and how contract cheating sites seek to undermine education with their aggressive and deceptive advertising. Without at least theoretically situating their employers in these other perspectives, educators in colleges and universities could find themselves and their students as unwitting pawns in a much larger and older game.

There are also potential risks in the way copyright issues related to AFS are pursued in higher education. For example, file-sharing sites may remove a file that an educational institution claims violated their copyright ownership, then simply repost a link directing users elsewhere (Martin & Newhall, 2013). There are also intricacies in the DMCA, such as lack of awareness or financial benefit, which have allowed some file-sharing sites to find safe harbour when faced with prosecution based on copyright issues. Finally, many feel that removal of academic files which violate copyright laws from file-sharing sites may simply "drive cheating underground, making detection harder" (Clarke & Lancaster, p. 223; see also Mansfield-Devine, 2010; Rogerson & Basanta, 2016).

Schools and academic integrity organisations could ultimately advocate for the mutually beneficial disruption of the predatory world of AFS. Martin and Newhall (2013) offer some ideas that institutions could consider in their approaches to copyright implications in AFS. "Avoid punishing people before they might reasonably be expected to know what they're doing is a crime" (p. 140) seems like good advice given that many students do not know about the legal implications of AFS. College and university policies could reflect this by having educative approaches to the issue. At the time of this writing, one university professor at an American institution where faculty hold copyright to their work took a stronger approach by suing a student who had uploaded exams to an AFS site (Associated Press, 2022). Part of the rationale for the lawsuit was that the tests contained copyright warnings against their reproduction.

Martin and Newhall (2013) also suggest having governments, specifically federal governments, pass laws that target the most prominent providers of AFS to shut down infringing sites and seize assets, which could tie in to existing and proposed legislation regarding contract cheating sites and their services being made illegal.

Copyright law may be leveraged to gain access to at least some of the popular AFS sites. In their foundational chapter on academic file-sharing, Rogerson and Basanta (2016) suggested that without access to the often closed communities of AFS, institutions are limited to four approaches in their dealing with it: policies, education for students, detection of shared and derivative assignments, and prevention through assessment design. Copyright law may be a fifth. Again, this not only contextualises copyright within academic integrity, but in the case where an institution owns the copyright to academic files and monitors their use, it alleviates some of the work otherwise placed on instructors trying to ensure copyright law compliance for academic files for which they are the copyright holder.

Leveraging Copyright Law Against AFS Sites

After a multi-institutional initiative to block access to AFS and contract cheating sites on institutional networks (Seeland et al., 2020), ACC gathered and analysed monthly data on the names and rates of access to dozens of sites. The first author of this chapter, in the role of Academic Integrity and Copyright Officer, chose one commonly accessed, US-based site that could be searched using an internet search engine to reveal over 200 academic files tagged as relevant to ACC.

Using the site's own copyright takedown notice information, Seeland sent a request for removal of all 200+ ACC files. Though it was felt that this would be unlikely to succeed, the reward of convenience would have made the little time it took well worth it. A DMCA Compliance Team Agent from the site responded quickly, writing that school, department, and other categories of mass takedowns were too broad, and that each individual file must be mentioned and accompanied by a site URL.

Although some information could be gathered through free previews, the number of free previews was limited. To gather the required information for all ACC files required an account, as access to the site was restricted. Seeland created an "educator" account, the process for which required a verification period of over two weeks. Once this happened, the same Compliance Team Agent agreed to provide 30 free "unlocks" to facilitate the gathering of required information. While this was not enough to open each file, the site provided further unlocks for responding to a pop-up survey and labelling the file as "helpful," which it was in the context of this process. Adding unlocks this way allowed the information-gathering process to continue.

Sorting the ACC files by date, Seeland prioritised files that appeared as ones that students might still be able to use for purposes of academic misconduct. Some of the files were up to two years old, making it less likely that the assessment was still being used, and that the student who had uploaded it was still enrolled in the college, where the longest programme is two years.

The diversity of the files was surprising. Along with completed assignments helpfully prefaced by title pages including student names, there were slide decks, assignment instructions, handouts, and even screenshots of students' digital calendars complete with their names. Many of the completed assignments were replete with spelling and other errors such that their use in any capacity would likely result in low grades. All files were categorised as "homework help" and "test prep."

As the files were explored in depth, the information required by the site for takedown had to be extracted and organised for efficiency. The information required included the file name, uploader name, and site URL for the file. Surprisingly, many user accounts comprised actual student names that could be verified in ACC's email contact list. This made one wonder whether the students using this site did not realise there were copyright and academic integrity issues, despite many receiving education on both of these aspects, including AFS specifically. The prospect of receiving unlock credits to find completed assignments for one reason or another could also have been a motivation, and there was also the possibility that the students simply did not care about copyright compliance or school policy.

Now came a pivotal moment. While copyright compliance was the lever with which access to the site was gained, not every file was a copyright concern. For example, assignment instructions with the ACC logo and slides created by instructors were especially obvious cases of copyright law violation as, when asked in relation to the files as well as at professional development sessions on AFS, no instructors indicated that they gave students permission to upload to AFS or other sites. On the other hand, it was determined in the course of discussions with instructors and their administrators that files consisting only of student writing in the form of assignments, without the instructions or questions contained, were issues of academic misconduct.

In accordance with Martin and Newhall's (2013) thought on not punishing individuals over copyright issues and targeting the disruption of sites rather than potentially positioning institutions as another merely commercial entity like the music and film industries, the files related solely to copyright were organised and entered into the site's takedown forms. A handy feature was the ability to have multiple files in one takedown request, and with the required information already organised, the process was one of quick copying and pasting. Of the over 200 ACC files on the site, 22 were deemed copyright violations and added to a single takedown request. A mere two days later, the site responded by email with notification that all files had been removed from public access, which we confirmed. For the files related to academic misconduct, 17 were linked to the School of Business, 6 to Hospitality and Tourism, and 3 to Health and Human Services. The Chairs of each area were contacted and they confirmed if the assignments were in use, by which instructor, and in some cases due to the title page or real student username from the file-sharing site, if the student was still enrolled at the college.

At the time of this process, the academic integrity policy at ACC included a type of academic misconduct called "facilitating academic dishonesty." The instructors involved did not feel that other students had used the uploaded assignments in any capacity. It was decided that students who had uploaded files to the file-sharing site would receive the sanctions at this level, which were minor and educative in that they included being told about the copyright and policy implications of uploading to such sites. These students, however, were flagged as first "offenders" and consequences for subsequent academic misconduct incidents would be more severe. Most of the classes in which the students were studying also had a workshop to clarify the differences between copyright compliance and academic misconduct related to AFS using anonymised case studies. Almost all students who uploaded files to the site had uploaded multiple files, and as such, most had their user accounts terminated by the site as per its own policy related to repeated copyright violations.

As instructors were now aware that some of their assignments had been compromised, they were not only more vigilant in trying to identify this type of misconduct, but perhaps more importantly were now eager to refresh assignments to make sharing and uploading less appealing to students. Instructors and Chairs involved in this process became much more interested in matters related to academic integrity, and in some cases began participating in the ACC Academic Integrity Advisory Committee. An educative module on related policy in an orientation course for all full-time students now contains information to clarify these intricacies for students. A remedial module with related materials for students having engaged in this type of academic misconduct has been created.

A recent policy revision changed the name of this type of AFS misconduct to "facilitating academic misconduct" rather than "facilitating academic dishonesty" and clarified both the meaning and educative nature of the sanctions. Intentional sharing of assignments, or misconduct involving tests and exams, both on and off AFS sites, would fall under a higher level or different type of misconduct, depending on the situation. This aligns with Bretag et al. (2019b) in that sharing behaviours like the indiscriminate uploading of notes to an AFS site fall lower on the outsourcing spectrum, with providing or receiving exam assistance on the higher and more serious end of the spectrum.

In applying the crucial research and evidence generated by universities, colleges, and the practitioners working at them, do often seem to be able to implement change with an agility less common at universities. This institutional agility is further enabled at colleges where the copyright of learning materials is owned by the institution. Although their focus was on colleges in Australia, the US, and the UK, Bretag and Harper (2020) called for more research on the college environment in general—be that students or educators—in relation to contract cheating and, more broadly, academic integrity. Perhaps this chapter will provide a small step towards their suggestion that "university educators would benefit from the opportunity to learn from college staff in a number of areas" (Bretag & Harper, 2020, p. 135).

Conclusion

AFS remains a growing and problematic issue in academic integrity. Copyright compliance provides a lever to access file-sharing sites that are often otherwise restricted, and for institutions which own the copyright to their learning materials, contextualising it within academic integrity may increase institutional agility in academic integrity. Once accessed, the takedown process for files related to copyright violation is relatively simple and fast. Pursuing legal actions against individual students over copyright compliance may inadvertently cause colleges and universities to side with large entertainment companies in a financial battle against file-sharing, and exacerbate the commercialisation of higher education, especially among students who identify with the file-sharing culture. Taking an educative approach towards the impersonal type of AFS described here allows for students to learn about the process and contrasts it against serious forms of academic misconduct involving intentional ethical choices that may take place on the same websites, such as contract cheating and collusion. By monitoring AFS websites and pursuing copyright compliance for institution-owned resources, support staff can contribute to the maintenance of academic integrity at their institutions and generate yet another incremental improvement.

References

Associated Press. (2022, March 17). Professor sues student for posting final exam online. *Miami Herald.* https://www.miamiherald.com/news/business/article259485704.html

Bateman, C. R., Valentine, S., & Rittenburg, T. (2013). Ethical decision making in a peer-to-peer file sharing situation: The role of moral absolutes and social consensus. *Journal of Business Ethics, 115,* 229–240. https://doi.org/10.1007/s10551-012-1388-1

Bertram Gallant, T. (2016). Leveraging institutional integrity for the betterment of education. In T. Bretag (Ed.), *Handbook of academic integrity* (pp. 979–993). Springer. https://doi.org/10.1007/978-981-287-098-8_52

Bretag, T., & Harper, R. (2020). Contract cheating at colleges and other non-university higher education providers. In T. Bretag (Ed.), *A research agenda for academic integrity* (pp. 127–137). Edward Elgar Publishing. https://doi.org/10.4337/9781789903775

Bretag, T., Harper, R., Burton, M., Ellis, C., Newton, P., Rozenberg, P., Saddiqui, S., & van Haeringen, K. (2019a). Contract cheating: A survey of Australian university students. *Studies in Higher Education, 44*(11), 1837–1856. https://doi.org/10.1080/03075079.2018.1462788

Bretag, T., Harper, R., Burton, M., Ellis, C., Newton, P., van Haeringen, K., Saddiqui, S., & Rozenberg, P. (2019b). Contract cheating and assessment design: Exploring the relationship. *Assessment & Evaluation in Higher Education, 44*(5), 676–691. https://doi.org/10.1080/02602938.2018.1527892

Clarke, R., & Lancaster, T. (2013). Commercial aspects of contract cheating. In *Proceedings of the 18th ACM Conference on Innovation and Technology in Computer Science Education,* 219–224. https://doi.org/10.1145/2462476.2462497.

Curtis, G. J., McNeill, M., Slade, C., Tremayne, K., Harper, R., Rundle, K., & Greenaway, R. (2022). Moving beyond self-reports to estimate the prevalence of commercial contract cheating: An Australian study. *Studies in Higher Education, 47*(9), 1844–1856. https://doi.org/10.1080/03075079.2021.1972093

Danaher, B., Smith, M. D., & Telang, R. (2014). Piracy and copyright enforcement mechanisms. *Innovation Policy and the Economy, 14*(1), 25–61. https://doi.org/10.1086/674020

Dawson, P. (2021). *Defending assessment security in a digital world: Preventing e-cheating and supporting academic integrity in higher education.* Routledge.

Eaton, S. E. (2021). *Plagiarism in higher education: Tackling tough topics in academic integrity.* Libraries Unlimited.

Ellis, C., van Haeringen, K., Harper, R., Bretag, T., Zucker, I., & McBride, S. (2020). Does authentic assessment assure academic integrity? Evidence from contract cheating data. *Higher Education Research & Development, 39*(3), 454–469. https://doi.org/10.1080/07294360.2019.1680956

Harrison, D., Patch, A., McNally, D., & Harris, L. (2021). Student and faculty perceptions of study helper websites: A new practice in collaborative cheating. *Journal of Academic Ethics, 19,* 483–500. https://doi.org/10.1007/s10805-020-09373-2

John, N. A. (2014). File sharing and the history of computing: Or, why file sharing is called "file sharing". *Critical Studies in Media Communication, 31*(3), 198–211. https://doi.org/10.1080/15295036.2013.824597

Kezar, A., & Bernstein-Sierra, S. (2016). Commercialization of higher education. In T. Bretag (Ed.), *Handbook of academic integrity* (pp. 325–346). Springer.

Lancaster, T. (2020). Commercial contract cheating provision through micro-outsourcing websites. *International Journal for Educational Integrity, 16*(4). https://doi.org/10.1007/s40979-020-00053-7

Lancaster, T., & Cotarlan, C. (2021). Contract cheating by STEM students through a file sharing website: A COVID-19 pandemic perspective. *International Journal for Educational Integrity, 17*(1), 1–16. https://doi.org/10.1007/s40979-021-00070-0

Locquiao, J., & Ives, B. (2020). First-year university students' knowledge of academic misconduct and the association between goals for attending university and receptiveness to intervention. *International Journal for Educational Integrity, 16,* 5. https://doi.org/10.1007/s40979-020-00054-6

Mansfield-Devine, S. (2010). The perils of sharing. *Network Security, 2010*(1), 11–13. https://doi.org/10.1016/S1353-4858(10)70015-5

Martin, B., & Newhall, J. (2013). Criminal copyright enforcement against file-sharing services. *North Carolina Journal of Law & Technology, 15*(1), 101. vi.

McKenzie, A. (2019). *Enhancing academic integrity through quality assurance.* Paper presented at the Canadian Symposium on Academic Integrity, Calgary, Canada. http://hdl.handle.net/1880/110296

Mehta, G. (2020). *Proposal to install spyware in university libraries to protect copyright shocks academics.* https://www.codastory.com/authoritarian-tech/spyware-in-libraries/

Quality Assurance Agency for Higher Education. (2020). *Contracting to cheat in higher education: How to address essay mills and contract cheating.* https://www.qaa.ac.uk/docs/qaa/guidance/contracting-to-cheat-in-higher-education-2nd-edition.pdf

Rogerson, A., & Basanta, G. (2016). Peer-to-peer file sharing and academic integrity in the internet age. In T. Bretag (Ed.), *Handbook of academic integrity* (pp. 273–285). Springer.

Sano-Franchini, J. L. (2010). Intellectual property and the cultures of BitTorrent communities. *Computers and Composition, 27*(3), 202–210. https://doi.org/10.1016/j.compcom.2010.06.008

Seeland, J., Stoesz, B., & Vogt, L. (2020). Preventing online shopping for completed assessments: Protecting students by blocking access to contract cheating sites on institutional networks. *Canadian Perspectives on Academic Integrity, 3*(1). https://doi.org/10.11575/cpai.v3i1.70256

Siegfried, R. M. (2004). Student attitudes on software piracy and related issues of computer ethics. *Ethics and Information Technology, 6*, 215–222. https://doi.org/10.1007/s10676-004-3391-4

Stephens, J. M. (2016). Creating cultures of integrity: Multilevel intervention model for promoting academic honesty. In T. Bretag (Ed.), *Handbook of academic integrity* (pp. 995–1007). Springer.

Stoesz, B. M., Eaton, S. E., & Seeland, J. (2022). Critical thinking as an antidote to contract cheating. In S. E. Eaton, G. J. Curtis, B. M. Stoesz, K. Rundle, J. Clare, & J. Seeland (Eds.), *Contract cheating in higher education: Global perspectives on theory, practice, and policy*. Palgrave.

TEQSA. (2021). *How to respond to contract cheating: Detection and management.* https://www.teqsa.gov.au/how-respond-contract-cheating-detection-and-management

Velliaris, D. M., & Pierce, J. M. (2019). Cheaters beware: (re)designing assessment practices to reduce academic misconduct. In *Prevention and detection of academic misconduct in higher education* (pp. 1–38). IGI Global.

CHAPTER 6

The Encouragement of File Sharing Behaviours Through Technology and Social Media: Impacts on Student Cheating Behaviours and Academic Piracy

Ann M. Rogerson

Instances of student cheating can include the sharing and trading of assessment and course content by current and former students. Through peer-to-peer file sharing some of this work can end up presented as the work or answers of others by downloading the material and ultimately being submitted for grading. These activities are just some that can be considered as contract cheating behaviours (Bretag et al., 2019). After identifying some materials and their file sharing sources during grading, I took the opportunity to highlight that instances of students uploading and downloading academic content were an area of concern at a plagiarism conference in 2014 (Rogerson, 2014). During the conference I described the concept of file sharing as occurring when academic lecture materials, notes,

A. M. Rogerson (✉)
Faculty of Business and Law, University of Wollongong,
Wollongong, NSW, Australia
e-mail: annr@uow.edu.au

© The Author(s), under exclusive license to Springer Nature Switzerland AG 2022
S. E. Eaton et al. (eds.), *Contract Cheating in Higher Education*,
https://doi.org/10.1007/978-3-031-12680-2_6

assessment tasks, answers, and responses are shared, swapped, and traded over internet-based sites in fee, free, or barter (credit/exchange) arrangements (Rogerson, 2014; Rogerson & Bassanta, 2016). File sharing sites housing educational materials can also be known as "crowd sourcing sites, study aid sites and peer-to-peer platforms" (Lancaster & Cotarlan, 2021, p. 2) and have extended their range of materials to include e-books (Lee et al., 2019).

This chapter continues the discussion of student file sharing behaviours and their relationships to contract cheating and academic piracy when file sharing is facilitated through technology. I expand the discussion about the confusion that continues to exist for students when file sharing or sharing of content and materials appears to be acceptable behaviour or the norm in society (e.g., via social media). However, the sharing and trading of materials, content and answers are not considered a norm or permissible in all educational contexts (Rogerson & Bassanta, 2016). Sharing of materials can facilitate collusion, contribute to contract cheating and other breaches of academic integrity, as well as undermine copyright and acknowledgement practice (Dixon & George, 2021; Lancaster & Cotarlan, 2021; Rogerson & Bassanta, 2016). This chapter goes on to discuss the implications of file sharing behaviours beyond higher education, considering whether we as educators are sufficiently preparing students for organisational life where the sharing of organisational knowledge is not acceptable for proprietary, commercial confidentiality, or privacy reasons.

File Sharing and Academic Integrity

Encouragement of file sharing behaviours can occur on several fronts. Some are legitimate such as educators setting collaborative assessment tasks and students using social media to facilitate group work (e.g., Khan et al., 2016) and where it is recognised as a supportive communication mechanism to facilitate interactions with fellow students and teachers (Bretag et al., 2019). Social media platforms can also be incorporated to form part of the assessment task (e.g., Hull & Dodd, 2017). However, there is a darker side to file sharing where students are encouraged to upload educational content for profit, credit, or benefit regardless of whether or not the student holds the copyright or intellectual property ownership in the materials being shared (Dixon & George, 2021; Lancaster & Cotarlan, 2021; Rogerson & Bassanta, 2016). Sharing sites operating in this manner are exploiting the 'sharing economy' (Richardson, 2015), promoting themselves as providing help and assistance when in fact these sites are facilitating contract cheating (Lancaster & Cotarlan, 2021).

In examining the concept of student academic file sharing with Giselle Bassanta in a chapter titled 'Peer-to-Peer File Sharing and Academic Integrity in the Internet Age' in the *Handbook of Academic Integrity* (Bretag, 2016), we noted that the "lines are blurring between what is and is not appropriate to share, inform, re-use, trade, swap, or sell in an academic context" (Rogerson & Bassanta, 2016, p. 275). If anything, measures of appropriateness have become even blurrier with software providers such as Apple® and Microsoft® providing prompts in programs and applications that encourage users to 'copy, paste, share' when they hover over words and phrases. Although the software providers advertise that the functionality is designed to facilitate transferring of material between personal devices, this type of language tacitly legitimises sharing behaviour as something that is a normal practice. Further tacit endorsement is established when institutions provide students with free user licences to programs provided by these companies and students use computers and handheld devices for study and assessment.

SOCIAL ASPECTS OF SHARING

The global COVID-19 pandemic has increased and accelerated the use of technology in educational contexts and shifted educational activities from the campus and classroom to home and computer-mediated social spaces (Eaton, 2020). The social connectedness students usually achieve by coming to campus also assists with engaging in institutional resources and services to support their learning (Won et al., 2021). When these interactions are missing, however, students must rely on other methods to connect. As students turn to social media to replace physical social connectedness, they may also reach out for help, or seek interactions that can facilitate collaborative learning, and the transfer of resources (Ansari & Khan, 2020). When coupled with social media platforms that promote content based on search word algorithms, the sites seeking to profit from hosting file sharing communities merely need to promote their services through a social media platform to reach new potential contributors and users, therefore extending their ethically questionable practices.

This is where the key difference is in the academic integrity space. Sharing sites masquerading as sharing centres are designed to profit owners, who employ 'aggressive marketing practices' (White, 2020). Students sharing information (and in many cases materials where they do not own the copyright) are doing so to gain profit or credit to spend, barter, or exchange to gain information, and in the end seeking an unfair advantage over fellow students. Students are not necessarily aware or educated in how to distinguish between for profit versus sanctioned sharing or genuine support sites promoted by their educational institution. Using the language of help and support adds a notion of legitimacy to the operation of sharing sites whilst they seek to undermine the very operations they are trying to imitate (Lancaster & Cotarlan, 2021; Rogerson & Bassanta, 2016).

Student Help-Seeking Behaviours and Social Media

The help-seeking literature provides a useful insight into the motivations that underpin student help-seeking behaviours. Instrumental help-seeking behaviours indicate that a student is seeking help to reduce the subsequent need for assistance, for example not needing explanation or clarification. In comparison, executive help-seeking behaviours (also referred to as expedient help-seeking behaviours) refer to students seeking the answers to problems as a way of avoiding doing the work themselves (Bailey & Withers, 2018; Karabenick, 2004; Nelson-le Gall, 1985). Therefore, social media platforms provide a way to connect the help-seeking and help-giving through facilitating connections via technology. Some studies prior to the COVID-19 pandemic examined how students used social media for peer-to-peer knowledge sharing purposes (Asterhan & Bouton, 2017), how Twitter® was used to improve learning experiences (Hull & Dodd, 2017), or how instant messaging assisted students to clarify ambiguities while establishing social bonding (Nkhoma et al., 2018). However, even prior to the pandemic other studies had already established the link between deviant social media behaviour and breaches of academic integrity (Amigud & Lancaster, 2019) and collective cyber-cheating behaviours (Parks et al., 2018).

While the notion of 'helping' others may contribute to students participating in unauthorised or illegal file sharing activities, there is also the issue of helping as a potential neutralisation factor. Neutralisation techniques are a form of deviant consumer behaviour where individuals excuse or justify their actions to alleviate their guilt associated with a specific action which would breach societal norms and the norms they usually espouse (Harris & Daunt, 2011). Deviant behaviours are neutralised through techniques such as denying responsibility by placing the blame for the action on others, denying that there is victim associated with the action, and placing the demands of social groups and associations ahead of society at large (Sykes & Matza, 1957). In a study of e-book piracy, it was noted how individuals who use neutralisation techniques are "more inclined to blur their moral boundaries" to justify their actions to use the internet for "free download, uploading, creating or sharing of electronic books" (Lee et al., 2019, p. 302). Through the use of neutralisation techniques "feelings of guilt or shame from participation in digital piracy" are removed (Lee et al., 2019, p. 302). It could be that students' notions of helping others, or responding to requests for assistance over social media platforms, overcome their sense of judging whether sharing material that they do not own is wrong or has the potential to be misused to breach the policies and principles associated with academic integrity.

Technology, Social Media, and File Sharing

The internet and social media platforms have accelerated the access to and accessibility of content but educating students about what is and is not appropriate to share has not kept pace with the breadth, extent, and growth of sharing facilitated by technology. The COVID-19 pandemic has driven education to rely on technology to take the place of in-person, on campus delivery of lectures, workshops, practicums, labs, or tutorials limiting opportunities for students to interact in the same physical location (Eaton, 2020).

However, social media platforms continue to deliver mechanisms for students to connect and stay connected, while on the flip side providing greater reach for sharing and cheating platforms and behaviours. The rapid transition to remote learning took place without the time for planning or consideration of the potential impact on student sharing behaviours or intentions. As indicated by articles issued over 2020 and 2021, sharing behaviours have increased, leading to academic integrity breaches of cheating and collusion (e.g., Comas-Forgas et al., 2021; Eaton, 2020; Lancaster & Cotarlan, 2021).

The internet-based sites encouraging students to share are appealing to them directly, or through social media to 'help' others while helping themselves. The use of language and persuasive rhetoric designed to attract and encourage engagement (Rowland et al., 2018) does not highlight the risks of participating in sharing behaviours of this nature, with the caveats and disclaimers hidden in fine print or terms and conditions (Dixon

& George, 2020). Inappropriate or unsanctioned file sharing undermines the principles of academic integrity and in some cases breaks the law in jurisdictions where copyright provisions and intellectual property rights are upheld (Rogerson & Bassanta, 2016). If we are encouraging students to collaborate in some classes while trying to promote that students do not inappropriately share content they may have written up as notes or submitted for assessment, students can be left confused or conflicted as to what they should and should not do.

File Sharing as Academic Piracy

Piracy of media (e.g., music, movies, and images) has been identified as an issue with students (and others) with the inappropriate sharing or illegal use of intellectual property and sharing of content which has been described as 'digital piracy' (Jackman & Lorde, 2014). This type of sharing and use ignores the copyright holders' rights to income and royalties for creative content. The use of pirated content even for individual entertainment purposes is for personal gain for the user in access to content without paying a fee, or via a greatly reduced rate compared to a commercial and legal purchase (Tyrowicz et al., 2020). Although studies demonstrate that the presence of legal means of entertainment downloads reduces the instances of pirated media usage through relatively affordable subscription services such as Netflix® (Nhan et al., 2020), the question of cost was shown to influence the decision to access and use pirated content regardless of the legal implications of partaking in the activity (Jackman & Lorde, 2014; Lee et al., 2019). File sharing sites provide options to students to barter for content thereby negating the cost issue through uploading content to earn credit to download other content, while providing mechanisms for payment by piece or subscription (Dixon & George, 2021; Rogerson & Bassanta, 2016).

For those hosting the sites and sharing there is also the potential for further financial gain through revenue from advertising placed or promoted through the internet-based sites. This is no different from the approach of paraphrasing tool sites, which promote free but not necessarily quality services (Rogerson & McCarthy, 2017). Where file sharing sites are hosting, providing, bartering, or exchanging academic content not owned by an individual, it becomes another form of digital piracy, but more correctly academic piracy.

The peer-to-peer sharing sites, and those using them, will argue for the right of a student to share notes and answers to assessment tasks as it is their own copyright. However, the fact is that much of the content shared over the file sharing sites is the original work of an individual academic or educational institution. In addition, much of the content being uploaded to earn credit is already available to students for free via their institutional repositories. Reuse or exploitation of this work without permission for personal gain equates to academic piracy. Students do not hold the copyright in materials such as assessment or examination questions, exemplars, sample papers, course outlines, and lecture slides, yet file sharing sites accept this content without question and hold it behind membership paywalls. In trying to attract students to use the sites, the materials can be identified through subject and institutional searches over the internet (Dixon & George, 2021). Then begins the task of lodging Digital Millennium Copyright Act (DMCA) take-down notices (DMCA, n.d.) to have content removed. Unfortunately, the time to identify and then enact these take-down requests means that the content is available for access during assessment periods, which can be used inappropriately by students.

Implications for Future Practice

From an educational perspective academia needs to determine better ways to ensure that intellectual property of academics and the institution are better protected. This will mean cultivating and educating individuals about ways to guard content delivered and accessible online to make it less attractive as a target for sharing (Petrescu et al., 2018). This may include taking additional steps to watermark, add logos, disclaimers, or other commentary to make it more difficult for students to share content downloaded from the institutional learning platforms or websites (Sheridan & Rogerson, 2020). From a student perspective, students need to be educated about appropriate sharing versus inappropriate sharing just as we seek to enlighten students to the consequences of breaching academic and educational integrity.

Leveraging the socialisation of sharing practices to undermine the frameworks of appropriate use and authorial acknowledgement of the reuse of materials have implications far beyond education. While students bring their societal and educational norms into their learning experiences, and have those norms shaped and sometimes reinforced throughout their studies, they can equally retain those norms when transitioning to work and environments outside of education (Guerrero-Dib et al., 2020). Herein lies the danger that students are not necessarily cognisant or remaining aware of what is and is not appropriate to share and this area warrants further investigation.

There is a lack of awareness of what happens when data, intellectual property, or even ideas are shared through habit (such as norms established through social media usage) rather than acknowledging that organisational related information is proprietary information and therefore not shared or disclosed at the whim of an individual. Specific non-disclosure agreements may highlight to individuals that certain sets of data will place an organisation at risk if shared. However, the general requirements of confidentiality provisions that form part of employment contracts (specifying that information belongs to the organisation and is not to be shared without specific permission) are lesser known and more at risk of being breached. This risk is heightened where individuals rely on their previous experiences where they consider that sharing is considered a social and behavioural norm.

Therefore, what applies in a social setting does not necessarily translate to an educational or professional setting. Studies such as Guerrero-Dib et al.'s (2020) demonstrate that there is a link between breaches of academic integrity and future workplace ethical behaviour, although this study was confined to examining this phenomenon in relation to cheating, copying, falsification, the use of unauthorised support, and plagiarising or paraphrasing without the use of citations. The issue of inappropriate sharing of materials or use of shared materials was not incorporated into the study but would be of interest and use to both educators and organisations.

There are increasing calls that higher education institutions should better prepare individuals for their working lives beyond university (e.g., the 2020 Australian legislation around the Jobs Ready Graduate Package [https://www.dese.gov.au/job-ready/improving-higher-education-students]). Seeking to uphold academic standards through education about appropriate sharing behaviours is an urgent situation to be addressed particularly through educative approaches to managing academic integrity issues. Institutions also need to ensure that file sharing contexts of academic integrity breaches are covered in policies and procedures. The misappropriation of content that is not owned or authored by a student for sharing and/or personal gain is something that needs to be classified for what it is—academic piracy and couched on those terms to emphasise the inappropriate and illegal aspects of the behaviour.

Future Research

What is not clear is the impact that social media platforms and technology providers that openly encourage sharing behaviours with aspects of personal life have on students' intentions to share materials related to academic courses of study. This plays upon sharing as being a norm. Alarmingly, technology providers such as Apple® and social media platforms such as WhatsApp, Instagram, and Snapchat encourage sharing behaviours between individuals. There are no caveats or warnings about the risks of sharing certain materials or prompting a question whether the individual sharing content has the legal right to do so.

Consequently, future research looking at peer-to-peer file sharing in the education sphere should consider the copyright question (where this applies in relevant jurisdictions) and as the socialisation of sharing, and more particularly how file sharing as a normal practice is misleading in educational and professional contexts. This may be more difficult for students to understand where their country or jurisdiction does not have or uphold copyright provisions. Studies into the type and classification of file sharing as academic piracy may have a greater impact on developing an awareness and countering the practice. The success and reduction of piracy may provide some insight into how we can get students to understand and accept the inappropriateness of sharing and using content that they do not own. We also need a greater understanding of what materials are being shared, when decisions to share take place, and whether neutralisation notions such as 'helping others' contribute to an intention to participate in file sharing and academic piracy. Other studies could examine the effectiveness of discussions and assessment tasks that consider and demonstrate what is or is not appropriate to share.

Conclusion

The failure to properly educate students on appropriate and ethical sharing behaviours in educational contexts contributes to instances of academic misconduct and breaches of academic integrity through contract cheating. While peer interactions can benefit educational outcomes, they can also contribute to cases of collusion when the boundaries of support and assistance are not clear. The implications of unauthorised and inappropriate file sharing also carry broader risks to organisational knowledge management, privacy provisions, and the protection of intellectual property as demonstrated in cases of media (digital) piracy. This is a societal risk beyond the confines of academic and educational environments. The risk to organisational information loss and competitive advantage is real, just as the risk of file sharing in an academic environment diminishes the value placed on knowledge, intellectual property, and originality of thought and academic achievement. As noted in 2016, the imperative remains that we need to openly discuss and confront the issue and implications of file sharing with students while developing their capacity for discernment and judgement on what is and is not appropriate to share (Rogerson & Bassanta, 2016).

REFERENCES

Amigud, A., & Lancaster, T. (2019). 246 reasons to cheat: An analysis of students' reasons for seeking to outsource academic work. *Computers & Education, 134*, 98–107. https://doi.org/10.1016/j.compedu.2019.01.017

Ansari, J. A. N., & Khan, N. A. (2020). Exploring the role of social media in collaborative learning the new domain of learning. *Smart Learning Environments, 7*(1), 1–16. https://doi.org/10.1186/s40561-020-00118-7

Asterhan, C. S. C., & Bouton, E. (2017). Teenage peer-to-peer knowledge sharing through social network sites in secondary schools. *Computers & Education, 110*, 16–34. https://doi.org/10.1016/j.compedu.2017.03.007

Bailey, C., & Withers, J. (2018). What can screen capture reveal about students' use of software tools when undertaking a paraphrasing task? *Journal of Academic Writing, 8*(2), 176–190. https://doi.org/10.18552/joaw.v8i2.456

Bretag, T. (2016). *Handbook of academic integrity*. Springer. https://doi.org/10.1007/978-981-287-079-7

Bretag, T., Harper, R., Burton, M., Ellis, C., Newton, P., Rozenberg, P., Saddiqui, S., & van Haeringen, K. (2019). Contract cheating: A survey of Australian university students. *Studies in Higher Education, 44*(11), 1837–1856. https://doi.org/10.1080/03075079.2018.1462788

Comas-Forgas, R., Lancaster, T., Calvo-Sastre, A., & Sureda-Negre, J. (2021). Exam cheating and academic integrity breaches during the COVID-19 pandemic: An analysis of internet search activity in Spain. *Heliyon, 7*(10), e08233, 1–8. https://doi.org/10.1016/j.heliyon.2021.e08233.

Dixon, Z., & George, K. (2021). Monitoring uncharted communities of crowd-sourced plagiarism. *Journal of Academic Ethics, 19*(2), 291–301. https://doi.org/10.1007/s10805-020-09381-2

DMCA. (n.d.). *What is a DMCA takedown?* https://www.dmca.com/FAQ/What-is-a-DMCA-Takedown

Eaton, S. E. (2020). Academic integrity during COVID-19: Reflections from the University of Calgary. *International Studies in Educational Administration, 48*(1), 80–85. http://hdl.handle.net/1880/112293

Guerrero-Dib, J. G., Portales, L., & Heredia-Escorza, Y. (2020). Impact of academic integrity on workplace ethical behaviour. *International Journal for Educational Integrity, 16*(1), 1–18. https://doi.org/10.1007/s40979-020-0051-3

Harris, L. C., & Daunt, K. L. (2011). Deviant customer behaviour: A study of techniques of neutralisation. *Journal of Marketing Management, 27*(7–8), 834–853. https://doi.org/10.1080/0267257X.2010.498149

Hull, K., & Dodd, J. E. (2017). Faculty use of Twitter in higher education teaching. *Journal of Applied Research in Higher Education, 9*(1), 91–104. https://doi.org/10.1108/JARHE-05-2015-0038

Jackman, M., & Lorde, T. (2014). Why buy when we can pirate? The role of intentions and willingness to pay in predicting piracy behavior. *International Journal of Social Economics, 41*(9), 801–819. https://doi.org/10.1108/IJSE-04-2013-0104

Karabenick, S. A. (2004). Perceived achievement goal structure and college student help seeking. *Journal of Educational Psychology, 96*(3), 569–581. https://doi.org/10.1037/0022-0663.96.3.569

Khan, T., Kend, M., & Robertson, S. (2016). Use of social media by university accounting students and its impact on learning outcomes. *Accounting Education, 25*(6), 534–567. https://doi.org/10.1080/09639284.2016.1230880

Lancaster, T., & Cotarlan, C. (2021). Contract cheating by STEM students through a file sharing website: A Covid-19 pandemic perspective. *International Journal for Educational Integrity, 17*, 1–16. https://doi.org/10.1007/s40979-021-00070-0

Lee, B., Fenoff, R., & Paek, S. Y. (2019). Correlates of participation in e-book piracy on campus. *The Journal of Academic Librarianship, 45*(3), 299–304. https://doi.org/10.1016/j.acalib.2019.04.002

Nelson-le Gall, S. A. (1985). Motive–outcome matching and outcome foreseeability: Effects on attribution of intentionality and moral judgments. *Developmental Psychology, 21*(2), 332–337. https://doi.org/10.1037/0012-1649.21.2.332

Nhan, J., Bowen, K., & Bartula, A. (2020). A comparison of a public and private university of the effects of low-cost streaming services and income on movie piracy. *Technology in Society, 60*, 101213. https://doi.org/10.1016/j.techsoc.2019.101213

Nkhoma, C. A., Thomas, S., Mathews Zanda, N., Sriratanaviriyakul, N., Trang Huyen, T., & Vo, H. X. (2018). Measuring the impact of out-of-class communication through instant messaging. *Education & Training, 60*(4), 318–334. https://doi.org/10.1108/ET-12-2017-0196

Parks, R. F., Lowry, P. B., Wigand, R. T., Agarwal, N., & Williams, T. L. (2018). Why students engage in cyber-cheating through a collective movement: A case of deviance and collusion. *Computers & Education, 125*, 308–326. https://doi.org/10.1016/j.compedu.2018.04.003

Petrescu, M., Gironda, J. T., & Korgaonkar, P. K. (2018). Online piracy in the context of routine activities and subjective norms. *Journal of Marketing Management, 34*(3–4), 314–346. https://doi.org/10.1080/0267257X.2018.1452278

Richardson, L. (2015). Performing the sharing economy. *Geoforum, 67*, 121–129. https://doi.org/10.1016/j.geoforum.2015.11.004

Rogerson, A. M. (2014, June 16–18). Detecting the work of essay mills and file swapping sites: Some clues they leave behind [Conference presentation]. In *6th International Integrity and Plagiarism Conference*, Newcastle-on-Tyne, pp. 1–9. https://doi.org/10.1007/s40979-017-0021-6

Rogerson, A. M., & Bassanta, G. (2016). Peer-to-peer file sharing and academic integrity in the Internet age. In T. Bretag (Ed.), *Handbook of academic integrity* (pp. 273–285). Springer. https://doi.org/10.1007/978-981-287-098-8_55

Rogerson, A. M., & McCarthy, G. (2017). Using internet based paraphrasing tools: Original work, patchwriting or facilitated plagiarism? *International Journal for Educational Integrity, 13*(1), 1–15. https://doi.org/10.1007/s40979-016-0013-y

Rowland, S., Slade, C., Wong, K.-S., & Whiting, B. (2018). 'Just turn to us': The persuasive features of contract cheating websites. *Assessment & Evaluation in Higher Education, 43*(4), 652–665. https://doi.org/10.1080/02602938.2017.1391948

Sheridan, L., & Rogerson, A. M. (2020, March 6–8). Protecting our own copyright: Combating the piracy of academic content by students [Paper presentation]. In *International Center for Academic Integrity (ICAI) Conference*, Portland, OR, USA.

Sykes, G. M., & Matza, D. (1957). Techniques of neutralization: A theory of delinquency. *American Sociological Review, 22*(6), 664–670. https://doi.org/10.2307/2089195

Tyrowicz, J., Krawczyk, M., & Hardy, W. (2020). Friends or foes? A meta-analysis of the relationship between "online piracy" and the sales of cultural goods. *Information Economics and Policy, 53*, 100879. https://doi.org/10.1016/j.infoecopol.2020.100879

White, A. (2020, March 23). *Amanda White on education for and detection of contract cheating in virus times.* Campus Morning Mail. https://campusmorningmail.com.au/news/education-forand-detection-of-contract-cheating-in-the-age-of-covid-19/

Won, S., Hensley, L. C., & Wolters, C. A. (2021). Brief research report: Sense of belonging and academic help-seeking as self-regulated learning. *The Journal of Experimental Education, 89*(1), 112–124. https://doi.org/10.1080/00220973.2019.1703095

CHAPTER 7

Higher Education Assessment Design

Wendy Sutherland-Smith and Phillip Dawson

Technologies have disrupted educational experiences for both staff and students over many years. Institutions have adopted various technologies to maintain relevance for the increasingly digital world. This includes various elements of assessment design. To add to this disruption, COVID-19 has created further challenges for learning, teaching, and assessment. At a time where many nations have resorted to online delivery of all facets of education, in lieu of any face-to-face contact, assessments have necessarily been provided via technology. Such wholesale disruption to assessment regimes is confronting and stressful but also offers opportunities to reimagine assessment design in profoundly new ways. Although peer-reviewed evidence of an increase in rates of cheating during the global pandemic is only now emerging (e.g., Lancaster & Cotarlan, 2021), the hasty shift online has likely created just the right circumstances for students to outsource a variety of assessments for a multitude of reasons such as stress, increased isolation, boredom, struggling to cope with study, or trauma of life in lockdown.

W. Sutherland-Smith (✉) • P. Dawson
Centre for Research in Assessment and Digital Learning (CRADLE), Deakin University Australia, Geelong, VIC, Australia
e-mail: wsuther@deakin.edu.au; p.dawson@deakin.edu.au

© The Author(s), under exclusive license to Springer Nature Switzerland AG 2022
S. E. Eaton et al. (eds.), *Contract Cheating in Higher Education*,
https://doi.org/10.1007/978-3-031-12680-2_7

Assessment success is a key driver for students' actions. Students must pass assessments to progress through courses, no matter where they sit in the education hierarchy. As Boud (1995) observes, "Students can, with difficulty, escape from the effects of poor teaching, they cannot (by definition if they want to graduate) escape the effects of poor assessment" (p. 35). Therefore, as Ramsden (1992) states, assessment "always defines the actual curriculum" for students (p. 187). This means that assessments can drive choices students make about which tasks are essential to complete and which are not and allocate time and effort accordingly. Therefore, it is important to understand the assessment design features that motivate students to complete tasks or, perhaps, decide to outsource or contact cheat them.

In this chapter we use both the terms 'outsourcing' and 'contract cheating'. Contract cheating is when students can have original work produced for them by online auction sites, which they can submit as their own work. Often this involves payment (see Lancaster & Clarke, 2008). 'Outsourcing' includes online sites but also includes friends or family who can undertake part or whole of the assessment task. Outsourcing is a broader view than contract cheating (Awdry, 2021). This distinction is useful when considering research that indicates students do not just use auction sites or pay for assessments when submitting work that is not their own (Bretag et al., 2019; Rowland et al., 2018).

What we Know about Assessment and Contract Cheating

We can learn many lessons for assessment design from prior research about students outsourcing work and cheating on assessments. Some key findings we know are:

1. *Some task designs are more likely to be outsourced than others*
   Bretag et al. (2019) surveyed 14,086 students about outsourcing behaviours. They asked students about their perceptions of the likelihood of 13 different assessment tasks being contract cheated. Assessments included a range of tasks such as research essays, time limited tasks, small graded tasks (like weekly online quizzes), in-class tasks, real-world tasks, vivas (oral defences), and reflections. They found four tasks that were the least likely to be cheated or out-

sourced by students: in-class tests, personalised tasks, vivas, and reflections on practical placements. It is important to note that the researchers are not claiming that these four tasks cannot be outsourced, but rather that assessments designed to be personal, unique, seek student voice (reflections or orals), are less likely to be outsourced. The researchers also found that heavily weighted assessments, including invigilated exams, or those with short turnaround times were perceived by students to provide many cheating opportunities. Earlier research also found that students reported outsourcing invigilated exams "at higher rates than any other type of cheating" (Bretag et al., 2019, p. 685). Bretag et al. (2019) also claimed that students may seek to justify outsourcing unsupervised small tasks, like online quizzes, as they count little towards final grades and low weightings may signal a lack of importance in the students' assessment priorities. This is important when linked to Ramsden's (1992) idea that students decide what is essential assessment to complete and what is not in determining their own curriculum priorities.

2. *Authentic assessment design is not immune from cheating*

Bretag et al. (2019) also probed the oft-touted solution of deterring cheating or outsourcing—authentic assessment tasks. They found that students were least likely to outsource three assessment designs—those related to professional development skills; practicum reflections; and tasks where there is no right answer. The research team concluded that "it appears that authenticity alone is not sufficient for reducing the perception that an assessment task may be outsourced" (p. 687). Similarly, Baird and Clare's (2017) study found that a highly authentic task alone did not completely deter students from outsourcing behaviours. They implemented several interventions in response to contract cheating allegations in a large compulsory undergraduate unit of study. The researchers used rational choice theory from criminology, which centres on students weighing the risk in choosing whether to cheat or not in certain situations. After re-designing a 40% weighted task using interventions calculated to encourage students to complete the task themselves, they found academic integrity breaches decreased (from 183 to 27 cases) but did not cease entirely. The authors concluded that "the case study presented highlights the importance of assessment design to reduce contract cheating" (2017, p. 14). At a macro level,

Ellis et al. (2019) provided what is likely the most damning evidence for authentic assessment as an anti-contract cheating strategy: evidence from the cheating sites themselves that authentic assessments make up a significant proportion of assignments that are produced and sold.

3. *Invigilated exams are not a panacea to cheating*

Harper et al. (2021) examined students' self-reported cheating behaviours on various tasks as well as teachers' self-reported detection of cheating. Most interestingly, they found that students reported commonly cheating in exams, particularly multiple-choice exams, yet academic staff rarely detected exam cheating. Whilst students reported slightly fewer cheating behaviours in written assessments, academic staff detected more cheating, particularly in text dense tasks such as essays and reports. Whilst much debate raged in the academic community about whether returning to examinations would combat cheating, this study reports that students indicated they could, and did, cheat more on examinations than other forms of assessment.

This finding is of grave concern given the increasing number of multiple-choice tests and heavily weighted examinations permeating higher education as class sizes increase, marking staff decrease and computer-marked assessments (like multiple-choice exams) become an economic reality for institutions. When viewed through the lens of consequential validity—the impacts of an assessment beyond its ability to measure learning (Sambell et al., 1997)—student cheating behaviour cannot be divorced from the characteristics of an assessment. In the next section we explore what Self-Determination Theory (SDT), a theory of motivation, offers in relationship to student behaviour and motivation to cheat or not as a focus in rethinking assessment design.

Self-Determination Theory (SDT)

What motivates a student to complete, or not complete, an assessment task themselves should be an important consideration in assessment design. Historically, much of the thinking and practice in assessments have been predicated on the supposed motivating powers of marks and grades: that in exchange for payment in the form of a good mark, students will do the necessary work (Kohn, 1999). Building on behaviourism (Skinner,

1965) and social exchange theory (Emerson, 1976), a range of arguments have been mounted that external pressures can be used to motivate, shape, or control students' behaviour to do assessments themselves, either through rewards (such as competitive grades, prizes, or course entry) or through punishments (failure, institutional penalties, or denial of course entry).

Self-Determination Theory (SDT), we believe, is in stark contrast to theories underpinning many current manifestations of assessment design—high-stakes testing and performance accountability of teachers, assessment designers, and students. The idea that high-stakes rewards or punishments will motivate all parties in the learning journey to perform more effectively has been shown to be flawed (Boud et al., 2018; Ryan & Deci, 2020). We support SDT's proposition that high-stakes testing regimes increase pressure on students and can reduce their motivation and can "promote various types of 'gaming'" (2012, p. 431), which includes cheating and outsourcing of work to others.

We consider that SDT offers many institutions the opportunity to rethink assessment design placing the three basic psychological needs of students: autonomy, competence, and relatedness at the design core. These three elements act as "essential nutriments" (Deci & Ryan, 2012, p. 423) for student learning growth, motivation to undertake assessments, and well-being. As Ryan and Deci (2020) explain, *autonomy* means an individual's sense of ownership over their own actions, such as undertaking experiences of educative value. In educational settings, autonomy is undermined where a student feels externally controlled through reward and punishment systems. *Competence* refers to an individual's sense of succeeding or growing towards mastery of knowledge, content, and skills. It is supported by meaningful intellectual pursuits and challenges as well as positive, effective feedback. *Relatedness* means a person's sense of belonging or connection and is often achieved through feeling valued, respected, or cared about in learning environments. These three key interrelated needs fuel an individual's motivation (called autonomous motivation) which is key in a student's decision to complete assessments or not. In short, if students feel motivated and supported to undertake assessment tasks themselves, then they are more likely to do so, rather than outsource them.

One reason SDT is well suited as a theoretical base to explore outsourcing and cheating is that it can be applied across relationships between students, teachers, and assessment design. For example, SDT assumes that generally students are curious, keen to learn and gain knowledge or skills. This motivates them to high levels of function (autonomy) if they are engaged in meaningful learning tasks (competence) and are socially supported in their learning (relatedness). Assessment design can contribute to all three elements including structuring the necessary autonomy support from teachers. Of course, SDT recognises that some students do not display curiosity or engagement either some, or all the time, lack self-motivation and can display dissatisfaction. We consider rethinking assessment design with SDT at the heart may encourage disenfranchised students to engage in learning.

The nexus between teachers and assessment design is clear. Where teachers are perceived to support student learning and help them understand not only *what* they want students to learn but *why* the task is of educative value, they are supporting students' autonomous motivation to learn. By offering well-designed and inherently relevant assessments, teachers provide a structure for assessment performance (competence support) and are seen to care about student success in learning (relatedness support). For example, in addition to supplying a series of task instructions (what to learn), for teachers who also provide a meaningful rationale for the value of an assessment (why learn) with adequate support (care to learn), students are more likely to be motivated to complete the task themselves and forego cheating or outsourcing opportunities. However, not all behaviours result from students being interested or inherently motivated to complete activities or assessments. Sometimes students' motivations are controlled by external factors such as believing university education is only a means to a job, with no extrinsic value outside employment. It is unlikely these students will see the intrinsic educative value formative or summative tasks provide (intrinsic and extrinsic motivation are discussed in detail in Ryan & Deci, 2020). We are aware that many teachers currently find workarounds to support the needs of their learners despite institutional or bureaucratic barriers, including norm referenced assessments, mandated high-stakes examinations, rigidly controlled curricula (often set by accreditation authorities), and decreasing resources for needs-support and student-centred education. However, we believe an opportunity exists to broadly rethink assessment design to reduce the dependency on high-stakes tasks and channel educators' creativity in positive assessment design, rather than workarounds. Let us consider research studies that examine how student motivation, cheating, and assessment design play out in educational settings.

Student Motivation, Cheating, and Assessment

We need to be clear that most students do not engage in outsourcing or contract cheating and are not motivated to do so (Bretag et al., 2019). In 2019, Rundle et al. conducted a survey with 1204 students to probe why students say they do not engage in cheating on assessments. Using a rational choice perspective, meaning the reasons people give for ethical or unethical behaviours and decision-making, they found that students' moral beliefs, their perceptions of norms, and their motivation to learn were reasons they did not outsource assessments. Indeed, the researchers found that students' level of competence satisfaction related to their motivation for learning, and was a key reason they gave for deciding not to cheat. The authors also concluded that assessment design plays a role in disrupting opportunities for students to cheat and can increase their motivation to complete tasks themselves. By focussing on learning goals, assessment design may help students rationalise why they do not engage in cheating behaviours. However, some students may be motivated to cheat in certain situations.

In 2017, Anderman and Koenka explored students' motivations to cheat or not to cheat. They proposed three questions that underpin student learning: What is my purpose? Can I do this? What are the costs? They also considered how educators can support students to answer these questions themselves. To answer the first question, they suggest guiding students towards mastery of knowledge or skills as a primary purpose rather than focussing on grades or extrinsic rewards. This means designing assessments that focus on deep learning of material and allowing students to persist with tasks until they attain a level of mastery. Appropriate, timely feedback that supports students in deciding whether they have mastered the knowledge, content, or skill is critical. Anderman and Koenka argue that with mastery as the learning goal, there is no gain for the student in cheating as they are not progressing towards their own mastery goal. The authors contrast a focus on mastery with the many high-stress, high-stakes exam testing environments currently used and assert "cheating will be a more viable option for students" in exams (Anderman & Koenka, 2017, p. 100).

To answer the second question, Anderman and Koenka suggest supporting students to set short-term goals to reach mastery. We agree and believe this can be built into assessment design. Structuring tasks for small but consistent wins is likely to motivate students to continue to more challenging activities or tasks as part of the mastery goal. Assessment design can include creating co-operative student learning groups where all group members are striving for the common goal of mastery, rather than competing against each other for the highest grades. Part of the assessment design involves clear and consistent performance expectations being set and revisited by both educators and students. This is promoted and sustained through use of well-written rubrics and criterion-referenced performance expectations. Finally, Anderman and Koenka advise that the costs of cheating must be explicitly discussed with students, not only in terms of policies and regulations, but also in terms of the cost of the student's own learning and their future career or study aspirations. Explicit discussion between academic staff and students as well as between students themselves of the possible costs of cheating is widely advocated in the research literature. Whilst these ideas may appear highly aspirational and difficult to achieve at the learning/teaching interface, with the many challenges and constraints on educators, such as heavy workloads, large class sizes, lack of marking support, and other logistical considerations, restructuring assessment design to align more with mastery as the core goal is worthy of consideration to motivate students to do assignments themselves rather than outsource them. To illustrate this, two research studies using SDT in relation to student motivation and cheating are discussed.

Kanat-Maymon et al. (2015) conducted two experimental studies testing their theory that if the three needs of SDT (autonomy, competence, and relatedness) were not met, academic deception was likely. In the first study with 121 undergraduate students, the researchers manipulated the fulfilment of needs by providing different instructions about task completion to participant students. Some students had instructions that met all three needs and encouraged them to experiment and play. The other set of instructions allowed no choice or play and made it clear teachers had low expectations of students succeeding. Therefore, none of the SDT needs were met. Unsurprisingly, the researchers found that students who had their needs satisfied were less likely to cheat and those whose needs were not met were more likely to cheat. In the second study, 115 high school students all completed a set of questionnaires: (a) whether learning needs were met at school, (b) completing assessments, and (c) self-assessment on academic dishonesty. Students whose basic needs were met demonstrated higher levels of autonomous motivation and were less likely to engage in cheating behaviours. Indeed, the authors concluded that autonomously motivated students were more likely to view cheating as an impediment to genuine learning rather than see any gain from it.

In 2016, Oz et al. used SDT in an experimental design to investigate the reasons underlying students' motivations to achieve goals. Students may have the same goal but are motivated by different factors, such as personal satisfaction or a tangible reward, which may influence their learning outcomes. The researchers gave 212 undergraduate students a specific spatial drawing task and asked them to state their key achievement goal in undertaking the task as well as their reasons (autonomous or controlling) for goal satisfaction. The authors wanted to investigate whether students giving the same reasons for different goals would predict their motivation to cheat or not. Similar to other studies, the researchers found that the underlying autonomous (inward facing) reasons or controlling reasons (outward facing) were motivators in achievement goals and decisions to complete tasks themselves or not. There are implications for learning and assessment design: if completing a task is personally meaningful, interesting, enjoyable, and aligns with personal values, then students are more likely to be autonomously motivated—but if a task is only being completed because it is mandatory then this is associated with less autonomous motivation and more maladaptive coping strategies.

Similarly, Park (2020) surveyed 2360 Korean college students across two time points using goal content theory, a sub-set of Self-Determination Theory (SDT). The author examined whether students' motivations and goal content could predict serious and minor cheating behaviours. Goal content theory has two categories of goals—intrinsic goals that face inward, such as self-growth and personal values, and extrinsic goals that face outward, such as recognised success, financial gain, and external rewards. Intrinsic goals support the three pillars of individual need outlined in SDT: autonomy, competence, and relatedness. The author found that where intrinsic goals are satisfied, particularly self-growth, there was a negative association with cheating. However, the specific extrinsic goal of wealth was positively associated with minor cheating behaviours. The author concluded that goal content should be included in educational programmes and we suggest that this can be achieved within assessment design.

What Can Assessment Design Contribute?

Existing research suggests that both in theory and in practice, where assessment design meets the three SDT needs (autonomy, competency, and relatedness), students can achieve learning outcomes themselves, without resorting to outsourcing or contract cheating. Furthermore, student well-being is enhanced as they are succeeding in attaining learning outcomes, no matter how small the steps, gaining competency in knowledge and skills, and feeling supported and valued in the learning process by educators and peers.

Ryan and Deci (2020) suggest assessment design should include the educator's role in supporting autonomous motivation in students. They assert that promoting intrinsic motivation rather than external rewards and encouraging students to constructively participate in learning promotes this goal. They suggest that to support students' autonomous motivation and engagement, educators should be responsive to students' perspectives, provide clear opportunities for student ownership in assessments, and offer meaningful assessments. The authors advocate clear structure in tasks, which is distinguished from teacher-centred control. The difference is that a structured task: sets clear goals, is consistent in guidelines, uses flexible language, provides supporting information, and resources for student engagement, and encourages students in positive ways with timely, high-quality, meaningful feedback. Importantly, the assessment design should have a clear and meaningful rationale to enable students to perceive the value in undertaking the assessment task at all. Further, in supporting a sense of students' ownership of their work, they advocate there must be *real* choice, not tokenism. These supportive educator behaviours are designed to motivate students to complete assessments that are of educative value themselves, rather than outsourcing them to others. The authors contend that where such structure exists, empirical evidence shows higher autonomous motivation and application of self-learning with reduced anxiety in students. Indeed, the authors claim that permitting educators such autonomy also supports students' other needs of competency and relatedness and, importantly, student well-being and mental health. We consider this particularly important post-COVID, with concern about how effectively teachers and students will re-engage in face-to-face classes, group, and teamwork.

Ryan and Deci (2020) also outline factors that negatively affect learning growth. These include "excessive emphasis on grades, performance goals and pressures from high-stakes testing" (p. 5). They advocate for feedback that is meaningful to the student to help them improve. However, grades per se can negatively affect student motivation and learning as they are, most often, performance based, therefore competitive rather than motivating. Therefore, students can perceive performance goals as stressful and externally set to control motivation (get the highest grade), which can negatively affect student motivation. The authors advocate, along with other researchers, assessment design focussing on mastery goals, which build upon the student's existing knowledge base and extend it. They state, "this high-stakes reform approach, as long predicted by SDT … has been remarkably ineffective" (2020, p. 6). To conclude, they advocate SDT-based interventions in teacher education courses, which could also apply to tertiary academic staff in their professional development. They rely on several studies where these interventions have been applied and conclude that "interventions based on SDT have been strongly empirically supported relative to other theoretical perspectives" (2020, p. 6), not only enhancing student performance and motivation but nurturing student well-being. This statement on the strength of empirical support for SDT is very important; compared to much pedagogical theory there is replicated and directly traceable empirical support for each of the key claims of SDT (e.g., Howard et al., 2021).

A key feature of the success of motivating students to complete assessments themselves is the nature and quality of the tasks. Assessment tasks need to be meaningful and of educative value to cultivate autonomous motivation. Tasks of educative value (Dewey, 1999) are relevant to need, contemporary, and engaging. Where tasks are deemed by students as 'busy work', boring, unrelated, or irrelevant to their needs, they are less likely to be completed and perhaps more likely to be outsourced. Where the assessment design allows students a degree of participation or choice in decision-making and includes an ability for students to express their perspectives, this fosters students' autonomous motivation to complete tasks. It must be noted that this works where educators play a role in supporting learning goals, through methods already discussed. Ryan and Deci (2020) conclude that the 'what' students are asked to do in assessment tasks is not the only driving factor in students' growth to autonomy. It is equally important that the 'why' and also the 'how' students are asked to approach tasks are clear. Where teachers employ autonomous supportive strategies rather than controlling strategies students appear more motivated to complete the task themselves.

Pulfrey et al. (2019) investigated student goals and motivations to cheat in two settings. One was a controlled laboratory situation and the other a classroom. They used a combination of SDT and Achievement Goal Theory to examine whether students presented with assessment task instructions that had different goals (performance or mastery) and different teaching approaches (supportive autonomy or controlling) would influence cheating behaviours. They found that even small variations in task presentations can immediately influence the degree of cheating behaviour, therefore educators must be aware of any "hidden messages" (2019, p. 15) that may underpin assessment task instructions. The researchers also found that 'nudging' which involves "structuring choice to modify people's voluntary behavior in ways that can be predicted" (p. 15) can be applied to cheating behaviours. This suggests that students may be 'nudged' to behave more ethically where options are offered within the assessment task design. The framing of assessment tasks matters, not just the nature of the task themselves. Pulfrey et al. concluded that it is equally important to focus on the autonomy support as the mastery-goal approach. This is because students need teachers to support their growth to autonomous motivation as the pressures of external rewards, temptations to cut corners in busy lives, and achieve success to avoid shame are often present. We think this study adds weight to SDT as a theory that encompasses the roles of assessment design, learning, and teaching in a positive way.

Where to from Here?

From SDT and the studies discussed that test its approaches, we know that where students are motivated to do the work themselves, given meaningful tasks to work towards mastery goals, and supported by educators to do so, they are less likely to cheat or outsource. This is because outsourcing and cheating defeat the purpose of attaining the requisite knowledge and skills which the students themselves have decided are their key achievement goals. The benefit to educators of using SDT is that the learning relationship is more satisfying for teachers, as motivated students who complete tasks themselves to gain the knowledge or skills being taught can be rewarding for educators. In addition, where students succeed, teachers also succeed—whether that be personally rewarding or through the metrics used by institutions to measure successful teaching. It is true that SDT requires more work from teachers to initially design and structure assessment tasks to offer choice, be meaningful and explicitly related to knowledge or skill gain (thereby meeting the three needs of autonomy, competence, and relatedness). However, it can be said that much teacher time could be saved with fewer integrity breach allegations to prepare, as cheating and outsourcing behaviours decrease.

Finally, the global pandemic disruption challenged student-teacher engagement and assessment delivery in unforeseen ways. Technologies were implemented, often rapidly, to allow education to continue. The pandemic foregrounded discussion of cheating and students outsourcing their work, as teachers rushed to provide, guide, and mark assessments digitally and institutions scrambled to ensure technologies could cope with the total student cohort, and were secure and reliable. This major disruption to traditional assessments offers teachers and institutions an opportunity to reimagine assessment design focussing on mastery goals rather than performance goals. We propose Self-Determination Theory offers a pathway to achieve this end. Ultimately while it is up to students to make the decision to cheat or to complete a task with integrity, it is educators and institutions who create much of the circumstances that shape their motivation.

REFERENCES

Anderman, E. M., & Koenka, A. C. (2017). The relation between academic motivation and cheating. *Theory Into Practice, 56*(2), 95–102. https://doi.org/10.1080/00405841.2017.1308172

Awdry, R. (2021). Assignment outsourcing: moving beyond contract cheating. *Assessment & Evaluation in Higher Education 46*(2) 220–235. https://doi.org/10.1080/02602938.2020.1765311

Baird, M., & Clare, J. (2017). Removing the opportunity for contract cheating in business capstones: A crime prevention case study. *International Journal for Educational Integrity, 13*(1), 6. https://doi.org/10.1007/s40979-017-0018-1

Boud, D., Ajjawi, R., Dawson, P., & Tai, J. (2018). *Developing evaluative judgment in higher education: Assessment for knowing and producing quality work*. Routledge.

Boud, D. (1995). Assessment and learning: Contradictory or complementary. In P. Knight (Ed.), *Assessment for learning in higher education* (pp. 35–48). Kogan Page.

Bretag, T., Harper, R., Burton, M., Ellis, C., Newton, P., van Haeringen, K., Saddiqui, S., & Rozenberg, P. (2019). Contract cheating and assessment design: Exploring the relationship. *Assessment & Evaluation in Higher Education, 44*(5), 676–691. https://doi.org/10.1080/02602938.2018.1527892

Deci, E. L., & Ryan, R. M. (2012). Self determination theory. In P. A. van Lange, A. Kruglanski, & R. Tory (Eds.), *Handbook of theories of social psychology* (pp. 416–437). SAGE.

Dewey, J. (1999). *Education and experience*. Free Press.

Ellis, C., van Haeringen, K., Harper, R., Bretag, T., Zucker, I., McBride, S., Rozenberg, P., Newton, P., & Saddiqui, S. (2019). Does authentic assessment assure academic integrity? Evidence from contract cheating data. *Higher Education Research & Development, 39*(3), 454–469. https://doi.org/10.1080/07294360.2019.1680956

Emerson, R. M. (1976). Social exchange theory. *Annual Review of Sociology, 2*, 335–362.

Harper, R., Bretag, T., & Rundle, K. (2021). Detecting contract cheating: Examining the role of assessment type. *Higher Education Research & Development, 40*(2), 263–278. https://doi.org/10.1080/07294360.2020.1724899

Howard, J. L., Bureau, J., Guay, F., Chong, J. X. Y., & Ryan, R. M. (2021). Student motivation and associated outcomes: A meta-analysis from self-determination theory. *Perspectives on Psychological Science, 1745691620966789*. https://doi.org/10.1177/1745691620966789

Kanat-Maymon, Y., Benjamin, M., Stavsky, A., Shoshani, A., & Roth, G. (2015). The role of basic need fulfillment in academic dishonesty: A self-determination theory perspective. *Contemporary Educational Psychology, 43*, 1–9. https://doi.org/10.1016/j.cedpsych.2015.08.002

Kohn, A. (1999). *Punished by rewards: The trouble with gold stars, incentive plans, A's, praise, and other bribes*. Houghton Mifflin Harcourt.

Lancaster, T., & Clarke, R. (2008). The phenomena of contract cheating. In T. Roberts (Ed.), *Student plagiarism in an online world: Problems and solutions* (pp. 144–159). IGI Global. https://doi.org/10.4018/978-1-59904-801-7.ch010

Lancaster, T., & Cotarlan, C. (2021). Contract cheating by STEM students through a file sharing website: A covid-19 pandemic perspective. *International Journal for Educational Integrity, 17*(3). https://doi.org/10.1007/s40979-021-00070-0

Oz, A., Lane, J. F., & Michou, A. (2016). Autonomous and controlling reasons underlying achievement goals during task engagement: Their relation to intrinsic motivation and cheating. *Educational Psychology, 36*(7), 1160–1172. https://doi.org/10.1080/01443410.2015.1109064

Park, S. (2020). Goal contents as predictors of academic cheating in college students. *Ethics & Behavior, 30*(8), 628–639. https://doi.org/10.1080/10508422.2019.1668275

Pulfrey, C. J., Vansteenkiste, M., & Michou, A. (2019). Under pressure to achieve? The impact of type and style of task instructions on student cheating. *Frontiers in Psychology, 10*(1624). https://doi.org/10.3389/fpsyg.2019.01624

Ramsden, P. (1992). *Learning to teach in Higher Education*. Routledge.
Rowland, S., Slade, C., Wong, K.-S., & Whiting, B. (2018). 'Just turn to us': the persuasive features of contract cheating websites. *Assessment & Evaluation in Higher Education, 43*(4), 652–665. https://doi.org/10.1080/02602938.2017.1391948
Rundle, K., Curtis, G., & Clare, J. (2019). Why students do not engage in contract cheating. *Frontiers in Psychology, 10*, 2229. https://doi.org/10.3389/fpsyg.2019.02229
Ryan, R. M., & Deci, E. L. (2020). Intrinsic and extrinsic motivation from a self-determination theory perspective: Definitions, theory, practices, and future directions. *Contemporary Educational Psychology, 61*, 101860. https://doi.org/10.1016/j.cedpsych.2020.101860
Sambell, K., McDowell, L., & Brown, S. (1997). "But is it fair?": An exploratory study of student perceptions of the consequential validity of assessment. *Studies in Educational Evaluation, 23*(4), 349–371. https://doi.org/10.1016/S0191-491X(97)86215-3
Skinner, B. F. (1965). *Science and human behavior*. Simon and Schuster.

CHAPTER 8

Critical Thinking as an Antidote to Contract Cheating

Brenda M. Stoesz, Sarah Elaine Eaton, and Josh Seeland

Underdeveloped critical thinking skills have been highlighted in news reports of a surge in academic cheating during the COVID-19 pandemic as educators and students pivoted from traditional classrooms to emergency remote teaching and learning. Universities reported four times more academic cheating than in previous years (Garcia, 2020), with contract cheating increasing ten-fold (Rossiter, 2020). These reports suggest that critical thinking abilities are generally deficient in society—that many individuals are unable to make decisions about the most appropriate and ethical courses of action (Flores et al., 2012). In this chapter, we briefly

---

B. M. Stoesz
University of Manitoba, Winnipeg, MB, Canada
e-mail: Brenda.Stoesz@umanitoba.ca

S. E. Eaton (✉)
University of Calgary, Calgary, AB, Canada
e-mail: seaton@ucalgary.ca

J. Seeland
Assiniboine Community College, Brandon, MB, Canada
e-mail: seelandjl@Assiniboine.net

© The Author(s), under exclusive license to Springer Nature Switzerland AG 2022
S. E. Eaton et al. (eds.), *Contract Cheating in Higher Education*,
https://doi.org/10.1007/978-3-031-12680-2_8

describe the indirect evidence for relationships between underdeveloped critical thinking skills and use of contract cheating services (i.e., outsourcing academic work to third parties; Clarke & Lancaster, 2006). Although government and educational institutions in some jurisdictions have implemented or are working to implement laws, policies, and other high-level strategies to combat contract cheating (TEQSA, 2017; Newton & Lang, 2016; QAA, 2020; Seeland et al., 2020), strengthening students' critical thinking abilities at the course level is also necessary. Therefore, we also describe several pedagogical strategies that support the development of critical thinking skills (Niu et al., 2013), and how using these strategies could reduce temptations to engage in contract cheating.

Defining Critical Thinking

Critical thinking involves the ability to analyse, synthesize, and evaluate information and apply these skills and strategies responsibly to various situations to determine the best course of action (Halpern, 2001; Profetto-McGrath, 2003). Employers view critical thinking "as an important practical capacity, manifested in the avoidance of mistakes and making the right decisions, self-correction and self-regulation, and social responsibility" (Penkauskiene et al., 2019, p. 807). Individuals with effective critical thinking skills and dispositions are able to avoid doing "blatantly stupid things" (Butler et al., 2017, p. 39) and make good decisions consistently that lead to more positive and fewer negative life events (Butler, 2012; Butler et al., 2017) and greater life satisfaction (Siebert et al., 2020). Due to its value to individuals, employers, and society, the ability to think critically is an important goal of education (Arum et al., 2011).

Contract Cheating and Underdeveloped Critical Thinking Skills

The rapid shift to online learning during the COVID-19 pandemic coincided with students making more requests for solutions to questions on formal assessments. Lancaster and Cotarlan (2021) estimated that the use of file-sharing or "homework help" sites increased by about 75% during the pandemic in the fields of computer science, physics, chemistry, and engineering. The dramatic increase in contract cheating has increased motivation to implement strategies, such as blocking access to contract cheating websites (Seeland et al., 2020), text-matching software (Rogerson, 2017), e-proctoring (Hill et al., 2021), visual inspection of assignments (Dawson & Sutherland-Smith, 2019), and statistical or computational authorship attribution techniques (Halvani et al., 2019; Rudzewitz, 2016) and other forensic methods (Johnson & Davies, 2020), to discourage outsourcing behaviour.

To understand the associations between underdeveloped critical thinking skills and the rise in contract cheating more fully, we must appreciate why students choose to engage in contract cheating. Using discourse analysis, Amigud and Lancaster (2019) identified justifications for outsourcing academic work in Twitter messages and categorized them as the inability to persevere, lower academic aptitude, low self-discipline, personal issues, and competing objectives. Many justifications suggested that students have difficulty managing their academic workload and other academic issues, which are the most common sources of stress for postsecondary students (Akgun & Ciarrochi, 2003; Yang et al., 2021). During the pandemic, academic stress was worsened by fears of infection and separation from academic environments (Yang et al., 2021). Higher stress levels interfere with learning and critical thinking processes (Misra et al., 2020), which reduce students' ability to make appropriate choices regarding academic work. High stress and reduced ability to make good decisions, combined with the persuasiveness of contract cheating suppliers (Rowland et al., 2018), are bound to increase the temptation to outsource assignments.

In contrast, successful students have developed characteristics and strategies that support their learning and ability to resist temptations to cheat. This may be because their ability to cope with increasing stress developed as they acquired more effective critical thinking skills (Misra et al., 2020; Okide et al., 2020). During the pandemic, student success may have depended on the ability to adapt to online learning, adjust study routines, and self-monitor progress (McAllister & Watkins, 2012). Further indirect evidence for the link between contract cheating and poor reasoning comes from studies measuring perceptions of the value of intellectual endeavours and the ability to think critically (Eigenberger & Sealander, 2001; Frunzaru et al., 2018) and correlations with beliefs about academic misconduct (Elias, 2009) and classroom incivility (Laverghetta, 2018). When students view critical thinking and intellectual pursuits as unimportant (Eigenberger & Sealander, 2001), they are more likely to report that academic cheating is not unethical (Elias, 2009).

Pedagogies for Critical Thinking Skill Development

Concerns have arisen that universities view critical thinking and other transversal skills too narrowly as the transfer of cognitive skills within specific domains (Barnett, 1997) without considering real-world complexities (Kay & Greenhill, 2011). The specifist view contends that deep content knowledge and critical thinking skills are intertwined within a particular domain, and that set of knowledge and skills is different from those practised in another domain. The generalist view argues that broad sets of universal skills can be learned in any context and then applied to any other context (Liu et al., 2014; Moore, 2004). Some argue that the generalist view has resulted in the offering of generic critical thinking courses in postsecondary education (Penkauskiene et al., 2019), which may be equally ineffective. Instead of relying on general and specific approaches to developing critical thinking skills, integrated, combinatory approaches that encourage educators to use pedagogies from various viewpoints and that are developmentally appropriate for students at different educational levels (Abrami et al., 2008; Burbach et al., 2004; Ikuenobe, 2001) may be more successful in supporting student learning. In addition, these same critical thinking skills development strategies are also important for promoting academic integrity (Morris, 2016). Below, we summarize six strategies for supporting the development of critical thinking and how each can be used to reduce contract cheating.

Scaffolding

Scaffolding involves breaking lessons, learning activities, or assignments into smaller, more manageable chunks in which the knowledge or skills learned in an earlier chunk are built upon in the chunk that follows. Scaffolding involves providing students with more support in early chunks and reducing supports and increasing students' responsibility to complete activities when there is evidence that they can complete activities on their own (Makmur et al., 2019). Earlier chunks may involve the presentation of examples, asking students to share their prior knowledge and skills, providing opportunities to ask questions, and front-loading vocabulary and other background information. By incrementally building on prior knowledge and skills, students may feel less overwhelmed by the quantity of content and skills that they are required to learn. Scaffolding can also foster self-efficacy and self-regulated learning, components of critical thinking, thereby decreasing and preventing stress, hopelessness, fear, and anxiety (Grothérus et al., 2019) and reducing temptations to cheat. Another benefit of scaffolding is the ability to observe and gather evidence of learning as it unfolds. Having a deep understanding of students' level of understanding and style of communicating their learnings enables instructors to more easily and accurately identify probable cases of contract cheating when it does occur.

An important limitation of scaffolding is that students may ignore the scaffolds and jump to the next stage before they are ready to do so. To limit the tendency to skip ahead prematurely, it is important to add value to each stage. Ideally, that value comes from the intrinsic reward of learning and mastering each stage, but students often need external rewards (e.g., grades) as a supplementary motivator. The challenge is to find the right reward level—too much and the stage has been set for cheating, too little and students may not take the scaffolded learning activity or assessment strategy seriously. Other challenges with scaffolding include the time required to plan suitable activities and the potential marking/grading load associated with each stage in scaffolded assignments. However, carefully planned scaffolded activities can result in greater learning, better experiences for students with less frustration, and reduced or quicker end of term grading of final assignments.

Case Studies
Case studies can be used to lead students through the process of analysing to support the development of critical thinking skills (McDade, 1995). Effective cases are carefully constructed to the level of the student by providing facts in a particular order but end before the story concludes. This structure provides opportunities for speculation, analysis by identifying key characters, issues, and variables at play in a case, and crafting possible solutions. Students are often asked to put themselves in others' shoes for "ascertaining resources, constituencies, and constraints; determining sources and nature of conflicts, and the dynamics of behavior; isolating decisions to be made; identifying alternatives; and anticipating and assessing consequences of decisions and actions" (McDade, 1995, p. 9). Providing students with prompts for critically analysing cases can be helpful for students who have difficulty beginning these types of learning activities (see Miles & Spies-Butcher, 2012).

Effective case studies are non-linear and complex, do not have one clear solution, can pose several ethical dilemmas, and are ideal for exploring students' views and thought processes around contract cheating. Beginning with contract cheating scenarios or scenarios involving other types of academic misconduct (Foxe et al., 2022; Penaluna & Ross, 2022) can also serve as a foundational exercise before moving into cases that allow students to explore course-specific content. Students could also write their own case studies about academic integrity and contract cheating that are then randomly distributed to other students. Encouraging students to examine the details of cases and the possible outcomes may also be a way for students to think about their role in society outside of the educational context. Collections of cases and accompanying discussion questions are freely available online with topics ranging from cheating and copyright issues to environmental and health scenarios (e.g., McCombs School of Business The University of Texas at Austin, 2021).

Using case studies can be challenging for instructors who have not been trained to implement them or who are not comfortable assessing students' exploration of the grey areas of real-world, complex cases that have no one correct answer. Case studies can also be difficult to use because preparing stories suitable for given sets of learning objectives can be labour-intensive and time-consuming (Mostert, 2007). Moreover, students may require advance preparation before examining cases and stories for the activities more engaging and useful in the synchronous learning context. Therefore, using case study approaches for supporting the development of critical thinking skills may need to be combined with scaffolded and flipped approaches so that students come prepared with solid foundations of relevant knowledge and skills before attempting to analyse cases. Although advance preparation positively impacts students' learning and development of critical thinking compared to the traditional lecture (Dehghanzadeh & Jafaraghaee, 2018), students may resent the time and effort it takes to prepare for learning activities involving case studies.

Problem-Based Learning
Problem-based learning shares the characteristics of scaffolding and case studies in that students' previous knowledge and experiences can be used to solve real-life problems relevant to a course (Flores et al., 2012). Problem-based learning is an active and collaborative learning approach where students are required to connect course content to a problem and is distinguished from case-based learning in that learners are required to "discover" on their own (Srinivasan et al., 2007). Problem-based learning, like case studies, can help students to explore the grey areas of problems and think creatively about how to solve them. In doing so, students

develop the skills to make decisions and explore possible outcomes. Problems involving outsourcing academic work to third parties and the grey areas of academic file-sharing and homework help can encourage students to analyse, evaluate, and ultimately make decisions about whether to use these services and in which contexts they are appropriate or inappropriate. Problem-based learning requires students to be prepared with the foundational knowledge and skills required to tackle a problem. When students lack the relevant knowledge and skills, they may find it difficult to move forward in their discussions with other students and in their thinking to solve problems. As a result, problem-based learning can take more time and can induce anxiety in some students.

Discussion
Successful dialogue requires participation and interaction among students and must be facilitated skilfully by the instructor. The instructor must model being a discussant rather than being perceived as the authority on a topic. The ability to speak in multiple contexts and about various topics is an important skill for students. Students enrolled in courses using discussion for processing ideas develop more advanced critical thinking (Mayo, 2002), and oral and written communication (Dallimore et al., 2008) skills. Discussion can also enhance relationships between instructors and students and amongst students, providing more satisfaction with the academic experience and learning environment. Using discussion about contract cheating, students can learn about the knowledge, understanding, and perspectives of other students, which can help them to further their own understandings. A limitation of discussion is that students may be reluctant to share their views if they feel ill-prepared to contribute to the discussion, or fear cold-calling or being judged by other students. This strategy may also be more challenging to employ in online courses. To address these limitations, instructors can provide students with advanced notice about the topics, provide relevant pre-readings, and outline the ground rules for discussion sessions that include the procedures for participation and expectations for showing respect for others and their ideas. For online courses, it is essential that the instructor is an active participant in the discussions and encourages students to engage actively in the process to reap the benefits (Wilson et al., 2007).

Reflection

Reflection is argued to be a key component of teaching students how to think critically (Colley et al., 2012). Reflection requires that students think about their own thinking and what factors influence their thinking. Reflection has been parsed into various types, including content-based, metacognitive, self-authorship, and transformative (see Grossman, 2009). In content-based reflection, students consider how their experiences relate to specific learning objectives. Metacognitive reflection is the awareness and knowledge of one's own thinking and how that applies to solving complex problems. Self-authorship reflection is the understanding that one's thoughts and feelings impact how one perceives the world and its challenges. Transformative reflection is knowing why you think what you think, which supports "learning to be more socially responsible, self-directed, and less dependent on false assumptions" (Kiely, 2005, p. 7). Reflective practice increases self-awareness, creating thinking, and encourages active engagement in learning processes.

Reflective exercises involving contract cheating and other ethical dilemmas can be used to encourage students to understand and challenge their internal assumptions about academic integrity and misconduct and why these assumptions must be evaluated continuously. Students should also be encouraged to reflect on how they can take responsibility for their good or poor decisions based on their assumptions (Flores et al., 2012; Vučković et al., 2020). Students are less likely to outsource assignments requiring reflection or those that are personalized and unique (Bretag et al., 2019). Reflection, however, requires time to think about experiences and how it applies to academic work, and some students may not know how to approach this type of learning exercise. Reflection may also require that students have experienced relevant events or thoughts/feelings, and if they have not, the reflective exercise can be challenging. Educators may also be under the misconception that reflection does not need to be taught explicitly, therefore, they may not provide students with guidelines for doing so. Educators can support students in reflective practice by providing clear concrete guidelines and several opportunities to practice.

Supporting Self-Regulation and Self-Control
Self-regulation along with self-efficacy predicts critical thinking abilities (Uzuntiryaki-Kondakçi & Çapa-Aydin, 2013) and behaviours associated with acting with academic integrity (McAllister & Watkins, 2012; Rundle et al., 2019). Educators can support the development of self-regulation

skills and self-control by supporting effective time management, communicating due dates clearly, and requiring regular interaction with course content. Educators can also support self-regulation by encouraging the use of learning strategies, such as organization and elaboration, and providing specific directions for getting help before it is too late. By increasing self-regulation and self-control abilities, students become more skilled at monitoring their behaviour associated with their goals, comparing that behaviour or performance to a criterion, and adjusting as necessary. These actions will also reduce stress, which is an important determinant of cheating behaviour.

Conclusion

Increases in academic misconduct, including contract cheating, may be related to changes in the purpose of education from one of "personal development ..., cultivating informed and active citizens, developing intrinsically valuable knowledge, and serving society through public interest ... [to] serving society through economic development" (Conrad & Openo, 2018, p. 5). COVID-19 has highlighted this shift in the purpose of education and exacerbated the problems that many have observed in educational systems and in society over the past several decades. In this chapter, we discussed evidence for the relationships between underdeveloped critical thinking skills and the rise in use of contract cheating services. Much of this evidence is indirect, therefore, we call on researchers to corroborate the link between critical thinking and reduced contract cheating. The absence of original research in this area, however, should not prevent educators from implementing pedagogical practices that focus on the development of critical thinking skills. Educators at all levels and disciplines are encouraged to use effective teaching strategies to support the explicit development of critical thinking skills during the entire span of students' educational careers. Doing so will equip students with knowledge and skills to make better decisions in their academic work and to grapple with ethical issues beyond campus boundaries.

References

Abrami, P. C., Bernard, R. M., Borokhovski, E., Wade, A., Surkes, M. A., Tamim, R., & Zhang, D. (2008). Instructional interventions affecting critical thinking skills and dispositions: A stage 1 meta-analysis. *Review of Educational Research, 78*(4), 1102–1134. https://doi.org/10.3102/0034654308326084

Akgun, S., & Ciarrochi, J. (2003). Learned resourcefulness moderates the relationship between academic stress and academic performance. *Educational Psychology, 23*, 287–294. https://doi.org/10.1080/0144341032000060129

Amigud, A., & Lancaster, T. (2019). 246 reasons to cheat: An analysis of students' reasons for seeking to outsource academic work. *Computers and Education, 134*(September 2018), 98–107. https://doi.org/10.1016/j.compedu.2019.01.017

Arum, R., Roksa, J., & Cho, E. (2011). *Improving undergraduate learning: Findings and policy recommendations from the SSRC-CLA longitudinal project*. 22. http://www.eric.ed.gov/ERICWebPortal/contentdelivery/servlet/ERICServlet?accno=ED514983%5Cn; http://www.eric.ed.gov/ERICWebPortal/detail?accno=ED514983

Australian Government: Tertiary Education Quality and Standards Agency (TEQSA). (2017). *Good practice note: Addressing contract cheating to safeguard academic integrity* (Issue October). https://www.teqsa.gov.au/latest-news/publications/good-practice-note-addressing-contract-cheating-safeguard-academic

Barnett, R. (1997). *Higher education: A critical business*. McGraw-Hill Education.

Bretag, T., Harper, R., Burton, M., Ellis, C., Newton, P., van Haeringen, K., Saddiqui, S., & Rozenberg, P. (2019). Contract cheating and assessment design: Exploring the relationship. *Assessment & Evaluation in Higher Education, 44*(5), 676–691. https://doi.org/10.1080/02602938.2018.1527892

Burbach, M. E., Matkin, G. S., & Fritz, S. M. (2004). Teaching critical thinking in an introductory leadership course utilizing active learning strategies: A confirmatory study. *College Student Journal, 38*(3), 482–493.

Butler, H. A. (2012). Halpern critical thinking assessment predicts real-world outcomes of critical thinking. *Applied Cognitive Psychology, 26*(5), 721–729. https://doi.org/10.1002/acp.2851

Butler, H. A., Pentoney, C., & Bong, M. P. (2017). Predicting real-world outcomes: Critical thinking ability is a better predictor of life decisions than intelligence. *Thinking Skills and Creativity, 25*(July), 38–46. https://doi.org/10.1016/j.tsc.2017.06.005

Clarke, R., & Lancaster, T. (2006). Eliminating the successor to plagiarism: Identifying the usage of contract cheating sites. *Paper Presented at the Second International Plagiarism Conference*.

Colley, B. M., Bilics, A. R., & Lerch, C. M. (2012). Reflection: A key component to thinking critically. *The Canadian Journal for the Scholarship of Teaching and Learning, 3*(1). https://doi.org/10.5206/cjsotl-rcacea.2012.1.2

Conrad, D., & Openo, J. (2018). *Assessment strategies for online learning: Engagement and authenticity.* AU Press.

Dallimore, E. J., Hertenstein, J. H., & Platt, M. B. (2008). Using discussion pedagogy to enhance oral and written communication skills. *College Teaching, 56*(3), 163–172. https://doi.org/10.3200/CTCH.56.3.163-172

Dawson, P., & Sutherland-Smith, W. (2019). Can training improve marker accuracy at detecting contract cheating? A multi-disciplinary pre-post study. *Assessment and Evaluation in Higher Education, 44*(5), 715–725. https://doi.org/10.1080/02602938.2018.1531109

Dehghanzadeh, S., & Jafaraghaee, F. (2018). Comparing the effects of traditional lecture and flipped classroom on nursing students' critical thinking disposition: A quasi-experimental study. *Nurse Education Today, 71*(March), 151–156. https://doi.org/10.1016/j.nedt.2018.09.027

Eigenberger, M. E., & Sealander, K. A. (2001). A scale for measuring students' anti-intellectualism. *Psychological Reports, 89*(2), 387–402. https://doi.org/10.2466/pr0.2001.89.2.387

Elias, R. Z. (2009). The impact of anti-intellectualism attitudes and academic self-efficacy on business students' perceptions of cheating. *Journal of Business Ethics, 86*(2), 199–209. https://doi.org/10.1007/s10551-008-9843-8

Flores, K. L., Matkin, G. S., Burbach, M. E., Quinn, C. E., & Harding, H. (2012). Deficient critical thinking skills among college graduates: Implications for leadership. *Educational Philosophy and Theory, 44*(2), 212–230. https://doi.org/10.1111/j.1469-5812.2010.00672.x

Foxe, J. P., Miller, A., Farrelly, G., Hui, V., Nubla, D., & Schindler-Lynch, C. (2022). Visual plagiarism: Seeing the forest and the trees. In S. E. Eaton & J. Christensen Hughes (Eds.), *Academic integrity in Canada: An enduring and essential challenge* (pp. 267–289). Springer International Publishing. https://doi.org/10.1007/978-3-030-83255-1_14

Frunzaru, V., Vătămănescu, E. M., Gazzola, P., & Bolisani, E. (2018). Challenges to higher education in the knowledge economy: Anti-intellectualism, materialism and employability. *Knowledge Management Research and Practice, 16*(3), 388–401. https://doi.org/10.1080/14778238.2018.1493368

Garcia, J. (2020, September 30). QUT reports four times more cheating as exams go online [online]. *Brisbane times.* https://www.brisbanetimes.com.au/national/queensland/qut-reports-four-times-more-cheating-as-exams-go-online-20200930-p560m3.html

Grossman, R. (2009). Structures for facilitating student reflection. *College Teaching, 57*(1), 15–22. https://doi.org/10.3200/CTCH.57.1.15-22

Grothérus, A., Jeppsson, F., & Samuelsson, J. (2019). Formative scaffolding: How to alter the level and strength of self-efficacy and foster self-regulation in a mathematics test situation. *Educational Action Research, 27*(5), 667–690. https://doi.org/10.1080/09650792.2018.1538893

Halpern, D. F. (2001). Assessing the effectiveness of critical thinking instruction. *The Journal of General Education, 50*(4), 270–286. https://www.jstor.org/stable/27797889

Halvani, O., Winter, C., & Graner, L. (2019). Assessing the applicability of authorship verification methods. *ACM International Conference Proceeding Series.* https://doi.org/10.1145/3339252.3340508.

Hill, G., Mason, J., & Dunn, A. (2021). Contract cheating: An increasing challenge for global academic community arising from COVID-19. *Research and Practice in Technology Enhanced Learning, 16*(1). https://doi.org/10.1186/s41039-021-00166-8

Ikuenobe, P. (2001). Teaching and assessing critical thinking abilities as outcomes in an informal logic course. *Teaching in Higher Education, 6*(1), 19–32. https://doi.org/10.1080/13562510020029572

Johnson, C., & Davies, R. (2020). Using digital forensic techniques to identify contract cheating: A case study. *Journal of Academic Ethics, 18*(2), 105–113. https://doi.org/10.1007/s10805-019-09358-w

Kay, K., & Greenhill, V. (2011). Twenty-first century students need 21st century skills. In G. Wand & D. M. Gut (Eds.), *Bringing schools into the 21st century* (pp. 41–65). Springer.

Kiely, R. (2005). A transformative learning model for service-learning: A longitudinal case study. *Michigan Journal of Community Service Learning, 12*(1), 5–22.

Lancaster, T., & Cotarlan, C. (2021). Contract cheating by STEM students through a file sharing website: A Covid-19 pandemic perspective. *International Journal for Educational Integrity, 17*(1), 1–16. https://doi.org/10.1007/s40979-021-00070-0

Laverghetta, A. (2018). The relationship between student anti-intellectualism, academic entitlement, student consumerism, and classroom incivility in a sample of college students. *College Student Journal, 52*(2), 278–282.

Liu, O. L., Frankel, L., & Roohr, K. C. (2014). Assessing critical thinking in higher education: Current state and directions for next-generation assessment. *ETS Research Report Series, 2014*(1), 1–23. https://doi.org/10.1002/ets2.12009

Makmur, W., Susilo, H., & Indriwati, S. E. (2019). Implementation of guided inquiry learning with scaffolding strategy to increase critical thinking skills of biology students' based on lesson study. *Journal of Physics: Conference Series, 1227*(1). https://doi.org/10.1088/1742-6596/1227/1/012003

Mayo, J. A. (2002). Dialogue as constructivist pedagogy: Probing the minds of psychology's greatest contributors. *Journal of Constructivist Psychology, 15*(4), 291–304. https://doi.org/10.1080/10720530290100505

McAllister, C., & Watkins, P. (2012). Increasing academic integrity in online classes by fostering the development of self-regulated learning skills. *The Clearing House: A Journal of Educational Strategies, Issues and Ideas, 85*(3), 96–101. https://doi.org/10.1080/00098655.2011.642420

McCombs School of Business The University of Texas at Austin. (2021). *Ethics unwrapped*.

McDade, S. A. (1995). Case study pedagogy to advance critical thinking. *Teaching of Psychology, 22*(1), 9–10. https://doi.org/10.1207/s15328023top2201_3

Miles, B., & Spies-Butcher, B. (2012). Short exercise practice 1: Critical analysis–reading.

Misra, S., Roberts, P., & Rhodes, M. (2020). Information overload, stress, and emergency managerial thinking. *International Journal of Disaster Risk Reduction, 51*(August), 101762. https://doi.org/10.1016/j.ijdrr.2020.101762

Moore, T. (2004). The critical thinking debate: How general are general thinking skills? *Higher Education Research and Development, 23*(1), 3–18. https://doi.org/10.1080/0729436032000168469

Morris, E. J. (2016). Academic integrity: A teaching and learning approach. In T. Bretag (Ed.), *Handbook of academic integrity* (pp. 1037–1054). Springer. https://doi.org/10.1007/978-981-287-098-8

Mostert, M. P. (2007). Challenges of case-based teaching. *The Behaviour Analyst Today, 8*(4), 434–442.

Newton, P. M., & Lang, C. (2016). Custom essay writers, freelancers and other paid third parties. In T. Bretag (Ed.), *Handbook of academic integrity* (pp. 249–271). Springer. https://doi.org/10.1007/978-981-287-079-7

Niu, L., Behar-Horenstein, L. S., & Garvan, C. W. (2013). Do instructional interventions influence college students' critical thinking skills? A meta-analysis. *Educational Research Review, 9*, 114–128. https://doi.org/10.1016/j.edurev.2012.12.002

Okide, C. C., Eseadi, C., Ezenwaji, I. O., Ede, M. O., Igbo, R. O., Koledoye, U. L., Ekwealor, N. E., Osilike, C., Okeke, N. M., Igwe, N. J., Nwachukwu, R. U., Ukanga, L. P., Olajide, M. F., Onuorah, A. E., Ujah, P., Ejionueme, L. K., Abiogu, G. C., Eskay, M., & Ugwuanyi, C. S. (2020). Effect of a critical thinking intervention on stress management among undergraduates of adult education and extramural studies programs. *Medicine, 99*(35), e21697. https://doi.org/10.1097/MD.0000000000021697

Penaluna, L.-A., & Ross, R. (2022). How to talk about academic integrity so students will listen: Addressing ethical decision-making using scenarios. In S. E. Eaton & J. Christensen Hughes (Eds.), *Academic integrity in Canada:*

An enduring and essential challenge (pp. 393–409). Springer International Publishing. https://doi.org/10.1007/978-3-030-83255-1_20

Penkauskiene, D., Railiene, A., & Cruz, G. (2019). How is critical thinking valued by the labour market? Employer perspectives from different European countries. *Studies in Higher Education, 44*(5), 804–815. https://doi.org/10.1080/03075079.2019.1586323

Profetto-McGrath, J. (2003). The relationship of critical thinking skills and critical thinking dispositions of baccalaureate nursing students. *Journal of Advanced Nursing, 43*(6), 569–577. https://doi.org/10.1046/j.1365-2648.2003.02755.x

Quality Assurance Agency (QAA). (2020, October 35). *Contracting to cheat in higher education: How to address essay mills and contract cheating, 2nd edition.* https://www.qaa.ac.uk/docs/qaa/guidance/contracting-to-cheat-in-higher-education-2nd-edition.pdf

Rogerson, A. M. (2017). Detecting contract cheating in essay and report submissions: Process, patterns, clues and conversations. *International Journal for Educational Integrity, 13*(1), 10. https://doi.org/10.1007/s40979-017-0021-6

Rossiter, S. (2020, June 21). Cheating becoming an unexpected COVID-19 side effect for universities [online]. *CBC news.* https://www.cbc.ca/news/canada/edmonton/cheating-becoming-an-unexpected-covid-19-side-effect-for-universities-1.5620442

Rowland, S., Slade, C., Wong, K. S., & Whiting, B. (2018). 'Just turn to us': The persuasive features of contract cheating websites. *Assessment and Evaluation in Higher Education, 43*(4), 652–665. https://doi.org/10.1080/02602938.2017.1391948

Rudzewitz, B. (2016). Exploring the intersection of short answer assessment, authorship attribution, and plagiarism detection. *Proceedings of the 11th Workshop on Innovative Use of NLP for Building Educational Applications,* 235–241. https://doi.org/10.18653/v1/w16-0527.

Rundle, K., Curtis, G. J., & Clare, J. (2019). Why students do not engage in contract cheating. *Frontiers in Psychology, 10,* 2229. https://doi.org/10.3389/fpsyg.2019.02229

Seeland, J., Stoesz, B. M., & Vogt, L. (2020). Preventing online shopping for completed assessments: Protecting students by blocking access to contract cheating websites on institutional networks. *Canadian Perspectives on Academic Integrity, 3*(1), 55–69. https://doi.org/10.11575/cpai.v3i1.70256

Siebert, J. U., Kunz, R. E., & Rolf, P. (2020). Effects of proactive decision making on life satisfaction. *European Journal of Operational Research, 280*(3), 1171–1187. https://doi.org/10.1016/j.ejor.2019.08.011

Srinivasan, M., Wilkes, M., Stevenson, F., Nguyen, T., & Slavin, S. (2007). Comparing problem-based learning with case-based learning: Effects of a major curricular shift at two institutions. *Academic Medicine, 82*(1), 74–82. https://doi.org/10.1097/01.ACM.0000249963.93776.aa

Uzuntiryaki-Kondakçi, E., & Çapa-Aydin, Y. (2013). Predicting critical thinking skills of university students through metacognitive self-regulation skills and chemistry self-efficacy. *Educational Sciences: Theory & Practice, 13*(1), 666–670.

Vučković, D., Peković, S., Blečić, M., & Đoković, R. (2020). Attitudes towards cheating behavior during assessing students' performance: Student and teacher perspectives. *International Journal for Educational Integrity, 16*(1), 1–28. https://doi.org/10.1007/s40979-020-00065-3

Wilson, B. M., Pollock, P. H., & Hamann, K. (2007). Does active learning enhance learner outcomes? Evidence from discussion participation in online classes. *Journal of Political Science Education, 3*(2), 131–142. https://doi.org/10.1080/15512160701338304

Yang, C., Chen, A., & Chen, Y. (2021). College students' stress and health in the COVID-19 pandemic: The role of academic workload, separation from school, and fears of contagion. *PLoS One, 16*(2 February), 1–16. https://doi.org/10.1371/journal.pone.0246676

CHAPTER 9

Contract Cheating and the Dark Triad Traits

Lidia Baran and Peter K. Jonason

As with many socially undesirable traits or tendencies like cheating in academic contexts (e.g., racial prejudice), there are two main classes of explanations: the person and the environment (e.g., Hodson & Dhont, 2015; Koehn et al., 2019). The most appealing of these are environmentally deterministic models focused on contextual influences. Relevant researchers—often experimentalists—manipulate how environmental features change people's willingness or actual commission of cheating. Researchers inspired by this line of reasoning focus on issues like the behaviour of others (Malesky et al., 2021; Schuhmann et al., 2013), honour codes (Irlenbusch et al., 2020; Tatum et al., 2018), the risk of detection (Kajackaite & Gneezy, 2017; Thielmann & Hilbig, 2018), and the expected benefits (Ludwig & Achtziger, 2021; Markiewicz & Gawryluk, 2020) to explain the mechanisms that lead to cheating. The appeal of such

L. Baran (✉)
Institute of Psychology, University of Silesia in Katowice, Katowice, Poland
e-mail: lidia.baran@us.edu.pl

P. K. Jonason
Department of General Psychology, University of Padua, Padua, Italy

Institute of Psychology, University of Cardinal Stefan Wyszyński, Warsaw, Poland
e-mail: peterkarl.jonason@unipd.it

an approach is that it gives the impression (true or not) that one can reduce the undesirable behaviour in question. As experimentalists, they often intentionally or unintentionally downplay the role of the second class of explanations. That is, through random assignment, individual and naturally occurring group differences are minimised as error. But maybe such phenomena are not errors. Instead, they could provide meaningful, further information about who cheats.

Understanding who cheats starts with the assumption that not all people are equally likely to cheat regardless of pushes from contextual forces. Individual differences researchers investigate sex differences (Whitley et al., 1999), personality traits like perfectionism (Błachnio et al., 2021), and impulsivity (McTernan et al., 2014), or attitudes towards cheating (Pulfrey & Butera, 2016). With the fuller elucidation of *who* cheats, researchers can better home in on the specific mechanisms for who cheats and why, providing the potential for well-tailored "remedies" for cheating when desired.

Unfortunately, research on the role of personality traits in this area is limited because of a tendency for researchers to be a bit too general in their approach. Instead of focusing on specific personality traits that might bear strong relationships with cheating, researchers tend to focus on broad-band traits like the Big Five traits (i.e., extraversion, conscientiousness, agreeableness, neuroticism, and openness to experience). Although interesting, they may be insufficient to understand aversive behaviours like cheating. Much of this generality centres on the fact that the most trusted taxonomy of personality is descriptive, not predictive, in nature. However, over the last 20 years, a growing body of literature has examined the nature, development, and consequences of three relevant socially aversive personality traits, the Dark Triad of psychopathy, narcissism, and Machiavellianism (Furnham et al., 2013; Paulhus & Williams, 2002). This is not to say that these traits are new to the field of psychology, but instead, it was not until recently that these traits have been consistently studied in nonclinical populations, the kinds of populations that are likely to engage in cheating (e.g., higher education students). Therefore, in this chapter, we detail the research and relevance of the Dark Triad traits in understanding cheating, including contract cheating, to provide deeper insights into who cheats to better inform efforts to reduce cheating.

The Dark Triad Traits and Cheating

There is a growing collection of socially undesirable traits under investigation today (Zeigler-Hill & Marcus, 2016) thanks to simplified self-report measures (see Jonason, 2022) like the Dark Triad Dirty Dozen (Jonason & Webster, 2010), the Short Dark Triad (Jones & Paulhus, 2014), and the brief measure of personality pathologies from the *Diagnostic and Statistical Manual* (American Psychiatric Association, 2013). We focus here on the Dark Triad traits only given the nascent state of work on sadism and spitefulness, and doubts about whether they provide meaningfully more explanatory power over the others, especially psychopathy (Jonason & Zeigler-Hill, 2018; Jonason et al., 2017). The three traits are associated with a sense of grandiosity, egotism, fragile self-esteem, and self-centeredness (i.e., narcissism; Turner & Webster, 2018); with manipulative behaviour, self-interest, exploitation of others, and a ruthless lack of morality (i.e., Machiavellianism; Jones, 2016); and with recklessness, cruel and callous attitudes, antisocial selfish behaviour, and a lack of remorse (i.e., psychopathy; Cale & Lilienfeld, 2002). The traits are correlated with an array of other traits and behaviours that may hint at their likely correlations with contract cheating, including relationship infidelity (Jones & Weiser, 2014), limited self-control (Jonason & Tost, 2010), petty crime (Lyons & Jonason, 2015), impulsivity (Jones & Paulhus, 2011), future discounting (Jonason et al., 2010), competitive social attitudes (Jonason, 2015), and "cutting corners" at work (Jonason & O'Connor, 2017).

Indeed, there is evidence that the Dark Triad traits are related to cheating in the academic context. Self-reported tendency to commit acts of academic dishonesty was correlated positively with psychopathy, Machiavellianism, and narcissism (Cheung & Egan, 2020; Zhang et al., 2019), although from all of them, only psychopathy remained a predictor of cheating when controlling for the shared variance among the traits. Similar results were obtained when the indicator of academic dishonesty was not students' self-reports, but instead the reports from cheating detection software. For example, Nathanson et al. (2006) used a program to indicate possible cheating student pairs based on their responses in five (Study 1) and two (Study 2) multiple-choice exams administered throughout a course. Both studies showed that students with higher levels of the Dark Triad traits were more likely to give answers like those of the people sitting near them during exams. Williams et al. (2010) measured the tendency to plagiarise assignments by evaluating two essays assigned to students with the text-matching program TurnitIn. The program provides percentage estimates of plagiarism based on comparing a sample document with other papers and documents available online in their repository. Papers submitted by students scoring high in the Dark Triad traits (psychopathy in particular) had a greater degree of overlap, and, therefore, evidence a greater potential for being plagiarised. Consistent with self-report studies, psychopathy was the strongest predictor of cheating on an exam and plagiarising assignments.

A more detailed understanding of the relationship between the Dark Triad traits and students' tendency to engage in dishonest behaviour in the academic context is derived from studies analysing each of those traits and their facets separately. In the case of psychopathy, research shows that the primary (i.e., low anxiety through genetic predispositions), but not the secondary (i.e., high anxiety in response to environmental stimuli), subtype predicts self-reported tendency to commit various types of academic misconduct (Coyne & Thomas, 2008; Enweh et al., 2021; Ternes et al., 2019). The triarchic model of psychopathy postulates its three dimensions—disinhibition, boldness, and meanness—from which the last two positively predict declared frequency of academic dishonesty (Baran & Jonason, 2020; Ljubin-Golub et al., 2020). Out of narcissism facets, individual differences in feelings of superiority and authority, but not being special, were related to cheating on exams and assignments (Brunell et al., 2011). Lastly, in the case of Machiavellianism, students with a tendency to disregard moral standards, but not desire for status, declared engaging more frequently in deviant academic behaviours (Barbaranelli et al., 2018).

The fact that the propensity for academic dishonesty is linked to selected dimensions of the Dark Triad traits has led researchers to look for specific mechanisms mediating these relationships. Williams et al. (2010) found that unrestrained agency and moral inhibition mediated the relationship between psychopathy and academic cheating. Psychopathic students strive for academic success (i.e., high grades or scholarships) without regard to fairness or others, which might lead them to cheat to achieve that success. They also devalue integrity, which does not act as a deterrent to cheating and therefore allows them to act on impulses towards dishonest actions. Research by Baran and Jonason (2020) explained that mechanism further by showing that individual differences in a mastery-goal orientation mediated the relationship between disinhibition, meanness, and academic dishonesty. Rebelliousness and susceptibility to boredom characteristic of students with a high level of meanness might lead them to be less prone to strive towards mastery in an academic context and, as a result, cheat to achieve academic goals. Disinhibited students exhibit an inability to control impulses, making it difficult for them to strive for achievement through learning and acquiring knowledge, which leads to cheating without regard for the consequences. In the case of the meanness aspect of psychopathy, Ljubin-Golub et al. (2020) showed that high levels of that facet, associated with low acceptance of social norms and moral values, leads to a more lenient attitude towards cheating and, by this, to more frequent academic cheating. Lastly, students with a high level of primary psychopathy exhibited low confidence in their capacity to be successful in academic tasks and, therefore, were prone to commit cheating to achieve the goals of their academic programme (Enweh et al., 2021).

The exhibitionism facet of narcissism, reflecting a desire for admiration, was related to experiencing less guilt over cheating, which may inflate reports of cheating on exams and assignments (Brunell et al., 2011). It seems then that students who want to impress others with their academic success are willing to cheat to achieve such success and can do it because of a lack of remorse over their actions. Menon and Sharland (2011) suggest that narcissistic students might hold a positive attitude towards academic cheating but only if they are prone to exploit others.

In the case of Machiavellianism, one of its potential facets—amoral manipulation—leads to academic cheating through a surface approach to learning and a moral disengagement mechanism (Barbaranelli et al., 2018). Students who tend to manipulate others and disregard integrity to reach their goals might use a moral disengagement mechanism to deactivate moral self-regulation and, by this, be able to engage in academic transgressions. Moreover, this tendency may be amplified when students with high amoral manipulation want to get their academic tasks done with minimal effort and thus accomplish this by cheating, justified through disengagement from moral norms.

The Dark Triad Traits and Contract Cheating

If we assume that contract cheating is a specific manifestation of cheating in general, it should be reasonable to predict that students characterised by the Dark Triad traits will engage in contract cheating. This type of academic dishonesty includes paid or free outsourcing of academic work such as exams, tests, or written assignments (Rundle et al., 2019). Participation of a third party might involve assistance from a friend, family member, another student, a paid service, or assignment mill and include help in writing papers, completing assignments, or taking tests/exams (actual or online) for another person (Bretag et al., 2019). Based on these characteristics, engaging in contract cheating might be tempting for students characterised by high rates of Dark Triad traits for several reasons.

First, the general tendency to break the rules related to narcissists' low integrity (O'Reilly III & Doerr, 2020), psychopaths' low moral inhibition (Williams et al., 2010), and Machiavellians' amorality (Barbaranelli et al., 2018) makes students characterised by those traits ideal candidates for circumventing academic assessment process through contract cheating. Second, and more specifically, psychopathic, narcissistic, and Machiavellian individuals tend to exploit others for their benefit (Black et al., 2014), which includes choosing friends who help achieve specific goals (i.e., psychopathy), are easily exploited (i.e., Machiavellianism), or possess useful qualities such as high intelligence (i.e., narcissism; Jonason & Schmitt, 2012). That means that manipulating others to complete their academic assignments might be one of the strategies that students with high Dark Triad traits easily adopt in the academic context. Third, engaging someone else in cheating by paying them to write a paper might be perceived as a situation with a low risk of being caught in which those characterised by the Dark Triad traits are likely to cheat (Jones & Paulhus, 2017). Fourth, the lack of guilt experienced by narcissists, Machiavellians, and psychopaths (Curtis et al., 2022; Schröder-Abé & Fatfouta, 2019) makes them more prone to commit contract cheating. For example, by using moral disengagement and neutralisation mechanisms, they can justify paying somebody to do their work because there is no salient victim of their actions and no need for remorse (Egan et al., 2015; Furtner et al., 2017).

There are also specific qualities characteristic of each of the Dark Triad traits that might be related to a greater likelihood of engaging in contract cheating. Machiavellians, who cheat strategically and perceive it as a useful method to achieve their goals, might see contract cheating as a business-like (pragmatic) and valid method for "cutting corners" through outsourcing their academic work (Harrison et al., 2018; Jones & Paulhus, 2017). Narcissistic individuals might resort to paying somebody to do their work or buying assignments to confirm their superiority and receive high grades, especially in situations when their academic accomplishments are mediocre and their self-perceived worth is threatened (Williams et al.,

2010; Zhang et al., 2019). On the other hand, students high in psychopathy might be inclined to pay or manipulate other students to take an exam for them because of their tendency to engage in dishonest actions even when the risk of being caught is high (Jones & Paulhus, 2017). They also may outsource their work because of low motivation to acquire academic knowledge resulting from the need for immediate gratification and lack of impulse control (Baran & Jonason, 2020).

The few studies conducted so far confirm the relationship between the Dark Triad traits and contract cheating. Machiavellian and narcissistic students report a tendency to hire someone else when engaged in cheating (Esteves et al., 2021). Curtis et al. (2022) showed that students with high levels of psychopathy and Machiavellianism declared more acceptable attitudes towards contract cheating and subjective norms favouring cheating, which predicted their intention to engage in that type of academic dishonesty.

Contract Cheating as a Social Pathology

Academic dishonesty, including contract cheating, can be viewed as pathological behaviour because of its unethical and socially damaging nature. Outsourcing tasks that should be completed by the student violates the academically accepted principles of pursuing knowledge and respecting academic laws and customs. Contract cheating makes it possible to pass subjects and achieve high grades despite objectively poor knowledge and skills, leading to low suitability of the student as a specialist after graduation (Curtis et al., 2022). Treating cheating as a pathology leads to a search for its possible sources, which may include relatively stable personality traits associated with tendencies to act in a certain way. As we have shown, high levels of psychopathy, Machiavellianism, and narcissism might act as such sources because they lead to engaging in dishonest behaviours and are a risk factor for engaging in contract cheating. Therefore, to counteract contract cheating, it would be necessary to reduce the chances of manifesting behaviours characteristic of the Dark Triad and/or take measures leading to potential changes in personality.

Lowering the likelihood of exhibiting dishonest behaviours might be accomplished by:

- increasing the risk of being caught cheating and increase benefits from performing the task without help from a third party (for students high in Machiavellianism),
- using penalties that may damage self-image, like receiving a final grade or public denouncement indicating that contract cheating was the cause of a student failing a course (for students high in narcissism),
- planning the method of verifying the student's knowledge in such a way that it would not be possible to outsource work to someone else (for students high in psychopathy).

Interventions dedicated to change at the personal level may, in turn, focus on morality and academic skills. To increase the chance of contract cheating being seen by students characterised by the Dark Triad traits as inappropriate, if not unethical, it would be necessary to appeal to the elements responsible for their moral decision making. For psychopaths, this would mean addressing their immature decision-making processes linked to neural (Glenn et al., 2009) and genetic (Campbell et al., 2009) factors that lead to low concern for morality. In the case of Machiavellians, whose decision making appears to be more gist-based (Carre & Jones, 2017), interventions should focus on their flexible moral beliefs. Decision making by narcissists seems to be unrelated to their moral development but rather to social approval, which means that implementing changes might involve working on socially desirable system of morality (Jonason et al., 2015). On the other hand, focusing on improving students' academic skills might lead to adopting mastery-oriented motivation rather than surface-approach to learning or experiencing a sense of academic self-efficacy rather than lack of confidence, which mediates the relationship between the Dark Triad traits and academic dishonesty (Baran & Jonason, 2020; Barbaranelli et al., 2018; Enweh et al., 2021).

Contract Cheating as a Pseudopathology

As noted above, there are two approaches common to research on cheating, but they both can be found in two larger epistemological frameworks. Sociocultural models of behaviour envision—although rarely expressed this way—people as the victims of institutional (e.g., economics), social (e.g., class), or contextual (e.g., shortage of time) forces. In this way, people are seen as part of stimulus and response systems where cheating is a response that necessarily follows from particular conditions.

However, the sociocultural approach typically ignores the role of personal agency, which is where evolutionary models step in. One particular model is relevant here. Life history theory (Wilson, 1975) was originally used to describe differences between species in terms of how organisms allocate finite resources in time and metabolic energy towards the two most fundamental Darwinian tasks of survival (i.e., somatic) and reproduction (i.e., mating). When applied to people, this theory may account for within-species differences or personality traits (Figueredo & Rushton, 2009). Unlike traditional models of cheating that treat it as a social pathology, conceptualising cheating within this model suggests that even socially aversive traits might be "rational" adaptive processes allowing individuals to calibrate expenditures of time and resources (i.e., a pseudopathology; Crawford & Anderson, 1989). The costs of cheating may be perceived as delayed and suffered by others, and therefore, less important for those characterised by a "fast" life history strategy like those characterised by the Dark Triad traits. This may mean that if the individual is getting some success out of cheating, communal efforts to reduce cheating will be relatively ineffective. Calling cheating a "pathology" may actually obscure the origins and genuine motivations for cheating through humans' tendencies to detect and punish cheaters in social contracts (Cosmides et al., 2005).

Conclusions

The psychological analysis of human behaviour is usually based on attempts to accurately describe, explain, predict, and control it. This gives psychologists a chance to understand why people take certain actions and how, if needed, they might be changed. As we have shown, in the case of academic dishonesty, answering the question of who cheats enables both an understanding of the mechanism leading to that behaviour and possible ways to reduce it. The results of the research conducted so far clearly indicates that students characterised by the Dark Triad traits are likely to cheat and that the mechanisms responsible for this may be the pragmatic profitability of cheating (i.e., Machiavellianism), the desire to maintain a certain image (i.e., narcissism), or low self-control (i.e., psychopathy). They may be also particularly likely to outsource academic tasks because of their tendency to manipulate and exploit others and to break the rules for their own benefit without feeling guilty.

The way to counteract contract cheating, undertaken by students with high levels of the Dark Triad traits, depends on a chosen theoretical approach to academic dishonesty. Treating cheating as a social pathology results in a search for ways to eliminate or reduce the impact of its causes on behaviour. Treating cheating as a pseudopathology leads, in turn, to seeking ways to make the interests of the individual and the system compatible. No matter the paradigm, a fuller understanding and more effective means to reduce academic dishonesty, including contract cheating, must consider individualised interventions which can best be gleaned by an examination of different people, situated within contexts.

References

American Psychiatric Association. (2013). *Diagnostic and statistical manual of mental disorders* (5th ed.). https://doi.org/10.1176/appi.books.9780890425596

Baran, L., & Jonason, P. K. (2020). Academic dishonesty among university students: The roles of the psychopathy, motivation, and self-efficacy. *PLoS One, 15*, e0238141. https://doi.org/10.1371/journal.pone.0238141

Barbaranelli, C., Farnese, M. L., Tramontano, C., Fida, R., Ghezzi, V., Paciello, M., & Long, P. (2018). Machiavellian ways to academic cheating: A mediational and interactional model. *Frontiers in Psychology, 9*, 695. https://doi.org/10.3389/fpsyg.2018.00695

Black, P. J., Woodworth, M., & Porter, S. (2014). The big bad wolf?: The relation between the dark triad and the interpersonal assessment of vulnerability. *Personality and Individual Differences, 67*, 52–56. https://doi.org/10.1016/j.paid.2013.10.026

Błachnio, A., Cudo, A., Kot, P., Torój, M., Oppong Asante, K., Enea, V., et al. (2021). Cultural and psychological variables predicting academic dishonesty: A cross-sectional study in nine countries. *Ethics & Behavior, 32*(1). https://doi.org/10.1080/10508422.2021.1910826

Bretag, T., Harper, R., Burton, M., Ellis, C., Newton, P., Rozenberg, P., Saddiqui, S., & van Haeringen, K. (2019). Contract cheating: A survey of Australian university students. *Studies in Higher Education, 44*, 1837–1856. https://doi.org/10.1080/03075079.2018.1462788

Brunell, A. B., Staats, S., Barden, J., & Hupp, J. M. (2011). Narcissism and academic dishonesty: The exhibitionism dimension and the lack of guilt. *Personality and Individual Differences, 50*, 323–328. https://doi.org/10.1016/j.paid.2010.10.006

Cale, E. M., & Lilienfeld, S. O. (2002). Sex differences in psychopathy and antisocial personality disorder: A review and integration. *Clinical Psychology Review, 22*, 1179–1207. https://doi.org/10.1016/S0272-7358(01)00125-8

Campbell, J., Schermer, J. A., Villani, V. C., Nguyen, B., Vickers, L., & Vernon, P. A. (2009). A behavioral genetic study of the dark triad of personality and moral development. *Twin Research and Human Genetics, 12*, 132–136. https://doi.org/10.1375/twin.12.2.132

Carre, J. R., & Jones, D. N. (2017). Decision making, morality, and Machiavellianism: The role of dispositional traits in gist extraction. *Review of General Psychology, 21*, 23–29. https://doi.org/10.1037/gpr0000093

Cheung, Y. K., & Egan, V. (2020). The HEXACO-60, the dark triad, and scholastic cheating. *Psychological Reports, 124*(6). https://doi.org/10.1177/0033294120961071

Cosmides, L., Tooby, J., Fiddick, L., & Bryant, G. A. (2005). Detecting cheaters. *Trends in Cognitive Sciences, 9*, 505–506. https://doi.org/10.1016/j.tics.2005.09.005

Coyne, S. M., & Thomas, T. J. (2008). Psychopathy, aggression, and cheating behavior: A test of the Cheater–Hawk hypothesis. *Personality and Individual Differences, 44*, 1105–1115. https://doi.org/10.1016/j.paid.2007.11.002

Crawford, C. B., & Anderson, J. L. (1989). Sociobiology: An environmentalist discipline? *American Psychologist, 44*, 1449–1459.

Curtis, G. J., Clare, J., Vieira, E., Selby, E., & Jonason, P. K. (2022). Predicting contract cheating intentions: Dark personality traits, attitudes, norms, and anticipated guilt and shame. *Personality and Individual Differences, 185*, 111277. https://doi.org/10.1016/j.paid.2021.111277

Egan, V., Hughes, N., & Palmer, E. J. (2015). Moral disengagement, the dark triad, and unethical consumer attitudes. *Personality and Individual Differences, 76*, 123–128. https://doi.org/10.1016/j.paid.2014.11.054

Enweh, I. I., Onyedibe, M. C. C., & Onu, D. U. (2021). Academic confidence mediates the link between psychopathy and academic dishonesty. *Journal of Academic Ethics*. https://doi.org/10.1007/s10805-021-09426-0

Esteves, G. G. L., Oliveira, L. S., de Andrade, J. M., & Menezes, M. P. (2021). Dark triad predicts academic cheating. *Personality and Individual Differences, 171*, 110513. https://doi.org/10.1016/j.paid.2020.110513

Figueredo, A. J., & Rushton, J. P. (2009). Evidence for shared genetic dominance between the general factor of personality, mental and physical health, and life history traits. *Twin Research and Human Genetics, 12*, 555–563. https://doi.org/10.1375/twin.12.6.555

Furnham, A., Richards, S. C., & Paulhus, D. L. (2013). The dark triad of personality: A 10 year review. *Social and Personality Psychology Compass, 7*, 199–216. https://doi.org/10.1111/spc3.12018

Furtner, M. R., Maran, T., & Rauthmann, J. F. (2017). Dark leadership: The role of leaders' dark triad personality traits. In M. Clark & C. Gruber (Eds.), *Leader development deconstructed: Annals of theoretical psychology* (pp. 75–99). Springer. https://doi.org/10.1007/978-3-319-64740-1_4

Glenn, A. L., Raine, A., & Schug, R. A. (2009). The neural correlates of moral decision-making in psychopathy. *Molecular Psychiatry, 14*, 5–6. https://doi.org/10.1038/mp.2008.104

Harrison, A., Summers, J., & Mennecke, B. (2018). The effects of the dark triad on unethical behavior. *Journal of Business Ethics, 153*, 53–77. https://doi.org/10.1007/s10551-016-3368-3

Hodson, G., & Dhont, K. (2015). The person-based nature of prejudice: Individual difference predictors of intergroup negativity. *European Review of Social Psychology, 26*, 1–42. https://doi.org/10.1080/10463283.2015.1070018

Irlenbusch, B., Mussweiler, T., Saxler, D. J., Shalvi, S., & Weiss, A. (2020). Similarity increases collaborative cheating. *Journal of Economic Behavior & Organization, 178*, 148–173. https://doi.org/10.1016/j.jebo.2020.06.022

Jonason, P. K. (2015). How "dark" personality traits and perceptions relate to racism in Australia. *Personality and Individual Differences, 72*, 47–51. https://doi.org/10.1016/j.paid.2014.08.030

Jonason, P. K. (2022). *Shining light on the dark side of personality: Measurement properties and theoretical advances.* Hogrefe.

Jonason, P. K., Koenig, B., & Tost, J. (2010). Living a fast life: The dark triad and life history theory. *Human Nature, 21*, 428–442. https://doi.org/10.1007/s12110-010-9102-4

Jonason, P. K., & O'Connor, P. J. (2017). Cutting corners at work: An individual differences perspective. *Personality and Individual Differences, 107*, 146–153. https://doi.org/10.1016/j.paid.2016.11.045

Jonason, P. K., & Schmitt, D. P. (2012). What have you done for me lately? Friendship-selection in the shadow of the dark triad traits. *Evolutionary Psychology, 10*. https://doi.org/10.1177/147470491201000303

Jonason, P. K., Strosser, G. L., Kroll, C. H., Duineveld, J. J., & Baruffi, S. A. (2015). Valuing myself over others: The dark triad traits and moral and social values. *Personality and Individual Differences, 81*, 102–106. https://doi.org/10.1016/j.paid.2014.10.045

Jonason, P. K., & Tost, J. (2010). I just cannot control myself: The dark triad and self-control. *Personality and Individual Differences, 49*, 611–615. https://doi.org/10.1016/j.paid.2010.05.031

Jonason, P. K., & Webster, G. D. (2010). The dirty dozen: A concise measure of the dark triad. *Psychological Assessment, 22*, 420–432. https://doi.org/10.1037/a0019265

Jonason, P. K., & Zeigler-Hill, V. (2018). The fundamental social motives that characterize dark personality traits. *Personality and Individual Differences, 132*, 98–107. https://doi.org/10.1016/j.paid.2018.05.031

Jonason, P. K., Zeigler-Hill, V., & Okan, C. (2017). Good v. evil: Predicting sinning with dark personality traits and moral foundations. *Personality and*

Individual Differences, 104, 180–185. https://doi.org/10.1016/j.paid.2016.08.002

Jones, D. N. (2016). The nature of Machiavellianism: Distinct patterns of misbehavior. In V. Zeigler-Hill & D. K. Marcus (Eds.), *The dark side of personality: Science and practice in social, personality, and clinical psychology* (pp. 87–107). American Psychological Association. https://doi.org/10.1037/14854-005

Jones, D. N., & Paulhus, D. L. (2011). The role of impulsivity in the dark triad of personality. *Personality and Individual Differences, 51*, 679–682. https://doi.org/10.1016/j.paid.2011.04.011

Jones, D. N., & Paulhus, D. L. (2014). Introducing the short dark triad (SD3) a brief measure of dark personality traits. *Assessment, 21*, 28–41. https://doi.org/10.1177/1073191113514105

Jones, D. N., & Paulhus, D. L. (2017). Duplicity among the dark triad: Three faces of deceit. *Journal of Personality and Social Psychology, 113*, 329–342. https://doi.org/10.1037/pspp0000139

Jones, D. N., & Weiser, D. A. (2014). Differential infidelity patterns among the dark triad. *Personality and Individual Differences, 57*, 20–24. https://doi.org/10.1016/j.paid.2013.09.007

Kajackaite, A., & Gneezy, U. (2017). Incentives and cheating. *Games and Economic Behavior, 102*, 433–444. https://doi.org/10.1016/j.geb.2017.01.015

Koehn, M. A., Jonason, P. K., & Davis, M. D. (2019). A person-centered view of prejudice: The big five, dark triad, and prejudice. *Personality and Individual Differences, 139*, 313–316. https://doi.org/10.1016/j.paid.2018.11.038

Ljubin-Golub, T., Petričević, E., & Sokić, K. (2020). Predicting academic cheating with Triarchic psychopathy and cheating attitudes. *Journal of Academic Ethics, 18*, 377–393. https://doi.org/10.1007/s10805-019-09338-0

Ludwig, J., & Achtziger, A. (2021). Cognitive misers on the web: An online experiment of incentives, cheating, and cognitive reflection. *Journal of Behavioral and Experimental Economics, 94*, 101731.

Lyons, M., & Jonason, P. K. (2015). Dark triad, tramps, and thieves: Psychopathy predicts a diverse range of theft-related attitudes and behaviors. *Journal of Individual Differences, 36*, 215–220. https://doi.org/10.1027/1614-0001/a000177

Malesky, A., Grist, C., Poovey, K., & Dennis, N. (2021). The effects of peer influence, honor codes, and personality traits on cheating behavior in a university setting. *Ethics & Behavior, 1-11*. https://doi.org/10.1080/10508422.2020.1869006

Markiewicz, Ł., & Gawryluk, K. (2020). Cheating among children: Temptation, loss framing, and previous cheating. *Journal of Behavioral Decision Making, 33*, 151–165. https://doi.org/10.1002/bdm.2150

McTernan, M., Love, P., & Rettinger, D. (2014). The influence of personality on the decision to cheat. *Ethics & Behavior, 24*, 53–72. https://doi.org/10.1080/10508422.2013.819783

Menon, M. K., & Sharland, A. (2011). Narcissism, exploitative attitudes, and academic dishonesty: An exploratory investigation of reality versus myth. *Journal of Education for Business, 86*, 50–55. https://doi.org/10.1080/08832321003774772

Nathanson, C., Paulhus, D. L., & Williams, K. M. (2006). Predictors of a behavioral measure of scholastic cheating: Personality and competence but not demographics. *Contemporary Educational Psychology, 31*, 97–122. https://doi.org/10.1016/j.cedpsych.2005.03.001

O'Reilly, C. A., III, & Doerr, B. (2020). Conceit and deceit: Lying, cheating, and stealing among grandiose narcissists. *Personality and Individual Differences, 154*, 109627. https://doi.org/10.1016/j.paid.2019.109627

Paulhus, D. L., & Williams, K. M. (2002). The dark triad of personality: Narcissism, Machiavellianism, and psychopathy. *Journal of Research in Personality, 36*, 556–563. https://doi.org/10.1016/S0092-6566(02)00505-6

Pulfrey, C., & Butera, F. (2016). When and why people don't accept cheating: Self-transcendence values, social responsibility, mastery goals and attitudes towards cheating. *Motivation and Emotion, 40*(3), 438–454.

Rundle, K., Curtis, G. J., & Clare, J. (2019). Why students do not engage in contract cheating. *Frontiers in Psychology, 10*, 2229. https://doi.org/10.3389/fpsyg.2019.02229

Schuhmann, P. W., Burrus, R. T., Barber, P. D., Graham, J. E., & Elikai, M. F. (2013). Using the scenario method to analyze cheating behaviors. *Journal of Academic Ethics, 11*, 17–33. https://doi.org/10.1007/s10805-012-9173-4

Schröder-Abé, M., & Fatfouta, R. (2019). Shades of narcissistic dishonesty: Grandiose versus vulnerable narcissism and the role of self-conscious emotions. *Journal of Economic Psychology, 71*, 148–158. https://doi.org/10.1016/j.joep.2018.06.003

Tatum, H. E., Schwartz, B. M., Hageman, M. C., & Koretke, S. L. (2018). College students' perceptions of and responses to academic dishonesty: An investigation of type of honor code, institution size, and student–faculty ratio. *Ethics & Behavior, 28*, 302–315. https://doi.org/10.1080/10508422.2017.1331132

Ternes, M., Babin, C., Woodworth, A., & Stephens, S. (2019). Academic misconduct: An examination of its association with the dark triad and antisocial behavior. *Personality and Individual Differences, 138*, 75–78. https://doi.org/10.1016/j.paid.2018.09.031

Thielmann, I., & Hilbig, B. E. (2018). Daring dishonesty: On the role of sanctions for (un) ethical behavior. *Journal of Experimental Social Psychology, 79*, 71–77. https://doi.org/10.1016/j.jesp.2018.06.009

Turner, I. N., & Webster, G. D. (2018). Narcissism and dark personality traits. In A. Hermann, A. Brunell, & J. Foster (Eds.), *Handbook of trait narcissism* (pp. 195–203). Springer. https://doi.org/10.1007/978-3-319-92171-6_21

Whitley, B. E., Nelson, A. B., & Jones, C. J. (1999). Gender differences in cheating attitudes and classroom cheating behavior: A meta-analysis. *Sex Roles, 41*, 657–680.

Williams, K. M., Nathanson, C., & Paulhus, D. L. (2010). Identifying and profiling scholastic cheaters: Their personality, cognitive ability, and motivation. *Journal of Experimental Psychology: Applied, 16*, 293–307. https://doi.org/10.1037/a0020773

Wilson, E. O. (1975). *Sociobiology: The new synthesis.* Harvard University Press.

Zeigler-Hill, V., & Marcus, D. K. (2016). The dark side of personality: Science and practice in social, personality, and clinical psychology. *American Psychological Association.* https://doi.org/10.1037/14854-001

Zhang, J., Paulhus, D. L., & Ziegler, M. (2019). Personality predictors of scholastic cheating in a Chinese sample. *Educational Psychology, 39*, 572–590. https://doi.org/10.1080/01443410.2018.1502414

CHAPTER 10

Contract Cheating: The Influence of Attitudes and Emotions

Guy J. Curtis and Isabeau K. Tindall

Folk wisdom would suggest that our attitudes provide a good indication of what we will do in the future. If we think progressive political causes are important, we will be more likely to protest in favour of progressive political issues, and if students think cheating is wrong, they will be less likely to cheat. However, the relationship between attitudes and behaviour is more complex than our intuitions would suggest. For example, sometimes attitudes and behaviour are unrelated, and at other times our attitudes follow our actions and not the other way around. In this chapter, we discuss how understanding students' engagement in contract cheating can be informed by research on the relationship between academic misconduct attitudes and behaviours. We then extend on this discussion to consider how

G. J. Curtis (✉)
School of Psychological Science, University of Western Australia, Crawley, WA, Australia
e-mail: guy.curtis@uwa.edu.au

I. K. Tindall
Centre for Transformative Work Design, Curtin University, Perth, WA, Australia
e-mail: Isabeau.Tindall@curtin.edu.au

© The Author(s), under exclusive license to Springer Nature Switzerland AG 2022
S. E. Eaton et al. (eds.), *Contract Cheating in Higher Education*,
https://doi.org/10.1007/978-3-031-12680-2_10

emotions, both felt and anticipated, may influence attitudes towards, and engagement in, contract cheating.

Attitudes and Contract Cheating

A study on student cheating was one of the earliest to question the intuitive idea that attitudes predict behaviour. Corey (1937) gave his introductory educational psychology students a pencil-and-paper questionnaire concerning their attitudes towards cheating in college exams. The questionnaires were covertly marked with pin pricks so that students were later identifiable. Through the semester, Corey (1937) gave his students a series of five tests on the course content. These tests were collected and scored, and scores were recorded. Students were not told that the tests had been scored. The next week, the tests were returned to students for them to ostensibly grade themselves and report their self-scored mark to the teacher. Students awarded themselves an average of one to two additional, unearned, points per test. In other words, low-level cheating was common. However, there was no significant relationship between the strength of students' attitudes towards cheating measured in the questionnaires and the extent of their cheating behaviour.

For some time, Corey's (1937) study, and similar findings, flummoxed psychology researchers who anticipated a positive relationship between attitudes and behaviour. Even in contemporary research, we see examples of discordant attitudes towards academic misconduct and students' behaviour. For example, recent research found that 11% of students admitted to uncited word-for-word plagiarism, despite 98% considering it to be a serious academic misconduct breach (Curtis & Tremayne, 2021). This means that most of the 11% of students who engaged in verbatim copying considered it to be serious academic misconduct but did it anyway. Research has clarified some of the ways in which attitudes and behaviour interact. In the next few sections, we outline these interactions between attitudes and behaviour, and the implications of these for understanding contract cheating.

Cognitive Dissonance

When people's behaviour is inconsistent with their attitudes they feel psychological discomfort, or dissonance, which they often resolve by changing their attitudes to become more consistent with their behaviour. This phenomenon, called cognitive dissonance, was first described by Festinger (1957), and provides a good account of how attitudes can be formed and changed. Imagine, for example, that you have neutral political views, but your best friend invites you to attend a progressive protest with them. After the protest, you may feel that your friend asking you to come was insufficient justification for your attendance. You feel some mental discomfort at the fact that you protested about something you were ambivalent about. To resolve this discomfort, you decide that you really do want to save the whales and ban nuclear weapons.

In the context of academic misconduct, cognitive dissonance suggests that students may become more favourable towards cheating after they do it than before they did it, despite what their previous attitudes might be (Stephens, 2017; Storch & Storch, 2003). Consider Corey's (1937) study. His students expressed attitudes against cheating but then found that throughout the semester they could cheat undetected by awarding themselves inflated marks on five tests. Some of these students may have reasoned with themselves that if they do not take the opportunity to cheat when their classmates might, they would be at a disadvantage, and, therefore, they had to cheat. In this situation, cognitive dissonance may occur for students who cheated after initially expressing attitudes against cheating, thus these students might have moderated their attitude to be more positive towards cheating. However, we will never know if this occurred in Corey's (1937) study because he did not re-test his students' attitudes to cheating after they had the opportunity to cheat. Nonetheless, a positive change in attitudes towards cheating after cheating has occurred fits well with literature showing that students cheat despite knowing that it is wrong and considering it to be serious (e.g., Curtis & Tremayne, 2021; Stephens, 2017). In the context of contract cheating, it is possible that students expressing positive attitudes towards contract cheating are more likely to have already engaged in contract cheating than students expressing a negative attitude (i.e., attitudes may be evidence of past behaviour).

Cognitive dissonance has been proposed as a useful mechanism for promoting socially acceptable attitudes and behaviours. For example, eliciting egalitarian statements from men who hold strongly sexist attitudes causes a weakening of these attitudes (Swann et al., 1988). However, the small amount of relevant research to date suggests little impact of such strategies on academic misconduct (e.g., Vinski & Tryon, 2009), and no research has yet examined whether cognitive dissonance can counteract contract cheating.

Implicit and Explicit Attitudes

Another reason why attitudes and behaviour sometimes misalign is because people can hold differing explicit (or conscious) and implicit (or nonconscious) attitudes about the same thing. Explicit attitudes are those that people can tell you about when you ask them and are typically measured on self-report surveys. Implicit attitudes, however, are more elusive and psychologists have developed various methods to assess their presence, which often involves examining how quickly people categorize various words as "good" versus "bad" (e.g., Gawronski & Hahn, 2019). Importantly, sometimes implicit attitudes can be better predictors of behaviour than explicit attitudes (Kocan & Curtis, 2009).

Returning to Corey's (1937) study, it is possible that his students, while explicitly opposed to cheating, were implicitly more accepting of it. However, as with cognitive dissonance, there is scant research on implicit attitudes towards academic misconduct, and what does exist has found no relationship between implicit attitudes and cheating behaviour (Sanecka & Baran, 2015). Nonetheless, the potential connection between implicit contract cheating attitudes and contract cheating behaviour deserves further investigation.

General and Specific Attitudes

Extroverts are not always outgoing and introverts are not always shy and quiet. The difference between an extroverted person and an introverted person is how they will tend to behave across a number of situations over time, with the extroverted person being more frequently outgoing than the introverted person (Locke et al., 2017). Similarly, attitudes are often a guide to how people will generally act across a range or situations but cannot determine how they will act in specific situations (Epstein, 1983). Thus, we find that people who have a negative attitude towards cheating tend to cheat less across a range of situations than people who have a positive attitude towards cheating (Beck & Ajzen, 1991). However, in any given situation many immediate influences can impact what a person does more than their attitudes do (e.g., their current needs and the likely consequences of their behaviour). Because of this, general attitudes are unreliable predictors of specific behaviours in specific situations. On the flip side, highly specific attitudes, such as whether a student thinks it is okay to cheat on a particular test, are more predictive of their behaviour. Returning to Corey's (1937) study, students were asked about their general attitude towards cheating in exams, not their specific attitude towards cheating in the tests they were given in their course. Extending the idea of general and specific attitudes to contract cheating, we may expect that on aggregate students who are opposed to contract cheating will be less likely to engage in it, but general attitudes towards contract cheating will not be a strong predictor of students' choice to cheat on any specific assessment.

The Theory Planned Behaviour (TPB)

The theory of planned behaviour (TPB) is a model that draws on other predictors of people's actions, in addition to attitudes, to better explain their behaviour than can be achieved by looking at their attitudes alone (Ajzen, 1991). As the name suggests, the TPB is a framework used to understand causes of intentional behaviour rather than behaviours that occur without forethought. Thus, the TPB is a useful model for considering contract cheating because it is nearly impossible to imagine a situation where a student engages in contract cheating accidentally. Can you imagine a student saying, "Whoops, I tripped over and before I knew it, I had inadvertently uploaded my assessment details into a website, asked for someone to write my assignment before the due date, and then entered my credit card details in order to pay them"?

The TPB states that attitudes are one of three predictors of intentions, with intentions predicting behaviour. In addition to attitudes, the two other predictors of intentions are subjective norms (what we think other people will do or should do in the situation) and perceived behavioural control (how much we think we can change our behaviour in the situation) (Ajzen, 1991). Intentions are an important step to consider when predicting voluntary behaviour, for example, a student may intend to engage in contract cheating, but subsequently be unable to find anyone to write their assignment for them. The TPB is presented in Fig. 10.1 with added emotion-related factors, which we discuss later.

Once again, considering Corey's (1937) study, although students' attitudes and behaviours were examined, the other components of the TPB were not. Through the course of Corey's study, a social norm may have developed among the students that minor cheating in self-scored tests was acceptable. In addition, although students may have expressed an attitude opposed to cheating, the ease of cheating on self-scored tests may have enhanced their perception that the behaviour was controllable.

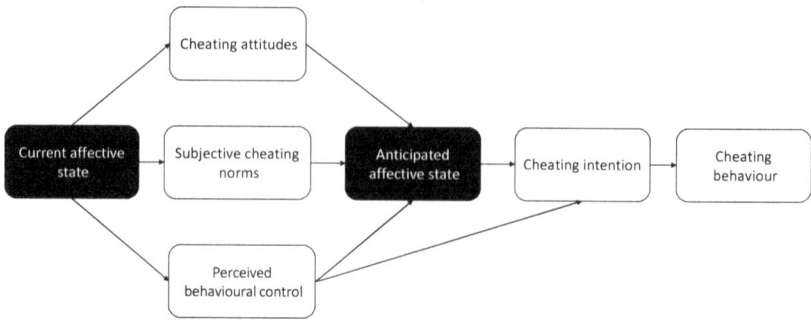

Fig. 10.1 The theory of planned behaviour (TPB) applied to contract cheating (white filled boxes) and extended to include current and anticipated affective states (black filled boxes)

The TPB has proven to be a reliable model for predicting students' engagement in plagiarism and cheating (Chudzicka-Czupała et al., 2016; Curtis et al., 2018; Uzun & Kilis, 2020). Indeed, one of the first studies to test the TPB indicated that the theory could successfully predict students' engagement in academic misconduct (Beck & Ajzen, 1991). Thus, because the TPB is good at modelling how attitudes predict academic misconduct, and is particularly suited to predicting volitional behaviour, we expect that it can reliably predict students' engagement in contract cheating.

In several studies of academic misconduct, the TPB has been extended to include other possible predictors of plagiarism and cheating in addition to attitudes, norms, perceived behavioural control, and intentions. For example, Stone et al. (2010) found that emotional stability and conscientiousness predicted attitudes, norms, and perceived behavioural control and contributed to the prediction of academic misconduct. Curtis et al. (2018) found that self-control (i.e., the ability to resist temptation) could replace perceived behavioural control within a TPB model when predicting plagiarism. Uzun and Kilis (2020) found that students' feelings of moral obligation to avoid plagiarism predicted their plagiarism intentions separately from their attitudes. Together, these studies suggest that other factors can be considered within a TPB framework to predict contract cheating. Particularly important psychological factors that may fit within the TPB and add to its ability to predict contract cheating are current and anticipated emotions.

Affective States, Attitudes, and Contract Cheating

Student life is filled with many potential opportunities for advancement and joy, but can also bring vast amounts of stress and emotional turmoil. Moods and emotions (collectively called affective states) can shape people's moment-to-moment decisions (Forgas, 1995), with this being especially true for younger people (Arain et al., 2013). Typical undergraduate students are under 25 years of age, yet the human brain's decision-making capacity and ability to cope with emotional challenges are not fully developed until around 25 years (Giedd et al., 1999). Thus, it is no surprise that people, particularly those under 25 years of age, including most undergraduate students, sometimes make bad decisions that are affected by their emotions.

The remainder of this chapter outlines how felt emotions and anticipated emotions can interact with attitudes to influence the likelihood of students deciding to engage in contract cheating. There are some good reasons why it is important to understand the potential impact of students' emotions on their decision to cheat. First, as mentioned, being a student is a time of potential emotional volatility. A study of over 5000 higher education students found that they had, on average, higher levels of stress, depression, and anxiety than members of a wider community sample (Larcombe et al., 2016). Second, there is existing evidence suggesting that felt and anticipated emotions can influence engagement in unethical behaviour generally (Zhang et al., 2020), and academic misconduct specifically (Sierra & Hyman, 2006). Finally, as any psychologist will tell you, emotions are changeable and manageable. Thus, there are several actions institutions and individuals can take to attenuate the influence of emotions on cheating. In the next sections, we elaborate on the impact of current and anticipated affective states, and attitudes, on contract cheating behaviour, with reference to the modified TPB in Fig. 10.1.

Current Affective States

Based on research in psychology, students' current affective states can reasonably be expected to influence their attitudes towards cheating, their subjective norms concerning cheating, and their perception that cheating is within their control. These relationships are represented in Fig. 10.1 by the arrows from current affective state to the original TPB factors.

Affective states can influence general evaluations, such as attitudes, in ways that are congruent or incongruent with people's moods (Forgas, 1995). For example, people feeling anxious may evaluate someone else as more threatening and negative (Curtis & Locke, 2005) or as more positive (Ciarrochi & Forgas, 1999). Affective states can also influence the way in which people think, such that they may process information more deeply or more superficially, or in ways that better help them manage their moods or adapt to the environment (Curtis, 2013; Forgas, 1998). Recent research on academic misconduct has found that students' attitudes towards plagiarism are related to their affective states. For example, four studies have found that negative emotionality is related to more positive attitudes towards plagiarism (Fu & Tremayne, 2021; Tindall & Curtis, 2020; Tindall et al., 2021). Thus, it is entirely conceivable that affective states would influence attitudes towards contract cheating.

The influence of affective states on information-processing may alter perceived norms. A perceived norm may form around simple rules of thumb that people rely on when feeling emotional, such as how easily examples can be brought to mind (Park & Banaji, 2000). When a student is feeling stressed and they attempt to estimate how common cheating is among their peers, they may recall an example of a friend who cheated and assume cheating is common. Indeed, Tindall and Curtis (2020) found that negative emotions were not just related to plagiarism attitudes but also to perceiving plagiarism as more common. Subsequently, Tindall et al. (2021) found that the impact of negative emotions on students' perceived norms predicted both their intentions regarding, and engagement in, academic misconduct.

It is likely that the different affective states students experience will have different influences on their attitudes. As noted above, studies have found that negative emotions were related to more positive attitudes towards plagiarism. This finding is consistent with behaviour in other contexts, for example, negative emotions are related to more unethical behaviour in the workplace (Samnani et al., 2014). However, would feeling happy make a student more favourable (i.e., more positive) towards plagiarism and other forms of misconduct? Research on emotion and cheating suggests not. In an experiment where people could cheat by completing an easier task than the one that they were assigned, happiness made no difference to how many people cheated (DeSteno et al., 2019). Moreover, people feeling gratitude were less likely to cheat (DeSteno et al., 2019). The impact of gratitude on cheating seems to be consistent with Bretag et al.'s (2019) finding that contract cheating engagement is related to dissatisfaction with the learning and teaching environment. If students are grateful to teachers, they may be less inclined to cheat.

Moods and emotions can also influence the extent to which behaviours are perceived to be controllable. Anxiety and sadness are associated with thinking of the world as being uncontrollable (Fiske et al., 1996; Seligman, 1972). Thus, it is possible that students' current emotions will influence the extent to which they see their ability to complete their own assessment work as being controllable. For example, a student who is feeling extremely stressed may feel that completing an assignment themselves is beyond their control, which may then influence both their intention to cheat and how they expect to feel about cheating.

Anticipated Affective States

A great deal of human decision-making is driven by anticipated emotions. We often want to do things that we think will make us feel happy (Gilbert, 2006). A student, for example, might think that they will feel happier if they submit an assignment done by someone else because it will give them time to do other things, such as concentrate on other subjects they find more interesting. In addition to seeking good feelings, people seek to minimize bad feelings. People often want to do things that they think will help them avoid negative emotions (Kermer et al., 2006). If a student submits an assignment written by someone else, they might think that they will avoid the emotional blow that comes from failing if their own work is not good enough. On the other hand, if they submit an assignment written by someone else, they might think that they will feel guilt-ridden even if they are never caught. Thus, anticipated emotions, depending on what emotion is anticipated, may influence students' decisions to cheat or to not cheat (Rundle et al., 2019).

As it turns out, people are good at anticipating what emotions future events might elicit (Gilbert, 2006). Referring to Fig. 10.1, if a student has an unfavourable attitude towards cheating, they might anticipate feeling guilty if they do cheat, and be correct in anticipating this emotion. If a student perceives that contract cheating is uncommon, they may anticipate feeling more guilty if they break this behavioural norm. And, if a student believes they have a choice to do something other than cheating, they may anticipate feeling more guilty if they do.

Although people are good at predicting what their emotional reactions to future events will be, we are less good at anticipating how intensely future events will influence our feelings and we reliably overestimate how long our emotional reactions to future events will last (Gilbert, 2006). Thus, a student who anticipates feeling guilty about submitting an assignment that was written by someone else may incorrectly guess the level of guilt they will feel and overestimate the duration of this guilt. This tendency to overestimate the duration of negative emotions in response to future events provides a safeguard against risk-taking (Gilbert, 2006), which might incidentally be helpful in the context of academic integrity since it may help some students talk themselves out of cheating.

Returning to Fig. 10.1 and the TPB more directly, there is substantial evidence that anticipated moral emotions (such as guilt and shame) add to the capacity of this model to predict intentions and behaviour (Rivis et al., 2009). Specifically in the context of academic integrity, Hsiao (2015) found that adding anticipated positive and negative affect to the TPB added to the prediction of students' intention to cheat in tests or exams. More recently, Curtis et al. (2022), found that anticipated guilt mediated the relationship between attitudes, norms, and intentions to engage in contract cheating. However, referring to Fig. 10.1, both Hsiao (2015) and Curtis et al. (2022) stopped short of assessing whether cheating intentions were related to cheating behaviours.

Conclusion

Psychology research and theories tell us a great deal about attitudes, emotions, behaviour, and how they interact. Much of this knowledge has already been applied to help understand academic misconduct such as plagiarism and cheating in tests. However, almost no research has extended the findings on attitudes and emotions from psychology to contract cheating. In this chapter, we have outlined many ways that attitudes and emotions, separately and together, may help us understand, predict, and reduce students' engagement in contract cheating.

In sum, the process of cognitive dissonance might help us explain why students rationalize engagement in a highly unethical behaviour like contract cheating. Differences between implicit attitudes, explicit attitudes, specific attitudes, and general attitudes may help us explain why students' expressed attitudes will not always predict their behaviour. Similarly, the TPB gives us a more thorough framework for understanding what factors in addition to attitudes are important when predicting contract cheating. As we have argued, moods and emotions that students feel, and expect to feel, can further add to the TPB to provide a better understanding of contract cheating. These predictions and speculations, however, need to be tested in future research. From the theory and evidence so far, educators should take the following practical advice from this chapter: (1) emphasize to students the importance of academic integrity to help shape their attitudes, subjective norms, and anticipated emotions associated with cheating; (2) secure assessment so that cheating is difficult, and thus perceived as hard to control; (3) seek to reduce the stress associated with study and assessment.

References

Ajzen, I. (1991). The theory of planned behavior. *Organizational Behavior and Human Decision Processes, 50*(2), 197–211. https://doi.org/10.1016/0749-5978(91)90020-T

Arain, M., Haque, M., Johal, L., Mathur, P., Nel, W., Rais, A., Sandhu, R., & Sharma, S. (2013). Maturation of the adolescent brain. *Neuropsychiatric Disease and Treatment, 9,* 449–461. https://doi.org/10.2147/NDT.S39776

Beck, L., & Ajzen, I. (1991). Predicting dishonest actions using the theory of planned behavior. *Journal of Research in Personality, 25*(3), 285–301. https://doi.org/10.1016/0092-6566(91)90021-H

Bretag, T., Harper, R., Burton, M., Ellis, C., Newton, R., Saddiqui, S., & van Haeringen, K. (2019). Contract cheating: A survey of Australian university students. *Studies in Higher Education, 44*(11), 1837–1856. https://doi.org/10.1080/03075079.2018.1462788

Chudzicka-Czupała, A., Grabowski, D., Mello, A. L., Kuntz, J., Zaharia, D. V., Hapon, N., Lupina-Wegener, A., & Börü, D. (2016). Application of the theory of planned behavior in academic cheating research–cross-cultural comparison. *Ethics and Behavior, 26*(8). https://doi.org/10.1080/10508422.2015.1112745

Ciarrochi, J. V., & Forgas, J. P. (1999). On being tense yet tolerant: The paradoxical effects of trait anxiety and aversive mood on intergroup judgments. *Group Dynamics, 3*(3), 227–238. https://doi.org/10.1037/1089-2699.3.3.227

Corey, S. M. (1937). Professed attitudes and actual behavior. *Journal of Educational Psychology, 28*(4), 271–280. https://doi.org/10.1037/h0056871

Curtis, G. J. (2013). Don't be happy, worry: Positive mood, but not anxiety, increases stereotyping in a mock-juror decision-making task. *Psychiatry, Psychology and Law, 20*(5), 686–699. https://doi.org/10.1080/13218719.2012.729019

Curtis, G. J., Clare, J., Vieira, E., Selby, E., & Jonason, P. K. (2022). Predicting contract cheating intentions: Dark personality traits, attitudes, norms, and anticipated guilt and shame. *Personality and Individual Differences, 185,* 111277. https://doi.org/10.1016/j.paid.2021.111277

Curtis, G. J., Cowcher, E., Greene, B. R., Rundle, K., Paull, M., & Davis, M. C. (2018). Self-control, injunctive norms, and descriptive norms predict engagement in plagiarism in a theory of planned behavior model. *Journal of Academic Ethics, 16*(1). https://doi.org/10.1007/s10805-018-9309-2

Curtis, G. J., & Locke, V. (2005). The effect of anxiety on impression formation: Affect-congruent or stereotypic biases? *British Journal of Social Psychology, 44*(1), 65–83. https://doi.org/10.1348/014466604X23464

Curtis, G. J., & Tremayne, K. (2021). Is plagiarism really on the rise? Data from four 5-yearly surveys. *Studies in Higher Education, 46*(9), 1816–1826. https://doi.org/10.1080/03075079.2019.1707792

DeSteno, D., Duong, F., Lim, D., & Kates, S. (2019). The grateful don't cheat: Gratitude as a fount of virtue. *Psychological Science, 30*(7), 979–988. https://doi.org/10.1177/0956797619848351

Epstein, S. (1983). Aggregation and beyond: Some basic issues on the prediction of behavior. *Journal of Personality, 51*(3), 360–392. https://doi.org/10.1111/j.1467-6494.1983.tb00338.x

Festinger, L. (1957). *A theory of cognitive dissonance.* Stanford University Press.

Fiske, S. T., Morling, B., & Stevens, L. E. (1996). Controlling self and others: A theory of anxiety, mental control, and social control. *Personality and Social Psychology Bulletin, 22*(2), 115–123. https://doi.org/10.1177/0146167296222001

Forgas, J. P. (1995). Mood and judgment: The affect infusion model (AIM). *Psychological Bulletin, 117*(1), 39–66. https://doi.org/10.1037/0033-2909.117.1.39

Forgas, J. P. (1998). On being happy and mistaken: Mood effects on the fundamental attribution error. *Journal of Personality and Social Psychology, 75*(2), 318–331. https://doi.org/10.1037//0022-3514.75.2.318

Fu, K. W., & Tremayne, K. S. (2021). Self-efficacy and self-control mediate the relationship between negative emotions and attitudes toward plagiarism. *Journal of Academic Ethics.* https://doi.org/10.1007/s10805-021-09415-3.

Gawronski, B., & Hahn, A. (2019). Implicit measures: Procedures, use, and interpretation. In G. D. W. H. Blanton & J. M. LaCroix (Eds.), *Measurement in social psychology* (pp. 29–55). Routledge/Taylor & Francis Group.

Giedd, J. N., Blumenthal, J., Jeffries, N. O., Castellanos, F. X., Liu, H., Zijdenbos, A., Paus, T., Evans, A. C., & Rapoport, J. L. (1999). Brain development during childhood and adolescence: A longitudinal MRI study. *Nature Neuroscience, 2*(10), 861–863. https://doi.org/10.1038/13158

Gilbert, D. T. (2006). *Stumbling on happiness.* Knopf.

Hsiao, C. H. (2015). Impact of ethical and affective variables on cheating: Comparison of undergraduate students with and without jobs. *Higher Education, 69*(1), 55–77. https://doi.org/10.1007/s10734-014-9761-x

Kermer, D. A., Driver-Linn, E., Wilson, T. D., & Gilbert, D. T. (2006). Loss aversion is an affective forecasting error. *Psychological Science, 17*(8), 649–653. https://doi.org/10.1111/j.1467-9280.2006.01760.x

Kocan, S. E., & Curtis, G. J. (2009). Close encounters of the initial kind: Implicit self-esteem, name-letter similarity, and social distance. *Basic and Applied Social Psychology, 31*(1), 17–23. https://doi.org/10.1080/01973530802659752

Larcombe, W., Finch, S., Sore, R., Murray, C. M., Kentish, S., Mulder, R. A., Lee-Stecum, P., Baik, C., Tokatlidis, O., & Williams, D. A. (2016). Prevalence and socio-demographic correlates of psychological distress among students at an Australian university. *Studies in Higher Education, 41*(6), 1074–1091. https://doi.org/10.1080/03075079.2014.966072

Locke, K. D., Church, A. T., Mastor, K. A., Curtis, G., Sadler, P., McDonald, K., de Vargas-Flores, J., Ibáñez-Reyes, J., Morio, H., Reyes, J. A. S., Cabrera, H. F., Arias, R. M., Rincon, B. C., Arias, N. C. A., Muñoz, A., & Ortiz, F. A. (2017). Cross-situational self-consistency in nine cultures. *Personality and Social Psychology Bulletin.* https://doi.org/10.1177/0146167217704192.

Park, J., & Banaji, M. R. (2000). Mood and heuristics: The influence of happy and sad states on sensitivity and bias in stereotyping. *Journal of Personality and Social Psychology, 78*(6), 1005–1023. https://doi.org/10.1037/0022-3514.78.6.1005

Rivis, A., Sheeran, P., & Armitage, C. J. (2009). Expanding the affective and normative components of the theory of planned behavior: A meta-analysis of anticipated affect and moral norms. *Journal of Applied Social Psychology, 39*(12), 2985–3019. https://doi.org/10.1111/j.1559-1816.2009.00558.x

Rundle, K., Curtis, G. J., & Clare, J. (2019). Why students do not engage in contract cheating. *Frontiers in Psychology, 10*(3389). https://doi.org/10.3389/fpsyg.2019.02229

Samnani, A. K., Salamon, S. D., & Singh, P. (2014). Negative affect and counterproductive workplace behavior: The moderating role of moral disengagement and gender. *Journal of Business Ethics, 119*(2), 235–244. https://doi.org/10.1007/s10551-013-1635-0

Sanecka, E., & Baran, L. (2015). Explicit and implicit attitudes toward academic cheating and its frequency among university students. *Polish Journal of Applied Psychology, 13*(2), 69–92. https://doi.org/10.1515/pjap-2015-0030

Seligman, M. E. (1972). Learned helplessness. *Annual Review of Medicine, 23*(1), 407–412. https://doi.org/10.1146/annurev.me.23.020172.002203

Sierra, J. J., & Hyman, M. R. (2006). A dual-process model of cheating intentions. *Journal of Marketing Education, 28*(3), 193–204. https://doi.org/10.1177/0273475306291464

Stephens, J. M. (2017). How to cheat and not feel guilty: Cognitive dissonance and its amelioration in the domain of academic dishonesty. *Theory Into Practice*, *56*(2), 111–120. https://doi.org/10.1080/00405841.2017.1283571

Stone, T. H., Jawahar, I. M., & Kisamore, J. L. (2010). Predicting academic misconduct intentions and behavior using the theory of planned behavior and personality. *Basic and Applied Social Psychology*, *32*(1), 35–45. https://doi.org/10.1080/01973530903539895

Storch, E. A., & Storch, J. B. (2003). Academic dishonesty and attitudes towards academic dishonest acts: Support for cognitive dissonance theory. *Psychological Reports*, *92*(1), 174–176. https://doi.org/10.2466/pr0.2003.92.1.174

Swann, W. B., Pelham, B. W., & Chidester, T. R. (1988). Change through paradox: Using self-verification to alter beliefs. *Journal of Personality and Social Psychology*, *54*(2), 268–273. https://doi.org/10.1037/0022-3514.54.2.268

Tindall, I. K., & Curtis, G. J. (2020). Negative emotionality predicts attitudes toward plagiarism. *Journal of Academic Ethics*, *18*(1), 89–102. https://doi.org/10.1007/s10805-019-09343-3

Tindall, I. K., Fu, K. W., Tremayne, K., & Curtis, G. J. (2021). Can negative emotions increase students' plagiarism and cheating? *International Journal for Educational Integrity*, *17*(25). https://doi.org/10.1007/s40979-021-00093-7

Uzun, A. M., & Kilis, S. (2020). Investigating antecedents of plagiarism using extended theory of planned behavior. *Computers and Education*, *144*, 103700. https://doi.org/10.1016/j.compedu.2019.103700

Vinski, E. J., & Tryon, G. S. (2009). Study of a cognitive dissonance intervention to address high school students' cheating attitudes and behaviors. *Ethics and Behavior*, *19*(3), 218–226. https://doi.org/10.1080/10508420902886692

Zhang, H., Shi, Y., Zhou, Z. E., Ma, H., & Tang, H. (2020). Good people do bad things: How anxiety promotes unethical behavior through intuitive and automatic processing. *Current Psychology*, *39*(2), 720–728. https://doi.org/10.1007/s12144-018-9789-7

CHAPTER 11

Applying Situational Crime Prevention Techniques to Contract Cheating

Joseph Clare

This chapter outlines a toolkit for contract cheating prevention that builds on what we know has worked in a criminal justice context: the situational crime prevention (SCP) framework. Initially, the theoretical foundation for SCP will be discussed, along with the evidence that this approach produces sustainable, scalable crime prevention outcomes that are independent of detection and apprehension of offenders. Following this, the relevance of SCP for academic integrity (generally) and contract cheating (specifically) is explained. The chapter then demonstrates how to use the SCP toolkit in creative ways to reduce the opportunity for contract cheating in a tertiary setting, drawing parallels to strategies discussed through out this edited collection. The chapter concludes by explaining that SCP is a process that needs to be committed to as an ongoing strategy for reducing and removing contract cheating opportunities.

J. Clare (✉)
School of Law, University of Western Australia, Crawley, WA, Australia
e-mail: joe.clare@uwa.edu.au

© The Author(s), under exclusive license to Springer Nature Switzerland AG 2022
S. E. Eaton et al. (eds.), *Contract Cheating in Higher Education*,
https://doi.org/10.1007/978-3-031-12680-2_11

Moving beyond Definition, Measurement, and Detection: The Problem of Preventing Contract Cheating

Much of the current research into contract cheating has focused on defining what it is that we are concerned about (e.g., Bretag et al., 2019; Newton, 2018), measuring the extent to which this problem is occurring (e.g., Bretag et al., 2019; Curtis & Clare, 2017), and looking at ways of detecting those engaging in this practice (e.g., Rogerson, 2017). These are all important endeavours and they are all crucial for developing targeted prevention strategies. However, these current strategies are likely highly ineffective at catching those involved in contract cheating (Gong & Lee, 2021) and are largely unrelated to why others choose not to cheat (Rundle et al., 2019). Consequently, it is also important to broaden the research focus beyond understanding and catching offenders, focusing instead on preventing cheating behaviours from occurring.

In exploring options for prevention, some fundamental characteristics of contract cheating are important to emphasise. It is clear that the norm is not to cheat (Curtis et al., 2021), that students cheat more on some types of assessments than others (Bretag et al., 2019), and that students who cheat once are likely to do so on multiple occasions (Curtis & Clare, 2017). There is also evidence indicating that easy opportunities to cheat increase the likelihood of students engaging in academic misconduct (Hodgkinson et al., 2015).

When thinking about these patterns and the role that opportunity plays in contract cheating it is important to reflect on the role opportunity plays in deviance in other contexts, particularly with respect to crime. It is clear from criminological research that the norm is not to offend and that even the most motivated offenders still only offend when they are presented with the appropriate context and opportunity (Eck, 2015). Furthermore, a large percentage of crime is perpetrated by a very small number of offenders (Martinez et al., 2017), crime problems cluster non-randomly in time and place (Eck, 2015), and repeat victimisation accounts for a very large proportion of the total victimisation experience (SooHyun et al., 2017). In short, a small group of people offend a lot, they do this in a small time/space window, and they repeatedly target a small number of potential (highly suitable) targets.

Felson and Clarke (1998) build on these patterns to propose the ten principles of crime opportunity, which are: (1) opportunities play a role in causing all crime; (2) crime opportunities are highly specific; (3) crime opportunities are concentrated in time and space; (4) crime opportunities depend on everyday movements of activity; (5) one crime produces opportunities for another; (6) some products offer more tempting crime opportunities; (7) social and technological changes produce new crime opportunities; (8) crime can be prevented by reducing opportunities; (9) reducing opportunities does not usually displace crime; and (10) focused opportunity reduction can produce wider declines in crime. As Eck and Eck (2012) explain:

> Rather than consider crime as the result of a few people with constant high propensities to offend—as is typically assumed in assistance and coercive crime policies—the opportunity perspective focuses on proximal situations: people choose whether to offend. The sound bite version of this perspective is "opportunity makes the thief" (Felson & Clarke, 1998). If people who offend have stable propensities, they cannot act on them unless there is an opportunity to do so. If people have unstable propensities to offend, proximal circumstances not only provide opportunities but also can trigger offending by providing temptations. In either case, the immediate situation matters. (p. 284)

With respect to criminological theory, this opportunity perspective is supported by the rational choice perspective (Clarke & Cornish, 1985). The rational choice perspective makes several important assumptions (comprehensively expanded by Cornish & Clarke, 2017) that are relevant to contract cheating. First, it is assumed that offenders make 'bounded' rational choices, constrained by cognitive capacity, time, imperfect information, and the context-specific balance of perceived costs (risk/effort) and benefits (rewards) of their actions. Second, the immediate risk-reward-effort equation influences decision-making much more than the long-term consequences of being apprehended for offending. Third, offending decisions can be influenced by factors that occur before, during, and after the offending action (with the offending decision unfolding like a 'crime script') meaning there are opportunities for prevention by reducing opportunity at all these time points. Finally, this perspective posits that anyone *could* offend provided the immediate contextual ratio of risk-reward-effort makes it boundedly rational for that person. All of these assumptions are supported by extensive offender-focused research.

Relating these assumptions to what is known about contract cheating, there are obvious connections. When considering the assumption that crime results from the interaction of motivation and situation, context matters and motivation to contract cheat are situationally dependent. Pre-COVID-19, this was demonstrated by hypothetical decision-making studies that found students were prepared to cheat when the risk of detection was low and/or the reward was high (Ogilvie & Stewart, 2010; Rigby et al., 2015). Most recently, this has been demonstrated by the dramatic increase in frequency of cheating behaviours during the pandemic (Dey, 2021). Pre-pandemic, 3.5% of postsecondary students were estimated to have engaged in contract cheating at least once (Curtis & Clare, 2017). More recently, analysis of Chegg usage by computer science, mechanical engineering, electrical engineering, physics, and chemistry students revealed a 196% increase in requests posted during 2020 (compared to the same duration 12 months earlier, before the onset of the pandemic, Lancaster & Cotarlan, 2021). Although some of these students may have cheated anyway, the increased stresses caused by COVID-19 have clearly caused other students to act in a situationally influenced way. Further to this, contract cheating is always a choice. The factors that increase the likelihood of making this choice (Rundle et al., 2019, 2020) do not force students to log into online essay mills with their assignment questions and credit cards. People engage in contract cheating because they think it will be beneficial to them. Finally, as with other crime, opportunity plays a powerful role in engaging in contract cheating. Much has been written about the growth and proliferation of online essay mills (e.g., Warren, 2021), acting to increase availability for repeat cheaters and the cheat-curious. We know from other crime contexts that many opportunities increase frequency of offending for offenders and the risk of offending for typically law-abiding individuals (Clarke, 2017).

As outlined in the ten principles of opportunity and crime (above), the assumptions of the rational choice perspective offer a useful (and reasonably optimistic) foundation for developing targeted contract cheating prevention strategies. If offenders make context-specific choices to offend (or not) based on the immediate perceived ratio of risk, reward, and effort involved, then (a) offending is not inevitable and (b) the risk-reward-effort ratios can be manipulated to make offending less rational (Cornish & Clarke, 1986, 2017). Thankfully, it is not essential to understand 'why' an unwanted behaviour occurs to prevent the behaviour. A classic example to demonstrate this point, responsible for ubiquitous, sustained, dramatic reductions in vehicle theft around the world, was the introduction of electronic vehicle immobilisers (Farrell et al., 2014). It was not necessary to understand the motivations, personality dispositions, and developmental circumstances of would-be vehicle thieves to make this change happen. Instead, a targeted, opportunity-focused prevention strategy was implemented preventing cars from being stolen in traditional ways. These rational choice perspective principles underpin the 25 techniques of SCP, which have consistently been highly effective in reducing crime problems for over four decades through altering offending opportunities by increasing the risk and effort involved, reducing the reward and provocations for crime, and removing the excuses for doing the wrong thing (see Table 11.1 from Clarke, 2017, for a comprehensive discussion of this framework, and https://popcenter.asu.edu for a collection of successful case studies across a wide range of crime contexts).

Hodgkinson et al. (2015) were the first to explicitly examine the utility of the SCP framework for the prevention of academic misconduct issues. Through a review of research Hodgkinson et al. identified three broad categories of academic dishonesty: plagiarism, cheating on tests, and collusion, each with different problem characteristics and involving different offending strategies. Using the 25 SCP techniques outlined in Table 11.1, Hodgkinson et al. proposed a range of strategies that could be used (in isolation or combination) to address these varying types of academic integrity problems. For example, to reduce the opportunity for cheating on tests, it would be possible to simultaneously: (a) target harden (increasing the effort involved) by ensuring exam papers are kept locked/supervised and documents are encrypted and/or password protected; (b) extend guardianship during exams (increasing the risk of cheating) by utilising additional proctors and/or having students grade each other's work in groups; (c) conceal targets (reducing the rewards of trying to cheat) by avoiding re-using exams and/or not returning completed exams for students to keep; (d) reduce frustration and stress involved with completing exams (reducing provocations for cheating) by ensuring assessments are fair, clear, and sufficient time is provided; and (e) setting clear rules about exams (removing excuses for cheating) by having and implementing university regulations and warning students not to engage in cheating behaviours at the start of each exam.

Moving from the hypothetical to the applied and focusing specifically on contract cheating behaviours, Baird and Clare (2017) demonstrated the utility of the SCP framework for removing the opportunity for

Table 11.1 The 25 techniques of situational crime prevention, with crime prevention examples of each technique (from Clarke, 2017)

Increase effort	Increase risk	Reduce rewards	Reduce provocations	Remove excuses
1. Target harden • Steering column locks and ignition immobilisers • Anti-robbery screens • Tamper-proof packaging	6. Extend guardianship • Go out in group at night • Leave signs of occupancy • Carry mobile phone	11. Conceal targets • Off-street parking • Gender-neutral phone directories • Unmarked armoured trucks	16. Reduce frustrations and stress • Efficient lines • Polite service • Expanded seating • Soothing music/muted lights	21. Set rules • Rental agreements • Harassment codes • Hotel registration
2. Control access to facilities • Entry phones • Electronic card access • Baggage screening	7. Assist natural surveillance • Improved street lighting • Support whistle-blowers	12. Remove targets • Removable car radios • Women's shelters • Pre-paid cards for pay phones	17. Avoid disputes • Separate seating for rival soccer fans • Reduce crowding in bars • Fixed cab fares	22. Post instructions • 'No parking' • 'Private property' • 'Total fire ban'
3. Screen exits • Tickets needed for exit • Export documents • Electronic merchandise tags	8. Reduce anonymity • Taxi driver IDs • 'How's my driving?' Decals • School uniforms	13. Identify property • Property marking • Vehicle licensing and parts marking • Cattle branding	18. Reduce temptation and arousal • Controls on violent pornography • Prohibit racial slurs	23. Alert conscience • Roadside speed display boards • Signatures for customs declarations • 'Shoplifting is stealing'
4. Deflect offenders • Street closures • Separate bathrooms for women • Disperse pubs	9. Use place managers • CCTV for double-deck busses • Two clerks for convenience stores • Reward vigilance	14. Disrupt markets • Monitor pawn shops • Controls on classified ads • License street vendors	19. Neutralise peer pressure • 'Idiots drink and drive' • 'It's OK to say no' • Disperse school troublemakers	24. Assist compliance • Easy library check out • Public lavatories • Litter receptacles

(*continued*)

Table 11.1 (continued)

Increase effort	Increase risk	Reduce rewards	Reduce provocations	Remove excuses
5. Control tools/weapons • 'Smart' guns • Restrict spray paint sales to juveniles • Toughened beer glasses	10. Strengthen formal surveillance • Red light cameras • Burglar alarms • Security guards	15. Deny benefits • Ink merchandise tags • Graffiti cleaning • Disabling stolen mobile phones	20. Discourage imitation • Rapid repair of vandalism • Censor details of modus operandi	25. Control drugs and alcohol • Server intervention programs • Alcohol-free events

contract cheating in a business capstone unit. After discovering an ongoing and coordinated contract cheating problem within a specific unit, using the process for implementation outlined in the next section, the opportunity to cheat was reduced by simultaneously and systematically adjusting a wide range of assessment elements. Opportunity adjustments included introducing invigilation for online tests (increasing effort by deflecting offenders), introducing updated, bespoke case studies (reducing rewards by concealing targets), distributing academic misconduct information to students at the start of the unit (reducing provocations by reducing temptation and arousal), and implementing an anonymous whistle-blower type feedback facility (increasing the risk by assisting natural surveillance from the student group). Not only was this intervention effective, but it also achieved this prevention goal without disadvantaging students who were not engaging in contract cheating (Baird & Clare, 2017). Designing out opportunities to cheat did not mean assessments were any harder for students who do the right thing.

As will be discussed below, simultaneously doing all possible things to reduce the opportunity is the best approach to implementing SCP. Furthermore, as mentioned above, these prevention gains can be achieved without relying on detection, apprehension, and prosecution. This is particularly important in a contract cheating context, given that much of the purchased work has the potential to be original, and, as such, would not be flagged by text-matching software. Drawing on this, the next section of this chapter examines the process of designing and implementing SCP with a view to helping practitioners reduce the opportunity for contract cheating in other academic contexts.

Looking for Creative Ways to Reduce Contract Cheating Opportunities

This section examines how the lessons learned from applying the SCP process to crime prevention can be translated to developing contract cheating prevention interventions. Four main elements to this process will be explained: (1) the importance of focusing on specific types of contract cheating; (2) try to develop an understanding of how contract cheating is being committed; (3) commit to an action-research model to address the specific problem, where you learn from, and build on imperfect responses; and (4) utilise all available solutions, remembering problems can be prevented by altering opportunities before, during, and after they occur. Each of these elements are expanded, below.

Focus on Specific Types of Contract Cheating

Being specific about the problem to be prevented is key. In a crime context, to be effective, SCP needs to address a meaningful category of similar crimes. For example, within the high-level category of vehicle crime there are several distinct sub-problems. Stealing from cars will have distinct motivations, skill sets, time/place locations, and require different resources in comparison to stealing cars themselves. Within the theft of cars category, further meaningful distinctions will exist relating to the types of cars targeted, the process of stealing the cars, and the reason the cars are being stolen (Clarke, 2017). In a similar way, it is important to be clear about the type of contract cheating that is being targeted by the prevention effort. Some clues exist in the literature in relation to this. For example, Lim and See (2001) asked students to consider 21 types of academic misconduct, and Bretag et al. (2019) asked respondents to consider contract cheating with respect to 13 different assessment tasks. Developing a typology of meaningful categories of contract cheating relates back to the importance of definition, but also includes distinct characteristics relating to how cheating is occurring and what resources are involved.

Understand how Contract Cheating Is Being Committed

Building on these meaningful categories of contract cheating problems, it is necessary to discover as much as possible about how this cheating is taking place in the current opportunity context. Electronic vehicle immobilisers were effective in preventing a large proportion of vehicle theft because they make it much harder to steal cars the way offenders were doing it at the time. In a contract cheating context, learning how particular categories of cheating are being completed could be done through discussions with students (particularly offenders) about their experiences: what opportunities exist, how are they being exploited, and so on. As in Baird and Clare (2017), whistle-blower feedback could also clarify the current cheating environment. In addition to these approaches, it is also possible to adopt what is referred to within the crime prevention literature as a 'think thief' perspective (Ekblom, 1995), where one attempts to place themselves in the shoes of the offender to seek to understand how a particular crime type is done (e.g., Lasky et al., 2017, discuss this approach with respect to preventing shoplifting). For example, a student who wants to submit an essay purchased from a third-party must complete a process (including, but not limited to) (1) interacting with the third-party to obtain the contracted assignment, (2) submitting the contracted assignment, and (3) not getting caught for cheating. "Thinking like a student who intends to cheat" exposes the necessary sequence of events required to offend (the before, during, and after crime 'script' required to successfully complete the offending behaviour, e.g., Leclerc, 2017), which can identify points for potential opportunity-reducing interventions that can make the offending less rational (increasing risk/effort, reducing reward/provocations, and/or removing excuses).

Use an Action-Research Model to Address your Problem

SCP is a toolkit for developing a targeted solution—not a solution in its own right. As Clarke (2017) explains, "the problem-solving methodology is a form of 'action research' in which the problem is studied, hypotheses about the main determinants are developed, a range of solutions are identified and studied, the chosen measures are put into place, and the results are then evaluated" (p. 292). Several incremental target-hardening strategies were tried to deter vehicle theft (i.e., central locking, alarms, steering wheel locks, and mechanical immobilisers) before developing the in-built electronic immobiliser (Farrell et al., 2011). Furthermore, additional strategies (including a name-and-shame 'most stolen' car league table) were required to encourage manufacturers to become part of the vehicle theft prevention process (Laycock, 2004). Crime prevention efforts did not stop once the first intervention was found to be sub-optimal. Translating this to a contract cheating context, the lesson for academics is that if your current approach has not fixed the problem, learn from what you did, adjust your approach, and try again.

Consider a Variety of Solutions

In addition to revisiting existing detection strategies, it is crucial to broaden the range of interventions being used to combat the specific problem you are dealing with. As discussed, above, through developing a clearer understanding of how students are currently cheating, new points of intervention will be identified before, during, and after the cheating behaviour. As Clarke (2017) explains, "a [SCP approach] is more effective when it adopts a package of measures, each of which is directed to a particular point of the process of committing the crime" (p. 292). With this aim in mind, drawing together some of the other ideas discussed in this book, and using the 25 techniques within the SCP structure under the mechanisms of risk, reward, effort, provocations, and excuses, Table 11.2 provides a non-exhaustive set of interventions that could be tried by academics interested in changing the opportunity structure for specific contract cheating problems. Some interventions can be located within more than one technique-mechanism—this is not a problem as they are not intended to be mutually exclusive. Furthermore, some techniques are intended to reduce opportunity before cheating (e.g., blocking access to known cheating sites), some target the 'during' cheating phase (e.g., invigilation of online tests), and others focus on the aftermath of cheating (e.g., whistle blowing and post-assessment cross-questioning practices).

TAKE HOME MESSAGES FOR PRACTITIONERS SEEKING TO DEVELOP TARGETED PREVENTION STRATEGIES

This chapter concludes by emphasising that SCP is a process that needs to be committed to as an ongoing strategy for addressing contract cheating opportunities. Restating the words of Clarke (2017), "to conclude with a harsh fact: situational prevention might be easier to undertake than longer

Table 11.2 Placing a range of proposed interventions within the framework of the 25 techniques of SCP (adapted from Clarke, 2017)

Increase effort	Increase risk	Reduce rewards	Reduce provocations	Remove excuses
1. Target harden • Enhance staff education/training about contract cheating	6. Extend guardianship • Facilitate anonymous peer feedback (whistle blowing) • Implement post-assessment cross-questioning practices	11. Conceal targets • Use up-to-date and bespoke assessment tasks	16. Reduce frustrations and stress • Provide additional training and guidance, including optional extra practice of assessments • Scaffolding—Building skills and reducing the need to cheat (Stoesz et al., this book)	21. Set rules • Distribute academic misconduct and academic integrity information
2. Control access to facilities • Block access to known cheating websites	7. Assist natural surveillance • Facilitate anonymous peer feedback (whistle blowing)	12. Remove targets • Use up-to-date and bespoke assessment tasks	17. Avoid disputes • Clarify standards of proof required for confirming contract cheating	22. Post instructions • Distribute academic misconduct and academic integrity information • Provide additional training and guidance, including optional extra practice of assessments

(*continued*)

Table 11.2 (continued)

Increase effort	Increase risk	Reduce rewards	Reduce provocations	Remove excuses
3. Screen exits • Prevent exam papers and notes from leaving venues	8. Reduce anonymity • In-built identifiable electronic watermarks on university documentation • Require intact document properties • Require test/exam ID	13. Identify property • In-built identifiable electronic watermarks on university documentation	18. Reduce temptation and arousal • Distribute academic misconduct information • Avoid reusing assessments • Scaffolding—Building skills and reducing the need to cheat (Stoesz et al., this book)	23. Alert conscience • Distribute academic misconduct and academic integrity information
4. Deflect offenders • Block access to known cheating websites	9. Use place managers • Invigilation of online tests	14. Disrupt markets • Deny access to cheating sites	19. Neutralise peer pressure • Randomly allocate students to group work • Facilitate anonymous peer feedback (whistle blowing)	24. Assist compliance • Provide additional training and guidance, including optional extra practice of assessments
5. Control tools/weapons • Block access to known cheating websites	10. Strengthen formal surveillance • Utilise engagement metrics wherever possible • Increasing staff awareness of student progress (Stoesz et al., this book) • Implement post-assessment cross-questioning practices	15. Deny benefits • Enforce misconduct procedures whenever possible	20. Discourage imitation • Enforce misconduct procedures whenever possible • Publicise enforcement of misconduct procedures • Publicise detected cases and penalties	25. Control drugs and alcohol

term efforts to alter dispositions, but it can still be very difficult to implement" (p. 292). That said, there are enough success stories from other contexts to be confident that this is an avenue well-worth exploration in the contract cheating prevention context.

Some final points to note, for those who are thinking SCP approaches just push crime around the corner. Research evidence is clear that whole-scale crime displacement is rare (Johnson et al., 2014). Just as making it harder to break into one house does not make other houses more suitable for burglary, making one assignment less suitable for contract cheating does not increase the vulnerability of other assessment items. Instead, research has shown that the norm following targeted crime prevention implementation is a diffusion of crime prevention benefits, such that the benefits extend beyond the target of the intervention (Johnson et al., 2014). Translating this into academic misconduct, focusing on contract cheating may also reduce incidents of other types of academic misconduct. Finally, those seeking to explore the value of SCP for reducing opportunity to cheat in their units must remain aware that offending will adapt. Technologies are going to continue to emerge that are designed to circumvent existing prevention strategies. A SCP approach expects this, which is why it advocates for an ongoing action-research process.

References

Baird, M., & Clare, J. (2017). Removing the opportunity for contract cheating in business capstones: A crime prevention case study. *International Journal for Educational Integrity, 13*(6), 1–15. https://doi.org/10.1007/s40979-017-0018-1

Bretag, T., Harper, R., Burton, M., Ellis, C., Newton, P., Rozenberg, P., et al. (2019). Contract cheating: A survey of Australian university students. *Studies in Higher Education, 44*(11), 1837–1856. https://doi.org/10.1080/03075079.2018.1462788

Clarke, R. V. (2017). Situational crime prevention. In R. Wortley & M. Townsley (Eds.), *Environmental criminology and crime analysis* (2nd ed., pp. 286–303). Willan Publishing.

Clarke, R. V., & Cornish, D. B. (1985). Modeling offenders' decisions: A framework for research and policy. In M. Tonry & N. Morris (Eds.), *Crime and justice* (Vol. 6). University of Chicago Press.

Cornish, D. B., & Clarke, R. V. (1986). *The reasoning criminal: Rational choice perspectives on offending*. Springer-Verlag.

Cornish, D. B., & Clarke, R. V. (2017). The rational choice perspective. In R. Wortley & M. Townsley (Eds.), *Environmental criminology and crime analysis* (2nd ed., pp. 29–61). Routledge.

Curtis, G. J., & Clare, J. (2017). How prevalent is contract cheating and to what extent are students repeat offenders? *Journal of Academic Ethics*, 15(2), 115–124. https://doi.org/10.1007/s10805-017-9278-x

Curtis, G. J., McNeill, M., Slade, C., Tremayne, K., Harper, R., Rundle, K., & Greenaway, R. (2022). Moving beyond self-reports to estimate the prevalence of commercial contract cheating: An Australian study. *Studies in Higher Education*, 47(9), 1844–1856. https://doi.org/10.1080/03075079.2021.1972093

Dey, S. (2021). Reports of cheating at colleges soar during the pandemic. *npr.org*. Retrieved from https://www.npr.org/2021/08/27/1031255390/reports-of-cheating-at-colleges-soar-during-the-pandemic?s=09

Eck, J. E. (2015). Who should prevent crime at places? The advantages of regulating place managers and challenges to police services. *Policing: A Journal of Policy and Practice*, 9(3), 223–233. https://doi.org/10.1093/police/pav020

Eck, J. E., & Eck, E. B. (2012). Crime place and pollution: Expanding crime reduction options through a regulatory approach. *Criminology and Public Policy*, 11(2), 281–316. https://doi.org/10.1111/j.1745-9133.2012.00809.x

Ekblom, P. (1995). Less crime by design. *Annals of the American Academy of Political and Social Science*, 539(114–129).

Farrell, G., Tilley, N., & Tseloni, A. (2014). Why the crime drop? *Crime and Justice*, 43(1), 421–490. https://doi.org/10.1086/678081

Farrell, G., Tseloni, A., Mailley, J., & Tilley, N. (2011). The crime drop and the security hypothesis. *Journal of Research in Crime and Delinquency*, 48(2), 147–175. https://doi.org/10.1177/0022427810391539

Felson, M., & Clarke, R. V. (1998). *Opportunity makes the thief: Practical theory for crime prevention–Police Research Series, Paper 98*. https://popcenter.asu.edu/sites/default/files/opportunity_makes_the_thief.pdf

Gong, Y., & Lee, T. (2021). Why are universities catching only 1 in 100 cheaters when the real figure is much higher? *SBS Chinese*. https://www.sbs.com.au/chinese/english/why-are-universities-catching-only-1-in-100-cheaters-when-the-real-figure-is-much-higher

Hodgkinson, T., Curtis, H., MacAlister, D., & Farrell, G. (2015). Student academic dishonesty: The potential for situational prevention. *Journal of Criminal Justice Education*. https://doi.org/10.1080/10511253.2015.1064982

Johnson, S., Guerette, R. T., & Bowers, K. (2014). Crime displacement: What we know, what we don't know, and what it means for crime reduction. *Journal of Experimental Criminology*, 10(4), 549–571. https://doi.org/10.1007/s11292-014-9209-4

Lancaster, T., & Cotarlan, C. (2021). Contract cheating by STEM students through a file sharing website: A Covid-19 pandemic perspective. *International Journal for Educational Integrity*, 17(3). https://doi.org/10.1007/s40979-021-00070-0

Lasky, N. V., Fisher, B. S., & Jacques, S. (2017). 'Thinking thief' in the crime prevention arms race: Lessons learned from shoplifters. *Security Journal, 30*(3), 772–792. https://doi.org/10.1057/sj.2015.21

Laycock, G. (2004). UK car theft index: An example of government leverage. In M. G. Maxfield & R. V. Clarke (Eds.), *Understanding and preventing car theft–crime prevention studies* (Vol. 17, pp. 25–44).

Leclerc, B. (2017). Crime scripts. In R. Wortley & M. Townsley (Eds.), *Environmental criminology and crime analysis* (pp. 119–141). Willan Publishing.

Lim, V. K. G., & See, S. K. B. (2001). Attitudes toward, and intentions to report, academic cheating among students in Singapore. *Ethics and Behavior, 11*(3), 261–274. https://doi.org/10.1207/S15327019EB1103_5

Martinez, N. N., Lee, Y., Eck, J. E., & SooHyun, O. (2017). Ravenous wolves revisited: A systematic review of offending concentration. *Crime Science, 6*(10). https://doi.org/10.1186/s40163-017-0072-2

Newton, P. M. (2018). How common is commercial contract cheating in higher education and is it increasing? A systematic review. *Frontiers in Education, 3*(67). https://doi.org/10.3389/feduc.2018.00067/full

Ogilvie, J., & Stewart, A. (2010). The integration of rational choice and self-efficacy theories: A situational analysis of student misconduct. *The Australian and New Zealand Journal of Criminology, 43*(1), 130–155. https://doi.org/10.1375/acri.43.1.130

Rigby, D., Burton, M., Balcombe, K., Bateman, I., & Mulatu, A. (2015). Contract cheating and the market in essays. *Journal of Economic Behavior and Organization, 111*, 23–37. https://doi.org/10.1016/j.jebo.2014.12.019

Rogerson, A. M. (2017). Detecting contract cheating in essay and report submissions: Process, patterns, clues and conversations. *International Journal for Educational Integrity, 13*(10). https://doi.org/10.1007/s40979-017-0021-6

Rundle, K., Curtis, G., & Clare, J. (2019). Why students do not engage in contract cheating. *Frontiers in Psychology, 10*(15). https://doi.org/10.3389/fpsyg.2019.02229/full

Rundle, K., Curtis, G., & Clare, J. (2020). Why students choose not to cheat. In T. Bretag (Ed.), *A research agenda for academic integrity* (pp. 100–111). Edward Elgar Publishing.

SooHyun, O., Martinez, N. N., Lee, Y., & Eck, J. E. (2017). How concentrated is crime among victims? A systematic review from 1977 to 2014. *Crime Science, 6*(9). https://doi.org/10.1186/s40163-017-0071-3

Warren, C. (2021). The cheat is on. *Education Technology.*. https://edtechnology.co.uk/features/the-cheat-is-on/

CHAPTER 12

Presentation, Properties and Provenance: The Three Ps of Identifying Evidence of Contract Cheating in Student Assignments

Robin Crockett

PRESENTATION, PROPERTIES AND PROVENANCE: THE THREE PS OF IDENTIFYING EVIDENCE OF CONTRACT CHEATING IN STUDENT ASSIGNMENTS

Contract cheating is the term first proposed by Clarke and Lancaster (2006, 2007) to describe the act of a student submitting for assessment any work commissioned from a third-party and declaring it—explicitly or implicitly—as their own work. This activity, also termed *commissioning*, does not necessarily involve payment or reward. The term *ghost-writing* is sometimes used to describe the activity by a commissioned writer (*ghost-writer*). The term *essay mill* (see e.g., Cambridge English Dictionary online, n.d.) is sometimes used to describe a business that employs or acts

R. Crockett (✉)
Library & Learning Services, University of Northampton, Northampton, UK

Loughborough University, Loughborough, UK
e-mail: robin.crockett@northampton.ac.uk

© The Author(s), under exclusive license to Springer Nature Switzerland AG 2022
S. E. Eaton et al. (eds.), *Contract Cheating in Higher Education*,
https://doi.org/10.1007/978-3-031-12680-2_12

as a procurer for ghost-writers (Ellis et al., 2018; Medway et al., 2018; Rogerson, 2014). The term *assignment provider* is used herein as an all-embracing term for businesses that provide submissible assignments to students.

Some assignment providers advertise a multiplicity of 'value-added' features to imply higher quality and standards (Rowland et al., 2018). Others make few or no such claims (Newton, 2018; Sutherland-Smith & Dullaghan, 2019). Some assignment providers include disclaimers on their websites that students should use purchased work for guidance and not submission, others do not. However, it is often the case that such disclaimers, where present, are afforded significantly less emphasis and visibility than statements claiming the work provided is 'plagiarism free', implying 'undetectable'. At the time of writing (August–October 2021), contract cheating is increasing (Curtis, 2021). Furthermore, *essay bots* (i.e., artificial intelligence (AI) enabled writing software) present an emerging threat.

Institutions have to take appropriate action when cheating is identified to protect the integrity of their awards, and their reputations. However, it is not as simple as every student who commissions is motivated to cheat: Some assignment providers are actively and deliberately deceptive in their marketing to lure naive and inexperienced students. Consequently, institutions additionally have duties of care to their students to deter them from cheating practices and, where appropriate, rehabilitate those who become ensnared and seek advice and support to disentangle themselves and 'go straight'.

Furthermore, it is not as simple as dismissing contract cheating as an isolated problem with an occasional student who might commission an 'inconsequential' assignment. There can be major professional consequences: Would you want to be treated by a medic who had cheated their drug-dose-calculation assessments? (And if you think your students cannot cheat key assessments because you assess via formal examinations, think again.)

Lastly, there is the possibility of blackmail (Draper et al., 2021). A student when transacting is unlikely to think beyond the convenience of buying a supposedly undetectable assignment. However, as well as the risk of ordering information, however well anonymised by a student, subsequently identifying them, a commissioned assignment becomes traceable as soon as it is submitted via similarity-checking software. Another danger is assignment providers sending unredacted student 'testimonials', provided by identifiable student customers, to other students (Crockett & Maxwell, 2021).

Presentation

Generally, initial identification of ghost-written work is dependent on the alertness and awareness of graders/moderators (Bretag & Mahmud, 2009; Dawson & Sutherland-Smith, 2017; Lancaster & Clarke, 2007; Rogerson, 2017). Therefore, let us start with a hypothetical assignment that has caught your attention because it somehow looks wrong but is not showing the usual similarity-score indications of copying or collusion. The underlying questions regarding what to look for can be summarised as 'Is there visible information suggesting an assignment provider?', and 'Does it align with other student work?'

Handwritten Assignments

Although the focus in this chapter is electronic submissions, let us briefly consider handwritten assignments such as formal examination scripts or training-placement logbook-type assignments. The key question here can be summarised as 'Is the handwriting the student's normal handwriting, allowing for circumstances?'

With regard to examinations, compare with the student's other examination scripts. Indeed, so doing might reveal other handwritings corresponding to other third-parties commissioned for other examinations. With regard to logbooks, the expectation is that these are contemporaneous records and so can be disjointed accounts of events that might resolve over several entries with errors, inconsistencies, amendments and annotations. Thus, a logbook that has been handwritten from a commissioned document (possibly written after the events) can look too neat and tidy, too unflawed.

Similarity to Other Texts, Similarity Score

If the similarity score with bibliography excluded (as determined by similarity-checking software) is anomalously or atypically low, particularly if the assignment is well written and with unexpected wording where subject-specific terminology (jargon) would be expected, then that can indicate a commissioned assignment where a ghost-writer has made subject-oblivious edits to reduce the similarity score.

It is not possible to give a one-size-fits-all figure that indicates a similarity score of concern as this is dependent on factors such as the nature of the assignment and level of study. However, a straightforward guideline is to view as suspicious any similarity score that is anomalously lower than the others in the cohort, well below what is expected for a typical student writing the assignment. Another guideline is that some assignment providers advertise 'plagiarism free' guarantees indicating 5% or less similarity, bibliography excluded.

Placeholders and Markup

Some assignment providers include pro-forma title pages with placeholders or annotations for students to enter name and submission details before submitting. Similarly, some assignments are supplied with placeholders or annotations for students to enter specific details (e.g., locations and dates of placements). Some students miss this and submit commissioned files still containing unedited placeholders or non-deleted annotations. Sometimes, this and other information are hidden from normal view but can be revealed by toggling the track-changes and markup settings.

Furthermore, an assignment provider might deliberately insert a telltale ('Easter Egg') that indicates an assignment is not the work of the student. This can be as explicit as a sentence in the body of the assignment to the effect 'This essay was written by X' or can be stealthier such as a spurious reference in an unrelated subject area, something that is effectively impossible for a student researching the assignment to find and include or, indeed, miss when proof-reading.

Presentation and Formatting

Most people have their preferred settings when writing using their own device. Therefore, noting possibilities such as writing to a specified template or borrowing a computer, is there some aspect of basic document formatting for the assignment in question that is inconsistent with other work submitted by that student? For example, page size and margins, headers and footers, font face, size and styles (e.g., bold, italics), line and paragraph spacings and text alignment/justification. Also, consider whether it looks like a student-written document (i.e., a document prepared by someone who is learning) or more like a professionally produced and formatted document.

Phrasing, Spelling, Grammar and Punctuation

Everyone who writes English (or any language) has their own preferred turns of phrase, use of words and spelling preferences where alternative spellings exist. Some languages, notably but not exclusively English, have different national spelling conventions. Furthermore, everyone has their punctuation—and mispunctuation—habits, commonly apostrophes in English but also hyphens, commas versus dashes, colons versus semi-colons, single versus double quotes, single versus double spaces after full-stops and capitalisation of proper nouns. Therefore, are there identifiable differences in such aspects between the assignment in question and the student's other submissions that align with third-party authorship?

Writer 'Voice' and Focus

Voice, in this context, is an inclusive term covering aspects such as style, tone, vocabulary, level of approach and exposition of concepts. Some aspects of voice are characteristic of students at given stages of their learning and development, others are more individual. It is important to allow for differences in voice necessitated by different assignment briefs, but differences not thus accounted for can indicate a ghost-written assignment.

Consideration of voice, including whether the voice appears genuinely student or contrived by a professional writer to appear student-like, thus requires knowledge of the teaching materials and subject coverage, also of an individual student in question and their development as an independent learner. This can necessitate detailed consideration by several tutors familiar with the student and their submissions.

Furthermore, assignment providers mass-produce assignments and so expend minimal effort over short timescales to produce maximal output at acceptable quality. Thus, new assignments can be substantially assembled from parts of previous assignments, edited to minimise similarity. This can result in a well-voiced assignment, with good vocabulary at the expense of core-content and some unusual wording to minimise similarity, that misses a specific focus of the assignment brief.

While full consideration of computer coding assignments is beyond the scope of this chapter, coder voice can be considered in essentially the same way as writer voice. There are many programming languages and coders have their individual voices, albeit constrained by the restricted vocabularies and syntaxes of programming languages compared to human languages.

References

Many students, particularly early-stage students, find referencing non-straightforward. Use of reference management software can help but must be configured and learned. Thus, it is reasonable to expect in-text citations and reference lists to be presented using an acceptable referencing style/system but with some errors and inconsistencies.

Therefore, use of a referencing style/system not as specified for the assignment, or not an institutional or discipline standard, can align with a ghost-writer referencing in their default style, particularly if the references themselves are (near) perfectly presented. Furthermore, referencing that is anomalously 'too perfect', even if in a specified or expected style/system, can align with a ghost-writer. Conversely, inclusion of generic subject references but not appropriately specific to the core matter of the assignment, and/or cited at approximate places in the text rather than accurately placed, can align with a ghost-writer carrying-over references from previous similar assignments for efficiency at minimal effort. A ghost-writer carrying-over references from previous assignments can also be apparent in the reference list showing block-wise similarities (i.e., uninterrupted sequences of identical references) to one or more individual sources.

Essay-Bot Writing

Essay bots are online artificial intelligence (AI)-enabled software 'writing' tools. Described simply, these tools allow students to prepare assignments by button-clicking to accept phrases and sentences generated by the software according to its programming. Other than enter some initial text (e.g., an essay title or statement from an assignment brief), the student does no writing and simply button-clicks to accept the AI-suggested text. Such text is often characterised by well-written English (or other language) but verbose, containing circumlocutions, hyperbole, absences of insight, non-sequiturs, out-of-timeline reference points or inconsistent numerical ranges/comparisons. An essay-bot-generated assignment can appear as a set of loosely connected paragraphs, lacking flow with variably phrased repetition of content over successive (introductory) paragraphs, and grammatically correct sentences containing subject-inconsistent/disconnected clauses. In short, writing that could be termed 'uninsightfully robotic'. However, these AIs will develop and improve.

PROPERTIES

This section considers aspects of document properties and metadata that can be inspected using the built-in functionality of Microsoft Word and other document-processing apps. However, it is sometimes necessary to investigate document metadata in more detail, and that is outlined in the next section. In either case, as well as evidence in individual metadata items, are the metadata as a whole consistent with student authorship?

Where possible, download the student's originally submitted file from the Virtual Learning Environment (VLE). Where that is not possible, be careful when working with files forwarded by tutors and others as those can contain modified metadata. In that context, beware of some apps' default option to re-save (and thereby modify metadata) when closing a file opened solely to read/view/print.

File Type and Name

Is the file type (e.g., DOC, DOCX, ODT, PDF) consistent with other assignments submitted by the student? In the absence of a difference necessitated by the assignment in question, an anomalous file type can indicate different authorship. With regard to the filename, is that consistent with the student's other submitted assignments and/or does it have the appearance of a *human* filename or of an assignment-provider order reference? Filenames take a variety of forms, and each of us has our individual preferences, but assignment-provider filenames often include order references, for example, combinations of writer or customer IDs, cataloguing code, dates, word-limit, target grade, separated by hyphens and underscores. To illustrate, noting endless variations, *CE_0712-0715_2500.docx*, a combination of a two-character provider label, followed by commission and delivery dates (month, day), followed by word limit.

Document Properties (Properties...)

Open the file in an indicated app and check the document properties (metadata) via the built-in menu options. There are too many variations in details across different apps and operating systems to describe here but, Microsoft Office, LibreOffice (The Document Foundation) and others collate essentially the same information from DOC, DOCX and ODT files in different combinations. However, LibreOffice reports the actual timestamps embedded in documents whereas some other apps can report file-system timestamps. Note that metadata in PDFs are often sparse compared to DOC, DOCX and ODT, and are highly dependent on the PDF-creation software used.

Author-Name Fields
The expectation is that both creating-author (creator) and last-saving/modifying (last-modifier) author names correspond to the student. Where they do not, are there any good reasons such as the student borrowing a computer? Does an author name look like an assignment-provider ID? Blank author-name fields do not necessarily indicate anything improper and can arise from privacy settings or importing files from Cloud-based apps for submission.

If a student borrows a computer to start or finish an assignment then, unless they have their own account on that computer, the creator or last-modifier name respectively will reflect the owner of the computer. Thus, if a student habitually borrows computers, a portfolio of their assignments will show an overall pattern of varying author-names corresponding to the borrowed computers. Conversely, if a student habitually commissions and adds, for example, their title-page details to the commissioned files before submitting, a portfolio of their assignments will show an overall pattern of varying creator names with consistent last-modifier name(s) aligning with the student.

Timeline Information
This is essentially the created and last-modified/saved timestamps and revision/edit history. Very closely spaced timestamps (e.g., a few minutes apart) coupled with a very short editing time and small number of revisions can indicate that an assignment provider has made a clean copy for the student who has then, for example, opened the file to add their title-page details and then saved and submitted. However, some students make clean copies of their own entirely honest work for submission, which can give rise to similar time-line information.

Custom Properties and Other Fields
Other fields can contain name or identity information and custom properties are a combination of user-set and software-set fields and settings. It is not possible to give a definitive list of what to look for as the variations are

endless, but such fields can include email addresses, name/ID and organisation information, URLs, tell-tales of (unexpected) reference-management or word-processing software that has been used at some point in the document preparation.

Other Document Settings

As with anomalies in document-properties metadata, anomalies in other settings for which there are no good/obvious reasons associated with individual assignments can indicate different writers with different preferences using different apps. Therefore, are such settings consistent with the student's other submissions, or are there otherwise unexplained differences that align with a different authorship? More specifically, check the settings for page size, margins, headers and footers, line and paragraph spacings and alignments, font face and size and language(s).

Some software embeds user information in outputs. Therefore, check any software output (e.g., design and code files) for evidence of a third-party designer or coder—anything that does not align with the student. Also check whether the software and version used align with institutional student-licensing or is otherwise reasonably available to the student.

PROVENANCE

This section is somewhat more open-ended than the preceding sections: Simply, follow-up avenues of investigation that are suggested by what you see in a suspicious assignment.

XML: Looking inside Files

DOCX and ODT files are actually zip files of XML (eXtensible Markup Language) files of document text and settings, plus embedded files such as images and graphs/charts (sometimes with embedded spreadsheet files). It is possible to unzip these and inspect the XML files and embedded content. Doing this does not require specialist tools: Zip software and a text editor, as generally pre-installed on computers (and are readily available if not) are required. A code editor that can highlight XML markup can help but is not necessary.

Unzipping DOCX and ODT Files

How to unzip varies according to whether you are using Windows, macOS or Linux/BSD. It can be necessary, particularly on Windows, to change the filename from *filename.docx* or *filename.odt* to *filename.zip*. Whatever method you use, it is good practice to create a new empty directory/folder and unzip inside that to keep the unzipped contents collated.

Having unzipped the file, inspect the contents as appropriate. Although details will vary according to any embedded files and custom properties, you should see a list of files and folders with the basic directory-structure as shown in Fig. 12.1. Note that while both formats embed XML for spreadsheet-generated graphs, Microsoft Word also embeds the (Excel) worksheet in DOCX files.

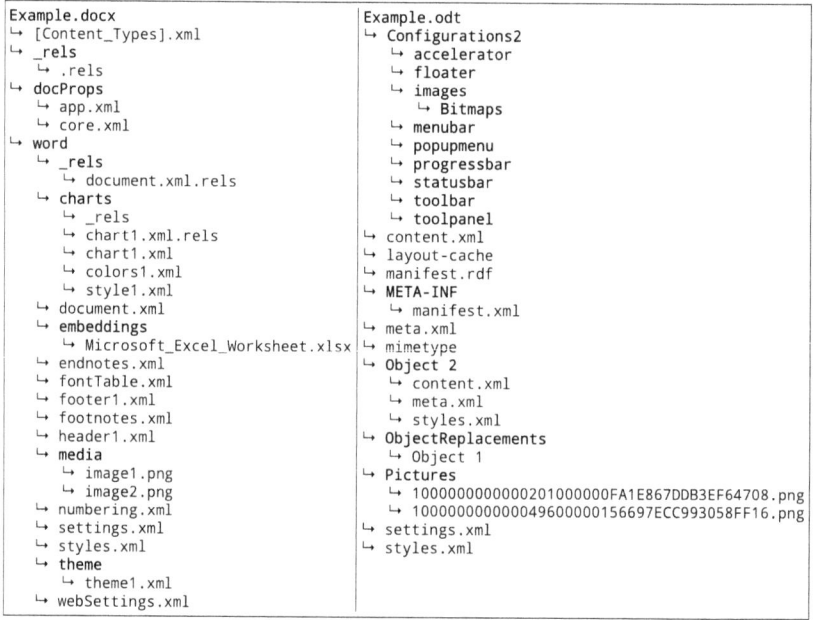

Fig. 12.1 The zipped file folder structures for DOCX (left) and ODT (right). Folder names are in bold and folder contents are indented (↳)

Further Document Properties and Settings

In DOCX files, the basic document properties are contained in the *core.xml* and *app.xml* files in the *docProps* folder, and any *custom.xml* file or any files in a *customXml* folder, if present, can contain useful information. The document text is in *document.xml*. In ODT files, the basic document properties are contained in the *meta.xml* file, as are (some) custom properties. The document text is in the top-level *content.xml* file. While empty fields can result from the use of privacy settings, or downloading a file from Cloud-based software, 'hacked' XML files generally indicate an attempt to remove information.

Embedded Files

There can be significant provenance information in an embedded file and its metadata, and sometimes in an associated field in the XML. Many images are cropped in the submitted file so that reader sees only what the writer intends to be visible, and it can be easier to check uncropped images in unzipped files than using an app's image cropping functionality. Embedded graphs/charts are often generated using spreadsheets, which can be embedded—with their metadata—in the file.

Open embedded files in indicated apps and check their metadata. In DOCX files, images are stored in the *media* folder, and embedded spreadsheets are in *embeddings*, both inside the *word* folder. In ODT files, images are stored in the *Pictures* folder.

It is not uncommon to find screenshots of the writer's desktop or app windows included in a file. These can reveal a lot of information regarding the user, for example, a name in an email tab, a user-account profile picture or a window that shows a non-student home directory path. To illustrate, noting endless variations, *C:\Users\contract-writer\commissions*. Sometimes date information revealed in a screenshot can pre-date the student's period of study, indicating work initially done at an earlier date.

Microsoft Word XML 'w:rsid' Tags

Whenever a document is opened for editing in Microsoft Word, a unique editing/writing XML *w:rsid* tag is allocated for that session. In DOCX files, the session edits in the *document.xml* file are annotated with the allocated tag (Johnson & Davies, 2020), and all session tags are listed in the *settings.xml* file. Those tags do not give any specific writer or timeline information but documents with tags in common very probably have editing/writing in common.

There are too many possibilities for there to be a one-size-fits-all figure that indicates a suspicious number of *w:rsid* tags in common. Completely distinct assignments are unlikely to have even one tag in common, but assignments independently prepared using the same formatted template will have template-formatting tags in common. Experience to date indicates that a template in common can account for up to approximately 10% of total tags in common, whereas files/assignments having about 60–70% or more tags in common probably have substantial common authorship. As appropriate, the actual tagged edits in the assignments' *document.xml* files should be compared.

Looking inside DOC Files
DOC files are binary files and, therefore, contain little human-readable text even if opened in a hexadecimal (hex) editor. In the general case, the best option to inspect any embedded files, or other content, is to convert the file to (or re-save it in) DOCX format and unzip, noting that some metadata might be updated by so doing.

Datasets

Assignment providers require predictable datasets that yield convenient results: Real data can be unpredictable and inconvenient. Therefore, check data that look 'too convenient' (e.g., a dataset that looks like a published dataset but with small amounts of noise added to individual data so as not to be identical while yielding the same 'safe' statistical analysis), or a survey/questionnaire where all the respondent numbers are multiples of, for example, 5 or 10.

Online Evidence

Many assignment providers have their own websites or are listed on others or use social media. Therefore, an online search for a suspect author-name in an assignment might reveal someone of (essentially) the same name promoted on the Internet as, for example, an academic content writer or advisor/tutor. An online search for the student name/ID can be productive: Some students leave such information (possibly including social-media profile picture) on such websites when commissioning or giving feedback.

Make sure to bookmark websites of interest and take screenshots of webpages at the time of discovery: Do not risk a website changing before you can return to it. Conversely, some freelancing websites leech off others and can reveal evidence of commissioning after it has disappeared from the primary site, and after an initial search.

Third-Party Access to a Student's VLE Accounts

Some assignment providers offer to 'do everything' for a price if the student grants them access to their VLE account(s). This can be tempting to students: It saves them from having to select and forward (or, indeed, read) course materials, or even to make the submission. The benefits to an assignment provider go beyond charging more money: They get access to valuable resources such as teaching materials and journals, plus similarity-checking software to help them fulfil 'plagiarism free' guarantees. Where this is suspected, check with institutional IT services whether there is evidence such as frequent accesses from unexplained/anomalous IP addresses, which can be location-checked using online look-up services.

Concluding Thoughts

I am not alone in tackling this subject and I commend TEQSA's guidance (TEQSA, 2020, 2021). Given the nature of the material, not everything I have covered is completely novel (and, indeed, some is what could be termed *common sense*). However, I hope I have brought a lot of information together in one place to help raise awareness and advance professional practice.

A ghost-written assignment might not show any typical tell-tales and, conversely, an entirely honest assignment could show some. Thus, the objective of an investigation is to collate a body of evidence to be considered *on balance of probabilities* (e.g., QAA, 2017, 2020; TEQSA, 2017) and not *proof beyond reasonable doubt*. In essence, the question being asked—and answered—with regard to assignments submitted by a student is whether it is more likely that (a) the student prepared those and the suspicious features arose coincidentally or (b) the student commissioned.

It is not (or should not be) necessary to establish precise third-party authorship in order to demonstrate that a student has, on balance of probabilities, commissioned. What is (or should be) necessary is to establish a body of evidence that demonstrates one or more submitted assignments have, on balance of probabilities, been written in whole or in part by someone other than the student.

It is generally appropriate to consider a portfolio of a student's submissions: Ghost-writing might only be revealed by otherwise unexplained inconsistencies amongst several assignments. Also, previously undetected contract cheating might be identified, and there is at least anecdotal evidence that students who commission tend to perceive it as a low-risk activity and commission repeatedly unless/until they are caught (Clarke & Lancaster, 2006; Ellis et al., 2018).

It is inappropriate to have any statute of limitations that unnecessarily limits investigation to (short) intervals around grading. Indeed, because evidence of contract cheating sometimes comes to light after grading, sometimes even years after graduation, any such statute of limitations is counter-productive and effectively a mechanism for letting culpable individuals escape sanctions.

Some contract cheating investigations are straightforward with clear evidence and take little time. However, others are complex involving several suspicious assignments submitted over an extended period containing a variety of evidence, possibly involving several students, requiring considerable effort and time (possibly weeks or longer) on the part of tutors and investigators to build a case and present it (Clarke & Lancaster, 2007).

It is not possible to design-out contract cheating from assignments (Ellis et al., 2019). Simply, there are now too many ways that assignment providers cater for student demands. For example, turn-around times of one to two hours or less (sometimes a couple of tens of minutes) mean time-constrained assessments are vulnerable, and incorporation of teaching materials and tutorial advice relayed by students over extended periods mean that assessments supposedly based on students' individual personal development are vulnerable.

Acknowledgements I gratefully acknowledge the late Robert (Bob) Clarke who first prompted my interest in contract cheating tell-tales, evidence trails and so on. All the discussions with support and encouragement I have received from the University of Northampton's team of contract cheating specialist investigators, and John Sinclair, Thomas Lancaster, Sandie Dann, Irene Glendinning, Michael Draper, Cath Ellis, Sarah Elaine Eaton, Guy Curtis and colleagues at Turnitin LLC.

REFERENCES

Bretag, T., & Mahmud, S. (2009, September 28–30). A model for determining student plagiarism: Electronic detection and academic judgement [Conference presentation]. *4th Asia Pacific Conference on Education Integrity (4APCEI)*, Wollongong. Journal of University Teaching and Learning Practice, 6(1), 49–60. http://ro.uow.edu.au/jutlp

Cambridge English Dictionary. (n.d.). Cambridge University Press. Accessed Feb 20, 2020, from https://dictionary.cambridge.org/dictionary/english/essay-mill

Clarke, R., & Lancaster, T. (2006, June 19–21). Eliminating the successor to plagiarism? Identifying the use of contract cheating sites [Conference presentation]. *Proceedings of the 2nd International Plagiarism Conference*.

Clarke, R., & Lancaster, T. (2007, July 26–27). Establishing a systematic six-stage process for detecting contract cheating. *Proceedings of the 2nd International Conference on Pervasive Computing and Applications*, 342–347. https://doi.org/10.1109/ICPCA.2007.4365466.

Crockett, R., & Maxwell, R. (2021). Ethical and privacy considerations of the marketing tactics used by some academic assignment providers: A case-study. *Proceedings of the European Conference on Academic Integrity and Plagiarism (ECAIP) 2021*. https://academicintegrity.eu/conference/conferenceproceedings/

Curtis, G. (2021). *1 in 10 uni students submit assignments written by someone else—and most are getting away with it*. The Conversation. https://theconversation.com/1-in-10-uni-students-submit-assignments-written-by-someone-else-and-most-are-getting-away-with-it-166410

Dawson, P., & Sutherland-Smith, W. (2017). Can markers detect contract cheating? Results from a pilot study. *Assessment & Evaluation in Higher Education., 43*(2), 286–293. https://doi.org/10.1080/02602938.2017.1336746

Draper, M., Lancaster, T., Dann, S., Crockett, R., & Glendinning, I. (2021). Essay mills and other contract cheating services: To buy or not to buy and the consequences of students changing their minds. *International Journal for Educational Integrity, 17*(13), 1–13. https://doi.org/10.1007/s40979-021-00081-x

Ellis, C., Zucker, I., & Randall, D. (2018). The infernal business of contract cheating: Understanding the business processes and models of academic custom writing sites. *International Journal for Educational Integrity, 14*(1), 1–21. https://doi.org/10.1007/s40979-017-0024-3

Ellis, C., van Haeringen, K., Harper, R., Bretag, T., Zucker, I., McBride, S., Rozenberg, P., Newton, P., & Saddiqui, S. (2019). Does authentic assessment assure academic integrity? Evidence from contract cheating data. *Higher*

Education Research & Development, 39(3), 454–469. https://doi.org/10.1080/07294360.2019.1680956

Johnson, C., & Davies, R. (2020). Plagiarism from a digital forensics perspective. In T. Foltýnek, C. Hill, & Z. Khan (Eds.), *Integrity in education for future happiness* (pp. 78–89). Mendel University Press. https://doi.org/10.11118/978-80-7509-772-9-0078

Lancaster, T., & Clarke, R. (2007). *Assessing contract cheating through auction sites–a computing perspective*. Proceedings of the 8th annual conference for information and computer sciences. 1–6. University of Southampton. https://citeseerx.ist.psu.edu/viewdoc/download?doi=10.1.1.453.8656&rep=rep1&type=pdf

Medway, D., Roper, S., & Gillooly, L. (2018). Contract cheating in UK higher education: A covert investigation of essay mills. *British Education Research Journal, 44*(3), 393–418. https://doi.org/10.1002/berj.3335

Newton, P. (2018). How common is commercial contract cheating in higher education and is it increasing? A systematic review. *Frontiers in Education, 3*(00067). https://doi.org/10.3389/feduc.2018.00067

QAA. (2017). *Contracting to cheat in higher education*. https://www.qaa.ac.uk/about-us/what-we-do/academic-integrity/

QAA. (2020). *Contracting to cheat in higher education* (2nd ed.). https://www.qaa.ac.uk/about-us/what-we-do/academic-integrity/

Rogerson, A. (2014, June 16–18). *Detecting the work of essay mills and file swapping sites: some clues they leave behind*. Proceedings of the 6th International Integrity & Plagiarism Conference. 1–9. https://ro.uow.edu.au/gsbpapers/434/

Rogerson, A. (2017). Detecting contract cheating in essay and report submissions: Process, patterns, clues and conversations. *International Journal for Educational Integrity, 13*(10), 1–17. https://doi.org/10.1007/s40979-017-0021-6

Rowland, S., Slade, C., Wong, K. S., & Whiting, B. (2018). 'Just turn to us': The persuasive features of contract cheating websites. *Assessment & Evaluation in Higher Education, 43*(4), 652–665. https://doi.org/10.1080/02602938.2017.1391948

Sutherland-Smith, W., & Dullaghan, K. (2019). You don't always get what you pay for: User experiences of engaging with contract cheating sites. *Assessment & Evaluation in Higher Education, 44*(8), 1148–1162. https://doi.org/10.1080/02602938.2019.1576028

TEQSA. (2017). *Good practice note: Addressing contract cheating to safeguard academic integrity*. https://www.teqsa.gov.au/latest-news/publications/good-practice-note-addressing-contract-cheating-safeguard-academic

TEQSA. (2020). *Substantiating contract cheating: A guide for investigators*. https://www.teqsa.gov.au/contract-cheating

TEQSA. (2021). *Substantiating contract cheating for symbol-dense, logical responses in any discipline, particularly mathematics*. https://www.teqsa.gov.au/contract-cheating

CHAPTER 13

"(Im)possible to Prove": Formalising Academic Judgement Evidence in Contract Cheating Cases Using Bibliographic Forensics

Cath Ellis, Ann M. Rogerson, David House, and Kane Murdoch

Introduction

There is a growing body of evidence attesting to the proportion of students who admit to engaging in contract cheating behaviours (see Bretag et al., 2019; Curtis & Clare, 2017; Curtis et al., 2022; Newton, 2018). But as

C. Ellis (✉)
School of the Arts and Media, Faculty of Arts, Design and Architecture, University of New South Wales, Sydney, NSW, Australia
e-mail: cath.ellis@unsw.edu.au

A. M. Rogerson
Faculty of Business and Law, University of Wollongong, Wollongong, NSW, Australia
e-mail: annr@uow.edu.au

Harper et al. (2021) point out "the rates of staff detection [...] seem incongruent with the rates of contract cheating reported by students" (p. 3). This low rate of detection is attracting media interest (see Denisova-Schmidt, 2019; Lee, 2019). As Dawson et al. (2019) explain: "websites selling contract cheating products [...] often claim that this form of cheating is undetectable" (p. 473; see also Lines, 2016; Rogerson, 2017). It is likely that incidents of contract cheating are being routinely suspected by academic teaching staff. In 2019, Harper et al. reported on a survey of academic teaching staff where just over two-thirds of respondents indicated that they had encountered at least one piece of assessment work that they suspected had been produced by someone other than the student but only half of them reported their concerns to an academic integrity decision maker (Harper et al., 2019). The dominant reason given (57.2%) was that they considered that contract cheating is impossible to prove (Harper et al., 2019).

This chapter contributes to the literature on contract cheating detection (see Clarke & Lancaster, 2007; Dawson et al., 2019; Dawson & Sutherland-Smith, 2018, 2019; Harper et al., 2021; Lines, 2016; Medway et al., 2018). It does so by considering the contribution academic staff can make by using an example of a particular domain of academic judgement: knowledge of the discipline area and the extant published literature on the topic. This is what Harper et al. refer to as "falsified or fictional references" (Harper et al., 2019, p. 1860) and Rogerson describes as "referencing and citation irregularities" (Rogerson, 2017, p. 3). We call this approach to contract cheating detection *bibliographic forensics*. We consider how academic judgement, in the form of bibliographic forensics, can contribute evidence to support contract cheating investigations.

D. House
University of New South Wales, Sydney, NSW, Australia
e-mail: david.house@unsw.edu.au

K. Murdoch
Macquarie University, Macquarie Park, NSW, Australia
e-mail: kane.murdoch@mq.edu.au

Identifying Contract Cheating

There are now several resources available to assist academic teaching staff to improve their ability to identify incidents of contract cheating. Rogerson (2017) identified a range of patterns and clues that are "evident in sections of body text and reference materials to identify irregularities" (p. 1). The two-year Contract Cheating and Assessment Design project adapted Rogerson's work along with a rubric developed by Felicity Prentice to create a guide to substantiating contract cheating (*Impossible to Prove? Substantiating Contract Cheating*, n.d.). Dawson has also produced a guide to assist academic markers (Dawson, n.d.).

Even with increasing research and these helpful resources, perceptions regarding the difficulty or impossibility of proving cases continue to prevail. Dawson and Sutherland-Smith (2018) provide an important reminder that "detection of contract cheating is not the same as successful prosecution of contract cheating" (p. 292). We propose clearer distinctions between the different stages of the detection process and suggest clear terminology to employ for those stages. We propose the term *incident* to refer to a situation in which contract cheating has occurred, regardless of whether it has been detected or not, and the term *suspicion* to refer to an academic marker having strong enough concerns that the student has not done some or all of the work themselves to warrant at least contemplating referring the incident to an academic integrity decision maker. We use the term *detection* to refer to a situation whereby an allegation of contract cheating has been upheld by an academic integrity decision maker.

The Role of Academic Judgement

A theme that runs throughout the detection literature is the role that academic judgement can play in providing evidence of sufficient probative value to support and uphold allegations of contract cheating. To return to the survey of academic teaching staff, six of the eight most common signals identified by staff who reported suspected incidents of contract cheating were a product of their academic judgement (Harper et al., 2019 p. 1860). Similarly, Rogerson's method for successful identification, examination, evaluation and confirmation of contract cheating emphasises paying attention to things that rely on academic judgement (Rogerson, 2017).

In this chapter we advocate for better recognition of the value of academic judgement and the role it can and, we argue, *should* play in the investigation and determination of incidents of contract cheating. In short, the purpose of this chapter is to propose how an academic's gut feeling that a student may not have done some or all of their assessment work themselves can contribute to a body of evidence of high probative value. This chapter proposes a partnership model between academic staff (on one side) and dedicated, specialist professional staff (on the other) as ideal. In this model, both partners bring specific skills, expertise and resources to the relationship and to their shared endeavour. Specialist professional staff in dedicated roles who have the remit to investigate academic misconduct referrals contribute administrative decision-making expertise alongside a detailed knowledge of institutional ordinances. They also draw on their experience of investigating how students make integrity mistakes (and conceal them) across different disciplines. They cannot, however, be expected to possess more than a passing knowledge of all subjects taught by their institution. On the other side of the partnership, academic staff (including casually employed teachers) should not be expected to know the fine details of academic misconduct procedures, but there is a wealth and depth of academic knowledge that only they can hold. Most obvious are:

- knowing the course learning design, content and the resources available to students undertaking it,
- knowing the discipline area and the extant published literature on the topic, and
- knowing the students and what is typically produced by them in the course of study.

Academic teaching staff are the eyes and ears on the ground; they interact with the students and are responsible for marking their assessable work. We now turn to consider specifically how the role that academic judgement can play in the investigation of contract cheating cases can be strengthened and formalised through the use of bibliographic forensics.

Bibliographic Forensics

We agree with Rogerson (2017) that analysing patterns and variations in how information is used and cited within and across work submitted by the same student can contribute valuable evidence to contract cheating investigations. As Rogerson infers, bibliographies and references in student assessment work are a rich source of information that can both trigger suspicion and contribute to a brief of evidence. She explores referencing and citation irregularities that, for various reasons, provide clues that should raise suspicion amongst academic teaching staff and presents them in a table. In this chapter, we build upon Rogerson's previous work in three ways. Firstly, we add to the explanations and examples that she provides for existing categories. Secondly, we add new categories to her table to provide an even more comprehensive list (Rogerson offers 9 categories and we extend it to 12). Thirdly, we add an additional column that offers some guidance on how referrals can be drafted and thereby can contribute to a brief of evidence. We present this in tabular form that augments Rogerson's original table. We distinguish between the information provided in Rogerson's original with unitalicised font and the additions we have made here in italicised font. The 12 categories we provide are not intended to be a template, although many academics may find bibliographic forensics to be a useful set of tools to start drafting referrals themselves (Table 13.1).

Discussion

The imperative to assure successful investigations of suspected incidents of contract cheating cannot be overstated. By 'successful' here, of course, we refer to investigation outcomes that correctly identify false positives while also keeping false negatives to a minimum. The unacceptable amount of damage that false positives inevitably do to the lives of falsely accused students goes without saying (see Ellis et al., 2020, p. 141). But false negatives create their own kind of damage in that they can generate discontent in academic staff who have invested time and effort in raising their concerns. This is in addition to the fact that students who have not undertaken their work with integrity are receiving credit for work and learning that they have not done themselves.

As suggested above, for our proposed partnership model to be effective, both partners need to bring their respective skills and expertise to the

Table 13.1 Bibliographic categories, explanations and examples with exemplar rationale

Category	Explanation/example	Exemplar rationale
1. Reference list provided without any in-text citations and/or direct quotation	Where a reference list is included without any in-text citations in the body text, there is no relationship between the sources and the use of sources. This may also indicate that a reference list has been borrowed from somewhere else and just placed at the end of the assessment task. It could also be driven by a perception that low or no text matches in a similarity report are a desirable outcome.	"My review of this paper reveals the student has failed to reference the sources in their bibliography throughout their paper. This is inconsistent with the assessment brief and other work submitted by the student. In my academic judgement, without reasonable explanation, this raises concerns that the student did not produce this assessment."
2. Reference list and in-text citations do not match	There is no relationship or correlation between the reference list and in-text citations. Usually an indicator of the body text being borrowed from another source, and placed with a reference list from another source.	"My comparison of the bibliography and the in-text citations in this paper reveals that they do not match each other. This is very unusual in my academic experience marking papers. In my view, it is possible that the student has tried to overstate the research they've done in preparing this work, or worse, that it is evidence that the student did not produce the work."
3. Inappropriate sources	Sources in the reference list may include sources such as sites selling essays (such as UK Essays) and example or sample assignments. In these cases the student has included the source information but does not understand that these are inappropriate sources to use.	"The references cited in this paper include websites which are, at best, file/assessment sharing services, and include services which sell papers students submit as their own. While it is possible the student simply does not appreciate this source material is inappropriate in an academic paper, this is also evidence that they have engaged with a website known for producing contract cheated work."
4. Irrelevant and fabricated sources	There may be entries in the reference list that are not relevant to the discipline, assessment topic or subject matter. The passage in the main body of the text has nothing to do with the information in the paper cited/referenced. References that have been made up. References that are used inappropriately. For example: an assessment on the cross-cultural concept of power distance (Hofstede, 1980) had a reference included on 'switchable distance-based impedance matching networks' that is electrical power distance. A novel being used to cite factual information.	"My review of this student's paper reveals several references that are not academically relevant to the topic. Having taught classes in this discipline for X study periods, it is also my academic judgement that no reasonable student reading/reviewing this source material, would mistake it for something relevant to the assessment task. In my view, it is possible that the student has tried to overstate the research they've done in preparing this work, or worse, that it is evidence that they did not produce the work."

5. Does not meet referencing/ bibliographic criteria requirements set for the assessment task Or far exceeds implicit bibliographic requirements.	Set criteria may include: Minimum/maximum number of references Type of references (journals/books/websites) Use of specific references/seminal papers/particular authors Date range of eligible references (e.g. post-2000 only) Observing where students do not meet the criteria provides another clue or observation point. Where a specific number of references was not required but the number in the bibliography far exceeds what is normally expected for a paper of this type/length. For example: where students are required to use journal articles from the year 2000 onwards and the reference list shows books from the 1980s this may be an indicator of using an old textbook as the source of their writing/references. It could be an indication that writers are using old references to avoid matches in Turnitin. This may also be an indicator that an order has been placed on a contract cheating site where the number of references can be stipulated. The student who has placed the order is unsure of what an appropriate volume of references would be and assumes that a large number gives an appearance of better quality scholarship.	"In my review of this paper I found it unusual that there were so few references for a paper of this level of sophistication. In my experience of marking this assessment over three terms, other student work submitted in this course of similar quality and sophistication normally have at least three times as many references as this one. At best this student has not cited the materials they have relied upon to compose this paper. Worse this may be evidence that the student did not write the paper." "Having reviewed this paper I was struck by the large volume of resources in the bibliography. For a paper of this length (xxxx words) I would normally expect to see no more than yy references. This paper has four times that amount. The fact that only half of them are directly cited in the main body of the paper makes me concerned that the student has overstated the research they've done in preparing this work, or worse, that it is evidence that they did not produce the work."
6. Access date on the internet/ dates on internet sources	A reference list entry for the current year with an access date of an older year should be noted as an irregularity, particularly where it is outside the student's candidature, or matches to the assignment due dates of a previous instance of the subject.	"The following references included in this student's bibliography show an access date which does not correspond with the current study period: [Reference A Reference B etc.] In my view, this is strong evidence that they have copied some of this paper from the work of another student or, worse, that they did not write the paper at all."

(continued)

Table 13.1 (continued)

Category	Explanation/example	Exemplar rationale
7. Presentation of references in foreign languages particularly where unrelated to the students' background Resources that are unavailable	While some students may include references from articles studied at other institutions, presentation of references unrelated to the student are worth noting. For example: An international student from South East Asia presented four references in Polish, referencing a Polish institution in Warsaw. Two were seminal papers available in English and referred to in class. The student had purchased essays written by someone in Poland, but due to poor English language skills did not review what they had purchased and did not detect the discrepancy. Reference to a Los Angeles Times article in the bibliography that included 'page unavailable in your region' as part of the reference.	"During my review of this paper I noted the student had referenced [Reference A]. This source material was one I'd never previously seen in running this subject and when I obtained a copy, it could only be acquired in a foreign language. In my view, unless the student can show that they read/speak this language, it is likely that they have tried to overstate the research they've done in preparing this work, or worse, that it is evidence that the student did not produce the work."
8. Old dated references linked to contemporary organisations or recent concepts/ findings	For example: A reference dated 1965 but citing Microsoft as the company being researched. A reference dated before a discovery took place or a theory published.	"My review of this student's paper reveals several references that are not logically possible. For instance there is a source referring to the use of [a technology] which has a publication date [x] years earlier than [the technology] was invented. While this may be a simple error on the part of the student it may be evidence that the student has overstated the research they've done in preparing this work, or worse, it may be evidence that the student did not produce the work."

| 9. Bibliographic 'mashups'/ Altered dates | A mix of bibliographic information (books, journals, news articles) within the one reference entry For example: Tribune, H. (2008) Engineering leadership and Anticipation in Australia. *Journal of Economy, Australia: Queensland Edition.* The journal does not exist, there are no state-based editions of journals and Tribune H ended up being the Herald Tribune. This particular example was sourced by the student from a student file-sharing site. The sharing site was located through a Google search. References in a bibliography are forward dated, for example, by ten years, saying the date of publication is 2013 but the resource was actually published in 2003. This can mean the source is not detected by Turnitin but makes the bibliography appear up-to-date. | "My review of the references the student used in this paper reveals that many either do not exist or have been altered to, for example, change the date from X to Y. You can see this on the Turnitin report where the dates are the only portions of the bibliography that are not matched to other sources. The consistency of these mistakes makes it unlikely to be mere typographical error. In my view, the likelier explanation is that the author has fabricated/altered these references to artificially deflate the Turnitin similarity score while appearing to be current or worse still that the student is not the author of this work." |
| 10. Unique or specific bibliographic markers | Proquest account IDs that are irregular and/or that do not match the institutional ID number. Every document downloaded from ProQuest from an institutional library includes an ID number that is unique to that library account. This appears in a bibliography if a referencing tool (e.g., Zotero) has been used to write the bibliography. If more than one account ID appears in a student's bibliography, it is evident that these resources have been accessed from more than one library. | "My review of the bibliography in this student's paper reveals that multiple ProQuest accounts have been used to obtain the source material. This is demonstrated by the varying proquest account IDs that appear in the references. The library has advised me that our institution's ProQuest ID number is [XXXXXX]. Since our students have free access to ProQuest through the library, I am concerned that the student may have acquired reference material inappropriately or worse that this is evidence that the student did not produce this work." |

(continued)

Table 13.1 (continued)

Category	Explanation/example	Exemplar rationale
11. Use of multiple referencing tools	Different referencing tools or systems being used within a paper: for example, footnotes being placed by using both the Microsoft word footnote tool and being typed in manually. Use of Microsoft citation manager being used for some references and not others. Different referencing tools or systems being used across multiple papers: for example, evidence of Mendeley, Zotero, Endnote, Microsoft Word citation manager in an earlier paper in the course and a later paper showing evidence of these not being used now.	"My review of this student's paper reveals that the author has employed multiple referencing tools within this paper. For example [Reference A] has most likely been copy/pasted from the library website into the document, while other references have been populated using Endnote. In my academic judgement, this is inconsistent and unusual. I have also reviewed two other papers this student has submitted in the same study period. One of those papers shows no signs of the use of a referencing tool, and the other has used a referencing tool consistently throughout. It is my academic opinion that this level of inconsistency, within and across these assessments, make it likely that the student is not the true author of some or all of these pieces of work."
12. Use of paraphrasing tools or sites	Turnitin showing partial matches in the bibliography with certain words replaced with similes in titles, journal names, for example, Global instead of International, Dynamic instead of Active. Author names in the main body or references changed to similes, for example, Geoff Crisp changed to Geoff Fresh. (see Rogerson & McCarthy, 2017)	"The following references included in this student's bibliography show that some words have been replaced in bibliographic data: [Reference A Reference B etc.] In my view, this is evidence that, at best, they have taken some or all of the material in this paper from another source and processed it through a paraphrasing tool or article spinner. At worst, it may be evidence that this student has not done some or all of this work themself."

relationship. To explain what that can look like in practice, we hypothesise that noticing an irregularity in a student's bibliography and/or referencing (such as those listed in our table) will in many cases provide a first point of suspicion or concern for an academic marker. The inevitable question that arises once that suspicion has been aroused is 'now what?' In our partnership model, the next step is for an academic staff member to refer their concerns to a professional staff investigation. But to do their job well, investigators need something tangible with which to work. We now turn to outline three key principles to achieve this outcome and propose how these principles can guide an academic staff member as they frame and organise their observations in a referral.

The first principle is that the information should be presented in a scholarly way such that all assertions based on academic judgement must be supported with evidence. In other words, just as an academic would represent their scholarly findings in a research paper, so too should they present their academic judgement in an academic misconduct referral. For instance, an assertion that 'this work contains fabricated references' needs to be accompanied by specific references to where this has occurred in the student's submitted work and evidence of the fabrication. In other words, it is not enough for an academic to feel suspicious; they should explain *why* they are and provide evidence to support their assertions. Importantly, this can and should draw on their experience. To inform what is the most probable explanation for their concerns, the referral should develop two hypotheses of what has happened: one if the facts are construed most favourably for the student, and the other where the facts are construed least favourably. This gives the investigator—and eventually the decision maker—a range of what is possible and thereby allows them to better answer the question of what is most probable.

The second principle is to get both the volume and validity of academic-judgement evidence right. On the one extreme, saying nothing more than 'this student could not have done this work' does not provide investigators with sufficient information. On the other extreme, academic staff should be dissuaded from investing time analysing aspects of students' submissions that do not rely on their academic judgement. Getting the balance of volume and validity right avoids providing too little evidence, on the one hand, or too much of the wrong type of evidence, on the other.

The final principle is one that is possibly the most difficult for academic staff to uphold: their academic-judgement evidence should be as objective, factual and dispassionate as possible. In our experience of referring and investigating contract cheating cases, we have frequently observed academic staff feeling personally affronted when a student engages in contract cheating behaviours in their class. While this reaction is understandable, allowing an emotive response into the discourse of the referral is unhelpful.

Following these three principles ensures that an assessment of a student's submissions by an academic will produce a piece of formal, discipline-appropriate, advice. Of course, a referral based on academic judgement—even when it is well supported with evidence—remains an opinion. But it constitutes a much more valuable opinion, when viewed from an evidentiary perspective, than suspicions without context. It is always important to remember that any decisions being made are done against a standard of proof which is 'balance of probability'.

The partnership model we propose—whereby professional expertise works in partnership with academic judgement—brings the twin benefits of efficacy and efficiency. Encouraging professional and academic colleagues to work together and to use their strengths allows them to share the workload and emotional burdens that inevitably accompany contract cheating matters. The partnership model represents a level of institutional maturity that is expected by our myriad stakeholders and allows us to continue to uphold the value which we should all hold most dear: our institutional academic integrity.

Conclusions

We conclude with observations about the approach we recommend in this chapter. Our first observation is that it is frequently difficult if not impossible to uphold an allegation based on one student submission alone. We advocate for an approach that considers other (and where possible all) submissions made by that student to the institution for assessment. This achieves two key objectives: firstly, it allows a wider body of evidence to be gathered and makes it more likely that improbable patterns of behaviour within and between student submissions may be observed; and secondly, it makes it more likely that other incidents of contract cheating behaviour are not being missed, thereby reducing the proportion of false negatives. Our second observation is that there will always be a range of ways to build a case depending on the discipline. Knowing, looking for and identifying markers that should trigger suspicion that are relevant to a particular discipline is a skill that all academic teaching staff should bring to their teaching practice. This is especially true for the example we have explored in this chapter—bibliographic forensics—which is, for instance, likely to be differently useful in 'STEM' and 'HASS' disciplines. Our third observation is that all briefs of evidence should be drafted with their ultimate 'audience' in mind. When a decision maker can better understand the reasoning behind a particular type of academic opinion (such as one derived from bibliographic forensics), this reasoning becomes accepted by those decision makers, thereby making it more likely that a suspected instance of contract cheating can go from 'impossible to prove' to 'proven'.

References

Bretag, T., Harper, R., Burton, M., Ellis, C., Newton, P., Rozenberg, P., Saddiqui, S., & van Haeringen, K. (2019). Contract cheating: A survey of Australian university students. *Studies in Higher Education, 44*(11), 1837–1856. https://doi.org/10.1080/03075079.2018.1462788

Clarke, R., & Lancaster, T. (2007). Establishing a systematic six-stage process for detecting contract cheating. *2nd International Conference on Pervasive Computing and Applications*, 342–347. https://doi.org/10.1109/ICPCA.2007.4365466

Curtis, G. J., & Clare, J. (2017). How prevalent is contract cheating and to what extent are students repeat offenders? *Journal of Academic Ethics, 15*(2), 115–124. https://doi.org/10.1007/s10805-017-9278-x

Curtis, G. J., McNeill, M., Slade, C., Tremayne, K., Harper, R., Rundle, K., & Greenaway, R. (2022). Moving beyond self-reports to estimate the prevalence of commercial contract cheating: An Australian study. *Studies in Higher Education, 47*(9), 1844–1856. https://doi.org/10.1080/03075079.2021.1972093

Dawson, P. (n.d.). Online learning good practice: The prevention of contract cheating in an online environment. *TEQSA*. https://www.teqsa.gov.au/sites/default/files/prevention-contract-cheating-in-online-environment-web.pdf?v=1587691121

Dawson, P., & Sutherland-Smith, W. (2018). Can markers detect contract cheating? Results from a pilot study. *Assessment & Evaluation in Higher Education, 43*(2), 286–293. https://doi.org/10.1080/02602938.2017.1336746

Dawson, P., & Sutherland-Smith, W. (2019). Can training improve marker accuracy at detecting contract cheating? A multi-disciplinary pre-post study. *Assessment & Evaluation in Higher Education, 44*(5), 715–725. https://doi.org/10.1080/02602938.2018.1531109

Dawson, P., Sutherland-Smith, W., & Ricksen, M. (2019). Can software improve marker accuracy at detecting contract cheating? A pilot study of the Turnitin authorship investigate alpha. *Assessment & Evaluation in Higher Education, 0*(0), 1–10. https://doi.org/10.1080/02602938.2019.1662884.

Denisova-Schmidt, E. (2019, April 20). What can universities do to stop students cheating? *University World News.* https://www.universityworldnews.com/post.php?story=20190415143459825

Ellis, C., van Haeringen, K., & House, D. (2020). Technology, policy and research: Establishing evidentiary standards for managing contract cheating cases. A research agenda for academic integrity. https://www.elgaronline.com/view/edcoll/9781789903768/9781789903768.00017.xml

Harper, R., Bretag, T., Ellis, C., Newton, P., Rozenberg, P., Saddiqui, S., & van Haeringen, K. (2019). Contract cheating: A survey of Australian university staff. *Studies in Higher Education, 44*(11), 1857–1873. https://doi.org/10.1080/03075079.2018.1462789

Harper, R., Bretag, T., & Rundle, K. (2021). Detecting contract cheating: Examining the role of assessment type. *Higher Education Research & Development, 40*(2), 263–278. https://doi.org/10.1080/07294360.2020.1724899

Impossible to prove? Substantiating contract cheating. (n.d.). Contract cheating and assessment design. https://cheatingandassessment.edu.au/wp-content/uploads/2018/07/EDUCATOR-RESOURCE-Substantiating-contract-cheating.pdf

Lee, G. (2019). FactCheck: Universities catch less than one per cent of 'bought in' essays, own records suggest. *Channel 4 News.* https://www.channel4.com/news/factcheck/factcheck-universities-catch-less-than-one-per-cent-of-bought-in-essays-own-records-suggest

Lines, L. (2016). Ghostwriters guaranteeing grades? The quality of online ghostwriting services available to tertiary students in Australia. *Teaching in Higher Education, 21*(8), 889–914. https://doi.org/10.1080/13562517.2016.1198759

Medway, D., Roper, S., & Gillooly, L. (2018). Contract cheating in UK higher education: A covert investigation of essay mills. *British Educational Research Journal, 44*(3), 393–418. https://doi.org/10.1002/berj.3335

Newton, P. M. (2018). How common is commercial contract cheating in higher education and is it increasing? A systematic review. *Frontiers in Education, 3.* https://doi.org/10.3389/feduc.2018.00067.

Rogerson, A. M. (2017). Detecting contract cheating in essay and report submissions: Process, patterns, clues and conversations. *International Journal for Educational Integrity, 13*(1), 1–17. https://doi.org/10.1007/s40979-017-0021-6

Rogerson, A. M., & McCarthy, G. (2017). Using Internet based paraphrasing tools: Original work, patchwriting or facilitated plagiarism? *International Journal for Educational Integrity, 13*(2), 2–15. https://doi.org/10.1007/s40979-016-0013-y

CHAPTER 14

Aligning Academic Quality and Standards with Academic Integrity

Irene Glendinning

INTRODUCTION

Few people would argue with the premise that if an educational institution has a problem with academic integrity, the standards and quality of their educational provision will be compromised. For example, if students who are avoiding learning by resorting to contract cheating, or bribing their way through school or university, are allowed to progress and ultimately graduate, then the educational standards of the institution, and its reputation, will become seriously undermined.

To address threats such as these, schools, colleges, and universities should develop a holistic institution-wide strategic approach to the assurance of quality and standards, underpinned by educational, academic and research ethics and integrity, as appropriate to their educational function and mission. However, research that I conducted demonstrates that very few countries and institutions have wide-ranging strategies approaching this ideal (Glendinning et al., 2019).

I. Glendinning (✉)
Coventry University, Coventry, UK
e-mail: ireneg@coventry.ac.uk

In this chapter, I first explore available evidence about what strategies for quality and standards educational institutions (schools, colleges, universities) are expected to adopt in different parts of the world, and to what extent these are aligned with academic integrity, and specifically addressing contract cheating. I then propose a framework for national guidance and holistic institutional compliance, which provides the necessary strategic integration of academic quality, standards and integrity, together with suggestions for how this should be implemented and applied to contract cheating.

Evidence Linking Quality Assurance and Academic Integrity

QA and Integrity from CIQG Research Results

In research I conducted with two colleagues on behalf of the Council for Higher Educational Accreditation's International Quality Group (CIQG), 64/69 questionnaire participants, who were either networks or reputable agencies responsible for external accreditation and quality assurance in different countries around the world, said that student assessment was central ($n = 34$), important ($n = 26$) or moderately important ($n = 4$) to their organisation (Glendinning et al., 2019).

Despite these responses, when asked about "contract cheating/use of essay mills/ghost-writing of [student] assignments", only 19/69 participants expressed either minor concerns (8), serious concerns (8) or thought this was a "major problem" (3) (Glendinning et al., 2019, p. 18). When asked about their concerns on "the proliferation of contract cheating companies" only 15 respondents expressed either minor concerns (7), serious concerns (6) or thought this was a major problem (2) (Glendinning et al., 2019, p. 18). Questions about plagiarism and cheating in exams generated a slightly higher rate of concerns, at 25/69 and 22/69 responses, respectively (see Fig. 14.1 for more detail). Questions about corruption in other aspects of higher education (regulation of higher education, teaching, admissions and recruitment, credentials and qualifications, research and academic publishing) yielded far fewer expressions of concern than those about student assessment.

The above results, plus additional feedback from respondents, suggest there is a high degree of complacency or denial about serious threats to

CORRUPTION IN ASSESSMENT

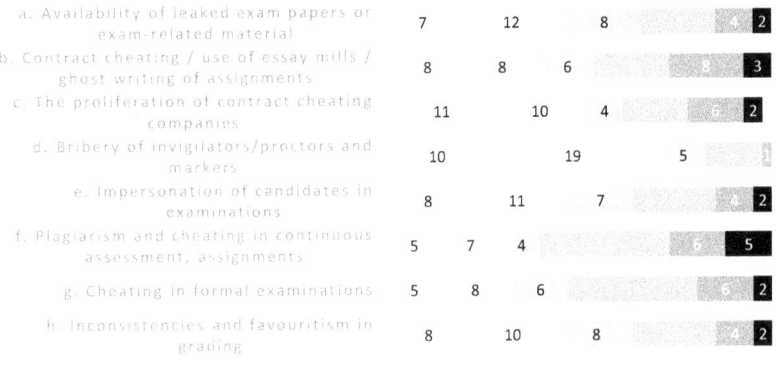

Fig. 14.1 CIQG project—Concerns from AQABs about corruption in student assessment, n = 69 (Glendinning, I., Orim, S., & King, A. (2019). Policies and Actions of Accreditation and Quality Assurance Bodies to Counter Corruption in Higher Education, published by CHEA/CIQG, 2019, p. 18: https://www.chea.org/quality-assurance-combatting-academic-corruption-resources)

academic integrity by many quality assurances and accreditation bodies (AQABs). I will next focus on examples of progress in three geographical regions: Europe, Australia and the USA.

QA and Integrity in the European Higher Education Area

The European Network of Quality Assurance set out expectations for how higher education (HE) institutions and quality assurance (QA) agencies operating in the European Higher Education Area (EHEA) should respond to academic quality and standards, encapsulated in this statement:

> Institutions should have a policy for quality assurance that is made public and forms part of their strategic management. Internal stakeholders should develop and implement this policy through appropriate structures and processes, while involving external stakeholders. (ENQA, 2015, p. 11)

This document includes four references to integrity. The first mention relates to institutional QA policies, in which "the institutional context and its strategic approach" should support "academic integrity and freedom and [be] vigilant against academic fraud" and involve "external stakeholders in quality assurance" (ENQA, 2015, p. 11).

The other three references to integrity relate to the professional integrity of the external agencies and agents themselves. Therefore, all HE institutions in EHEA countries should have both external oversight and institutional quality assurance policies that support academic integrity and challenge "academic fraud". Also, QA agencies operating in Europe need to take measures to safeguard their own standards and integrity.

An evaluation of compliance with the European Standards and Guidelines (ESG) was recently conducted on behalf of the European Commission (AIT & Bischof, 2019). In 57 interviews with "national authorities and quality assurance agencies" from EHEA countries the researchers' study found that while most QA agencies were confident that they were complying with the ESG, there were "differences in compliance among national QA systems based on their maturity" (AIT & Bischof, 2019, Executive Summary, p. 5). The survey also included responses from 1551 HE institutions, from 41 countries (AIT & Bischof, 2019, p. 17).

The evaluation report only mentions academic integrity once, specifically concerning Ukraine: "The development of effective internal QA systems [in Ukraine] is hindered by a lack of academic integrity, nepotism, corruption and rent seeking, low wages and the quality of teaching staff, and lack of investment in many Ukrainian HE institutions" (AIT & Bischof, 2019, p. 51).

This report refers to cross-border regulation by international QA agencies, requiring them to be listed on the European Quality Assurance Register (EQAR). The report gives some reassurance of progress since 2015 in developing internal and external QA systems across the EHEA, tempered by exceptions to this rule, including these:

- "the full integration of QA in the daily work within HE institutions is still a significant challenge in many countries, for example, Portugal, Malta, Cyprus, Bulgaria, Italy and Czech Republic" (AIT & Bischof, 2019, p. 31).
- 7% of HEI survey respondents, mainly from France (15) and Spain (24), had no QA strategy or plans to develop one (AIT & Bischof, 2019).

- In some countries the established policies are "not necessarily followed by staff", with examples: Italy, Bulgaria, Malta and the Czech Republic (AIT & Bischof, 2019, p. 29).
- In Bulgaria all HE providers have QA strategies, but for some "they exist mainly as a formality" (AIT & Bischof, 2019, p. 29).

The 2019 evaluation makes no mention of progress on implementing policies for academic integrity within institutional QA strategies.

The Bologna Process, which started in 1999, aims to harmonise standards and provision of HE across Europe. This statement comes from a recent communique: "Academic freedom and integrity, institutional autonomy, participation of students and staff in HE governance, and public responsibility for and of HE form the backbone of the EHEA" (EACEA, 2020, p. 158). This statement provides hope that the message has not been lost completely for Europe.

European funding has supported many research projects about academic integrity, including the highly successful European Network for Academic Integrity (ENAI, n.d.), through the European Commission, Council of Europe and national research councils. The 2019 evaluation of the ESG suggests scope for more research and development in Europe, especially towards integrating academic integrity, quality and standards.

QA and Academic Integrity in Australia

In the CIQG research Australia's Tertiary Education Quality and Standards Authority (TEQSA) expressed both interest in and concerns about most forms of corruption included in the questionnaire (Glendinning et al., 2019). TEQSA, in conjunction with the government and HE institutions in Australia, has taken action, over many years, to address some serious threats to integrity, including contract cheating, irregularities in admissions and sexual harassment.

Australia has an abundance of dedicated academic integrity researchers, with relatively easy access to research funding, due to the gravity attached to corruption and malpractice and to ensure that the quality, standards and reputation of their HE provision remain high.

The focus on integrity in Australia greatly intensified in 2014 after the "MyMaster scandal" (McNeilage & Visentin, 2014), followed by a shocking video from the Australian Broadcasting Corporation called "Degrees of Deception" (ABC, 2015; Besser & Cronau, 2015). This example demonstrates the power of investigative journalism to reveal corruption, in this case unethical admissions agents, admissions fraud, bribery, contract cheating and fraud in English language testing for international applicants to Australian universities. This was a shock to the entire Australian HE sector and a catalyst for change. The impact on Australia led to innovative research and many scholarly publications (including Bretag et al., 2019; Curtis et al., 2022; Dawson and Sutherland-Smith, 2018; Rogerson, 2017; Sutherland-Smith & Dullaghan, 2019), which in turn have had a profound influence on academic integrity in other parts of the world.

The introduction of Australian legislation against contract cheating in 2018 was the culmination of combined efforts by researchers, the HE sector, TEQSA and the government. Similar legislation was introduced in the Republic of Ireland in 2019 and in England in 2022. Austria introduced legislation banning essay mills in 2018 and early in 2022 Ukraine was planning their own legislative response.

QA and Academic Integrity in the USA

Academic integrity in the USA has been led by pioneers such as Donald McCabe (2016) and ongoing initiatives from the International Center for Academic Integrity (ICAI, n.d.). In my view, US HE providers are not at the forefront of good practice in quality assurance or systematically making connections between QA and academic integrity, compared to some other parts of the world. The concept of external scrutiny in the USA is usually about the distribution of grants and funding to HE providers or subject-based audits, rather than promoting academic standards and integrity.

The "Varsity Blues" sports admissions scandal had not emerged when we completed the CIQG research, but we did mention sports scholarships that made this scam possible (Glendinning et al., 2019), whereby underqualified students are routinely admitted to prestigious US universities on the basis of their sporting prowess, then allegedly given an easy ride on the academic requirements so they can remain in the varsity team (Downes, 2017). The common practice of preferential admission to the university for children of alumni, wealthy donors and politicians (Downes, 2017) implies that, given suitable contacts, the "Varsity Blues" parents could have followed this traditional but equally corrupt approach, without the need for bribing agents and faking sporting skills.

More positively, the USA is one of the few parts of the world where "academic integrity" is understood and part of the vocabulary in pre-university settings, often introduced through a similar "honour code" honesty system for students that is used in HE.

ACADEMIC INTEGRITY STRATEGIES

A high-level strategy for academic integrity in HE establishes the overarching priorities within an institution, which could be focused on punishment, deterrence or education. I agree with Bertram Gallant and Stephens (2020) who strongly recommend adopting an educational approach.

In the following discussion, input from government is presented first, then the role of QA agencies, followed by institutional strategies.

Government Input to Educational QA and Academic Integrity

The role of local or national government should be to ensure there are mechanisms in place to balance the needs to direct, guide, monitor, regulate and support institutions, while not overly encroaching on their autonomy for self-governance and identity at institutional levels.

Many governments delegate the responsibility for oversight of education to one or more regulatory bodies, typically quality assurance and accreditation bodies. In some countries, such as Russia, India, Spain and the Czech Republic, an external attestation committee or similar body, rather than the university, is responsible for confirming certain awards and appointments, particularly doctorate, habilitation or professorship, which is viewed by many experts in HE governance as encroaching on institutional autonomy.

External QA and Academic Integrity

An international network of QA bodies has developed a toolkit, which includes the characteristics of "An effective academic integrity framework" (INQAAHE et al., 2020). Stakeholders consist of government, QA agencies, management, staff, students and employers, surrounded by four elements: Policies and procedures, Recording and reporting, Cycle of improvement and Education for staff and students (INQAAHE et al., 2020, p. 7). The toolkit defines four dimensions of an external quality assurance process: Analysis, Assessment, Intervention and Education

(INQAAHE et al., 2020). In essence, the external QA should be designed to check whether the internal QA is appropriately established and operating as intended, rather than just viewed by either side as a box-ticking exercise. External QA input to an institution should be about "quality enhancement", to identify any weaknesses that can undermine institutional quality and standards, especially relating to academic integrity, so that timely improvements can be made.

The CIQG research confirmed that, even if AQABs are alert to the prospect of corruption and malpractice, their modus operandi means they are unlikely to uncover evidence of this in their routine oversight of institutions (Glendinning et al., 2019), typically involving a self-evaluation report or an institutional visit, with access to the institutional audit-trail of documentation. Institutions have ample opportunities to hide away any skeletons they may have, even allowing for an impromptu visit. The remit of an AQAB may be limited to exploring institutional policies, curricula and assessment methods, but the literature demonstrates that corruption can occur in a broader range of HE operational functions.

Our recommendations to QA bodies included the need to find alternative ways to uncover serious problems in governance and operations, or proactively explore any suggestions of impropriety (Glendinning et al., 2019).

The regulator for HE in England, the Office for Students (OFS), has recently conducted a review of the "reportable events" for education providers (OFS, 2020). As part of the quality monitoring process, all English HE providers are required to report certain types of events and evidence to the regulator. However, no mention was included of the need to report breaches to "integrity" or corruption and only one mention of "misconduct", specifically referring to "harassment and sexual misconduct" (OFS, 2020, p. 34).

On a more positive note, several AQABs are taking action. For example, Quality and Qualifications Ireland (QQI) has established a network of institutional representatives and a national panel of experts to assist institutions in developing their strategies and policies on academic integrity. The UK's QAA established a national Advisory Group on academic integrity in 2016, which has strong connections internationally on research into contract cheating. TEQSA provides effective leadership for the Australian HE sector, involving the researchers and experts in research and development (Curtis et al., 2022). All these QA agencies provide freely downloadable guidance and advice on a range of topics relating to contract cheating, addressing corruption and encouraging academic integrity (QAA, n.d.; QQI, n.d.; TEQSA, n.d.).

These organisations regularly work together and network internationally to share intelligence and good practice, which is an excellent way of disseminating advances and experiences in one country or region with a wide range of other countries. There could also be great benefits from initiating vertical networking, typically when HE QA bodies share their experiences with QA agencies concerned with non-university education, but there are very few examples of this type of cooperation.

It is well understood that school children of all ages are very likely to plagiarise or cheat in other ways if their teachers and parents do not tell them it is wrong; we know that secondary pupils are regularly targeted by homework help companies (Creasey, 2021) and essay mills (Jeffreys & Main, 2018). However, input and guidance from external QA bodies on academic integrity at pre-university education levels are limited. This is an area in need of more focus and research.

Institutional Quality Assurance and Academic Integrity

It is the responsibility of every HE provider to safeguard academic quality, standards and integrity, whether or not there is external scrutiny. Any institutional strategy for academic integrity should be part of or strongly connected to the quality strategy, apply institution-wide and carry unequivocal support and adequate resourcing from the highest levels of management. The strategic ethos of integrity should be explicitly embedded in statements about the institutional mission, commitment, aims and objectives of the institution.

The committee structure, reporting and authorisation for changes, and membership should be inclusive of different sections of the community. In some countries, universities are managed in devolved ways, with diverse policies applying at faculty level or in research institutes. This model is prevalent in Western Balkan countries (Foltýnek et al., 2017), but even in such circumstances, a consistent, institution-wide approach should still be the aim.

If an institution is serious about academic integrity, they should make available in the public domain a clearly worded statement of strategy, especially leadership on academic integrity. UK's QAA recently went one stage further, following the lead of TEQSA in Australia, by introducing the Academic Integrity Charter (QAA, n.d.). The charter commits signatories

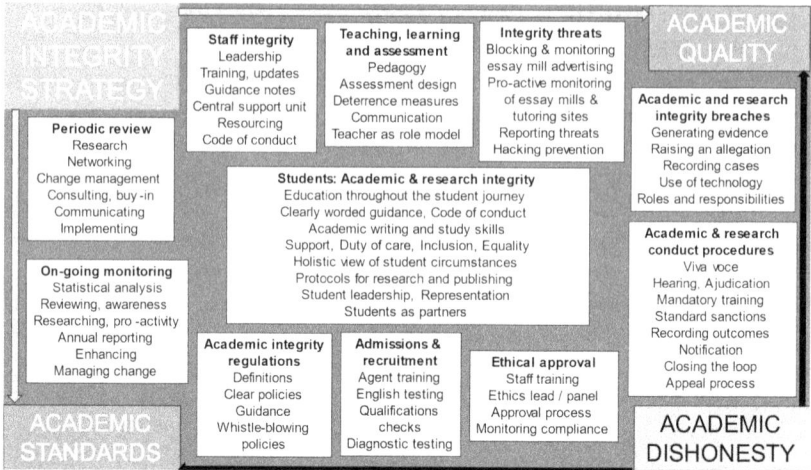

Fig. 14.2 Aligning institutional academic integrity strategy with quality and standards

to the Principles for Academic Integrity set out in Fig. 14.2. Member institutions were asked to sign the Charter, as a way of making a public commitment to their approach to academic integrity. Since it was published on 21 October 2020, over 200 institutions and other bodies have signed the Charter (QAA, n.d.—reflects a number of signatories on 8 August 2022). The QAA principles emphasise a holistic institutional approach, and engagement with and empowerment of both students and staff, encouraging them to take responsibility. The principles also advocate working with others in the sector as well as having consistent and effective policies.

The Charter was designed to complement guidance to HE providers on how to develop suitable policies to address contract cheating, coming from the perspective of a national agency responsible for quality and standards (QAA, 2020). The QAA guidance emphasises that taking action to address contract cheating applies to everyone, not just those with specialist roles relating to academic integrity.

The Academic Integrity Toolkit developed by a team from Australia (Bretag et al., 2020) provides guidance for HE providers about effective approaches to academic integrity, including the following characteristics of institutional policies:

- *Student engagement*
- *Robust decision-making systems*
- *Academic integrity education*
- *Academic integrity champions*
- *Record keeping for evaluation*
- *Regular review of policy and process*

The way QAA and TEQSA, together with other AQABs and networks, have guided and mobilised educational providers in their countries and beyond can serve as a model for HE regulators and QA bodies in other countries who are looking for inspiration on how to improve approaches to academic quality, standards and integrity. All the guidance acknowledges that students' views are an important element of the consultation and development process. There is also the need to conduct research, networking to share good practice and regularly update the guidance, as threats to integrity evolve and new threats emerge.

Towards a Framework on Academic Integrity Strategies and Policies

The toolkits, guidance, models and frameworks discussed so far provide a good starting point for developing a strategy. The framework I propose provides more detail about what policies should be included within an institutional academic integrity strategy and how to connect this to the institutional strategy on quality and standards. There are suggestions on how to refine these policies to address contract cheating. Figure 14.2 is the latest version of a framework, designed to encourage dialogue. This is still work-in-progress, and feedback is most welcome. The overarching strategic focus in this model is education.

The surrounding border of the diagram illustrates that a well-constructed institutional academic integrity strategy will have a positive impact on academic quality and standards. Conversely, failure to design and implement an effective strategy will risk the dominance of academic dishonesty, or worse, negative impacts on academic quality and standards. Within the border are 11 essential components required to create a well-balanced institutional response to academic integrity breaches.

Students: Academic and Research Integrity

Students and their education are central to the role of universities, colleges and schools, irrespective of the level of education. The power of students in supporting the academic integrity strategy cannot be overemphasised. In my experience, co-creation with students as partners and having students lead campaigns to promote the need for integrity can be especially valuable both for students and for the institution.

In this context, education includes appreciating institutional expectations and culture, consequences of making mistakes and developing the skills and knowledge in writing and study that are needed to progress and succeed. The education and training should not be a once-off event, on arrival or delivered through an academic integrity module. Instead, it should take place in the context of the study programme, at suitable points throughout the student journey.

Conversely, there is a need for support and guidance for students suspected of misconduct, irrespective of allegations against them, and to ensure they are treated fairly. A wide range of factors can influence student conduct, including previous education, family circumstances, health, disabilities and other personal problems. Although such factors should not constitute excuses for academic misconduct, an understanding of individual circumstances may influence the decision about what outcomes would be fair and appropriate for this specific student.

Integrity Threats

Finding suitable opportunities to open a dialogue with students about the many risks and dangers around contract cheating is an essential element of education about academic integrity. Students need to be made aware that when people rely on contract cheating, in any of its forms, they forfeit the moral right to graduate, because they have not demonstrated their own learning and achievements. Research by Bretag et al. (2019) suggest that many students do not appreciate how serious contract cheating is or the consequences of getting caught. In addition, they put themselves at the mercy of any ghostwriters or essay mills they used, who may disclose what they have done or share the student's personal data with other unscrupulous individuals and companies (Sutherland-Smith & Dullaghan, 2019; Yorke et al., 2020). Such threats will remain with the student forever. These are just a few of many powerful messages to students that should serve as disincentives to cheating.

Staff Integrity

Top left in Fig. 14.2 is about integrity by all staff, including institutional leaders, academic staff, administrative and professional support staff. Unfortunately, some academics do not set the required example to students, ranging from minor carelessness, such as forgetting to acknowledge sources, to more serious actions and forms of corruption, including helping students to cheat, demanding or accepting bribes or favours from students or their parents in return for admission or higher grades, or working for or operating essay mills. Unethical and corrupt behaviour of this nature by academic staff is particularly difficult to uncover and prove, but having a carefully designed and well-publicised whistle-blowing policy can help. There is a need to protect the identity of informers to encourage them to report their concerns, but to remain aware of the possibility of false and vindictive accusations.

Unethical conduct by a member of (academic or other) staff within an educational institution should be handled through a different process than the academic or ethical misconduct by students, because there are broader implications for staff about their professionalism, fitness and competence to practise in their staff role and whether they can be trusted. Whatever the local policies, it is important that the related procedures are clearly defined, accessible and transparent.

The latest QAA guidance (2020) advocates establishing a central academic integrity office (AIO) to provide leadership within the institution, responding to complex issues, including contract cheating. Ideally the AIO should have access to a wide range of expertise, including technological solutions, analytical methods, remain in tune with international research and development, coordinate academic integrity training for staff and students and develop training materials and guidance.

Academic and Research Integrity Breaches and Procedures

The reporting of allegations and management of hearings are purposely placed on one side of the diagram—to acknowledge that, although an essential component of the policies, the main focus should be on education and support. An institution should have transparent procedures that are well understood by staff and students. It is important to ensure these are consistently applied and that outcomes are consistent, proportionate and fair. It is in the long-term interests of the institution to include appropriate additional training for the student as a mandatory component of the outcomes for upheld academic misconduct cases.

Training for academic staff is essential. They are on the front line for spotting suspicions and anomalies during teaching and supervision of students and when evaluating their work. Contract cheating is one of the hardest types of academic misconduct to detect, even with access to intelligent technology, checklists (TEQSA, 2021) and years of experience. Even when the suspicions are strong, it can be very time-consuming and require considerable skills in detection and computer forensics to gather evidence and make a case that convinces decision-makers. As a result, many contract cheating cases go unnoticed. Even if a tutor suspects cheating, they may not have the will or the time to pursue it, especially if they believe it will be dismissed as "no case to answer" by the panel. But training can improve detection and evidence gathering (Dawson & Sutherland-Smith, 2018).

If it is relatively easy for an academic to report suspicions, ideally with expert assistance on hand with guidance and support to assemble the evidence, then cases are more likely to be detected. Academics and decision-makers, including deans, academic integrity/conduct officers, student advisers, librarians and panel members, all need to understand the nature of contract cheating and how to interpret any evidence presented. Most critically, everyone involved needs to know what is meant by "on balance of probability", based on academic judgement, otherwise well-substantiated cases may not be recognised as such. For serious integrity violations, such as contract cheating, it is advisable that the decisions are taken by a panel of academics and/or academic managers, possibly a student representative, all of whom have been trained for this specific role (QAA, 2020).

The onus is on institutions to find ways to ensure that any sanctions applied for academic integrity breaches are consistent, proportionate and fair. There are different ways that this can be achieved, but at the heart of every approach is a standard set of rules and guidance connected to either a formula, table of options or set of metrics, that must be followed by everyone when making the decisions. There is also the need for training for those tasked with making the decisions, especially when deciding the level of severity of the student conduct and factoring the broader context, including any previous history.

Recording of cases and outcomes is a vital part of the process. If there is no record of a case, there can be no accounting for second and possibly serial breaches of integrity. It is important to monitor and be aware if a student is not responding positively to the measures in place to deter academic misconduct, so alternative actions can be considered, ultimately, if all other measures fail, leading to permanent exclusion of the student.

Some institutions will immediately expel a student found to have resorted to contract cheating. The QAA guidance (2020) recommends education, support and guidance for first cases of integrity breaches, which is also my advice, even for contract cheating, combined with the need to complete a new replacement piece of work, with maximum grade set to the basic pass mark. If the student's conduct does not improve, or if a case of systematic contract cheating is discovered towards the end of the student's programme or after graduation, then expulsion and/or retraction of the degree must be considered.

Teaching, Learning and Assessment

The teaching, learning and assessment strategy and an appreciation of how decisions on curriculum and assessment design, and details such as submission rules, can either serve as a deterrent or driver for academic dishonesty. This element is an integral and vital part of the academic integrity strategy, particularly in the light of the recent moves to online and remote learning and changes to assessment methods. Tutors designing assessments need to remain mindful of the impact on integrity and minimise opportunities for cheating, as well as evaluating whether students have achieved the learning outcomes. Those in teaching roles implicitly set the standards that their students should aspire to. The level of professionalism, integrity and ethical conduct demonstrated by teachers provides the underlying climate of integrity for their students. Although a well-designed assessment cannot eliminate the prospect of contract cheating, such as individual or practical or creative tasks, conducted in class or controlled environment where possible, can make it more difficult for work to be contracted out. Evaluation methods such as viva voce examinations and in-person oral presentations, plus monitoring student progress and checking of drafts during the development of the work can help to improve authenticity. However, we must acknowledge that this type of approach requires considerably more time and resources than many institutions are able to provide.

Regulations for Academic Integrity and Ethical Approval

Ethical approval is separated from other educational requirements in Fig. 14.2, because these policies and procedures apply to everyone who conducts research, students, academic staff and researchers. They also apply to students enrolled in research and higher degree programmes and any staff involved in or supervising research. In some institutions where we have conducted research, this is a neglected or weakly defined element of the institutional strategy and in others this is the most strongly developed part of the strategy and policies. We also found that the emphasis varies, with some institutions not concerned about allegations of academic misconduct by undergraduate students and others only making checks at the final dissertation stage. If integrity only counts at the final hurdle to a degree, the student may miss out on vital guidance, support and learning during their journey to the qualification goal. Conduct relating to integrity in ethics and research is an essential life skill and therefore a key area for regular training for students, researchers, teachers and supervisory staff. This is not just about ethical approval; it concerns the whole process of conducting research and working with, respecting and supporting other researchers. It may also include protocols for applying for research funding and integrity in publishing and dissemination of research results. Ethical approval should not be viewed by researchers as the end point. There needs to be ongoing monitoring and a requirement for regular reviews and reappraisal of any research project lasting more than one year.

Admissions and Recruitment

An underlying cause of some cases of contract cheating is when students are admitted to an HE institution without the required qualifications or skills (AACRAO, 2005). This could happen if fake or undeserved qualifications have been included on an application (Watson, 2017); an English language test result may have been fraudulently obtained (Norman, 2018), or there may have been bribery to unfairly gain admission (Downes, 2017; Fursova & Simons, 2014; Kakuchi, 2018). As discussed earlier, there are well-documented cases of recruitment agents falsifying credentials to secure their commission (Watson, 2017). If a student does not have the necessary fundamental skills to succeed, they are likely to struggle and ultimately will fail. Alternatively, they can find ways to progress by asking someone else to do the work for them, for payment or favours.

There are documented cases of students who seek admittance to HE with fake qualifications, to access student loans or visas, with no intention of engaging in learning or completing their own assessment (Watson, 2017).

HE providers need to be mindful of this very serious threat to integrity. One essential step for all HE institutions is to ensure that all recruitment agents are very carefully vetted and required to attend regular training, including conflicts of interest and integrity, as exemplified by a recently introduced Australian code of conduct (Australian Government, 2018). Interviewing applicants and entrance examinations are common ways to check on credentials and skills before students are offered a place. However, when this is not possible, especially for late applicants and international students, a diagnostic formative writing exercise, for all newly admitted students, can be a very effective way to identify students who may not meet the required educational standards, or have special learning requirements that have not been discussed earlier. This formative work provides a very useful exemplar for comparison if there are doubts about authorship in a later assignment.

Periodic Review and Ongoing Monitoring

The remaining two boxes of Fig. 14.2 relate to quality monitoring and enhancement. These are fundamental to the link between integrity, quality and standards (QAA, 2020). Developing academic integrity policies and procedures is not a one-off process. Regulations and procedures must be adjusted on a regular basis as the threats to integrity evolve and new threats emerge. Even in a large institution with highly devolved procedures and decision-making, measures are needed for ongoing monitoring and reporting to ensure consistency and fairness, such as benchmarking of decisions. It is recommended, based on my personal experience, to have a steering committee, with broad representation from across the institution, to monitor and quickly resolve operational problems. The same committee can monitor and evaluate annual data, reporting to the institutional committee for quality and standards. A major periodic review of academic integrity policies should be instigated at least every five years, or more frequently if the strategy is not having the desired effect.

This framework is largely inward-facing and focused on student conduct, teaching, learning and assessment. Omissions from this framework include external influences, safeguarding integrity in partnership work and overseas operations, all of which would be valuable topics for further research.

Conclusions

The bottom line for an institution is to ensure that steps are taken to create a culture of integrity, ideally with education for every member of the institutional community. Academic integrity needs to be central to the institutional strategy, supported through external guidance from QA or accreditation bodies and/or ministries of education. Measures need to be taken to minimise misconduct and corruption. I hope that, in due course, all institutions will adopt fair, consistent and transparent policies that do not just focus on detection and dealing with academic misconduct.

Integrity in all aspects of education and the fight against corruption is the responsibility of everyone who cares about quality and standards in education. As advocated in almost all the guidance I have referred to, working with students as partners, listening to their viewpoints and allowing them to lead initiatives can be a very productive way to fight corruption and enhance integrity.

References

AACRAO. (2005). *Guide to Bogus Institutions and Documents*. American Association of Collegiate Registrars and Admissions Officers. https://www.aacrao.org/resources/newsletters-blogs/aacrao-connect/article/aacrao-publication-bogus-institutions-and-documents

ABC. (2015). *Degrees of deception*. Four Corners Video. Australian Broadcasting Corporation ABC. http://www.abc.net.au/4corners/stories/2015/04/20/4217741.htm

AIT, & Bischof, L. (2019). 'Study to evaluate the progress in quality assurance systems in the area of higher education in the Member States and on cooperation activities at European Level', (Austrian Institute of Technology, Directorate-General for Education, Youth, Sport and Culture (EC)). Publications Office of the European Union. https://doi.org/10.2766/352582

Australian Government. (2018). *National code of practice for providers of Education and Training to Overseas Students*. https://internationaleducation.gov.au/regulatory-information/Pages/National-Code-2018-Factsheets-.aspx

Bertram Gallant, T., & Stephens, M. (2020). Punishment is not enough: The moral imperative of responding to cheating with a developmental approach. *Journal of College and Character, 21*(2), 57–66. https://doi.org/10.1080/2194587X.2020.1741395

Besser, L., & Cronau, P. (2015). *Degrees of deception*. Transcript of Four Corners Video, Australian Broadcasting Corporation ABC, 20th April 2015. Transcript. http://www.abc.net.au/4corners/stories/2015/04/20/4217741.htm

Bretag, T., Harper, R., Saddiqui, S., Ellis, C., Newton, P., Rozenberg, P., & van Haeringen, K. (2019). Contract cheating: A survey of Australian university students. *Studies in Higher Education, 44*(11), 1837–1856. https://doi.org/10.1080/03075079.2018.1462788

Bretag, T., Curtis, G., McNeill, M., Slade, C. (2020). *Academic integrity toolkit.* https://www.teqsa.gov.au/academic-integrity-toolkit

Creasey, S. (2021). When does 'homework help' become cheating? *Times Educational Supplement,* 15th October 2021. https://www.tes.com/magazine/article/when-does-homework-help-become-cheating

Curtis, G. J., Slade, C., Bretag, T., & McNeill, M. (2022). Developing and evaluating nationwide expert-delivered academic integrity workshops for the higher education sector in Australia. *Higher Education Research & Development, 41*(3), 665–680. https://doi.org/10.1080/07294360.2021.1872057

Dawson, P., & Sutherland-Smith, W. (2018). Can markers detect contract cheating? Results from a pilot study. *Assessment & Evaluation in Higher Education, 43*(2), 286–293. https://doi.org/10.1080/02602938.2017.1336746

Downes, M. (2017). University scandal, reputation and governance. *International Journal of Educational Integrity.* https://edintegrity.springeropen.com/track/pdf/10.1007/s40979-017-0019-0

EACEA. (2020). *The European Higher Education Area in 2020 – Bologna process implementation report.* https://op.europa.eu/en/publication-detail/-/publication/c90aaf32-4fce-11eb-b59f-01aa75ed71a1/language-en/format-PDF/source-search

ENAI. (n.d.). *European Network for Academic Integrity.* https://www.academicintegrity.eu/

ENQA. (2015). European Standards and Guidelines (ESG) for Higher Education. http://www.enqa.eu/wp-content/uploads/2015/11/ESG_2015.pdf

Foltýnek, T., Dlabolová, D., Glendinning, I., Lancaster, T., & Linkeschová, D. (2017). *South East European project on policies for academic integrity, project report,* commissioned by Council of Europe, April 2017. http://www.plagiarism.cz/seeppai/Final-report_SEEPPAI.pdf

Fursova, V., & Simons, G. (2014). Social problems of modern Russian higher education: The example of corruption. *International Education Studies, 7*(10), 25–31.

Glendinning, I., Orim, S., & King, A. (2019). *Policies and Actions of Accreditation and Quality Assurance Bodies to Counter Corruption in Higher Education,* published by CHEA / CIQG 2019. Executive summary, full report and media coverage: https://www.chea.org/quality-assurance-combatting-academic-corruption-resources

INQAAHE, TEQSA, & QBBG. (2020). *Toolkit to support quality assurance agencies to address academic integrity and contract cheating.* https://www.teqsa.gov.au/sites/default/files/inqaahe-teqsa-qbbg-academic-integrity-toolkit-v1-0.pdf?v=1594958272

Jeffreys, B., & Main, E. (2018). *The YouTube stars being paid to sell cheating*, 1st May 2018. https://www.bbc.co.uk/news/education-43956001

Kakuchi, S., (2018). Bribery allegations shakes higher education sector. *University World News*, 12th July 2018. http://www.universityworldnews.com/article.php?story=20180712132556849

McCabe, D. (2016). Cheating and honor: Lessons from a long-term research project. In T. Bretag (Ed.), *Handbook of academic integrity* (pp. 187–198). Springer. https://doi.org/10.1007/978-981-287-098-8_35

McNeilage, A., & Visentin, L. (2014, November 12). Students enlist MyMaster website to write essays, assignments. *The Sydney Morning Herald*. http://www.smh.com.au/national/education/students-enlist-mymaster-website-to-write-essays-assignments-20141110-11k0xg

Norman, G. (2018). Chinese student to be deported after paying $3,000 to imposter. *Fox News*, April 5th 2018. http://www.foxnews.com/us/2018/04/05/chinese-student-to-be-deported-after-paying-3000-to-impostor-to-help-her-get-into-american-university.html

OFS. (2020). Consultation on the Office for Students' approach to reportable events. *Analysis of responses to consultation and decision*. Office for Students, 20th October 2021. https://www.officeforstudents.org.uk/publications/consultation-on-ofs-approach-to-reportable-events-analysis-of-responses-and-decision/

QAA. (2020). *Contracting to cheat in higher education* (2nd ed.). https://www.qaa.ac.uk/docs/qaa/guidance/contracting-to-cheat-in-higher-education-2nd-edition.pdf

QAA. (n.d.). *Academic Integrity Charter*. https://www.qaa.ac.uk/about-us/what-we-do/academic-integrity/charter

QQI. (n.d.). *Quality and qualifications Ireland*. https://www.qqi.ie/

Rogerson, A. (2017). Detecting contract cheating in essay and report submissions: Process, patterns, clues and conversations. https://ro.uow.edu.au/cgi/viewcontent.cgi?referer=&httpsredir=1&article=2344&context=buspapers

Sutherland-Smith, W., & Dullaghan, K. (2019). You don't always get what you pay for: User experiences of engaging with contract cheating sites. *Assessment & Evaluation in Higher Education*, *44*(8), 148–1162. https://doi.org/10.1080/02602938.2019.1576028

TEQSA. (2021). *Substantiating contract cheating: A guide for investigators* https://www.teqsa.gov.au/sites/default/files/substantiating-contract-cheating-guide-investigators.pdf

TEQSA. (n.d.). https://www.teqsa.gov.au/

Watson, R. (2017). Student loan scandal. *BBC Panorama*, broadcast 13th December 2017. http://www.bbc.co.uk/programmes/b09g5ll c

Yorke, J., Sefcik, L., & Veeran-Colton, T. (2020). Contract cheating and blackmail: A risky business? *Studies in Higher Education*, *47*(1), 53–66. https://doi.org/10.1080/03075079.2020.1730313

CHAPTER 15

Addressing Contract Cheating Through Staff-Student Partnerships

Thomas Lancaster

Contract cheating has been widely presented in the academic literature as representing a threat to the integrity of academic qualifications (Bretag, 2019; Draper & Newton, 2017; Lancaster & Clarke, 2016). Often the conversation surrounding contract cheating strays away from academic integrity and instead focuses on how to stop students from succumbing to academic misconduct. Such an approach can miss the wider focus of a successful educational community, which recognises that students are invested in their own learning.

Common solutions to contract cheating presented in the literature can take many forms. Discussions in the field consider the design of assessments, detection methods for contract cheating, legal solutions, student education and student support, to give just a few examples (Dawson & Sutherland-Smith, 2018; Draper & Newton, 2017; Morris, 2018; Rogerson, 2017). It is likely that a mixture of all these solutions will be necessary to address the harm caused by the contract cheating industry.

T. Lancaster (✉)
Department of Computing, Imperial College London, London, UK
e-mail: thomas@thomaslancaster.co.uk

© The Author(s), under exclusive license to Springer Nature Switzerland AG 2022
S. E. Eaton et al. (eds.), *Contract Cheating in Higher Education*, https://doi.org/10.1007/978-3-031-12680-2_15

On top of knowing about solutions, an understanding of the reasons why students end up contract cheating is useful for educators.

This chapter dives further into the contract cheating world by proposing another solution to be added to the mix. This solution takes as its premise that students themselves are active investors in their own learning. Some students feel strongly about contract cheating and other forms of academic misconduct and do not appreciate other students getting an unethical advantage, even though they may be reluctant to report this (Bretag et al., 2019; Waltzer et al., 2021). Some students may not feel properly equipped to say no to contract cheating when an opportunity for unfair help is offered to them. The idea of staff of all types working together in partnership to address contract cheating closely matches one of the most basic considerations of academic integrity; that is, academic integrity is not the responsibility of any single individual but requires the support of the whole educational community (Eaton, 2022; Lancaster, 2021b). In this chapter, the word staff is considered in a global sense to encompass educators, professional support staff, academic management and anyone involved in the student journey.

The idea of using staff-student partnerships to address contract cheating is not one that has been widely addressed in the academic literature, although examples of how this can work have been given in publications, presented in talks and can be found on social media (Lancaster, 2020, 2021c). As such, example citations are given where appropriate, but they do not always take a traditional research format, and this chapter also contains elements of reflective practice, relying heavily on the experiences of the author as an academic integrity practitioner. The chapter is intended to provide ideas for students and staff alike who are looking to raise awareness of contract cheating at their own institution and beyond, or who wish to innovate with the way that such issues are explored across the higher education sector.

The chapter draws inspiration from the student academic partners movement (Freeman et al., 2014). Originally developed in 2009 as a partnership between the Students' Union and the Centre for Enhancement of Learning and Teaching at Birmingham City University, UK, the scheme aimed to challenge the power dynamic between staff and students and encourage all parties to have ownership of the educational development process. In the first iteration of the scheme over the 2009/2010 academic year, 51 students were involved in paid positions, partnered with 32 staff. As Freeman et al. (2014) discussed, to be successful the scheme relied on institutional support from the uppermost levels, the ability of staff and students to take ownership and autonomy of the process, as well as mechanisms to help everyone involved make sense of what was meant by collaboration.

Similar schemes have since been developed at other institutions. These include, for example, the StudentShapers scheme at Imperial College London (n.d.), UK. This has led to the development of academic integrity and contract cheating-related research papers and other teaching resources. Examples produced through the StudentShapers scheme are included in this chapter.

This chapter takes the following structure. First, discussion points intended to help introduce the importance of contract cheating to students are presented. Then ideas to involve students in academic integrity innovations and developments are provided, all of which can be applied within the contract cheating space. The chapter also considers the use of awareness-raising events for contract cheating and methods to help students develop into academic integrity champions.

Involving Students in the Discussion About Contract Cheating

It seems unnecessary to provide a detailed background on what contract cheating is in a book devoted to the issue. But some context devoted to how contract cheating affects students is useful. This can also serve as the basis for a discussion between staff and students in a partnership approach. It may also be useful for students wishing to engage in discussion with their peers.

First, it should be recognised that contract cheating is not a standalone issue. Contract cheating is one of many types of academic misconduct that a student could knowingly or unknowingly commit during their academic studies. Generally speaking, it may be possible for a student to plagiarise accidentally, perhaps if they lack a proper understanding of how academic referencing should be used in practice. It is much harder for a student to accidentally contract cheat, but are there nuances here? Sometimes contract cheating providers present themselves as tutoring services (Draper & Newton, 2017; Lancaster & Cotarlan, 2021). A student may start work for themselves, but not realise that having a third party make substantial changes to that work is not acceptable. Further, the discussions around contract cheating can often be made murkier by a discussion of a financial exchange. Some students may think it acceptable for a family member to become involved in the production of assessed work as there is no money changing hands, but this still means that the person being assessed is not the person who completed the assignment.

A related discussion surrounds how academic integrity can be promoted as the cornerstone of academia and the guiding principles within which everyone, staff and students alike, should try and operate. It is very difficult to talk about contract cheating without also discussing academic integrity. There are many benefits to students of them completing their own work, not least a sense of personal satisfaction and an understanding of material that may be relied upon in later assessments or future employment. Academic integrity can easily be discussed in parallel with sessions on ethics. The concepts involved can sometimes seem alien to students, so it can help to bring in parallel examples from other areas of their life. For example, students can be asked how they feel about players in popular online games buying advantages that they themselves do not have access to.

A framework for categorising the impact of contract cheating as a social issue, developed by Khan et al. (2020), can provide a useful starting point for discussion. Khan et al. (2020) classify the impact of contract cheating in three ways, the immediate direct impact on the student, the longer-term impact on the student post the completion of their course and the subsequent impact on the wider surrounding society. Table 15.1 shows their findings, all of which are evidence-based.

Khan et al. (2020) focus their discussion of social impact on the case where a student contact cheats and does not get caught. A corresponding study by Pitt et al. (2020) reveals that the impact of contract cheating on students is also heavy if this is detected and the student is put through an academic misconduct hearing. They reveal that students find the experience challenging and stressful and worry about the damage to their

Table 15.1 The categorised impact of contract cheating as a social issue (Khan et al., 2020)

Direct	Long-term	Surrounding
• The student has not benefitted from lessons taught in class • Anxiety • Low self-esteem • Loneliness	• Difficulty in finding jobs or holding on to them • Depression • Suicide	• Shortage of skills and knowledge impacting family and economy • Unethical practices at workplaces

reputation. Students say they often feel unable to tell their family about the situation and so have to bear any financial burden from a proven contract cheating case for themselves.

There are also risks to students if they choose to engage with the wider contract cheating industry. The industry markets heavily to students, often using deceptive practices (Amigud, 2020; Lancaster, 2019). Students may not receive work they have paid for or it may not be of the quality they expected (Lines, 2016; Sutherland-Smith & Dullaghan, 2019). There is a heavy risk to students that they are open to scams and blackmail once they have provided their personal details to a provider working in a deceptive industry (Lancaster & Gupta, 2021; Yorke et al., 2020). In some jurisdictions providing contract cheating services is illegal and so students are helping to fuel criminal enterprises (Amigud & Dawson, 2020; Draper & Newton, 2017). If nothing else, a student who has contract cheated may become dependent on services like these since they have missed out on necessary learning. This is borne out by research showing many student customers as repeat buyers (Clarke & Lancaster, 2006; Curtis & Clare, 2017). This situation is one that is regularly exploited by the contract cheating industry.

A final area worth exploring with students is how contract cheating expands beyond essay mills. Research using the contract cheating terminology dates back to 2006 (Clarke & Lancaster, 2006). Much of the growth of the contract cheating problem can be traced back to the modern Internet era, but it was not new then. Dating back to the 1970s and earlier, students could purchase original solutions for the assessment tasks they had been sent by mail or telephone (Stott, 1976).

The contract cheating industry also continues to evolve as to how it presents itself to students. File-sharing sites, such as Chegg, that allow students to buy solutions also pose a substantial threat, and students may not realise that their use could be considered in the same league as essay mill use (Lancaster & Cotarlan, 2021; Rogerson & Basanta, 2016).

Assessment Co-design with Students

One of the drivers for contract cheating is that students do not always feel engaged with their learning (Bretag et al., 2019). If a student is disinterested in a subject, or feels what is being taught is not relevant to them or their future, this can give the student an incentive to turn to the contract cheating industry.

The co-design approach allows students to become more actively involved in their own learning, including determining what type of assessment will work best for them and will also allow them to meet module learning outcomes. The idea is that by taking ownership of the assessment process, students will not only feel empowered to complete assessments for themselves but also be able to ensure that the tasks set match their own interests.

There are many recommendations in the literature regarding how to make co-designed teaching innovations work, including those by Roschelle et al. (2006). They recommend seven characteristic features of such an approach, all of which can be interpreted with the need to reduce the risk of contract cheating in mind.

1. Co-design takes on a concrete, tangible innovation challenge.
2. The process begins by taking stock of current practice and classroom contexts.
3. Co-design has a flexible target.
4. Co-design needs a bootstrapping event or process to catalyse the team's work.
5. Co-design is timed to fit the school cycle.
6. Strong facilitation with well-defined roles is a hallmark of co-design.
7. There is central accountability for the quality of the products of co-design.

Roschelle et al.'s (2006) recommendations suggest that the scheduling of the assessment development should fit within the standard module teaching and learning period, rather than needing students to have to engage in additional work. They also note that students may not know how to construct an identifiable assessment problem or even what the scale of an appropriate problem should be. That means that help from instructors is needed here. The authors suggest that a workshop approach works well.

Assessment co-design is not without its challenges. The idea can be counter-intuitive to students, who are used to having assessments laid out for them. There is no reason why students should automatically know what makes a good assessment. But it seems likely that successful teaching and learning innovations can be developed by leveraging student knowledge and experience. The idea of assessment co-design seems worth exploring further although it can never hurt for instructors to have a backup plan in mind.

Students as Research Partners

There are many ways to get students involved as researchers in contract cheating-related questions. Traditionally, research into academic integrity can be conducted by PhD students, but there is no reason why such research cannot include undergraduate students and taught masters' students. These are the groups primarily considered in this section.

One traditional way of engaging students as contract cheating researchers has been to have students work on tasks for this field as part of their capstone project. For example, as part of computer science projects, the author has collaborated with students to work on detecting contract cheating through stylometric analysis and by developing systems to generate questions for instructors to ask students based on work they said they had written. The author has also participated in student films about contract cheating being developed by media students as part of their final project for that specific discipline (Hicking, 2020; Ma, 2020; Menon, 2017).

An alternative research approach has become enabled through schemes affording students the opportunity to be employed to develop research and resources in collaboration with staff partners. Two such schemes operating at Imperial College London, UK, which the author has participated, include the StudentShapers scheme and the Undergraduate Research Opportunity Programme (UROP). Such schemes allow the staff partner to draw upon the skills of the student which may match up well with theirs. They also allow the students to add specific ideas as to how the contract cheating industry operates which may only really be easily accessible to them as a student.

As well as getting experience working on a research project, the student partner may benefit from attending conferences, presenting their ideas to a wider audience, speaking to the media or getting an academic publication. For example, one StudentShapers' project led to the publication of a paper investigating contract cheating through a file-sharing site (Lancaster & Cotarlan, 2021), a paper that has also been widely covered by the media and has led to the student partner's name being mentioned in the UK's House of Commons to support proposed legal changes surrounding contract cheating provision. UROP-related research by computer science students has led to machine learning approaches being applied to large contract cheating-related data sets, drawing upon the technical experience of student partners.

It is worth noting that such research needs to be developed as a collaboration, rather than assuming that students can just go ahead and complete studies without guidance. Particularly at undergraduate level, students are likely to be inexperienced at conducting research and writing research papers. Such an approach can only ever really be successful when it is presented as a true staff-student partnership.

Academic Integrity Modules (Beyond Referencing)

In many institutions, a lot of work goes into teaching students how to write, reference and avoid plagiarism. That is largely essential core knowledge, particularly where students arrive at university from a variety of backgrounds and instructors need to ensure that they are all equipped for success. Often, such teaching will also include coverage of the fundamental values of academic integrity, accompanied by work to help students to have an ethical awareness relevant to their field of study.

An approach developed at Imperial College London, UK, and outlined by Lancaster (2021a), goes beyond helping undergraduate students to understand the fundamentals of academic integrity, and instead teaches them about academic integrity research and provides support for them to complete their own research projects in the field. As the previous section indicated, students are very capable of completing research into contract cheating, particularly where the backing of an experienced practitioner is available.

The *Academic Integrity in STEMM* module, taken by students across largely science, technology and medicine-based disciplines, provides an introduction to academic integrity for students who are not research specialists. The first iteration of the module saw this delivered online due to COVID-19, using a largely flipped curriculum approach. This included pre-recorded video lectures and carefully selected background reading with integrated class discussion activities. Students were introduced to academic integrity research through a thematic structure, including research case studies being presented. Guest lectures from practitioners at other institutions were also included to help students to see how academic integrity extended beyond their immediate institution.

Several parts of the module are directly related to contract cheating research. One week of the module was devoted to contract cheating, showcasing some of the main research findings in the field. Students were also encouraged to attend external talks and activities relating to contract cheating that were happening alongside the module. A student research panel was also arranged, with several of the participating students having previously worked on contract cheating research projects. This was an approach that proved to be both engaging and inspiring for students.

For module assessment, students were required to undertake reflective tasks as well as to participate in an interdisciplinary research project. To make the research fit within the time frame available, students were encouraged to find existing data to analyse, whether this was in the form of policy documents, research papers, social media posts or other such sources. Data relating to contract cheating would seem to fit perfectly here and would also serve to continue to raise awareness about the problem.

Since the module was first developed, other institutions have expressed interest in developing a similar optional module to use across their institution. Such a module would appear to provide a good alternative approach to interest students into not only understanding contract cheating but also actively researching it, whilst also developing core skills to feed back into their own disciplines.

Awareness-Raising Events

One of the most successful methods for getting students involved in advocating against contract cheating is also one of the simplest ones. It involves talking with students about contract cheating as part of an educational partnership of equals.

The International Day of Action against Contract Cheating has run annually since October 2016 (International Center for Academic Integrity [ICAI], n.d.). The global organisation for the event is led by a staff and student committee from the ICAI. Many of the ideas about activities to include in the event come directly from students.

Much of the focus is on individual institutions. The approaches used in each of these institutions will differ, but they can include encouraging academics to discuss contract cheating in class, running stalls, playing contract cheating-related games with students, inviting guest speakers and holding competitions. Institutions are also encouraged to join in with international activity facilitated online, for instance by encouraging staff and students to post whiteboard declarations on social media stating why they do not engage in or support contract cheating.

The ICAI also commonly hosts online activities. This might include broadcasting webinars, holding panel discussions, running online games or hosting student poster design competitions. In 2020, during the COVID-19 pandemic, ICAI ran 20 hours of live broadcasts on contract cheating, bringing together many prominent speakers and quality assurance body representatives from around the world. These broadcasts also included contributions from student partners.

For institutions that prefer to not lead their messaging with a discussion on contract cheating, it is also possible to bill this event as being about academic integrity. Some institutions have extended upon the original concept of the International Day of Action against Contract Cheating to include an entire Academic Integrity Week.

Many of the most successful local implementations of the International Day of Action against Contract Cheating have been seen where these have been organised by student groups themselves. In other instances, the local arrangements have been organised by students and staff partners. The best approaches all seem to rely on putting students at the heart of the academic integrity discussion as the real advocates of change.

Student Involvement Throughout Academic Integrity Procedures

A final consideration for improving the sector approach to address contract cheating is the movement towards students themselves becoming academic integrity champions. This is recognised through work they conduct with their peers, through student unions and by participating in academic integrity decision-making processes within institutions. Such active involvement represents a way to ensure that the student voice regarding contract cheating is fully heard and that fairness of process is achieved.

Many student unions have themselves started to lead the way in discussing contract cheating with students themselves. This has already been seen through the awareness-raising events and support sessions mentioned in the previous section, but also through social media campaigns and additional support put into place when a student is suspected of having contract cheated and is involved in an ongoing investigation.

Students themselves can provide support for other students in a more formalised way. Often a student will feel more comfortable discussing their concerns with another student than with a member of staff. A student who themself has been through a contract cheating investigative procedure can also often be an ideal person to mentor other students, as evidenced by Pitt et al. (2020).

When academic institutions develop new procedures and policies surrounding contract cheating, students themselves should be called upon to both play an active role in procedural design and check that the procedures are fair and understandable. Often archaic languages can be hidden inside policies and procedures which are not accessible to students, causing unintentional misunderstandings.

There are also many examples now of institutions where student representatives form part of the panel that makes a decision during an academic misconduct investigation. One such case is at the University of Sussex, where panels consist of two university staff members and one elected student representative (University of Sussex Students' Union, n.d.). This helps to ensure that the correct processes are being followed and sensible decisions made, particularly in cases of contact cheating where a proven allegation could lead to a student being unable to continue with their programme of study.

CONCLUSIONS

This chapter has reviewed the opportunities for students and staff to work in partnership to both promote academic integrity and reduce contract cheating. There are many examples of good work in this area going on around the world, including through students themselves taking the initiative and setting up their own networks helping to put academic integrity at the heart of the educational discussion.

Getting staff-student partnerships to work flawlessly is not without challenge, but it is possible, it is worthwhile, and it is something that should be encouraged.

The introduction drew upon the experiences of student academic partners scheme participants, noting the importance of institutional buy-in for any collaborative approach of this type to be successful. For academic integrity and contract cheating initiatives, institutional buy-in is of crucial importance. It is very easy for institutions to decide that it is best not to speak out about contract cheating for fear of getting unwanted publicity. Such an approach is simply unfair to everyone involved, including all the students who want the best from their education. To make sense of contract cheating, a collaborative approach between students and staff offers the only sensible route forwards.

Acknowledgements The author wishes to acknowledge and thank all the student partners whose experience has helped with the shaping of this chapter.

References

Amigud, A. (2020). Cheaters on Twitter: An analysis of engagement approaches of contract cheating services. *Studies in Higher Education*, 45(3), 692–705. https://doi.org/10.1080/03075079.2018.1564258

Amigud, A., & Dawson, P. (2020). The law and the outlaw: Is legal prohibition a viable solution to the contract cheating problem? *Assessment & Evaluation in Higher Education*, 45(1), 98–108. https://doi.org/10.1080/02602938.2019.1612851

Bretag, T. (2019). Contract cheating will erode trust in science. *Nature*, 574(7780), 599–600. https://doi.org/10.1038/d41586-019-03265-1

Bretag, T., Harper, R., Burton, M., Ellis, C., Newton, P., van Haeringen, K., & Rozenberg, P. (2019). Contract cheating and assessment design: Exploring the relationship. *Assessment & Evaluation in Higher Education*, 44(5), 676–691. https://doi.org/10.1080/02602938.2018.1527892

Clarke, R., & Lancaster, T. (2006, June 19–21). Eliminating the successor to plagiarism? Identifying the usage of contract cheating sites [Conference presentation]. *Proceedings of 2nd International Plagiarism Conference*, Newcastle, UK.

Curtis, G., & Clare, J. (2017). How prevalent is contract cheating and to what extent are students repeat offenders? *Journal of Academic Ethics*, 15(2), 115–124. https://doi.org/10.1007/s10805-017-9278-x

Dawson, P., & Sutherland-Smith, W. (2018). Can markers detect contract cheating? Results from a pilot study. *Assessment & Evaluation in Higher Education*, 43(2), 286–293. https://doi.org/10.1080/02602938.2017.1336746

Draper, M., & Newton, P. (2017). A legal approach to tackling contract cheating? *International Journal for Educational Integrity*, 13(11). https://doi.org/10.1007/s40979-017-0022-5

Eaton, S. E. (2022). Contract cheating in Canada: A comprehensive overview. In S. E. Eaton & J. Christensen Hughes (Eds.), *Academic integrity in Canada: An enduring and essential challenge* (pp. 165–187). https://doi.org/10.1007/978-3-030-83255-1_8

Freeman, R., Millard, L., Brand, S., & Chapman, P. (2014). Student academic partners: Student employment for collaborative learning and teaching development. *Innovations in Education and Teaching International*, 51(3), 233–243. https://doi.org/10.1080/14703297.2013.778064

Hicking, S. (2020). *Reading between the lines: Exploring the essay mill industry* [Video]. YouTube. https://youtu.be/r_8QajLHp-k

Imperial College London. (n.d.). *StudentShapers*. https://www.imperial.ac.uk/students/studentshapers

International Center for Academic Integrity. (n.d.). *IDOA International Day of Action Against Contract Cheating*. https://academicintegrity.org/events-conferences/idoa-international-day-of-action-against-contract-cheating

Khan, Z., Hemnani, P., Raheja, S., & Joshy, J. (2020). Raising awareness on contract cheating–lessons learned from running campus-wide campaigns. *Journal of Academic Ethics, 18*(1), 17–33. https://doi.org/10.1007/s10805-019-09353-1

Lancaster, T. (2019). Social media enabled contract cheating. *Canadian Perspectives on Academic Integrity, 2*(2), 7–24. https://doi.org/10.11575/cpai.v2i2.68053

Lancaster, T. (2020). Academic discipline integration by contract cheating services and essay Mills. *Journal of Academic Ethics, 18*(2), 115–127. https://doi.org/10.1007/s10805-019-09357-x

Lancaster, T. (2021a, March 1–4). *Developing an academic integrity research module for undergraduate students* [Conference presentation]. International Center for Academic Integrity Conference 2021. Virtual conference.

Lancaster, T. (2021b, June 22–23). *The power of academic integrity communities* [Keynote address]. Canadian Symposium on Academic Integrity 2021. Virtual presentation.

Lancaster, T. (2021c, October 18). *Academic integrity: The student partnership approach* [Keynote address]. National Academic Integrity Week (Ireland). Virtual presentation.

Lancaster, T., & Clarke, R. (2016). Contract cheating: The outsourcing of assessed student work. In T. Bretag (Ed.), *Handbook of academic integrity* (pp. 639–654). https://doi.org/10.1007/978-981-287-098-8_17.

Lancaster, T., & Cotarlan, C. (2021). Contract cheating by STEM students through a file sharing website: A Covid-19 pandemic perspective. *International Journal for Educational Integrity, 17*(3). https://doi.org/10.1007/s40979-021-00070-0

Lancaster, T., & Gupta, R. (2021, June 9–11). *Contract cheating and unauthorised homework assistance through Reddit communities* [Conference presentation]. European Conference on Academic Integrity and Plagiarism 2021. https://academicintegrity.eu/conference/

Lines, L. (2016). Ghostwriters guaranteeing grades? The quality of online ghostwriting services available to tertiary students in Australia. *Teaching in Higher Education, 21*(8), 889–914. https://doi.org/10.1080/13562517.2016.1198759

Ma, L. (2020, August). *Desperate measures* [Video]. YouTube. https://youtu.be/_g5mrcZYbmg

Menon, A. (2017, July 10). *At your service* [Video]. YouTube. https://youtu.be/91VoX0m1EBs

Morris, E. J. (2018). Academic integrity matters: Five considerations for addressing contract cheating. *International Journal for Educational Integrity, 14*(1), 1–12. https://doi.org/10.1007/s40979-018-0038-5

Pitt, P., Dullaghan, K., & Sutherland-Smith, W. (2020). "Mess, stress and trauma": Students' experiences of formal contract cheating processes. *Assessment & Evaluation in Higher Education, 46*(4), 659–672. https://doi.org/10.1080/02602938.2020.1787332

Rogerson, A. M. (2017). Detecting contract cheating in essay and report submissions: Process, patterns, clues and conversations. *International Journal for Educational Integrity, 13*(1), 1–17. https://doi.org/10.1007/s40979-017-0021-6

Rogerson, A., & Basanta, G. (2016). Peer-to-peer file sharing and academic integrity in the internet age. In T. Bretag (Ed.). *Handbook of academic integrity* (pp. 273–285). https://doi.org/10.1007/978-981-287-098-8_55

Roschelle, J., Penuel, W., & Shechtman, N. (2006). Co-design of innovations with teachers: Definition and dynamics. *ICLS '06: Proceedings of the 7th International Conference on Learning Sciences*, Bloomington, Indiana.

Stott, L. (1976). Integrity in public education. *The Journal of Educational Thought (JET)/Revue de la Pensée Educative*, 132–141. https://doi.org/10.11575/jet.v10i2.43865

Sutherland-Smith, W., & Dullaghan, K. (2019). You don't always get what you pay for: User experiences of engaging with contract cheating sites. *Assessment & Evaluation in Higher Education, 44*, 1148–1162. https://doi.org/10.1080/02602938.2019.1576028

University of Sussex Students' Union. (n.d.). *Academic misconduct panels*. https://sussexstudent.com/support/academic-misconduct/misc-panels

Waltzer, T., Samuelson, A., & Dahl, A. (2021). Students' reasoning about whether to report when others cheat: Conflict, confusion, and consequences. *Journal of Academic Ethics*, 1–23. https://doi.org/10.1007/s10805-021-09414-4

Yorke, J., Sefcik, L., & Veeran-Colton, T. (2020). Contract cheating and blackmail: A risky business? *Studies in Higher Education*. https://doi.org/10.1080/03075079.2020.1730313

CHAPTER 16

The Extortionate Cost of Contract Cheating

Terisha Veeran-Colton, Lesley Sefcik, and Jonathan Yorke

Originally defined by Clarke and Lancaster (2006), contract cheating is now a well-recognised part of the higher education landscape (Bretag et al., 2019c). Contract cheating happens when a student submits a piece of work that was completed for them by a third party, whom they may or may not have paid (Harper et al., 2019). It is a deliberate and fraudulent behaviour that seeks personal gain at the expense of academic integrity (Rundle et al., 2020).

Although contract cheating scandals tend to attract broad media coverage (Fellner, 2020; Visentin, 2015), relatively little attention has been given to the personal, professional, and financial consequences and their multiple points of impact on students. Through the lens of a fictitious (but plausible) contact cheating scenario, this chapter examines these multiple points of impact, identifying potential approaches that can be taken to discourage contract cheating. A similar approach has been applied by Bens (2022).

T. Veeran-Colton (✉) • L. Sefcik • J. Yorke
Curtin University, Bentley, WA, Australia
e-mail: terisha.veeran-colton@curtin.edu.au

Scenario

The following scenario was constructed by the authors from accounts of cheating posted to discussion boards and published in literature (Curtis & Clare, 2017; Ellis et al., 2020; Gilmore, 2009; Yorke et al., 2022). It is fictitious and anonymous but based on real-life experience, where the consequences of contract cheating are not always immediate.

Experience as a Student

I (Student X) was a diligent student in high school and was accepted into a good university, but once there, I struggled. No one tells you how different the pressures of university are compared to high school. Even though the assessments were supposed to be completed individually, I would often work with a group of classmates to make life easier. One group-member who was struggling financially started offering to do assignments for a small fee. I was having a hard time, it was convenient, and it did not seem too unethical since I was helping a friend (and lightening my workload at the same time). I was not planning on this being a regular thing. It was just going to be a few times and I thought the chances of getting caught were low, since it would be hard for the university's text-matching software to detect original work.

Semesters passed and the assessment requirements kept mounting. Balancing studies with a part-time job was becoming too much for me. Life felt stressful. Feeling there was little other choice, I continued to pay to get help with my assignments. I felt like a victim of circumstance and so cheating became a habit, I guess. The promise of a passing grade was difficult to reject. Other students it seemed, felt the same, as my friend now had a lucrative business and was always busy. So much so, that I had to find someone on the web to help me instead. Eventually I had to pay someone to sit my final exams since I did not understand much of the coursework by the end. Although the pandemic has been horrible at least it meant that all my exams were now online so it was much easier to get someone to do my exams for me. At the time, I thought it was a necessary means to an end, as I was certain to land a good job with such good grades and then I could start fresh.

Experience After Graduation

I am now employed at a successful tech start-up; but start-ups are fast-paced and I am struggling. My lack of knowledge and skills is becoming obvious to my colleagues and supervisor. Things are not going well and to make matters worse, I received a worrying email from the website I once used for assignment help. They threatened that if I did not pay them more money, they would tell the university about the assignments. The problem is that life in this city is expensive and I simply cannot afford to pay them. I decided not to pay, because I thought there was a good chance they were bluffing.

A few months later, I received allegations of cheating from my university. It turns out the website owners told the university. The university reviewed my work and they found more evidence of contract cheating by using some technology that was not available when I was a student. This linked my other assignments to my friend who I originally paid for help. Now we are all being sent details about disciplinary hearings with the possibility of our degrees being cancelled. Unfortunately, my employer found out and people at work are talking. I am scared I will lose my job. I feel that my world is unravelling, and I am horrified because I will need to explain this to my family and partner. I do not know where to start.

Figure 16.1 illustrates the flow of events depicted in the scenario and identifies possible factors, decision points, and consequences. There are various factors that can influence an initial decision to cheat. Unfortunately, consequences of contract cheating can be significantly delayed, which may

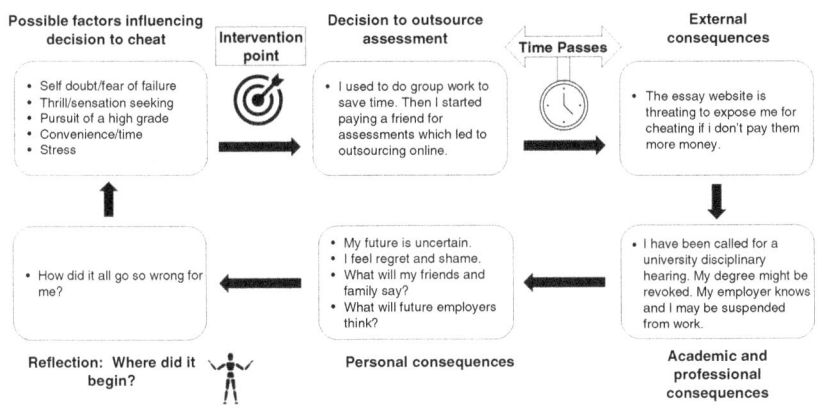

Fig. 16.1 Graphical representation of the contract cheating scenario

lull students into a false sense of security, thereby encouraging further use of cheating services.

Analysis

Consistent with the observation that contract cheating is a social issue that has immediate, long-term, and surrounding effects (Khan et al., 2020), the personal, academic, financial, and other consequences of contract cheating in the scenario are analysed. Figure 16.2 takes these four classifications and further breaks down the first three into sub-categories identifying related themes within each category. Inevitably, consequences depicted in Fig. 16.2 are not mutually exclusive: disciplinary action can evoke an emotional response that affects a student's social and emotional wellbeing, and it also can materially affect their reputation and future prospects.

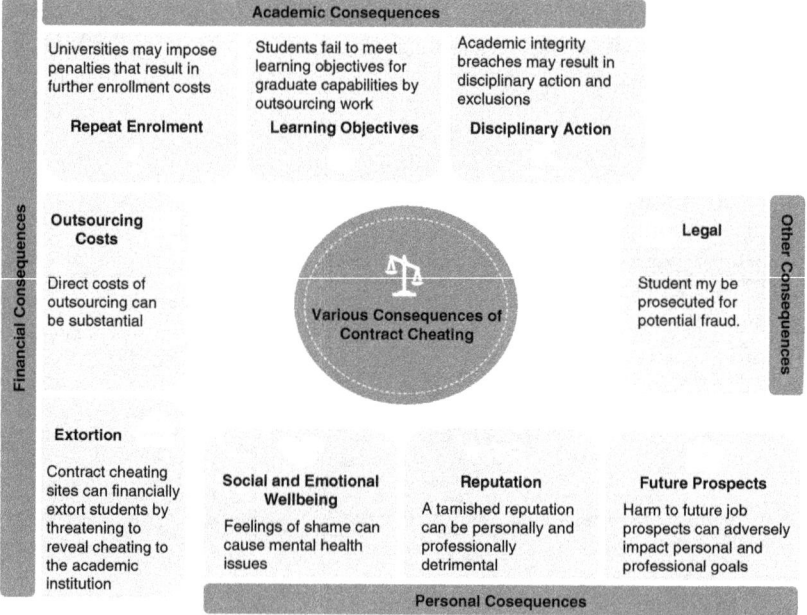

Fig. 16.2 Consequences of contract cheating broken down into sub-themes

Personal Consequences

Personal consequences spanned three sub-categories: social and emotional wellbeing; reputation; and future prospects (Fig. 16.2). Personal consequences are self-imposed costs that result from engaging in morally conflicting behaviour that affects one's conscience (Grasmick & Bursik, 1990). The danger is that students may rationalise personal consequences if they do not fully appreciate how these could affect them later in life. Student X felt personal consequences only after they had graduated university and joined the working world.

Social and Emotional Wellbeing

Yorke et al. (2022) suggest that for some students the decision to cheat stems from anxiety and self-doubt about academic ability, possibly precipitated by self-imposed or familial pressure to succeed (Rowland et al., 2018). Student X was failing at work because of a lack of foundational skills and knowledge stemming from their failure to meet the learning objectives in university due to outsourcing their disciplinary work. As a result, they felt a degraded sense of self-worth. Ironically, cheating was initially argued to improve self-worth with the aim of helping them to obtain good grades and a lucrative job. Feelings of self-worth may fluctuate over time, making individuals potentially vulnerable to psychological issues such as depression (Crocker, 2002; Orth et al., 2006; Tangney et al., 2011). In this case, it was difficult for Student X to anticipate this emotional consequence for their future self. Student X felt regret when they were contacted by the university about outsourcing their assessments and believed that had they not cheated they would be in a better position (Cowley, 2017; Taylor, 1996), with the skills to do their job.

Student X felt shame in the workplace when their colleagues became aware of their cheating behaviour at university, and then this shame extended into their personal life when they had to explain the situation to their partner and family (Poelmans et al., 2008). Shame is an emotion that tends to amplify if ignored (TED, 2011, 2012), an important data point to consider for our most vulnerable students.

Shame, guilt, and remorse are *moral emotions* (Taylor, 1996) that may have the potential to mediate behaviour. For instance, the fear of embarrassment or shame may deter certain behaviours (Cochran et al., 1999). Curtis et al. (2022) connect students' anticipated shame and guilt with contract cheating intentions. For this reason, institutions have at times considered naming and shaming offenders: "we should name and shame because that's the best way to learn that there's no fun in this and there's no gain" (Matchett, 2020, para. 2). This deterrence strategy is not without risks given the ethical considerations related to the privacy and rights of students. We also note the social and emotional consequences of public shaming outlined in Ronson (2015).

Reputation
The literature on contract cheating emphasises the damage that can be wrought on the higher education sector. The MyMaster issue exposed several universities whose students engaged in contract cheating, leading to intervention from the Australian Tertiary Education Quality and Standards Agency (TEQSA; Bretag et al., 2019a; Visentin, 2015).

However, with the exception of Pitt et al. (2020), the majority of studies have focused on aspects other than the personal impact of cheating on the individual student. According to Raub and Weesie (1990), reputation is defined through past behaviour: it is contingent on the perceptions and judgements of those around us and is socially mediated (Emler, 1990). Put simply, our behaviour affects how others perceive us and their judgements are made based on these perceptions.

Gilmore (2009) asserted that "plagiarism makes an announcement to the world" (p. 36), showing that reputational consequences of plagiarism increase in severity with academic level (Table 16.1).

Being caught for contract cheating sends a strong message to a student's immediate social circle, family, and teachers, suggesting that Student

Table 16.1 Consequences of plagiarism in relation to age, reproduced from Gilmore (2009)

Grade level	Consequences of plagiarism
Below 6th grade	Discussion, correction
6–8	Correction, rewriting
9–10	Correction, rewriting, grade penalties
11–12	Rewriting, failure on the assignment
College undergraduate	Rewriting, failure (assignment or course), expulsion
Graduate student	Expulsion
Professional	Loss of job/contract, legal penalties, loss of professional reputation

X may behave unethically and dishonestly. Pitt et al. (2020) have shown that students who have endured disciplinary action for contract cheating do not emerge unscathed, highlighting themes of reputational damage and rumours leading to stress and anxiety as their peers and teachers perceived them differently once they were caught. Students continuing with study felt less respected by their peers and teachers (Pitt et al., 2020).

Future Prospects
Universities treat contract cheating as a serious event and the academic consequences that students experience for a breach can be detrimental to their professional futures. Academic misconduct may bar progression into fields where honesty and integrity are professional obligations, including law (Bieliauskaitė, 2014), social work (Saunders, 1993), and nursing (Fontana, 2009). A record of misconduct may narrow career pathways for students.

Student X was caught for contract cheating at a life stage where their onward career choices arguably would be the narrowest, as they were already qualified in a specific field. Their professional reputation was damaged by poor performance at work, and being investigated for contract cheating had led other colleagues and their supervisor to doubt their credibility. Student X was viewed through the lens of their past behaviour, which resulted in negative perceptions of their character and values. Student X's professional future was potentially in jeopardy, especially if there was a university decision to rescind the degree, as this would leave them without a formal tertiary qualification having entered a profession that depended upon it.

Academic Consequences

Academic consequences of cheating include risks of failure to acquire learning outcomes, disciplinary action, and the need to repeat enrolments (Fig. 16.2).

Learning Objectives
The value of tertiary education can be understood on both macro and micro levels. At a macro level, tertiary education shapes our socio-economic world (Salmi et al., 2002). On a micro level, a tertiary qualification carries personal benefits as it can provide broader access to job opportunities and the ability to earn an income that can support other life

goals (Rose, 2013). If the skills and knowledge derived from learning are framed as the currency needed for future success, then contract cheating undermines both macro and micro levels.

A fixed mindset of *I must get a high grade at any cost* may lead to inappropriate behaviour prioritising grade success over learning. On the other hand, students with a growth mindset, "who believe their talents can be developed (through hard work, good strategies and input from others)" (Dweck, 2016, para. 2), are less likely to be involved in cheating than students with a fixed mindset who focus on success at all costs (Thomas, 2017; Yu et al., 2021). This suggests that an emphasis on learning within a growth mindset is a key component to combatting contract cheating.

Disciplinary Action

Outcomes and penalties for contract cheating cases vary based on the nature of academic integrity breach (TEQSA, 2017). However, common academic consequences for incidents of contact cheating include formal warnings, failing a unit, requirements to repeat units, being suspended, being expelled or excluded from university, or having a degree rescinded (Curtin University, 2020b; Griffith University, 2020; University of Sydney, 2020).

Pitt et al. (2020) argue that disciplinary action related to contract cheating can be regarded as one of "the most challenging experience[s] of the student's life" (p. 663) and that students in their study generally managed the stress and financial implications of the situation in isolation without disclosing the incident to their family. Therefore, disciplinary action has consequences for the social and emotional wellbeing sub-category located under personal consequences (Fig. 16.2), as well as potential financial consequences from requirements to repeat unit enrolments as discussed in the next section.

Financial Consequences

This category included consequences associated with outsourcing work, repeated enrolments, and extortion (Fig. 16.2).

Direct Outsourcing Costs

Student X experienced direct costs of purchasing assessments and hiring impersonators to sit examinations. Using data analysed from Twitter, Amigud and Lancaster (2020) found that students in the United States are willing to pay approximately US$33.32 per 1000 words for a typical contracted assessment such as an essay, but the costs are much higher if impersonators are involved. We note that impersonation costs are likely to be much higher for face-to-face or remote invigilated examinations, compared to non-invigilated online alternatives such as electronic tests and quizzes.

Repeated Enrolment
There are financial implications if a student is required to repeat an affected programme or unit. Pitt et al. (2020) describe the impacts of financial costs experienced by two students. Both were too ashamed to tell their families that they had to repeat their studies, and they had to save for a considerable amount of time (months) to be able to afford the approximately US$3000 cost to retake the unit after a determination of contract cheating.

Extortion
Student X's predicament worsened when the contract cheating website attempted to extort money long after they had completed their initial financial transaction. Extortion is "antagonistic with one party benefitting at the expense of the other" (Khalil et al., 2010, p. 180). Extortion in contract cheating gained prominence in Australia in 2018 when TEQSA reported that contract cheating websites were attempting to extort students who had previously used their services (Ross, 2018). Heightened concerns about contract cheating led to the passing of the TEQSA Amendment—Prohibiting Academic Cheating Services Bill 2019 which makes "providing and advertising academic cheating services subject to offences and civil penalty provisions under the *TEQSA Act*" (Ferguson, 2019, p. 3).

In a study of 587 Australian students, Yorke et al. (2022) subsequently reported that only 8.2% ($n = 48$) had heard of contract cheating-related extortion, indicating that students were largely unaware of this possibility. When asked how they would manage being extorted in this way, 27.4% ($n = 161$) reported that "they would do nothing and hope that the contract cheating service would not follow through with the threat" (Yorke et al., 2022, p. 8); much like Student X.

Other Consequences

Contract cheating students may be subjected to costs associated with fines and legal proceedings (Draper & Newton, 2017). According to Steel (2017), students could potentially be criminally prosecuted for fraud, forgery, and conspiracy to defraud due to contract cheating. The costs of legal representation can be substantial.

How Can HEIs Help Prevent These Consequences?

Researchers have identified some complex and variable drivers that lead to cheating behaviour (Amigud & Lancaster, 2019; Franklyn-Stokes & Newstead, 1995; McCabe et al., 1999). Rowland et al. (2018) summarised these as "academic, societal, family and/or intrinsic pressures to succeed, high stress levels, the wish to 'help a friend', time, peer pressure, fear of failure, laziness, unpreparedness, apathy and the sense that 'everybody does it'" (p. 653). Figure 16.1 illustrates that some of the reasons for outsourcing were related to stress and lack of time, convenience of outsourcing, self-doubt and fear of failure, and pursuit of a high grade. Within this complex and multifaceted terrain, what possibilities should institutions consider?

Culture of Academic Integrity and Support Services

A student's decision to cheat may be influenced within a supportive institutional culture that values academic integrity in conjunction with mechanisms that make it difficult for students to contract cheat. Policy frameworks and good practices have been discussed at length in Bretag et al. (2011), Bretag and Mahmud (2016), TEQSA (2017), and Morris (2018). Initiatives that destigmatise the process of asking for help may encourage a more open discourse around the pressures of university life.

Student educational programmes that open a dialogue about the potential complexity and pitfalls of contract cheating represent another avenue worth pursuing. For some, the decision to cheat is a moral one; for others, it may be risk-based. Raised awareness of risks may be helpful, given that 50% of students that initially chose to contract cheat in a hypothetical scenario changed their decision after risks of extortion were introduced (Yorke et al., 2022).

Campus campaigns have been successful in increasing student awareness about contract cheating (Khan et al., 2020). Media-rich campaigns and initiatives using comic strips to succinctly disseminate information about contract cheating can be engaging and informative (Charles Darwin University, 2020; Curtin University, 2020a). Peer-to-peer learning and mentoring from recently graduated students through social media have also been successful in raising awareness on contract cheating (Khan et al., 2020).

Undetected cheating can lead to resentment from students that are doing the work themselves. Whilst detection of contract cheating can be difficult, Dawson and Sutherland-Smith (2018) have shown that staff can more reliably detect contract cheating if provided with suitable guidance. Harper et al. (2019) suggest that the teaching and learning environment and supportive collegial relationships between educators and students are critical components that are necessary if contract cheating is to be addressed.

Assessment Design

Although contested, so-called authentic assessment approaches have been seen to improve academic integrity (Bretag et al., 2019b). However, most assessments can be readily outsourced (Ellis et al., 2020). This suggests that what is needed is more *effective* assessment design strategies that support integrity from multiple angles.

Baird and Clare (2017) provide a helpful synopsis of potential strategies that may alter the cheating dynamic so that the risk and effort involved with cheating is costlier than the potential benefits. Potential strategies include using anonymous feedback forums so students have a method for reporting cheating behaviour; creating more individualised assessments; providing opportunities for formative assessment practice; teaching targeted academic misconduct information to students; ensuring educators are taught academic integrity concepts and how to identify misconduct; avoiding assessment reuse; and most importantly implementing multiple interventions in conjunction (Baird & Clare, 2017).

Conclusion

The diverse consequences of contract cheating have been explored within our scenario, identifying personal, academic, financial, and other risks to students. At a broader level, unskilled graduates create reputation risks to institutions and the sector, highlighting the importance of quality assurance mechanisms for HEIs (Sutherland-Smith & Dullaghan, 2019).

At an institutional level, staff professional development activities could improve the awareness and detection of contract cheating. At a course level, coordinators should foster a consistent approach to academic integrity and its connection to employability. Within units, assessment approaches should consider academic integrity risks from the outset in terms of assessment design.

We recognise that students often face difficult life choices, given the stresses of university and personal life. Some of the approaches we have outlined have the potential to be transformative. Given that the costs and consequences of contract cheating can be literally extortionate, such transformation is sorely needed.

References

Amigud, A., & Lancaster, T. (2019). 246 reasons to cheat: An analysis of students' reasons for seeking to outsource academic work. *Computers & Education, 134*, 98–107. https://doi.org/10.1016/j.compedu.2019.01.017

Amigud, A., & Lancaster, T. (2020). I will pay someone to do my assignment: An analysis of market demand for contract cheating services on Twitter. *Assessment & Evaluation in Higher Education, 45*(4), 541–553. https://doi.org/10.1080/02602938.2019.1670780

Baird, M., & Clare, J. (2017). Removing the opportunity for contract cheating in business capstones: A crime prevention case study. *International Journal for Educational Integrity, 13*(6), 1–15. https://doi.org/10.1007/s40979-017-0018-1

Bens, S. (2022). Helping students resolve the ambiguous expectations of academic integrity. In S. E. Eaton & J. Christensen Hughes (Eds.), *Academic integrity in Canada. Ethics and integrity in educational contexts* (Vol. 1, pp. 377–392). Springer. https://doi.org/10.1007/978-3-030-83255-1_19

Bieliauskaitė, J. (2014). On the way to professionalism – The promotion of law students' academic integrity. *Procedia – Social and Behavioral Sciences, 116*, 4229–4234. https://doi.org/10.1016/j.sbspro.2014.01.922

Bretag, T., Harper, R., Burton, M., Ellis, C., Newton, P., Rozenberg, P., Saddiqui, S., & van Haeringen, K. (2019a). Contract cheating: A survey of Australian university students. *Studies in Higher Education, 44*(11), 1837–1856. https://doi.org/10.1080/03075079.2018.1462788

Bretag, T., Harper, R., Burton, M., Ellis, C., Newton, P., van Haeringen, K., Saddiqui, S., & Rozenberg, P. (2019b). Contract cheating and assessment design: Exploring the relationship. *Assessment & Evaluation in Higher Education, 44*(5), 676–691. https://doi.org/10.1080/02602938.2018.1527892

Bretag, T., Harper, R., Rundle, K., Newton, P. M., Ellis, C., Saddiqui, S., & van Haeringen, K. (2019c). Contract cheating in Australian higher education: A comparison of non-university higher education providers and universities. *Assessment & Evaluation in Higher Education, 45*(1), 125–139. https://doi.org/10.1080/02602938.2019.1614146

Bretag, T., Mahmud, S., Wallace, M., Walker, R., James, C., Green, M., East, J., McGowan, U., & Partridge, L. (2011). Core elements of exemplary academic integrity policy in Australian higher education. *International Journal for Educational Integrity, 7*(2), 3–12. https://doi.org/10.21913/IJEI.v7i2.759

Bretag, T., & Mahmud, S. (2016). A conceptual framework for implementing exemplary academic integrity policy in Australian higher education. In T. Bretag (Ed.), *Handbook of academic integrity* (pp. 463–480). Springer. https://doi.org/10.1007/978-981-287-098-8_24

Charles Darwin University. (2020). *Academic integrity at CDU: Student information.* https://www.cdu.edu.au/sites/default/files/academic-integrity/docs/episode_01_copy_time.pdf

Clarke, R., & Lancaster, T. (2006, June 19–21). *Eliminating the successor to plagiarism: Identifying the usage of contract cheating sites* [Paper presentation]. Second International Plagiarism Conference. The Sage Gateshead, Tyne & Wear, United Kingdom. https://citeseerx.ist.psu.edu/viewdoc/download?doi=10.1.1.120.5440&rep=rep1&type=pdf

Cochran, J. K., Chamlin, M. B., Wood, P. B., & Sellers, C. S. (1999). Shame, embarrassment, and formal sanction threats: Extending the deterrence/rational choice model to academic dishonesty. *Sociological Inquiry, 69*(1), 91–105. https://doi.org/10.1111/j.1475-682X.1999.tb00491.x

Cowley, C. (2017). Regret, remorse and the twilight perspective. *International Journal of Philosophical Studies, 25*(5), 624–634. https://doi.org/10.1080/09672559.2017.1381410

Crocker, J. (2002). Contingencies of self-worth: Implications for self-regulation and psychological vulnerability. *Self and Identity, 1*(2), 143–149. https://doi.org/10.1080/152988602317319320

Curtin University. (2020a). *Academic integrity.* https://students.curtin.edu.au/essentials/rights/academic-integrity/

Curtin University. (2020b). *Contract cheating.* https://students.curtin.edu.au/essentials/rights/academic-integrity/contract-cheating/

Curtis, G. J., & Clare, J. (2017). How prevalent is contract cheating and to what extent are students repeat offenders? *Journal of Academic Ethics, 15*, 115–124. https://doi.org/10.1007/s10805-017-9278-x

Curtis, G. J., Clare, J., Vieira, E., Selby, E., & Jonason, P. K. (2022). Predicting contract cheating intentions: Dark personality traits, attitudes, norms, and anticipated guilt and shame. *Personality and Individual Differences, 185*, 111277. https://doi.org/10.1016/j.paid.2021.111277

Dawson, P., & Sutherland-Smith, W. (2018). Can markers detect contract cheating? Results from a pilot study. *Assessment & Evaluation in Higher Education, 43*(2), 286–293. https://doi.org/10.1080/02602938.2017.1336746

Draper, M. J., & Newton, P. M. (2017). A legal approach to tackling contract cheating? *International Journal for Educational Integrity, 13*(11), 1–16. https://doi.org/10.1007/s40979-017-0022-5

Dweck, C. (2016, January 13). Managing yourself: What having a 'growth mindset' actually means. *Harvard Business Review.* https://hbr.org/2016/01/what-having-a-growth-mindset-actually-means/

Ellis, C., van Haeringen, K., Harper, R., Bretag, T., Zucker, I., McBride, S., Rozenberg, P., Newton, P., & Saddiqui, S. (2020). Does authentic assessment assure academic integrity? Evidence from contract cheating data. *Higher Education Research & Development, 39*(3), 454–469. https://doi.org/10.1080/07294360.2019.1680956

Emler, N. (1990). A social psychology of reputation. *European Review of Social Psychology, 1*(1), 171–193. https://doi.org/10.1080/14792779108401861

Fellner, C. (2020). Ghost writers helping UNSW students to cheat on assessments, leaked report reveals. *The Sydney Morning Herald.* https://www.smh.com.au/national/nsw/cheating-unsw-students-hire-ghost-writers-from-messaging-site-wechat-to-complete-work-20200505-p54q3f.html

Ferguson, H. (2019). *Tertiary education quality and standards agency amendment* (Prohibiting academic cheating services) Bill 2019. Parliament of Australia. Department of Parliamentary Services. Bills Digest. 84, 2019–20. https://parlinfo.aph.gov.au/parlInfo/download/legislation/billsdgs/7182391/upload_binary/7182391.pdf;fileType=application%2Fpdf#search=%22r6483%22

Fontana, J. S. (2009). Nursing faculty experiences of students' academic dishonesty. *Journal of Nursing Education, 48*(4), 181–185. https://doi.org/10.3928/01484834-20090401-05

Franklyn-Stokes, A., & Newstead, S. E. (1995). Undergraduate cheating: Who does what and why? *Studies in Higher Education, 20*(2), 159–172. https://doi.org/10.1080/03075079512331381673

Gilmore, B. (2009). *Plagiarism: A how-not-to guide for students.* Heinemann.

Grasmick, H. G., & Bursik, R. J. (1990). Conscience, significant others, and rational choice: Extending the deterrence model. *Law & Society Review, 24*(3), 837–861. https://doi.org/10.2307/3053861

Griffith University. (2020). *What will happen to me if I cheat?* https://studenthelp.secure.griffith.edu.au/app/answers/detail/a_id/3299/~/what-will-happen-to-me-if-i-cheat%3F

Harper, R., Bretag, T., Ellis, C., Newton, P., Rozenberg, P., Saddiqui, S., & van Haeringen, K. (2019). Contract cheating: A survey of Australian university staff. *Studies in Higher Education, 44*(11), 1857–1873. https://doi.org/10.1080/03075079.2018.1462789

Khalil, F., Lawarrée, J., & Yun, S. (2010). Bribery versus extortion: Allowing the lesser of two evils. *The Rand Journal of Economics, 41*(1), 179–198. https://doi.org/10.1111/j.1756-2171.2009.00095.x

Khan, Z. R., Hemnani, P., Raheja, S., & Joshy, J. (2020). Raising awareness on contract cheating – Lessons learned from running campus-wide campaigns. *Journal of Academic Ethics, 18*(1), 17–33. https://doi.org/10.1007/s10805-019-09353-1

Matchett, S. (2020, October 20). "Name and shame" students who cheat says den Hollander. *Campus Morning Mail*. https://campusmorningmail.com.au/news/name-and-shame-students-who-cheat-says-den-hollander/

McCabe, D. L., Trevino, L. K., & Butterfield, K. D. (1999). Academic integrity in honor code and non-honor code environments. *Journal of Higher Education, 70*(2), 211–234. https://doi.org/10.1080/00221546.1999.11780762

Morris, E. J. (2018). Academic integrity matters: Five considerations for addressing contract cheating. *International Journal for Educational Integrity, 14*(15), 1–12. https://doi.org/10.1007/s40979-018-0038-5

Orth, U., Berking, M., & Burkhardt, S. (2006). Self-conscious emotions and depression: Rumination explains why shame but not guilt is maladaptive. *Personality and Social Psychology Bulletin, 32*(12), 1608–1619. https://doi.org/10.1177/0146167206292958

Pitt, P., Dullaghan, K., & Sutherland-Smith, W. (2020). 'Mess, stress and trauma': Students' experiences of formal contract cheating processes. *Assessment & Evaluation in Higher Education, 46*(4), 659–672. https://doi.org/10.1080/02602938.2020.1787332

Poelmans, S., Stepanova, O., & Masuda, A. (2008). Positive spillover between personal and professional life: Definitions, antecedents, consequences, and strategies. In K. Korabik, D. S. Lero, & D. L. Whitehead (Eds.), *Handbook of work-family integration* (pp. 141–156). Academic Press. https://doi.org/10.1016/B978-012372574-5.50011-9

Raub, W., & Weesie, J. (1990). Reputation and efficiency in social interactions: An example of network effects. *American Journal of Sociology, 96*(3), 626–654. http://www.jstor.org.dbgw.lis.curtin.edu.au/stable/2781066

Ronson, J. (2015). *So you've been publicly shamed*. Riverhead Books.

Rose, S. (2013). The value of a college degree. *Change: The Magazine of Higher Learning*, 45(6), 24–33. https://doi.org/10.1080/00091383.2013.842101

Ross, J. (2018, December 7). *Contract cheating websites 'blackmailing whistle-blowers'*. https://www.timeshighereducation.com/news/contract-cheating-websites-blackmailing-whistle-blowers

Rowland, S., Slade, C., Wong, K.-S., & Whiting, B. (2018). 'Just turn to us': The persuasive features of contract cheating websites. *Assessment & Evaluation in Higher Education*, 43(4), 652–665. https://doi.org/10.1080/02602938.2017.1391948

Rundle, K., Curtis, G. J., & Clare, J. (2020). Why students choose not to cheat. In T. Bretag (Ed.), *A research agenda for academic integrity* (pp. 100–111). Edward Elgar Publishing. https://doi.org/10.4337/9781789903775.00014

Saunders, E. J. (1993). Confronting academic dishonesty. *Journal of Social Work Education*, 29(2), 224–231. https://www.jstor.org/stable/41346381

Steel, A. (2017). Contract cheating: Will students pay for serious criminal consequences? *Alternative Law Journal*, 42(2), 123–129. https://doi.org/10.1177/1037969X17710627

Sutherland-Smith, W., & Dullaghan, K. (2019). You don't always get what you pay for: User experiences of engaging with contract cheating sites. *Assessment & Evaluation in Higher Education*, 44(8), 1148–1162. https://doi.org/10.1080/02602938.2019.1576028

Tangney, J. P., Stuewig, J., & Hafez, L. (2011). Shame, guilt and remorse: Implications for offender populations. *The Journal of Forensic Psychiatry & Psychology*, 22(5), 706–723. https://doi.org/10.1080/14789949.2011.617541

Taylor, G. (1996). Guilt and remorse. In R. Harre & G. W. Parrott (Eds.), *The emotions: Social, cultural and biological dimensions* (pp. 57–73). Sage.

TED. (2011, January 4). *Brené Brown: The power of vulnerability* [video]. YouTube. https://www.youtube.com/watch?v=iCvmsMzlF7o&t=31s

TED. (2012, March 17). *Brené Brown: Listening to shame* [video]. YouTube. https://www.youtube.com/watch?v=psN1DORYYV0

Tertiary Education Quality and Standards Agency. (2017). *Good practice note: Addressing contract cheating to safeguard academic integrity*. https://www.teqsa.gov.au/sites/default/files/good-practice-note-addressing-contract-cheating.pdf

Salmi, J., Millot, B., Court, D., Crawford, P., Darvas, M., Golladay, F., Holm Nielsen, L., Hopper, R., Markov, A., Moock, P., Mukherjee, H., Saint, W., Shrivastava, S., Steier, F., & Van Meel, F. (2002). *Constructing knowledge societies: New challenges for tertiary education*. The World Bank. https://doi.org/10.1596/0-8213-5143-5

Thomas, D. (2017). Factors that explain academic dishonesty among university students in Thailand. *Ethics & Behavior, 27*(2), 140–154. https://doi.org/10.1080/10508422.2015.1131160

University of Sydney. (2020). *Academic dishonesty and plagiarism.* https://www.sydney.edu.au/students/academic-dishonesty/contract-cheating.html

Visentin, L. (2015, March 18). MyMaster essay cheating scandal: More than 70 university students face suspension. *The Sydney Morning Herald.* https://www.smh.com.au/national/nsw/mymaster-essay-cheating-scandal-more-than-70-university-students-face-suspension-20150312-1425oe.html

Yorke, J., Sefcik, L., & Veeran-Colton, T. (2022). Contract cheating and blackmail: A risky business? *Studies in Higher Education, 47*(1), 53–66. https://doi.org/10.1080/03075079.2020.1730313

Yu, H., Glanzer, P. L., & Johnson, B. R. (2021). Examining the relationship between student attitude and academic cheating. *Ethics & Behavior, 31*(7), 475–487. https://doi.org/10.1080/10508422.2020.1817746

CHAPTER 17

The Rise of Contract Cheating in Graduate Education

Ceceilia Parnther

INTRODUCTION

Contract cheating and other forms of academic misconduct appear to be on the rise (Newton, 2018; Rigby et al., 2015). Over the last 15 years, research in the area has expanded from an initial definition of contracted cheating based on findings from a computer science study (Clarke & Lancaster, 2006) to an area of study including contract cheating in the context of most academic disciplines and assignments. A more recent definition of the phenomenon is provided by Draper and Newton (2017) as "a basic relationship between three actors: a student, their university, and a third party who completes assessments for the former to be submitted to the latter, but whose input is not permitted" (p. 1). Contract cheating represents a billion-dollar industry (BBC, 2019) and continues to expand. In a study of 130 contract cheating sites, Ellis et al. (2018) identified the practice's primary business models. The study finds three models:

C. Parnther (✉)
Department of Administrative and Instructional Leadership, School of Education, St. John's University, Queens, NY, USA
e-mail: parnthec@stjohns.edu

© The Author(s), under exclusive license to Springer Nature Switzerland AG 2022
S. E. Eaton et al. (eds.), *Contract Cheating in Higher Education*,
https://doi.org/10.1007/978-3-031-12680-2_17

freelance writers, the academic custom writing business owner, and master site owners. The models build on one another, increasing infrastructure and distributing revenue as companies combine the models.

Although most research describes undergraduates who engage in contract cheating, graduate students are also targeted by contract cheating marketing efforts, often thesis and dissertation writing. Russian media reports suggest essay mills were used in up to 10,000, or the equivalent of two-thirds of all dissertations conferred in 2006. In a study identifying the prevalence of contract cheating, Harper et al. (2021) found that text-based assignments were the top eight most frequently detected forms. The authors surmised that many elements of graduate study, such as research development, annotated bibliographies/literature reviews, research proposals, theses, and dissertations, are text-based.

Graduate students are a rising, sought-after subsection of higher education and the contract cheating customer base. Unfortunately, factors including an increase in a customer-driven higher education system (Guilbault, 2018) represent a diminishing return on investment. Furthermore, marketing that appeals to students disappointed in the graduate school experience makes graduate education susceptible to predatory markets (Newton, 2018). This chapter provides an overview of contract cheating related to graduate students, the rise of dissertation and thesis services in the contract cheating industry, and the risks these pose to graduate students. Implications and discussion conclude the chapter.

Graduate Students and Contract Cheating

Graduate students are a rising population (Higher Education Statistics Agency, 2022). Given a need for a highly skilled workforce, these credentials are desirable during economic downturns. Graduate education may also serve as a financial safety net for institutions with declining undergraduate enrolment, the value of graduate students who provide institutional labour, and the increase of working professionals seeking promotions or career changes (Paris, 2021). As a result, graduate programmes will continue to grow (Paris, 2021). In some cases, institutions struggle to support student populations with increasingly diverse needs. El Alfy and Abukari (2020) identify student support as service quality dimensions. Supports include academic services (course-related and instructor-related), administrative services, academic facilities (library and education technology), and student service resources. El Alfy and Abukari (2020) describe the challenge of increased admissions and perceptions of service quality in a qualitative study of students, administrators, faculty, and staff warning that increasing access through holistic admissions without refining services quality measures, such as tutoring or technological resources, presents challenges and erodes trust.

Graduate students may return to school with additional personal and professional responsibilities that challenge classroom engagement. Graduate student development literature indicates that students seek direct feedback, instruction, and relevant connections to their fields of interest or aspiration. Knowles et al. (2015) describe the adult learner as someone who needs to know what is expected, what will be assessed, and how the work relates to their needs and desires using the concept of andragogy. As outlined in practice, graduate students seek respect for their former experiences, personal lives, and time commitments. Nebulous concepts may prove incredibly challenging for graduate students with diverse educational experiences. Graduate students are more likely to succeed when approaches are personalised rather than standardised ones. However, research indicates that graduate students who feel disconnected from faculty or advisers may experience anxiety, stress, and dissatisfaction (Ballantine & Jolly-Ballantine, 2015). Merç (2016) describes the heightened anxiety associated with writing expectations of research findings, thesis, and dissertation writing common in graduate studies. In addition, students may be more likely to experience dissatisfaction and decreased trust in the institution (Newton & Lang, 2016). This may represent a threat to the perceived value of graduate education. These factors make the graduate student population especially susceptible to contract cheating. Contract cheating companies are methodical in their approaches to reaching students. Rowland et al. (2018) identified persuasive word patterns in a website study of contract cheating providers. Terms related to dishonesty and integrity were omitted. At the same time, persuasive words and phrases related to customer service, quality, and security were prominent. The study described both evidence that reassurance and problem resolution strategies are used as efforts to entice students.

Doctoral contract cheating is on the rise, and seeking contract cheating services has also increased (Amigud & Lancaster, 2020; Rigby et al., 2015). Google trend data shows that as of October 2021, the search term *dissertation/thesis writing service and dissertations/thesis ghostwriting* is at peak popularity or 100%. The same term was at 33% in 2016 (www.trends.google.com, 2022).

Industry Marketing

In response to increased demand for cheating services, the contract cheating market response is personalised to service the needs of graduate student writers. Companies craft advertisements appealing to the real challenges inherent in the expectations of graduate-level academic writing. A literature review by Kelly and Stevenson (2021) found themes related to the challenges doctoral students face, including "balancing work and personal life," "the complexity of doctoral academic writing," "self-efficacy," and "academic career progression" (pp. 368–369). The study presented in this chapter aimed to understand how contract cheating companies market services to graduate student writers in strategic response to unmet andragogical need, customer service orientation, and perceptions of blame that generate a neutralisation response concerning academic misconduct. Specifically, the study sought to explore the techniques and services offered to students writing dissertations and theses. Additionally, the study sought to understand the nature of the services offered, the unique efforts and characteristics used to appeal to the graduate student market, and the risks associated with contract cheating providers.

METHOD

Qualitative content analysis was used in this study; it is widely used in education research and is well suited to answer the research questions. In addition to describing the website contents, the method is valuable in understanding broad themes of a given unit of analysis. It may include visual, digital, and textual elements (Leech & Onwuegbuzie, 2008). As is standard in qualitative content analysis, it was necessary to be intentional in data collection by (1) engaging with the data points, (2) developing and using a coding scheme, (3) organising codes into themes, and (4) defining and presenting findings while answering the research questions guiding the study (Leech & Onwuegbuzie, 2008).

Data Collection

This study represents a review of active websites using the search terms *dissertation coaching*, *dissertation tutoring*, *dissertation/thesis writing*, and *dissertation consulting* appearing in Google, a search engine; Facebook, a social messaging system; Discord, an instant messaging and digital distribution application; and Reddit, an online discussion forum. Website data were captured in Excel, with pictures of the live sites captured in screenshots and saved to a cloud-based storage system between 11/2/21 and 11/12/21. Evidence of contract cheating was represented by language offering the service, the presence of a payment area to purchase a dissertation, or a link to order a completed dissertation requiring a consultation.

Company websites were searched by landing page, about us page, and any subpages including specific evidence related to (1) *tutoring or coaching services*, (2) *academic misconduct, integrity, or plagiarism*, (3) *writing services offered*, (4) *service offerings* that meet the definition of an evident or implied ability to engage in contract cheating, and (5) *additional content* related to graduate students. For clarity, editing, methodological consulting, and coaching services were not included in this analysis *in the absence of* direct evidence of contract cheating. In addition, coaching and consulting services that specifically state they do not write content for students were excluded. Finally, data collection was delimited to website advertising specifically to graduate students for dissertations or theses.

Data Analysis

Deductive codes were informed by the principles of andragogy, the practice of adult learning (Knowles et al., 2015). These include Self-Concept, or how a student understands what they need to do (and how they need to do it) independently; Adult Learner Experience, or how a student can use their life experiences to make sense of new information; Readiness to Learn, or a student's ability to fit learning into their full lives; Motivation to Learn, or a student's internal desires and motivations; and Goal Orientation to Learning, or a student's connection to problem-based learning. Ultimately, this theory guides four principles. First, adults see themselves as partners in learning and want to be involved; second, adult students rely heavily on personal experiences and those guide their approach to learning; third, adults prefer to learn concepts that are tied to their personal and professional interests; and fourth, within this contextualisation, subject mastery for adult students most often comes from their ability to solve relevant problems.

The principles, guided by the theory, were chosen not to assign age attributes to graduate learners but to acknowledge that graduate students embody unique experiences, motivations, and responsibilities that require the incorporation of students' perspectives, experiences, and responsibilities. This study includes concepts such as *respect, life experience,* and *practicality*. Additional emergent codes, informed by the websites themselves, included *legality, quality,* and *help*. In all, 65 codes were identified. First, pattern coding was completed by collapsing aligning codes, then by aspects of the sites, such as visual and textual advertising characteristics, evidence of audience, and contractual agreements. Advertising characteristics were further explored, including positive and negative language. For example, language relating to career advancement was categorised as positive, whereas language related to unsupportive mentors was negative. Codes were also organised by responsibility. For example, services that "help" students who cannot grasp a specific concept versus services that describe themselves as filling the void of an inattentive or unsupportive faculty advisor. Second, cycle pattern coding continued until saturation.

Findings

The websites or webpages included 102 websites, with 5 of these found through Reddit posts using the search terms listed in the *r/assignmenthelp* and *r/essayhelp* subreddits. Four were found through Discord ($n = 1$) and TikTok ($n = 3$). Finally, nine sites were found through Facebook groups using the same search terms. All of the sites contained text evidence of selling written dissertations and theses. The sites also refer to homework help, tutoring, and consulting.

On other sites, academic imagery, including subjects (individuals or animals) with glasses, textbooks, computers, and pieces of paper, represents scholarly activity. Images of success are depicted, replete with graduation caps, raised arms, and smiles. The imagery on the websites often depicts stressed students, frequently hunched over a computer, hands on their heads to depict a sense of frustration and helplessness. Contract cheating is heavily marketed as a solution.

Contract Cheating as a Solution to the Problems of Graduate Students

Students visiting these websites are invited through marketing to solve a problem. On every website, the dissertation/thesis is presented as a problem outside a student's control, at times even an insurmountable goal. Graduate student challenges are addressed, specifically related to work and family demands, the urgent need for a quality paper, time limitations, and the document's importance. Solutions were presented to problems classified as being related to instruction, student challenges, time constraints, and the importance of the work.

Instruction was depicted as marginal, with the most frequent descriptors related to the time and care faculty have for students. Examples of this include the following statements that are critical of professors and instructors "students pick just the worst instructor who keeps demanding impossible things" (rush-my-essay.com). Another example describes the independent and sometimes isolating experience of graduate study: "These so-called external PhD students are not integrated into the academic community and generally receive much less intensive supervision by the supervisor than students who attain their doctorates within the faculty" (dissertation-writingservice.com, 2022).

Additional language included critiques of expectations and support, including feedback "many professors do not provide constructive criticism of mistakes and even less corrections for those mistakes" (academicresearchandwriting.com) and suggesting that the expectation of research papers is an outdated concept. "The old-fashioned education system that refuses to acknowledge that the times have changed and that essays are no longer the best way to gauge knowledge and understanding" (smartassignmenthelp.com).

In both instances exemplified here, the solution providers pose is to circumvent the faculty or institutional relationship by using contract cheating services, relying on "experts" who have experience navigating the process. The companies make attempts first to capitalise on the fear and anxiety of struggling students. The design of the websites also appeals to a student's sense of helplessness rooted in their abilities. Specifically, the sites speak to loneliness, overwhelming, and despair. One site, speaking to all of these, presents the dissertation or theses as insurmountable, adding "accompanied by the long process of planning, research, and writing—it's possible that they don't have enough time to accomplish all their tasks. This throws many students in despair" (studybay.com).

This is presented as a type of commiseration or understanding. Once again, the companies presenting a solution to these negative feelings follow a prescriptive approach to comfort the student and remove personal responsibility. One such statement attempts to comfort students in distress "there is no need to panic! Would you believe it is easy to get help from a team of professional dissertation writers who specialise in your field?" (papersowl.com).

By providing comfort, the reader may feel that contract cheating provides a solution to the problem. Relatedly, assurances that the service will alleviate the concerns around instruction, relevance, and knowledge are reviled with language directly addressing the above-mentioned issues. Specifically, the services' knowledge, experience, and understanding act as a solution to the concerns rooted in misunderstanding and inadequate supervision. The sites suggest that these services may also provide the boost needed to succeed and perhaps enhance the writing process.

- Our writers know what your professors are looking for—they will produce you a legit, custom dissertation that is unique to your requirements (academized.com).
- We thus close the gap resulting from the lack of or insufficient supervision by the university and can help overcome certain types of writer's block or to clarify specific questions (dissertation-writingservice.com).
- We only work with highly qualified writers who are working or have been employed in the academic field and therefore know exactly what is important when writing a dissertation (dissertation-writingservice.com).

Reassurances of the providers' skill and efficiency are evident and appear multiple times on the websites. While the websites frame the problems plaguing graduate students as instruction and support, contract cheating services are presented as help, assistance, and support to struggling students. Additional challenges impacting the student experience directly align with the needs of graduate students. The sample showed concerns commonly referenced for adult students, specifically time, additional priorities, family obligations, and employment. As in the previous examples, the websites attempt to summarise the student experience. The sites appeal to the stress and helplessness students feel due to time constraints. Examples of this are clearly found on the home pages:

- Many graduate students have other full or part-time commitments (dissertation-writingservice.com).

- Those who are exhausted after a long day at work often do not have the motivation and energy they need to work out profound scientific theories in the evening or at the weekend (thesiswritingservice.net).
- The deadline is nearing, and it seems more urgent to hand it in on time than to start over (academized.com).

The websites most often refer to time, providing quick service and sharing options to speed up the process. Repeated indicators of this are found on the web pages and social media sites. A form requesting time requirements is listed on the overwhelming majority of the sites. In addition, chatbots ask about deadlines before providing quotes. Finally, in the narrative sections of the website, information reminds the reader of the problem. Examples of that include the following language:

- answer few questions about your assignment and deadlines to ensure that you'll get the perfect assignment right on time (kiwipapers.com).
- comprehensive service in a discrete, fast, and personalised manner (optimumresearchconsulting.com).

Service continued to be a demonstrated priority for the companies. Despite offering services that violate academic integrity, a significant amount of energy is spent ensuring potential customers of service, satisfaction, and potential rewards.

Contract Cheating as Performative Customer Service

Customer service is an integrated feature on nearly all ($N = 97$) websites. Chatbots welcome visitors to the screen within seconds of opening the homepage. Contact information in the form of a pop-up is a regular feature on the sites. Discounts with countdowns are prominently displayed, and "as low as" language is displayed to indicate low rates. While one site offers introductory rates as low as US$7 per page, the average advertised rate was approximately $13. Several sites note the importance of higher-quality work submitted for a graduate degree. Despite this, quotes for 150-page dissertations using a timeline of over 30 days resulted in quotes from US$3052 to US$6000. Additional discounts were offered in exchange for activities demonstrating interest, such as accepting cookies, adding an email address, or for repeat customers as an affiliate or loyalty bonus. Multiple revisions were a common feature across the sample.

Additional features included an almost universal 24/7 customer service claim, and most included assurances of confidentiality and a refund policy, as noted by when describing their services, "This personalised approach to dissertation assistance guarantees that you'll have one individual working with you throughout the process so that you can feel confident that our assistance will be tailored to your specific needs and preferences at every stage" (dissertation-editor.com).

The majority of the sites disparage the potential quality of alternative contract cheating providers, describing poor work, including grammatical and plagiarism errors. The websites warn of wasted money, poor service, and general dissatisfaction. The providers attempt to assuage concern about these problems with premium or add-on services. Plagiarism checking, writers described as experts with a related degree, and fast turnarounds were offered as premium options at varying price points.

Contract Cheating and the Perception of Expertise

While many websites were clear about their services, notable sites were included that initially appeared to be dissertation support and editing sites. These sites focused exclusively on the challenges, some even offering skill-building and support. For example, the mission statement of one company includes language on the advancement and promotion of academic and professional excellence, continuous learning, and development. Websites (N = 65) included overviews of each section of the dissertation/thesis process, including tips for each section and defence. In each case, these overviews were written as blog posts designed to appear scholarly, with information spanning from dedicated pages to each section of the traditional dissertation or thesis format to one-sentence summaries. On six web pages, downloadable dissertation guides were available.

The websites made promises to potential clients of access and satisfaction, including providing quality "nothing but exceptional top-quality work" (thewritingplanet.com), authenticity, for example, a "guarantee that all work delivered is completely original and unique" (collegeessay.org), and messaging ensuring that contracted writers will work tirelessly to alleviate pressure for busy students, stating "we work around the clock so that you don't have to…we can complete all coursework in an effective and efficient manner such that you are—cleared to begin your dissertation project" (approvalreadyconsulting.com).

By framing customer service as quality, the contract cheating providers attempt to distance themselves from the behaviour itself, positioning the student as a customer deserving a quality product provided by an expert. The language used throughout the websites focused on assurances of expertise, an interesting finding given that none of the sites limited the academic focus of the services they provide. A few sites presented themselves as consultants and coaches, despite clearly indicating they would write entire dissertations and theses for a fee. The companies suggest they have writers uniquely capable of writing a dissertation that represents the culmination of a degree programme. The websites include language around freelance expertise. These include describing training and certification when describing the writers. Most companies include mentions of English proficiency, PhDs, professional writers, certification programmes, and highly rated writers.

The websites reviewed were mixed in terms of the customers' ability to choose a writer. As related to graduate students, emphasis was placed on the experience of writers who develop dissertations and theses. The websites included language speaking to the significance of the writing and the importance of hiring highly skilled professionals. Premium services also included writers who were degree holders from highly selective institutions. There were clear differences in the marketing of essay services for undergraduate students, with language focused on low cost and time, compared to graduate students focused on investment and quality. The price points, based on page number, bear out that point. Graduate students were advised to request services in advance to ensure the "expert" had time to prepare the manuscript adequately. Contract cheating providers also suggest that they are highly familiar with national and state laws around dissertation and thesis writing services. In two cases, Australian students were forbidden from using the website.

Many of the websites in the study assure students that purchasing a dissertation or thesis is a legal activity. To illustrate this, the companies include sections related to academic integrity, plagiarism, and legality. Examples of this language include statements falsely denying legal risks. In one example, Essaybox.org describes the service as assistance, stating, "paying professional essay writers to write your essay is not illegal. It does not mean that you are cheating with the education system or doing academic cheating. It only means that you are trying to get help" (essaybox.org). The site goes on to explain their position, arguing that "taking help from the dissertation writing service is not illegal and cheating because our company offers 100 percent legal and legitimate work." In another instance, sharkpapers.com suggests that only papers with evidence of detected plagiarism are illegal, stating, "Working with a custom writing service or paying an essay writer becomes illegal when the writer is inexperienced and knows nothing about your course." The site goes on to list tools used to plagiarise, including recycling older papers and using content spinners as illegal actions. Despite these assurances, the websites carefully use language to describe property rights and liability.

Contract Cheating and Legal Issues

In language related to sales, the suggestion is that student customers own the papers they are purchasing and that any material they submit to be reviewed is theirs as well. This language represents a significant disconnect with the language used in the terms and conditions. While the language that suggests a guarantee of success, approval, and graduation, the terms and conditions, terms of use, and legal pages associated with most sites ($N = 78$) referred to the resulting deliverable as a document for research purposes only. While these were not uniquely linked to graduate students, the language made clear that companies were not responsible for the quality of the content. Language in these policies expressly included plagiarism and grammatical errors. The companies also indemnify themselves against all consequences related to misrepresentation of the work as the student's own. The language included in the vast majority of the terms and conditions suggested that the purchase of a dissertation or thesis was actually the purchase of a research or academic resource and should only be used as such. Some policies clearly state students should not alter the document in any way, including using the content in whole or part or placing their own names on the purchased document. Examples of these were found to clearly list these limitations:

- You cannot put your name on the completed Product. The Products delivered by our Company are for research and reference purposes only (anywritinghelp.com).
- We will not be held accountable if such unethical and illegal use of Our Products and Website content occurs (thecollegehawk.com).
- You can use our documents as a model to create your own piece of writing based on provided research results and using the documents as a motivation (essaywave.com).

Policies on the websites described academic integrity and academic honour as principles the companies uphold. An honour code on one website reads: "Essay Pro does not appreciate and will not engage in any type of academic dishonesty, nor facilitate cheating, the commitment of fraud, and the obtaining of unearned grades or degrees" (EssayPro.com).

The companies do not consider themselves responsible for the actions of freelance writers or third parties. In fact, the legal terms on almost all of the websites that include terms and conditions state the company has the right to keep and share personal information as necessary. The language contradicts the sales claims in price, use, and quality. The following language illustrates several points. First, the papers are not meant to be submitted to an educational institution, "the Paper is not to be used for obtaining any mark, grade or any achievement in any way connected with academics" (valiantwriters.com). Second, purchased papers are considered reference material "for investigation, quotation purposes, and/or to enable you to see how to correctly complete an assignment" (tameraresearch.com). Third, after using the referenced resource, the paper will be destroyed, "you agree to destroy any, and all delivered Products from the Company after Your research/reference purposes for the paper have been met" (writepaper.com). And fourth, prices are subject to change, even after the initial agreement, "We personally can decide that a different price is required for your Order than the one specified, we will notify you about it and offer a different fee" (fusionessay.com).

The companies, *not* the author or purchaser, retain clear rights to the purchased material. This position does not align with the common expectation that universities endorse a dissertation or thesis as an independently written and published work. In addition, the review of the terms and conditions demands the customer relinquish a right to privacy and ownership of any written material submitted to the website (or website affiliate links) for informational purposes. Further, ownership is a complicated maze involving the website entity, the larger company, and most often, a freelance writer. For example, language separates the website from the service, such as "this website is developed and advertised by affiliated partners working as independent contractors under the terms of an affiliate program" (justdomyessay.com).

The review of the *Terms and Conditions* indicates that a smaller number of private limited content management companies own nearly all of the sites, despite the countries they market to. The companies in this study are located in the United States, the United Kingdom, and outlying territories, Cyprus, and Bulgaria. On Facebook, there is also a presence of companies with holdings in Malaysia, Pakistan, and the Philippines. However, most of the companies maintain ownership of the contracted work, as stated in the following intellectual property statement from writ-ersscholar.com (2022):

> all exclusive material intellectual property rights for all Samples and any other intellectual property objects created in the process of cooperation with the Company shall belong to the Company in full scope, including but not limited to: the right to use, possess and dispose of the sample, and all previously submitted Sample projects of Writers, in any tangible medium of expression, now known or later developed, from which it can be perceived, reproduced, or otherwise communicated, either directly or with the aid of a machine or device, including without limitation the rights to archive, republish, edit, repackage or revise any intellectual property object in any manner as the Company sees fit.

Discussion

In a review of dissertation services, providers appeal to the emotions of stressed and frustrated students. The contract cheating business models identified by Ellis et al. (2018) are evident in the present study. Design features, terms, and conditions with shell company names, and promises of personalisation provide evidence. As related to andragogy, the companies appeal to the real worry and fear students are experiencing. Rather than describing abstract concepts, the companies identify problems and offer immediate solutions. Unfortunately, the balm they offer comes in the form of an excuse. Rather than acknowledging the consequence of not asking for help or waiting until the last minute, the discourse is framed to solely blame the institution or faculty member. Prior research on academic misconduct describes the phenomenon of misplaced responsibility as a justification for misconduct using neutralisation theory (Makarova, 2019; Sykes & Matza, 1957).

The contract cheating model prioritises immediate interaction and service through chatbots, email forms, and phone calls. Aligning with Rowland et al. (2018), companies present themselves as a solution to the problems students face, frequently referencing busy schedules, customer service, and convenience, important considerations often ignored in traditional academic settings. Likewise, andragogical approaches may also appeal to graduate students. Students may find consolation in website language. Content that focuses on achieving milestones and intrinsic motivators, including grades, degrees, and defences, represents opportunities for career advancement or a faster time to degree.

Additionally, graduate students may value being viewed as a customer, with experts waiting to serve and support them, further rationalising contract cheating as an outsourced service needed for success. Professional writers, time savings, and an investment rationalised as aligning with the importance of the project are intentional strategies used throughout the websites. In addition, graduate students find appeal in choosing the topic, the expert, and the company that will assist them. Capitalising on this, contract cheating companies begin interactions by asking the student what they need instead of leading with what they provide, besides the obvious. Reviews, pictures of writers, credentials, specific disciplines, and dissertation titles all aid in personalisation. Some specifically target the rapidly growing online degree market, describing their services as personalised and one-on-one.

Implications

Contract cheating for graduate students represents a significant threat to academic integrity, particularly in writing dissertations and thesis projects. Companies are agile and intentional in their approaches. Students may choose to engage in misconduct without fully understanding the consequences of their actions (Ellis et al., 2018). Perhaps more important is the fundamental disadvantage of misrepresenting their expertise. If the practice continues to grow, it will represent a much larger share of the early career research and development in college. Beyond this, students will not demonstrate their expertise, a skill often necessary in leadership and research positions. As previous research warns, faculty and graduate student research advisors should be aware of these websites and explain the model and the pitfalls of contract cheating to students (Ellis et al., 2018).

For students with limited social capital or experience with graduate study, these sites represent an especially significant risk. As participation in postgraduate education increases, the impasse between traditional understandings of what a student has been exposed to or has not continues to grow. Faculty and administrators should not assume that all students understand contract cheating, especially with website language painting institutions as adversarial and product ownership nebulous. This review indicates that contract cheating companies continue to expand and personalise their services in response to student demand. These providers represent themselves as content management organisations, often using multiple names and likenesses under one company. The companies rely on freelancers to avail themselves of responsibility yet host the identity, payment, and intellectual property data of both writer and student.

In most cases, the limited ownership of the documents may represent additional legal risks for any student choosing to misrepresent work as their own. The companies expressly warn of these risks, although students do not immediately see the terms and conditions associated with their actions. The details of the contract are not located easily. In addition, the rise in contract cheating providers' uses of alternative social media platforms further obscures the terms and conditions.

Becoming aware of the language on contract cheating sites allows instructors and graduate supervisors to be responsive by offering supportive alternatives. Interventions may include scaffolding the dissertation into smaller sections, expanding and differentiating academic supports based on student concerns and skill levels, writing supports, and demystifying the process to remove the fear and unknown. For example, inviting students to attend dissertation defences, providing exemplar materials, writing communities, and offering peer mentorship from recent alumni may offer students alternatives.

A larger conversation on dissertations and theses as a culminating assessment is also warranted. While the characteristics are field and institutional-specific, there is a case for critically reviewing the structure and intention of final assessments. The language used throughout the sites in this study demonstrates misunderstanding, frustration, fear, and helplessness with the process. Framing the utility of the culminating assessment assigns value and understanding. For example, some disciplines have instituted the three-article dissertation research development and synthesis utility. Students walk away with active manuscripts of publishable quality, and the required synthesis adds to the student's ability to refine a research agenda. While this is not a one-size-fits-all solution, it offers an alternative for demonstrating understanding. Teaching and learning in graduate education are often collaborative; however, the process of dissertation and thesis writing are independent endeavours. Most leaders and researchers rely on partnerships with others to address problems in research and practice. While individual competence is essential to demonstrate, contract cheating is dependent on the fear and isolation normalised as part of the process.

Institutions responding to instances of contract cheating must contend with several issues. First is educating faculty, graduate research advisors, and students on the risks of contract cheating. Secondly, institutions should guide on how issues of contract cheating at the graduate level are handled, given the heightened expectations inherent in graduate work. This guidance should include instruction on managing the discovery of the content, addressing potential legal ramifications of the discovery, and addressing student responsibility. The response to each will determine the perceived severity of the action, a student's level of culpability, and an institutional endorsement or rejection of academic misconduct. Graduate theses and dissertations are especially fraught with risk, as a university endorsement represents confirmation of authentic and original research. Finally, institutions that discover contracted student work have a responsibility to address academic fraud and clearly state the consequences for these behaviours, including degree revocation.

Future research should consider how graduate students understand the purposeful marketing language and design used to promote contract cheating services. Research should include studies that measure student understanding of the risks, including, but not limited to, identity theft, bribery and extortion, academic misconduct charges, failing grades, and programme dismissal. Mapping the larger contract cheating companies to their smaller shell companies, ongoing work by others may provide a better understanding of the landscape in the global marketplace. Lastly, a more extensive review of the terms and conditions, honour codes, and academic integrity policies on contract cheating websites may provide additional considerations for students considering using the services. The risks of outsourcing core competencies, including content, literature reviews, research design, and analysis, are substantial. Contract cheating threatens the trust necessary to develop a research or policy agenda. The services erode the ability to adequately assess preparation and refine teaching and advising. On the other hand, the results represent meaningful opportunities to learn how contract cheating companies make sense of the struggles of disconnected, intrinsically motivated students. Students who are supported and engaged see independent research as an opportunity to engage in personally meaningful and creative pursuits. Instead, those using contract cheating services remove themselves from contributing and are also willing to risk their academic reputation and identity to gain a credential. Educators should consider supporting students seeking meaningful gains in leadership and research opportunities by educating graduate students on the risks of contract cheating, reconsidering traditional assessment practices, and addressing the detrimental factors to their experience.

REFERENCES

Amigud, A., & Lancaster, T. (2020). I will pay someone to do my assignment: An analysis of market demand for contract cheating services on Twitter. *Assessment & Evaluation in Higher Education, 45*(4), 541–553. https://doi.org/10.1080/02602938.2019.1670780

Ballantine, J. H., & Jolly-Ballantine, J. A. (2015). Mentoring graduate students: The good, bad, and gray. *Journal on Excellence in College Teaching, 26*(2), 5–41.

BBC. (2019). *The Kenyan ghost writers doing 'lazy' Western students' work*. Retrieved from https://www.bbc.co.uk/news/av/world-africa-50126963/the-kenyan-ghost-writers-doinglazy-western-students-work

Clarke, R., & Lancaster, T. (2006, June). Eliminating the successor to plagiarism? Identifying the usage of contract cheating sites. In *Proceedings of 2nd international plagiarism conference* (pp. 1–13). Northumbria Learning Press.

Draper, M. J., & Newton, P. M. (2017). A legal approach to tackling contract cheating? *International Journal for Educational Integrity, 13*(1), 1–16. https://doi.org/10.1007/s40979-017-0022-5

El Alfy, S., & Abukari, A. (2020). Revisiting perceived service quality in higher education: Uncovering service quality dimensions for postgraduate students. *Journal of Marketing for Higher Education, 30*(1), 1–25. https://doi.org/10.1080/08841241.2019.1648360

Ellis, C., Zucker, I. M., & Randall, D. (2018). The infernal business of contract cheating: Understanding the business processes and models of academic custom writing sites. *International Journal for Educational Integrity, 14*(1), 1–21. https://doi.org/10.1007/s40979-017-0024-3

Guilbault, M. (2018). Students as customers in higher education: The (controversial) debate needs to end. *Journal of Retailing and Consumer Services, 40*, 295–298. https://doi.org/10.1016/j.jretconser.2017.03.006

Harper, R., Bretag, T., & Rundle, K. (2021). Detecting contract cheating: Examining the role of assessment type. *Higher Education Research & Development, 40*(2), 263–278. https://doi.org/10.1080/07294360.2020.1724899

Higher Education Statistics Agency. (2022). *Higher education student statistics: UK, 2020/21 - Where students come from and go to study* (Statistical Bulletin No. SB262). https://www.hesa.ac.uk/news/25-01-2022/sb262-higher-education-student-statistics/location

Kelly, A., & Stevenson, K. J. (2021). Students pay the price: Doctoral candidates are targeted by contract cheating websites. *International Journal of Doctoral Studies, 16*, 363–377. https://doi.org/10.28945/4757

Knowles, M. S., Holton, E., & Swanson, A. (2015). *The adult learner* (8th ed.). Routledge.

Leech, N. L., & Onwuegbuzie, A. J. (2008). Qualitative data analysis: A compendium of techniques and a framework for selection for school psychology research and beyond. *School Psychology Quarterly, 23*(4), 587. https://doi.org/10.1037/1045-3830.23.4.587

Makarova, M. (2019). Factors of academic misconduct in a cross-cultural perspective and the role of integrity systems. *Journal of Academic Ethics, 17*(1), 51–71. https://doi.org/10.1007/s10805-019-9323-z

Merç, A. (2016). Research anxiety among Turkish graduate ELT students. *Current Issues in Education, 19*(1), 1–15.

Newton, P. M. (2018). How common is commercial contract cheating in higher education and is it increasing? A systematic review. *Frontiers in Education, 3*(67). https://doi.org/10.3389/feduc.2018.00067

Newton, P. M., & Lang, C. (2016). Custom essay writers, freelancers and other paid third parties. In T. Bretag (Ed.), *Handbook of academic integrity* (pp. 249–272). Springer. https://doi.org/10.1007/978-981-287-098-8_38

Rigby, D., Burton, M., Balcombe, K., Bateman, I., & Mulatu, A. (2015). Contract cheating & the market in essays. *Journal of Economic Behavior & Organization, 111*, 23–37. https://doi.org/10.1016/j.jebo.2014.12.019

Rowland, S., Slade, C., Wong, K. S., & Whiting, B. (2018). 'Just turn to us': The persuasive features of contract cheating websites. *Assessment & Evaluation in Higher Education, 43*(4), 652–665. https://doi.org/10.1080/02602938.2017.1391948

Sykes, G. M., & Matza, D. (1957). Techniques of neutralization: A theory of delinquency. *American Sociological Review, 22*(6), 664–670. https://doi.org/10.2307/2089195

CHAPTER 18

Listening to Ghosts: A Qualitative Study of Narratives from Contract Cheating Writers from the 1930s Onwards

Sarah Elaine Eaton, Brenda M. Stoesz, and Josh Seeland

INTRODUCTION

Little is known about the individuals who supply services to the academic cheating industry. One of the best-known suppliers to the contract cheating industry is American, David (Dave) Tomar, who rose to fame in the 2010s. Tomar first wrote about working for the contract cheating industry under the pseudonym "Ed Dante" in an exposé for *The Chronicle of Higher Education* (Dante, 2010). A few years later, Tomar revealed his identity,

S. E. Eaton (✉)
University of Calgary, Calgary, AB, Canada
e-mail: seaton@ucalgary.ca

B. M. Stoesz
University of Manitoba, Winnipeg, MB, Canada
e-mail: Brenda.Stoesz@umanitoba.ca

J. Seeland
Assiniboine Community College, Brandon, MB, Canada
e-mail: seelandjl@Assiniboine.net

© The Author(s), under exclusive license to Springer Nature Switzerland AG 2022
S. E. Eaton et al. (eds.), *Contract Cheating in Higher Education*, https://doi.org/10.1007/978-3-031-12680-2_18

271

writing a book about his experiences working for the industry (Tomar, 2013). Although Tomar might have gained the most notoriety as a supplier to the industry, by no means is he the only, nor the first, to write about his experiences. It has already been established that the commercial contract cheating industry, operating at scale, can be traced back to the 1930s (see Benjamin, 1939; Buerger, 2002, Eaton, 2021).

In recent years, the mainstream media has reported on the contract cheating industry, spotlighting what it is like for individuals who work in it. Media reports often focus on non-white individuals, especially those from Kenya and other African or South Asian countries (see BBC, 2019; Kansara & Main, 2021; Simons, 2019; Sutherland, 2019). One media report claimed that "Kenya, which has large numbers of educated graduates but rampant unemployment, has established itself as the centre of the academic cheating universe" (Singh, 2021, n.p.). We urge caution against drawing conclusions that the industry is based mainly in Africa or South Asia, as this can lead to an assumption by those from Anglo-based countries that the contract cheating industry is located "elsewhere" and that those who supply services to it are "foreigners". Such thinking can foster racial discrimination that is already entrenched in educational and societal contexts. Leask (2006) highlighted the ways in which educators and administrators often make assumptions about students who plagiarize, noting that "students from 'other cultures' are frequently highlighted as being perpetrators of this crime against the academic community of enlightened Western scholars" (p. 183). To some extent, this same bias is propagated by mainstream media when covering the academic outsourcing industry, leading to an erroneous assumption that foreigners enable the corruption of the otherwise pristine Western systems of higher education (HE). Our historical analysis of mainstream media and other sources dating back decades reveals that this is not necessarily the case, and that the educational community should be just as attentive to the probability that individual suppliers to the industry can be from Western, English-speaking countries.

Few empirical studies exist about individual contract cheating contractors, with some corroborating what has been highlighted in the media, and others that present a broader and more nuanced view of this complex industry. We offer the examples of studies conducted by Sivasubramaniam et al. (2016) and Lancaster (2019) to illustrate this point. Sivasubramaniam et al. (2016) conducted a qualitative study in which they interviewed ten writers whom they had recruited through Facebook. The suppliers had all been international students educated in Western countries who returned to their (undisclosed) country of origin after their studies. Study participants had a minimum of a master's degree in a variety of disciplines, with STEM fields being the most prominent. A key finding of this study was that interviewees had "a clear understanding of their work. They know how to justify their existence as well as sustain and grow their business" (p. 12). Suppliers also felt justified in their actions, positioning themselves as helping the students who paid for their services.

In another study, Lancaster (2019) analysed publicly available information from 93 unique individuals supplying services through Fiverr.com, a micro-outsourcing site. Lancaster included nine non-mutually exclusive classifications of individuals who supply contract cheating services: (a) accidental writers; (b) business opportunists; (c) desperate individuals; (d) would-be academics; (e) internationally qualified academics; (f) career writers; (g) student peers; (h) previous graduates; and (i) family members and friends. Lancaster found that the top supplier had completed 716 orders, noting that 12 individuals had each completed 100 or more assignments, pointing to the likelihood that a small group of suppliers can produce high volumes of academic work. Although it was not possible to verify the writers' country of origin for certain, Lancaster (2019) concluded that the top countries were Kenya, the USA, and Pakistan.

Our study complements the existing body of literature by analysing the experiences of suppliers to the contract cheating industry either told through their own narratives or mediated through reporting conducted by others. In our chapter we focus on the individuals who work for the industry, rather than the companies themselves or the industry at large, as these aspects have already been covered in the literature (see Clarke & Lancaster, 2006; Draper & Newton, 2017; Ellis et al., 2018; Hersey and Lancaster 2015; Lancaster, 2016a, b; Lancaster & Clarke, 2014; Martin, 1972b; Owings & Nelson, 2014; White, 2016). One aspect of our study that is unique, to the best of our knowledge, is that no previous research has systematically studied historical written accounts of individuals supplying services to the contract cheating industry on a global scale. In this chapter we explore the lived experiences of these individuals as told in their own words or told to someone else.

We begin with a note about nomenclature. The term "ghostwriter" is used in both mainstream and research literature and may be the preferred term among those who supply services to the industry (see Sivasubramaniam et al., 2016). However, academic integrity scholars (Bertram Gallant,

2016; Eaton, 2021) have objected to the use of this term on the grounds that ghostwriting is viewed as a legitimate profession and terms such as "ghostwriter" normalize the misconduct. Instead, we use the term "supplier", proposed by Eaton (2021), to attenuate the normalization of enabling academic misconduct and focus more on the transactional nature of the relationship between the student and the individual or organization supplying the contract cheating services. For a more robust discussion on the terminology, see Eaton (2021).

Theory and Method

We conducted this study as a qualitative narrative inquiry following Clandinin's (2006, 2007) notion that stories are pragmatic and ontological artefacts. Connelly and Clandinin (1990) note that:

> … narrative is both phenomenon and method. Narrative names the structured quality of experience to be studied, and it names the pattern of inquiry for its study. To preserve this distinction we use the reasonably well-established device of calling the phenomenon "story" and the inquiry "narrative". Thus, we say that people by nature lead storied lives and tell stories of those lives, whereas narrative researchers describe such lives, collect and tell stories of them, and write narratives of experience. (p. 2)

For the purposes of this study, we focused on individual narratives from multiple individuals over time, as expressed in their mainstream media narratives. We subscribe to Dewey's (1897) view that an individual is situated within a group to which one belongs. Narrative inquiry holds the "potential for making a contribution to the study of human life" (Clandinin, 2006, p. 45). Through this study we aim to understand the stories of those who have lived experience supplying services to contract cheating companies. We have taken a morally agnostic stance on our work, and our intention is not to cast judgement on the individuals or the work they do, but rather to understand their lived experiences through their stories.

Data Sources

We selected accounts from individuals who have reported working as suppliers to the contract cheating industry. Their accounts have been published in newspapers, magazines, blogs, and books. We located these sources in a variety of ways including searching the ProQuest Historical Newspaper databases available through a university library, as well as drawing on contemporary news sources and books available to us. We consider primary sources to be those written by the suppliers themselves. We also consider secondary sources, which are accounts written by others based on interviews and conversations with the suppliers. We did not include sources written by those who had been interviewed by a contract cheating company for potential employment, but in the end did not work for them (see Boyd, 2016).

We do not claim to present an exhaustive selection of supplier accounts. Instead, we have endeavoured to locate as many primary and secondary source documents as possible. Unlike a systematic or scoping review, there is no easy way to find accounts written by suppliers to the contract cheating industry. This chapter is intended to provide a point of departure for continued dialogue rather than a conclusive set of generalizable findings. Because this study relies on published documents, no further permissions were required from our institutional research ethics boards. We were unable to test or verify the facts of the accounts and nor was this our purpose. Our focus was to understand the lived experience of these individuals, through their own words, or the stories they shared with others.

Results and Discussion

Our sources ($N = 12$) included both primary ($n = 9$) and secondary ($n = 3$) sources. We offer an overview of each source in Table 18.1 and we provide a deeper analysis of the stories, beginning with the primary sources, the stories written by suppliers in their own words, then moving into the stories as told by others, the secondary sources. We note that in our table, the term "author" is the person who wrote the story, which is not necessarily the same as the person whose story is told. We include the author in Table 18.1 for the purposes of locating the source documents in our reference list. We note there were more written accounts of lived experience writing for commercial academic outsourcing companies available since the turn of the millennium.

Use of Pseudonyms

Some individuals whose stories we included explicitly indicated they were using pseudonyms either when telling their own story ($n = 6$) or when

Table 18.1 Overview of sources

Type	Author	Date	Pseudonym	Academic background (self-identified)	Country of origin (self-identified/implied)
Secondary	Benjamin	1939	Yes	Not indicated	USA
Primary	O'Toole	1974	Yes	Liberal arts	Canada
Primary	Martin	1972a, b, c	Yes	Not indicated	USA
Primary	Gray	1977	Not indicated	Liberal arts (history) and communications	USA
Primary	Witherspoon	1995	Yes	History and political science	USA
Primary	Dante	2010	Yes	Not indicated	USA
Primary	Tomar	2013	No	Not indicated	USA
Primary	Mills	2017	Yes	Not indicated	UK
Secondary	Simons	2019	No	Computer science	Kenya
Primary	Anonymous	2021	Yes	Liberal arts (English literature)	USA
Secondary	CBC News	2021	Yes	Not indicated	Kenya
Primary	Singh	2021	No	English and business management	India

sharing it with someone else who wrote about their experiences ($n = 2$); and in one case we were unable to determine if the individual was using their real name or a pen name. Although we cannot speak to the motives that would lead someone to use a pseudonym, we note that "Dante" (2010), writing under a pseudonym, later revealed himself to be Tomar (2013). In cases where the gender of those recounting their story is indicated, we have used pronouns corresponding to their gender. We have used the gender-neutral pronouns they/them if we were unable to ascertain for certain the gender of the person.

Theme #1: Perceptions of Working for the Contract Cheating Industry

We found inconsistencies across individuals' stories regarding their feelings about working for the academic outsourcing industry, with reflections ranging from pride (Benjamin, 1939), to having no regrets whatsoever (Tomar, 2013), to indifference (Anonymous, 2021), to shame (O'Toole, 1974; Witherspoon, 1995).

Benjamin (1939) describes "Mr. Smith", the supplier he interviewed, as being "an amazing little man with a devastating self-confidence.... There's precious little Smith doesn't know, and absolutely nothing that stumps him" (p. 157). Benjamin notes that "Smith takes professional pride in giving a new slant to every assignment" (p. 158). Similar to Mr. Smith, Martin also operated his own business and supplied services himself. A self-professed former "teaching associate at 'one of America's best universities' and a staff member at a 'leading educational research institute'" (Martin, 1972a, p. 69), Martin wrote authoritatively about experience "gained first as a writer for three of the major Boston term paper companies, and later as president of the fourth" (p. 69). Martin (1972a) noted that his motivation for writing his three-part exposé in the *Boston Globe* was that stories written by others who did not work in industry "lacked preciseness" (p. 69) and he wanted to "set some facts straight" (p. 69). This points to Martin's desire for readers to have accurate information about the industry and demonstrated his confidence that he could provide that, based on his extensive first-hand experience.

In contrast, others (e.g., O'Toole, 1974; Witherspoon, 1995) described their work supplying services to the contract cheating industry as being the academic equivalent of working for the sex trade. O'Toole notes that within the contract cheating business model, it is the business owners, not the writers, who profit most from the work, "I know the whole business is dishonest and distasteful but I still get upset when conversation disparages the writers as money-grubbing sell-outs. People don't seem to realize that the writer is the loser in the whole sorry enterprise but must prostitute his knowledge if he wants to survive" (O'Toole, 1974, p. 45). He lamented, "The whoredom of writing is really quite humiliating. When you walk into the essay bank's office and exchange guilty glances with prospective buyers you must work up the gall to introduce your services (they may be bogus: nobody seemed eager to check my qualifications)" (O'Toole, 1974, p. 45). Similarly, Witherspoon (1995) opens her account by describing herself as "an academic call girl" (p. 45). She points that she can write on any variety of topics, saying, "The teaching assistants eat it up. I can do simple English or advanced jargon. Like other types of prostitutes, I am, professionally, very accommodating" (Witherspoon, 1995, p. 49).

These accounts of working for the contract cheating industry as being analogous to working in the sex trade industry may be shocking, and we counter by recommending caution, since these suppliers made no claims of working in the sex trade industry themselves and as such, lack the experiential knowledge to make accurate claims about the parallels they are drawing. O'Toole acknowledges that he did not enter the industry by force, saying instead that for some people, work in the contract cheating industry is preferable to less desirable jobs, such as washing dishes or working in the food processing industry. O'Toole noted, "I had already done my bit working in a fish packing plant for four years. Essay writing, at least allowed me the use of my mind" (p. 45).

Tomar (2013) describes himself this way: "I usually had weed resin under my fingernails. My hair hung down into my eyes. I was kind of grimy" (p. x). He goes on to describe himself as "a paper factory, a sweatshop of one, a warehouse of industrial machinery humming over an endless assembly line where the stack of incoming papers never gets smaller" (p. 2). Tomar expressed that he had no regrets, saying, "I have never felt guilty while doing this job" (p. 3). Addressing the reader directly he says, "Don't flip through these pages searching for remorse. It isn't there. But I have also not felt particularly proud. A writer does not aspire to this profession so that others can be praised (or ridiculed) for his work" (pp. 3–4). Of note here is that Tomar refers to working for the contract cheating industry as a "profession" (p. 4), a sentiment uttered decades earlier by "Mr. Smith" who described his "fields of work" (Benjamin, 1939, p. 158) covering a variety of academic disciplines.

Theme #2: Financial Aspects of Working for the Contract Cheating Industry

There was inconsistency across accounts about whether working for the contract cheating industry paid well. In some accounts individual writers are portrayed as being exploited by their employers, whereas others claimed that working for the contract cheating industry brought them financial stability. Mills (2017) commented, "Ghost-writing was not a lucrative post. To earn anything approaching a liveable income required writing as many works as possible. I would have to work on three or four briefs per week, for which I would be lucky to make £300 [GBP]" (n.p). In contrast, Gray (1977) commented, "I'm not particularly proud of what I do, but it is good money, enjoyable work and a painless way to keep my mind active" (p. 440). Gray differs from other individual suppliers who claimed that working for the contract cheating industry was not financially rewarding. Anonymous (2021) stated, "In the summer, it was never more than $500 [USD] a week for roughly 10 to 12 essays. But during the semester, it could be up to $2,000 a week for 30 to 40 projects—a numbing amount of writing, but a lot of cash" (n.p.).

Financial distress was an important motivator for some to work in the academic cheating industry. Tomar (2013) noted, "I am often asked how I got into this line of work. I can assure you, it happened quite organically. I hated school and I was broke" (p. 4). Similarly, Mills (2017) recounted that they turned to working in the contract cheating industry after unsuccessful attempts to secure other employment, including academic jobs, sharing this perspective: "I was in need of some—any—income, it seemed a reasonable option, especially after having had several unsuccessful interviews for academic jobs" (n.p.). Anonymous (2021) conveyed a similar sentiment saying, "many of my fellow essay writers themselves were in academia—they wrote papers for students because they couldn't make ends meet" (n.p.).

Some accounts contrasted the amount of money made by the individual writers with that made by the business owners. O'Toole (1974) reflected that "there is no money in essay writing, except for the essay bank owners, but there is *some* money in it" (p. 45, emphasis in original). The situation was similar in 2019. Simons (2019) reported, "Slaving away in 'essay factories' in Nairobi, the highly educated experts earn as little as a dollar an hour while their millionaire bosses cream off the profits—and cheating Western teenagers take the credit" (n.p.). This points to feelings of helplessness and disenfranchisement on the part of individual writers.

Although the theme of money and finances appeared across the accounts, we were unable to draw conclusions about a uniformity of experience with regards to individual earnings, with experiences ranging from satisfaction with the amount of money a person made to accounts of exploitation and struggling to make ends meet.

Theme #3: The Role of the Higher Education System in Enabling Contract Cheating

Of particular importance for our study was the consistency across accounts about the extent to which the higher education system creates the conditions for contract cheating to flourish. In the earliest known account from a contract cheating supplier, Mr. Smith points out that "most curricula overload the student" (Benjamin, 1939, p. 159), and being stressed out and overwhelmed can motivate students to hire someone to complete work on their behalf.

It is well known among those who study contract cheating that suppliers find loopholes in academic misconduct regulations by claiming that they provide only model essays or sample work. We found evidence that this practice of finding loopholes dates back almost a century. Quoting Mr. Smith, Benjamin (1939) wrote, "Many students hardly know what a good essay looks like. Professors as a rule fail to discuss them and do not let students read the essays submitted by other members of the class. My papers stand as models and examples for the students" (p. 160). Here Smith is positioning himself as providing help and support to students in ways that professors do not. Such rhetoric of help and support for students remains a common aspect of cheating advertising in the twenty-first century (see Crook & Nixon, 2021).

Mr. Smith was not alone in his use of what we have termed the "model essay loophole". For example, Gray (1977) commented:

> Although the students agree in principle that they will use the papers they buy as reference material only, it is a safe bet that they merely type their names on the title page provided and hand in what has been sent to them. How any instructor worth his contract can let something as flagrant as this pass by is beyond me. (p. 440)

The same is evident in a 2019 account. Simons (2019) observed that "many of these companies exploit a legal loophole, offering disclaimers saying they are to be used as a 'study guide' only, while simultaneously advertising 'guaranteed grades' and 'plagiarism free essays'" (n.p.). These three accounts (Gray, 1977; Benjamin, 1939; Simons, 2019) spanning 80 years show the consistency with which the model essay loophole has been exploited by the contract cheating industry. If there is one takeaway for educational institutions, it is to close this loophole because if they do not, they remain complicit in enabling the industry to flourish. The question of how to close this loophole is complex and beyond the scope of this chapter; however, high-level recommendations include having student supports that clearly articulate expectations and further, using a balance of probabilities model for misconduct investigations and case management.

In addition to the model essay loophole, Smith (1939) and Gray (1977) pointed out how contract cheating involves individual actors within the educational system, and specifically instructors. Smith spoke to poor assessment design and lack of flexibility in supporting students' learning. Simons commented on professors failing to identify or report academic misconduct, a practice that remains common in higher education (see Eaton, 2021). The role that poor assessment design plays was echoed by Witherspoon (1995) who observed that "certain courses seem to consist of teaching kids the use of jargon as though it were a substitute for writing or thinking well. Often there is an implied pressure to agree with the assigned book. And many are simply impossible to understand…" (p. 54).

Professors being indifferent to students or their learning was repeated across accounts, particularly those from recent years. Singh (2021) noted, "At the graduate and master's level, where assignments are mostly in the form of PowerPoint presentations, reports and data, I guess professors hardly pay attention to the writing style" (n.p.). Professors not caring about students was echoed by Anonymous (2021), who recounted their perceptions supplying services during COVID-19. They said that "many professors don't want to be bothered with students' struggles. As COVID marched on, so did the deadlines, and a lot of the professors were quite rigid with their rules. On the rubrics I would read from students, I remember seeing one that said, 'No missed deadlines. I don't want to hear your sob story" (n.p.). However, individual professors do not work in isolation, but rather within institutions that comprise the HE system as a whole which contributes to the problem. Witherspoon (1995) pointed out the role that large class size plays, as well as students with limited English receiving insufficient support. She observed, "People hand these papers in and don't get caught, people who have difficulty speaking complete sentences in English; perhaps this is because classes and even tutorials are so big they never have to speak" (p. 54).

Martin (1972b) summed up the role of higher education most succinctly, when he said, "Universities regard term paper companies as a weed that has suddenly afflicted them—they do not realize though, to what a large extent forces in the universities themselves have prepared the soil in which we grow" (p. 77). To contextualize this comment, as this book was under development in 2022, exactly 50 years after Martin's accounts of working for the contract cheating industry were published, the role that HE plays in enabling contract cheating must not be ignored.

Significance

Our study provides new insights into individuals who have supplied services to the contract cheating industry. Further, we have shown that accounts of individuals supplying commercial academic cheating services date back to the late 1930s, and at this point, it would be naïve to think that this is a new industry or that it only surfaced during the COVID-19 pandemic or even the internet age.

Limitations

We make no claims about our work being exhaustive. Although we endeavoured to be careful and thorough in our collection of primary and secondary data, we recognize that we have missed sources. Furthermore, all the studies we collected were written in English, and we acknowledge this as a limitation of our work. For this reason, we offer our study as an analysis of a collection of *some* stories, rather than *all* stories. We note that although individuals are situated within groups, such as a company one works for, and lived experience can be part of a larger collective experience, it is simultaneously individual. A full analysis of the individuals' motivations for entering the contract cheating industry is beyond the scope of this chapter but this would be an insightful line of inquiry to pursue in future research. Thus, our results cannot be generalized or universalized. The lived experience of one contract cheating supplier is not the lived experience of all of them.

Conclusions and Call to Action

Inconsistencies across these accounts show that, at least from a historical perspective, it is difficult to draw generalized conclusions about individuals' experiences working as suppliers to the contract cheating industry. Some found it financially rewarding, whereas others did not. Some were proud of the work they did, whereas others felt ashamed. When media accounts portray sensationalized experiences of individuals in Africa or Asia working in dismal conditions to supply services to the contract cheating industry, it is important to recognize that although such depictions might be emotionally compelling, they do not tell the whole story. As we analysed primary and secondary accounts of individuals working for the contract cheating industry, we found their experiences were diverse, and at times conflicting. It is important to resist generalizing or stereotyping what it is like to work as an individual supplier of academic cheating services or products.

At the same time, we cannot ignore that these 12 accounts spanning almost 100 years had one common thread. The higher education system—and those who work within it—continue to perpetuate the conditions in which the contract cheating industry has flourished. Those working in the higher education sector have, by and large, turned a blind eye to the role the higher education system itself has played, instead laying blame on the students or the suppliers. There is no question that students should be held responsible for acting with integrity, but this does not absolve educational institutions or those who work within them of their responsibilities for ensuring teaching, assessment, and administrative practices are ethical. We conclude with two calls to action. Firstly, more research into contract cheating needs to be conducted to understand the details of the industry and how it works. For this to occur, research must be supported through funding and resources to conduct such investigations. Secondly, we call on educational leaders to examine the ways in which their institutional practices enable the contract cheating industry to flourish and take concrete actions to ensure that student learning and success are the focus of teaching and assessment.

References

Anonymous. (2021, July 6). I signed up to write college essays for rich kids. I found cheating Is more complicated than I thought. https://slate.com/human-interest/2021/07/college-essay-writer-diary.html

BBC News. (2019). The Kenyan ghost writers doing 'lazy' Western students' work. https://www.bbc.com/news/av/world-africa-50126963/the-kenyan-ghost-writers-doing-lazy-western-students-work

Benjamin, R. (1939). Ghost goes to college. *The American Mercury*, 157–160. https://www.yumpu.com/en/document/view/7438935/the-american-mercury-june-1939-ludwig-von-mises-institute

Bertram Gallant, T. (2016). Response to White's 'Shadow scholars and the rise of the dissertation service industry'. *Journal of Research Practice*, *12*(1). http://jrp.icaap.org/index.php/jrp/article/view/553/452

Boyd, V. (2016, 1 August). The company that wanted me to write students' essays in return for cash. *Times Higher Education*. https://www.timeshighereducation.com/blog/company-wanted-me-write-students-essays-return-cash

Buerger, G. E. (2002). *The owl and the plagiarist: Academic misrepresentation in contemporary education*. (Ph.D.). Dalhousie University (Canada), Ann Arbor. Retrieved from ProQuest Dissertations & Theses Global database. (NQ75718)

CBC News. (2021, July 26). *As online education grows, the business of cheating is booming.* https://www.cbsnews.com/news/online-education-cheating-business/

Clandinin, D. J. (2006). Narrative inquiry: A methodology for studying lived experience. *Research Studies in Music Education, 27*(1), 44–54. https://doi.org/10.1177/1321103X060270010301

Clandinin, D. J. (Ed.) (2007). *Handbook of narrative inquiry: Mapping a methodology*. Sage.

Clarke, R., & Lancaster, T. (2006). *Eliminating the successor to plagiarism: Identifying the usage of contract cheating sites*. Paper presented at the Second International Plagiarism Conference, The Sage Gateshead, Tyne & Wear.

Connelly, F. M., & Clandinin, D. J. (1990). Stories of experience and narrative inquiry. *Educational Researcher, 19*(5), 2–14.

Crook, C., & Nixon, E. (2021). How internet essay mill websites portray the student experience of higher education. *The Internet and Higher Education, 48*, 100775. https://doi.org/10.1016/j.iheduc.2020.100775

Dante, E. (2010). The shadow scholar. *The Chronicle of Higher Education*. https://www.chronicle.com/article/The-Shadow-Scholar/125329

Dewey, J. (1897). My pedagogic creed. *Teachers Manuals, 25*, 3–18.

Draper, M. J., & Newton, P. M. (2017). A legal approach to tackling contract cheating? *International Journal for Educational Integrity, 13*(1), 1–16. https://doi.org/10.1007/s40979-017-0022-5

Eaton, S. E. (2021). *Plagiarism in higher education: Tackling tough topics in academic integrity*. Libraries Unlimited.

Ellis, C., Zucker, I. M., & Randall, D. (2018). The infernal business of contract cheating: Understanding the business processes and models of academic custom writing sites. *International Journal for Educational Integrity, 14*(1), 1–21. https://doi.org/10.1007/s40979-017-0024-3

Gray, C. (1977, March 6). Life in a term-paper factory. *New York Times*, 440.

Hersey, C., & Lancaster, T. (2015). *The online industry of paper mills, contract cheating services, and auction sites*. Paper presented at the Clute Institute International Education Conference. https://www.researchgate.net/publication/280830577_The_Online_Industry_of_Paper_Mills_Contract_Cheating_Services_and_Auction_Sites

Kansara, R., & Main, E. (2021). The Kenyans who are helping the world to cheat. *BBC News*. https://www.bbc.com/news/blogs-trending-58465189

Lancaster, T. (2016a). *Contract cheating: A workshop on the bespoke assessment industry*. Paper presented at the Learning and Teaching Conference, Faculty of Arts, Computing, Engineering and Sciences, Sheffield Hallam University, UK. https://www.slideshare.net/ThomasLancaster/contract-cheating-a-workshop-on-the-bespoke-assessment-industry-faculty-of-arts-computing-engineering-and-sciences-learning-and-teaching-conference-sheffield-hallam-university-16-september-2016

Lancaster, T. (2016b). *Contract cheating and the essay writing industry: Where does the money go? (Slides)*. Paper presented at the International Center for Academic Integrity, Athens, Greece.

Lancaster, T. (2019). Profiling the international academic ghost writers who are providing low-cost essays and assignments for the contract cheating industry. *Journal of Information, Communication and Ethics in Society, 17*(1), 72–86. https://doi.org/10.1108/JICES-04-2018-0040

Lancaster, T., & Clarke, R. (2014, July). *An observational analysis of the range and extent of contract cheating from online courses found on agency websites*. Paper presented at the 8th International Conference on Complex, Intelligent and Software Intensive Systems (CISIS 2014), Birmingham.

Leask, B. (2006). Plagiarism, cultural diversity and metaphor—Implications for academic staff development. *Assessment & Evaluation in Higher Education, 31*(2), 183–199. https://doi.org/10.1080/02602930500262486

Martin, D. (1972a, February 20). Who buys term papers? A dealer opens his files. *Boston Globe,* 69&77. Retrieved ProQuest Historical Newspapers: The Boston Globe.

Martin, D. (1972b, February 20). Why does the business flourish? *Boston Globe (1960–1989),* 77. Retrieved ProQuest Historical Newspapers: The Boston Globe.

Martin, D. (1972c, February 21). A seller of term papers looks at colleges, himself. *Boston Globe (1960-1989),* 20. Retrieved from ProQuest Historical Newspapers: The Boston Globe.

Mills, S. A. (2017, 12 December). The crumbling façade: my experience working for an essay mill. http://blogs.lse.ac.uk/impactofsocialsciences/2017/12/12/the-crumbling-facade-my-experience-working-for-an-essay-mill/

O'Toole, L. (1974, September 19). The essay game. *The Globe and Mail,* 45.

Owings, S., & Nelson, J. (2014). The essay industry. *Mountain Plains Journal of Business and Economics, 15,* 1–21.

Simons, J. W. (2019, August 23). Exclusive: Inside the African essay factories that churn out university coursework for 115,000 cheating British students every year. *Daily Mail UK.* https://www.dailymail.co.uk/news/article-7290333/amp/Inside-African-essay-factories-producing-essays-cheating-UK-students.html

Singh, S. K. (2021). I get paid to do homework for students around the world. *Vice.* https://www.vice.com/en/article/epnz8m/cheating-students-homework-exams-university-india

Sivasubramaniam, S., Kostelidou, K., & Ramachandran, S. (2016). A close encounter with ghost-writers: An initial exploration study on background, strategies and attitudes of independent essay providers. *International Journal for Educational Integrity*, *12*(1), 1–14. https://doi.org/10.1007/s40979-016-0007-9

Sutherland, T. (Writer). (2019). Exclusive investigation: Kenyan man says he wrote essays for Canadian students. *City News Toronto*. Rogers Media. https://toronto.citynews.ca/2019/02/19/cheating-at-u-of-t/

Tomar, D. (2013). *The shadow scholar: How I made a living helping college kids cheat*. Bloomsbury.

White, J. L. (2016). Shadow scholars and the rise of the dissertation service industry: Can we maintain academic integrity? *Journal of Research Practice*, *12*(1). Retrieved from http://jrp.icaap.org/index.php/jrp/article/view/536/448

Witherspoon, A. (1995). This pen for hire: On grinding out papers for college students. *Harper's Magazine*, *290*(June), 49–57.

CHAPTER 19

Assessment Brokering and Collaboration: Ghostwriter and Student Academic Literacies

Emma J. Thacker

BACKGROUND

As contract cheating continues to undermine the core mission of higher education, academics and administrators work to define the scope of the problem, study and promote a range of solutions. Contract cheating exists in several forms; however, all types engage a third party to complete academic work for credit or academic advantage (Clarke & Lancaster, 2006). Those individuals who provide the outsourced assignments are typically called ghostwriters. Other terms include academic writer (Walker, 2019) or individual supplier (Eaton, 2021). This chapter shares the findings from a study with a focus on contract cheating services provided by independent, freelance ghostwriters who write for students in Canadian higher education institutions.

The higher education system applies various approaches to support academic integrity and to reduce academic misconduct. Although there is no single effective solution, many scholars argue for a holistic approach that

E. J. Thacker (✉)
University of Toronto, Toronto, ON, Canada
e-mail: em.thacker@utoronto.ca

combines several strategies and has a focus on education and prevention (Macdonald & Carroll, 2006). Other detection and deterrence approaches appeal to technology, using text-matching and surveillance software (Dawson, 2020). Punitive responses typically align with institutional policies that determine sanctions for academic misconduct (Miron et al., 2021).

Cutri et al. (2021) have recommended that academic integrity knowledge be treated as a *threshold concept* (Meyer & Land, 2003). A threshold concept is "a core idea that is conceptually challenging for students, who struggle to grasp it—but once grasped, it radically transforms the students' perception of the subject" (Kent, 2016, p. 2). Others have recommended that institutions strengthen *assessment literacy* (Morris, 2018). Assessment literacy is more than an understanding of assessment practices and concepts, it is a "context-dependent social practice" that extends beyond teaching staff to students and includes the navigation of academic and cultural knowledge (Willis et al., 2013, p. 242). Although recommendations and best practices have been developed to address contract cheating (e.g., QAA, 2020), these typically align with traditional views of academic writing and are not contextualised within the Canadian higher education sector.

Literature Review

The phenomenon of contract cheating is not new; however, information and communication technology (ICT) is an important factor in the proliferation of services by providing innovative ways to engage and to transact an unauthorised academic assessment (Amigud & Lancaster, 2019a). Several studies have researched ghostwriters (e.g., Sivasubramaniam et al., 2016; Walker, 2019), however, very little has been designed with a qualitative focus on ghostwriting in the Canadian academic landscape (e.g., Chang, 2018).

In addition to studies about ghostwriters, researchers have attempted to understand various stakeholder perceptions, attitudes, and experiences of contract cheating (Bretag et al., 2019a; Eaton et al., 2019). Studies have also explored motivations for contract cheating (Amigud & Lancaster, 2019b) and why students choose not to cheat (Rundle et al., 2019). Contract cheating is now understood to be a global industry, operating in multiple languages, and at all levels of education. To this end, studies have explored the industry's business processes (Ellis et al., 2018) and advertising strategies (Rowland et al., 2018). Other contract cheating research has examined policy (Stoesz et al., 2019), assessment (Bretag et al., 2019b), and detection (Rogerson, 2017). Although Canadian contract cheating research has increased materially since 2018 (see Ahsan et al., 2021; Eaton & Edino, 2018), there is still a need for research with a focus on the ghostwriters themselves, and their literacy interactions with students studying at Canadian institutions.

Further to this, *literacy brokering* has yet to be used as a concept to explore contract cheating. More than translators, literacy brokers are individuals who support the transfer of knowledge that might otherwise be inaccessible, including cultural knowledge related to literacies (Raslie & Keong, 2017). In an academic context, the literacy broker will possess some "genre knowledge" (Perry, 2009, p. 257), and offer "some particular academic expertise derived from having prior academic experience" (Lee, 2018, p. 45), enabling and empowering them to interpret academic texts and literacy practices. These informal interactions support students' navigation of the academic domain, bridging gaps in knowledge to clarify the meaning of texts (Perry, 2009). Given the significant role of literacy across the education sector, it should be foregrounded to inform contextualised contract cheating prevention strategies in Canada.

Theoretical Framing

This study adopts an academic literacies approach (Lea & Street, 1998). This approach considers literacy as a constructed social practice, inextricably linked to cultural context. Literacy is then multiple—there are *literacies*. Literacies are much more than a cognitive skill set, they are ideological, never neutral, nor independent of the power structures and systems that sustain or marginalise them (Street, 1984). Literacies are often marginalised, disempowering students, especially in academic institutions where dominant literacies and discourses require access, are controlled and privileged. Dominant literacies are also adopted by educational policies and assessment frameworks (Park & Fallon, 2016). By contrast, vernacular literacies are informal (Barton, 2007), such as those everyday digital literacies used with social media (Lankshear & Knobel, 2008). This sociocultural perspective brings to bear the literacies on the margins, which reveal a deeper understanding of literacy events and practices in context (Heath, 1983). They are patterned by social institutions and power relations. Literacies research includes consideration of how the marginalising of literacies can lead to the creation of a "third space" (Moje et al., 2004, p. 1).

Third Space Theory (Bhabha, 1994) speaks to the informal, educational spaces found in-between dominant literacy domains and discourses that can provide opportunity for learning (Gutiérrez, 2008).

When exploring literacies, Bourdieu's (1986) notions of *capital* are useful, as Bourdieu sees all the world as a continual symbolic exchange of capital (Grenfell et al., 2012). Bourdieu outlines several forms of capital. The first is social capital which is the "sum of the resources, actual or virtual, that accrue to an individual or a group by virtue of possessing a durable network" (Bourdieu & Wacquant, 1992, p. 119). Second is economic capital, which includes assets such as property and money. The third is cultural capital, which "amounts to an irreducible amalgamation" of status, skills, and ability (Lareau & Weininger, 2003, p. 582). Cultural capital has further subcategories, such as institutionalised capital (e.g., academic credentials) (Bourdieu, 1986). Extending the notion of capital to the digital domain, the term *techno-capital* refers to the use of networked technology for social gains or mobility (Rojas et al., 2003). Theorising contract cheating through the lens of capital exposes hidden motivations, affordances, and constraints of the various study participants.

Research Question and Methods

The doctoral thesis that precedes this chapter addressed several questions about the phenomenon of contract cheating. Given space constraints, this chapter reports on one of the research questions: What is the nature of literacy brokering between ghostwriters and their student clients in Canadian higher education institutions?

Four methods of data collection were utilised including: semi-structured interviews (ghostwriters ($n = 11$), students ($n = 7$), and teaching staff ($n = 8$)); text and document collection (e.g., essays); a follow-up survey with key informants; and lastly, concept mapping (Novak & Gowin, 1984). Concept mapping of the "literacy social practice building blocks" (Hamilton, 2010, p. 11) uncovered patterns and connections and enhanced meaning making across the literacies domains (Mannion et al., 2007).

Findings

This section is divided by theme reflecting the two digital, social literacies practice themes that emerged from the data: collaboration and assessment brokering. Although these practices were not commonplace for freelance ghostwriters, they were patterned, and this finding is an important indicator of the landscape of Canadian contract cheating. It reflects the agency and resistance of students, and the social underpinnings of both assessment and the contract cheating industry. In this context, agency results from the student and ghostwriter interrelationship and exchange of capital (Bourdieu, 1986) and literacies (i.e., socially situated, academic, and digital literacies) within the digitally mediated environment. Collaboration and assessment brokering in contract cheating reflect the affordances and constraints of both techno-capital (Rojas et al., 2003) and academic literacies (Lea & Street, 1998).

Collaboration Between Student and Ghostwriter

In the context of academic misconduct, nonpermitted collaboration is often referred to as collusion (Barrett & Cox, 2005). This study views academic collaboration as a literacy event (Heath, 1983) that occurs between and/or among writers to produce an academic text, where the efforts of the writers may not be equal. The ghostwriters situated in Canada ($n = 5$) and Britain ($n = 1$) provided more examples and richer descriptions of collaboration with their clients, and were overall more agreeable to the practice, in contrast to those from abroad (i.e., India ($n = 1$), Kenya ($n = 3$)).

Xander (ghostwriter) acknowledged the practice of collaboration within his business, explaining that "some people want to do it live on Google Docs and it kind of interrupts my research process and writing process." Google Docs (a web-based, word-processing tool that allows real-time collaboration [Google, n.d.]) was typically mentioned as the application used to support this digital academic literacies practice. Xander did not see the request for collaboration as constructive to his own writing process but explained that "people do ask for that specifically." When Xander was asked why a student might ask to collaborate on a contractual, outsourced assignment, he commented that some students may want to "make it in their own style," or because they might "feel guilty about having used an essay service."

Xander's response rings true, however, the findings suggest additional or other motivations, and a more nuanced perspective than offered by Xander. Examples of collaboration were provided at many stages of the contract. There were examples of collaboration provided prior to the assignment writing beginning, throughout the writing process, and even after the student had received the final product. Collaboration heavily utilised digital literacies and other social modalities by engaging in feedback and discussion. Although Xander pointed to collaboration as a nuisance, he explained that it was also considered necessary at times to maintain the client relationship. The role of friendship to sustain and source work, and the ghostwriter identities of *writer* and *helper* surfaced continuously from the data.

The ghostwriters explained that some of their clients wanted to be included in the writing process, despite the contractual arrangement. None of the ghostwriting advertisements offered collaboration as an option or service. Camille (ghostwriter) described two types of student clients. One group will "pay you any amount of money and they just need you to finish it [the assignment]" and the other who "needed help in the work." Camille shared that for those she had decided needed "the help" she would "work together a little bit more … and so, there's more cooperation in that context, and I definitely have moments where we'll have five, six, seven, eight emails back and forth with redlining or blacklining or different markups." Camille's comments highlight collaborative writing and how these informal practices (e.g., use of track changes for feedback) could support learning (Storch, 2019).

Another example of collaboration was described without a financial payment arranged. Morgan, a fourth-year undergraduate student, shared a story of unsanctioned collaboration with her best friend and roommate, who had helped her to write an essay the evening it was due. She explained that her friend was very familiar with the essay topic, and she began to help because Morgan admitted she was "struggling to write the argument." Morgan explained that after a few suggestions from her best friend, she passed her the laptop to keep working.

Morgan's experience reveals several complex struggles of student writers and the strong temptation to accept help from a friend—struggles such as time management, writing competencies, and familiarity or connection with the assignment topic. It also reveals the multiple exchanges of capital between the two peer students. Collaboration is beneficial to both parties—cultural and embodied capital is exchanged for economic (or additional social capital); social capital is leveraged for institutionalised capital; and techno-capital facilitates these material and symbolic exchanges. Capital is acquired or developed for both throughout the process. For the student, working collaboratively with their ghostwriter may be a safe space and opportunity to learn informally. Literacies are "frequently acquired through processes of informal learning and sense making" (Barton et al., 2000, p. 8); however, the paid ghostwriters did not consider collaboration to be a significant factor in students' learning. Still, "writing practices construct rather than simply reflect knowledge" (Paxton & Frith, 2014, p. 174).

Assessment Brokering

In addition to collaboration, the ghostwriters provided description and examples of assessment brokering with their student clients. Assessment brokering is defined as "the informal process of seeking assistance, about some element of an academic assessment text or assessment practice" (Thacker, 2022). Assessment brokering occurs where there is a social relationship, such as between student peers, and with ghostwriters. A brokering trigger will precede a brokering event, which occurs where students are motivated to "make sense of their new literacy context and literacy practices" (Raslie & Keong, 2017, p. 2) by leveraging social capital, and the social relationships around them, in exchange for cultural capital (Bourdieu, 1986). Assessment brokering clustered under two themes or types, as described below.

The first type of assessment brokering is related to *assignment criteria* and includes seeking understanding about assignment requirements and assignment content. Each ghostwriter spoke of experiences when their clients asked them about the assignment criteria and sought some level of clarity about the outsourced assignment. When discussing assignment instructions and assignment design, Xander (ghostwriter) commented that it was a common issue with students to struggle with understanding what is required. He commented "that students often choose to use my services on the basis of complicated instructions from professors," also noting that "students feel overwhelmed by this and instead choose to hire a writer."

Students also sought their ghostwriter's knowledge on the assignment once the outsourced paper had been created. Sang (ghostwriter) noted that, "some students, they want you to go over it with them so they either want to meet you or they want to speak with you on the phone or through e-mails." Sang's description demonstrates a level of student engagement with the assignment, which contradicts the typical view of students who use these services—which is that there is a "fundamental rejection of the expected behavior of the students" (Steel, 2017, p. 129) and that students are "bypassing learning" (Lancaster, 2018, p. 72). This view omits from the landscape of those students who do seek to understand, despite the overall behaviour being characterised as misconduct. For Camille (ghostwriter), brokering interactions occurred more with students who had assignments related to a student's intended profession. She explained that some students had a desire to understand the content and demonstrated agency in the process. She explained that some students were "more hands on" and "they'll ask me questions and for clarification and come back and ask me if they've understood something properly after reading the work." This example of brokering demonstrates that student and ghostwriting relationships are not homogeneous, and some students are gaining more than the opportunity for institutional capital, they are gaining academic literacies, cultural capital, and finding "a sense of one's place" (Bourdieu, 1984, p. 466).

The second type of assessment brokering is related to *authorship* and includes seeking understanding about sources, citations, and referencing. Terry (ghostwriter) stated that "Canadian students, they will ask for all kind of clarification on what you have done on their work with references." Although this comment is doubtless painted with a broad stroke, Terry points to the brokering around authorship. Rowan (ghostwriter) had similar experiences. She explained that "quite a lot of the questions I get are about sources and where I find my sources ... two words man: Google and Wikipedia. A lot of people ask me how to do works cited." The ghostwriters often referred to citation and referencing as a "struggle" and "weak point" for their student clients, clarifying it as a troublesome concept and practice. Sawyer (ghostwriter) reported that her clients asked for this specifically. She commented that if she is given an essay to "rewrite," usually her clients will request that she add-in or correct in-text citations and references. Sawyer also pointed to circumstances where students were challenged with larger, institutional processes and practices for sourcing knowledge. She explained that a client had asked her about the sources she had used to write their assignment. She realised that the student was trying to work out "if they were capable of conducting the research themselves." Sawyer shared that the student "ended up returning to me for more services," acknowledging that "unfortunately, students often find large databases to be daunting and overwhelming."

Assessment brokering enables students to navigate assessments, increases pathways for informal academic literacies support, and enables meaning making. Similar to collaboration, it also demonstrates how student academic misconduct choices are shaped by the dominant and often contested literacy practices of assessment. The ghostwriter leverages their embodied capital (Bourdieu, 1986) found within their academic literacies to act as broker. Often building upon the social capital found within their peer networks first, and then, leveraging techno-capital, they exchange embodied capital for economic capital. The student, seeking to gain institutionalised capital, utilises the economic and social capital available to them to gain the academic literacies (actual, and those found symbolically in the academic credential).

Discussion

Not all students engaging in contract cheating are seeking an assessment broker or are benefiting from collaboration and brokering experiences with their ghostwriters. Xander (ghostwriter) commented, "The majority of my customers want nothing more than a simple transaction, no contact, other than getting the essay." Although not the norm, each ghostwriter did provide examples of collaboration and assessment brokering from their own experiences. The findings suggest that students are struggling with assessment literacy—in terms of authorship, but also the assignment criteria and form itself. This finding aligns with Zheng and Cheng (2015), who found that students engaged in contract cheating admitted to not understanding the requirements of the assignment, and also broadly with Bretag et al. (2019a), who found that contract cheating in Australian students was "primarily influenced by dissatisfaction with the teaching and learning environment" (p. 1848).

Further, these exchanges of various forms of capital reflect the pedagogical contours of invisible motivations, acts of resistance, and agency. Although a variety of individual contexts, cultural and institutional factors motivate cheating behaviours (see Walker & Townley, 2012), this study identifies the vulnerability of assessment literacy as one underlying factor, aligning with Morris's (2018) recommendation. The findings also support Harper et al. (2019) who found a disconnect between teaching staff and student perceptions—although the teaching staff believed they had prepared their students for an assignment, the students who engaged in contract cheating did not agree and reported a negative experience. Further to this, Amigud and Lancaster (2019b) found that "many students try completing the work themselves, but later succumb to situational pressures that influence their ability to complete the work" (p. 102). Through consideration of academic writing, referencing/citation, and academic integrity as threshold concepts (Meyer & Land, 2003), institutions can begin to approach contract cheating as an assessment literacy issue, rather than a moral or criminal one (Steel, 2017).

This study demonstrates that contract cheating has social underpinnings, despite the digitally mediated space. Like the Canadian landscape, Walker (2019) found the Kenyan contract cheating industry to be a "deeply networked and socially bound industry" (p. 21). Leveraging the safe and social opportunities provided by digital spaces, both students and ghostwriters alike leveraged techno-capital for other forms of cultural. There are also similarities with Raslie and Keong's (2017) who found that students engaged with technology to "facilitate the brokering process" (p. 14), and informal collaborative writing among peers.

Assessment brokering occurs in the liminal spaces, or at the boundaries of the academic domain. These findings are consistent with Sivasubramaniam et al. (2016) who found that ghostwriters had a "constant dialogue"

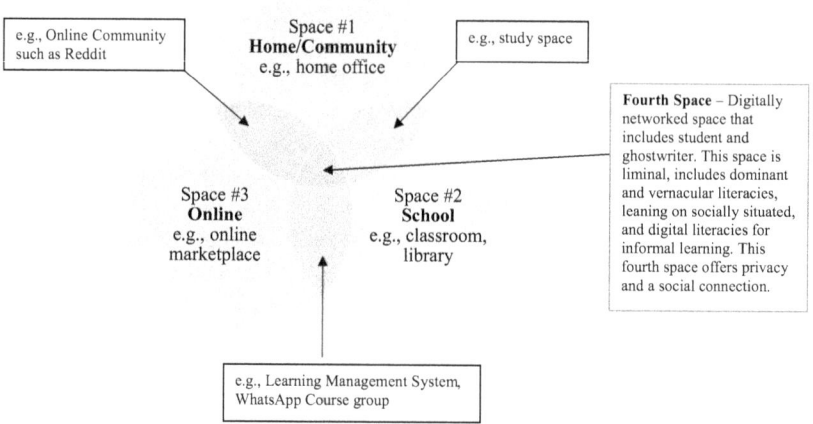

Fig. 19.1 Contract cheating literacies spaces, a fourth space

about the assignment with their clients (p. 10). Building on Moje et al.'s (2004) contributions, this study claims that collaboration and assessment brokering in this context make visible a "fourth space" (see Fig. 19.1; Fernández Ruiz et al., 2019, p. 1).

In the Canadian contract cheating landscape, this fourth space is "characterized by a flattening of power structures and hierarchies" (Thacker, 2022, p. 153). Revealed through the concept mapping technique, this fourth space is "where learning and discourse is relational and informal, and the online domain plays a significant role" (Thacker, 2022, p. 128). Within the fourth space, the opportunity is created for students to practice academic literacies, gain knowledge and understanding, and form their "writer identity" (Ivanič, 1998, p. 23). This finding challenges the view that contract cheating is a total rejection of learning. As Eaton (2021) and Valentine (2006) note, moral and ethical binaries are unhelpful and have implications for teaching and learning and for addressing academic misconduct.

Conclusion

This chapter highlights several contributions to the field. First, the novel term of assessment brokering which creates space for further exploration and understanding of the assessment literacy needs of both students and teaching staff. Second, although the study is not representative of all of Canada, this study demonstrates a more nuanced and critical view of contract cheating in Canada, challenging the binary view of students with respect to their learning and motivations that permeate the literature. Third, the freelance ghostwriting landscape is social, dependent upon digital literacies, and offers some students agency and informal learning within a fourth space. With efforts to prioritise assessment literacy, which includes the framing of academic integrity concepts, academic writing, and practices of authorship as threshold concepts (Meyer & Land, 2003), a contract cheating reduction strategy can support the core academic institutional mission.

References

Ahsan, K., Akbar, S., & Kam, B. (2021). Contract cheating in higher education: A systematic literature review and future research agenda. *Assessment & Evaluation in Higher Education.* https://doi.org/10.1080/02602938.2021.1931660

Amigud, A., & Lancaster, T. (2019a). I will pay someone to do my assignment: An analysis of market demand for contract cheating services on Twitter. *Assessment and Evaluation in Higher Education, 45*(4), 541–553. https://doi.org/10.1080/02602938.2019.1670780

Amigud, A., & Lancaster, T. (2019b). 246 reasons to cheat: An analysis of students' reasons for seeking to outsource academic work. *Computers & Education, 134*(June), 98–107. https://doi.org/10.1016/j.compedu.2019.01.017

Barrett, R., & Cox, A. (2005). 'At least they're learning something': The hazy line between collaboration and collusion. *Assessment & Evaluation in Higher Education, 30*(2), 107–122. https://doi.org/10.1080/0260293042000264226

Barton, D. (2007). *Literacy: An introduction to the ecology of written language* (2nd ed.). Blackwell.

Barton, D., Hamilton, M., & Ivanič, R. (2000). *Situated literacies: Reading and writing in context*. Routledge.

Bhabha, H. K. (1994). *The location of culture*. Routledge.

Bourdieu, P. (1984). *Distinction - A social critique of the judgment of taste*. (R. Nice, Trans.) Harvard. (Original work published 1979).

Bourdieu, P. (1986). The forms of capital. In J. G. Richardson (Ed.), *Handbook of theory and research for the sociology of education* (pp. 241–258). Greenwood. (Original work published 1983).

Bourdieu, P., & Wacquant, L. (1992). *An introduction to reflexive practice*. University of Chicago.

Bretag, T., Harper, R., Burton, M., Ellis, C., Newton, P., Rozenberg, P., Saddiqui, S., & van Haeringen, K. (2019a). Contract cheating: A survey of Australian university students. *Studies in Higher Education, 44*(11), 1837–1856. https://doi.org/10.1080/03075079.2018.1462788

Bretag, T., Harper, R., Burton, B., Ellis, C., Newton, P., van Haeringen, K., Saddiqui, S., & Rozenberg, P. (2019b). Contract cheating and assessment design: Exploring the relationship. *Assessment & Evaluation in Higher Education, 44*(5), 676–691. https://doi.org/10.1080/02602938.2018.1527892

Chang, D. H. (2018). Academic dishonesty in a postsecondary multilingual institution. *BC TEAL Journal, 3*(1), 49–62. https://doi.org/10.14288/bctj.v3i1.287

Clarke, R., & Lancaster, T. (2006). *Eliminating the successor to plagiarism? Identifying the usage of contract cheating sites*. [Paper presentation] Second International Plagiarism Conference, Gateshead, UK.

Cutri, J., Abraham, A., Karlina, Y., Patel, S. V., Moharami, M., Zeng, S., Manzari, E., & Pretorius, L. (2021). Academic integrity at doctoral level: The influence of the imposter phenomenon and cultural differences on academic writing. *International Journal for Educational Integrity, 17*(8), 1–16. https://doi.org/10.1007/s40979-021-00074-w

Dawson, P. (2020). *Defending assessment security in a digital world: Preventing e-cheating and supporting academic integrity in higher education.* Routledge.

Eaton, S. E. (2021). *Plagiarism in higher education: Tackling tough topics in academic integrity.* Libraries Unlimited.

Eaton, S. E., & Edino, R. I. (2018). Strengthening the research agenda of educational integrity in Canada: A review of the research literature and call to action. *International Journal for Educational Integrity, 14*(5), 1–21. https://doi.org/10.1007/s40979-018-0028-7

Eaton, S. E., Chibry, N., Toye, M. A., & Rossi, S. (2019). Interinstitutional perspectives on contract cheating: A qualitative narrative exploration from Canada. *International Journal for Educational Integrity, 15*(9), 1–17. https://doi.org/10.1007/s40979-019-0046-0

Ellis, C., Zucker, I. M., & Randall, D. (2018). The infernal business of contract cheating: Understanding the business processes and models of academic custom writing sites. *International Journal for Educational Integrity, 14*(1), 1–21. https://doi.org/10.1007/s40979-017-0024-3

Fernández Ruiz, M. R., Corpas Pastor, G., & Seghiri, M. (2019). Crossing the border between postcolonial reality and the 'outer world': Translation and representation of the third space into a fourth space. *Cultura, Lenguaje y Representación, 21*, 55–70.

Google. (n.d.). *Google docs - About.* https://www.google.ca/docs/about/

Grenfell, N., Bloome, D., Hardy, C., Pahl, K., Rowsell, J., & Street, B. V. (2012). *Language, ethnography, and education.* Routledge.

Gutiérrez, K. D. (2008). Developing a sociocritical literacy in the third space. *Reading Research Quarterly, 43*(2), 148–164. https://doi.org/10.1598/RRQ.43.2.3

Hamilton, M. (2010). Literacy in social context. In N. Hughes & I. Schwab (Eds.), *Teaching adult literacy: Principles and practice* (pp. 7–28). Open University.

Harper, R., Bretag, T., Ellis, C., Newton, P., Rozenberg, P., Saddiqui, S., & van Haeringen, K. (2019). Contract cheating: A survey of Australian university staff. *Studies in Higher Education, 44*(11), 1857–1873. https://doi.org/10.1080/03075079.2018.1462789

Heath, S. B. (1983). *Ways with words.*

Ivanič, R. (1998). *Writing and identity.* John Benjamins.

Kent, S. (2016). Threshold concepts. Taylor Institute for Teaching & Learning - University of Calgary. https://taylorinstitute.ucalgary.ca/sites/default/files/TI%20Guides/Threshold_Concepts_Guide.pdf

Lancaster, T. (2018). Profiling the international academic ghostwriters who are providing low-cost essays and assignments for the contract cheating industry. *Information, Communication and Ethics in Society, 17*(1), 72–86. https://doi.org/10.1108/JICES-04-2018-0040

Lankshear, C., & Knobel, M. (2008). *Digital literacies.* Peter Lang.
Lareau, A., & Weininger, E. B. (2003). Cultural capital in educational research: A critical assessment. *Theory and Society, 32,* 567–606. https://www.jstor.org/stable/3649652
Lea, M., & Street, B. (1998). Student writing in higher education: An academic literacies approach. *Studies in Higher Education, 23*(2), 157–173. https://doi.org/10.1080/03075079812331380364
Lee, S. (2018). Found in translation: How brokering practices support international students' learning. *Teachers and Curriculum, 18*(1), 41–51. https://doi.org/10.15663/tandc.v18i1.325
Macdonald, R., & Carroll, J. (2006). Plagiarism - A complex issue requiring a holistic institutional approach. *Assessment & Evaluation in Higher Education, 31*(2), 233–245. https://doi.org/10.1080/02602930500262536
Mannion, G., Ivanič, R., & LfLFE Research Group. (2007). Mapping literacy practices: Theory, methodology, methods. *International Journal of Qualitative Studies in Education, 20*(1), 15–30. https://doi.org/10.1080/09518390600924063
Meyer, J. H. F., & Land, R. (2003). Threshold concepts and troublesome knowledge: Linkages to ways of thinking and practicing within the disciplines. In C. Rust (Ed.), *Improving student learning: Improving student learning theory and practice.* OCSLD.
Miron, J. B., McKenzie, A., Eaton, S. E., Stoesz, B. M., Thacker, E. J., Devereaux, L., Persaud, N., Steeves, M., & Rowbotham, K. (2021). Academic integrity policy analysis of publicly funded universities in Ontario, Canada: A focus on contract cheating. *Canadian Journal of Educational Administration and Policy, 197,* 62–75. https://journalhosting.ucalgary.ca/index.php/cjeap/article/view/72082
Moje, E. B., Ciechanowski, K. M., Kramer, K., Ellis, L., Carrillo, R., & Collazo, T. (2004). Working toward third space in content area literacy: An examination of everyday funds of knowledge and discourse. *Reading Research Quarterly, 39*(1), 38–70. https://doi.org/10.1598/RRQ.39.1.4
Morris, E. J. (2018). Academic integrity matters: Five considerations for addressing contract cheating. *International Journal for Educational Integrity, 14*(15), 1–12. https://doi.org/10.1007/s40979-018-0038-5
Novak, J., & Gowin, D. (1984). Concept mapping for meaningful learning. In J. Novack & D. Gowin (Eds.), *Learning how to learn* (pp. 15–54).
Park, J., & Fallon, G. (2016). Notions of literacy in the K–12 school system in British Columbia education since 2002: A contested terrain. *Canadian Journal of Educational Administration and Policy, 179,* 1–38. https://journalhosting.ucalgary.ca/index.php/cjeap/article/view/42891
Paxton, M., & Frith, V. (2014). Implications of academic literacies research for knowledge making and curriculum design. *Higher Education, 67,* 171–182. https://doi.org/10.1007/s10734-013-9675-z

Perry, K. (2009). Genres, contexts, and literacy practices: Literacy brokering among Sudanese refugee families. *Reading Research Quarterly, 44*(3), 256–276. https://doi.org/10.1598/RRQ.44.3.2

Quality Assurance Agency for Higher Education (QAA). (2020). *Contracting to cheat in higher education: How to address contract cheating, the use of third-party services and essay mills* (2nd ed.). https://www.qaa.ac.uk/docs/qaa/guidance/contracting-to-cheat-in-higher-education-2nd-edition.pdf

Raslie, H., & Keong, Y. C. (2017). Literacy brokering among the international students of a public university. *Language Studies, 17*(1), 1–19. https://doi.org/10.17576/gema-2017-1701-01

Rogerson, A. (2017). Detecting contract cheating in essay and report submissions: Process, patterns, clues, and conversations. *International Journal for Educational Integrity, 13*(10), 1–17. https://doi.org/10.1007/s40979-017-0021-6

Rojas, V., Straubhaar, J., Roychowdhury, D., & Okur, O. (2003). Communities, cultural capital, and the digital divide. In E. Bucy & J. Newhagen (Eds.), *Media access: Social and psychological dimensions of new technology use* (pp. 107–130). Routledge. https://doi.org/10.4324/9781410609663

Rowland, S., Slade, C., Wong, K., & Whiting, B. (2018). 'Just turn to us': The persuasive features of contract cheating websites. *Assessment & Evaluation in Higher Education, 43*(4), 652–665. https://doi.org/10.1080/17449642.2017.1412178

Rundle, K., Curtis, G. J., & Clare, J. (2019). Why students do not engage in contract cheating. *Frontiers in Psychology, 10*(2229), 1–15. https://doi.org/10.3389/fpsyg.2019.02229

Sivasubramaniam, S., Kostelidou, K., & Ramachandran, S. (2016). A close encounter with ghostwriters: An initial exploration study on background, strategies, and attitudes of independent essay providers. *International Journal for Educational Integrity, 12*(1), 1–14. https://doi.org/10.1007/s40979-016-0007-9

Steel, A. (2017). Contract cheating: Will students pay for serious consequences? *Alternative Law Review, 42*(2), 123–129. 10.1177%2F1037969X17710627

Stoesz, B. M., Eaton, S. E., Miron, J., & Thacker, E. J. (2019). Academic integrity and contract cheating policy analysis of colleges in Ontario, Canada. *International Journal for Educational Integrity, 15*(4). https://doi.org/10.1007/s40979-019-0042-4

Storch, N. (2019). Collaborative writing. *Language Teaching, 52*(1), 40–59. https://doi.org/10.1017/S0261444818000320

Street, B. (1984). *Literacy in theory and practice*.

Thacker, E. J. (2022). *Contract cheating and academic literacies: Exploring the landscape* [Unpublished doctoral thesis]. Keele University.

Valentine, K. (2006). Plagiarism as literacy practice: Recognizing and rethinking ethical binaries. *College Composition and Communication, 58*(1), 89–109. http://www.jstor.org/stable/20456924

Walker, C. (2019). *The white-collar hustle: Academic writing & the Kenyan digital labour economy* [PhD thesis]. University of Oxford. https://ora.ox.ac.uk/objects/uuid:35c57129-11eb-4fad-a91f-65b2f3849b7a

Walker, M., & Townley, C. (2012). Contract cheating: A new challenge for academic honesty? *Academic Ethics, 10*, 27–44. https://doi.org/10.1007/s10805-012-9150-y

Willis, J., Adie, L., & Klenowski, V. (2013). Conceptualising teachers' assessment literacies in an era of curriculum and assessment reform. *Australian Educational Researcher, 40*, 241–256. https://doi.org/10.1007/s13384-013-0089-9

Zheng, S., & Cheng, J. (2015). Academic ghostwriting and international students. *Young Scholars in Writing, 12*, 124–133. https://repository.usfca.edu/rl_stu/1/

CHAPTER 20

Contract Cheating: A Summative Look Back and a Path Forward

Sarah Elaine Eaton, Brenda M. Stoesz, Josh Seeland, Guy J. Curtis, Joseph Clare, and Kiata Rundle

Contract cheating poses a significant threat to the integrity of education at all levels, but particularly higher education. Throughout *Contract Cheating in Higher Education: Global Perspectives on Theory, Practice, and Policy*, authors from around the world have examined various issues related to this specific type of academic misconduct, showing that it is not limited to one postsecondary institution or one country, but instead that contract cheating is a global problem. In this chapter, we draw throughlines to show the

---

S. E. Eaton (✉)
University of Calgary, Calgary, AB, Canada
e-mail: seaton@ucalgary.ca

B. M. Stoesz
University of Manitoba, Winnipeg, MB, Canada
e-mail: Brenda.Stoesz@umanitoba.ca

J. Seeland
Assiniboine Community College, Brandon, MB, Canada
e-mail: seelandjl@Assiniboine.net

© The Author(s), under exclusive license to Springer Nature Switzerland AG 2022
S. E. Eaton et al. (eds.), *Contract Cheating in Higher Education*,
https://doi.org/10.1007/978-3-031-12680-2_20

connections between the various chapters, highlighting major themes and contemplating next steps. This chapter is organised into four sections. First, we summarise key points raised throughout. Second, we highlight recommendations presented by contributors. Then, we acknowledge some limitations of the book, and we contemplate future work for contract cheating researchers, as well as educators, policy-makers, and others involved in understanding or dealing with contract cheating. Finally, we conclude with a clear call for sustained and sustainable plans to promote academic integrity and prevent contract cheating at local, national, and global levels.

Summary of Key Highlights

In this section, we summarise some of the key points raised throughout the book, highlighting the ways in which this book makes an original contribution to the field of academic integrity. We have organised this section under three key themes: (a) what we know about the contract cheating industry; (b) theoretical and research perspectives on contract cheating; and (c) how we can address contract cheating.

What We Know About the Contract Cheating Industry

Three chapters build on what we already know about the contract cheating industry. Eaton et al. (2022) analysed historical accounts written by individual suppliers to the industry. Although the number of sources examined was limited, the authors noted a significant finding consistent across nine decades of accounts written between the 1930s and 2020s: The contract cheating industry exists, in part, because higher education institutions and systems create the conditions that allow the industry to flourish.

G. J. Curtis
School of Psychological Science, University of Western Australia,
Crawley, WA, Australia
e-mail: guy.curtis@uwa.edu.au

J. Clare
School of Law, University of Western Australia, Crawley, WA, Australia
e-mail: joe.clare@uwa.edu.au

K. Rundle
Murdoch University, Murdoch, WA, Australia

Thacker (2022) gathered primary data from independent, freelance suppliers to the industry that showed that a continuum of collaboration between suppliers and students is not uncommon. At the one end of the continuum, students' collaboration with suppliers appears to be an attempt to understand assignment expectations and to be involved in the process of completing the assignment, which Thacker termed "knowledge brokering." Contract cheating falls at the other end of the outsourcing spectrum. Collaborative writing technologies (e.g., Google Docs) enable inappropriate collaboration with contract cheating suppliers.

Parnther (2022) provides insights into contract cheating among graduate students, a student population that has been historically understudied even among academic integrity researchers. Parnther provides evidence of the deceptive online marketing used by the contract cheating industry to target graduate students specifically. Parnther points out that companies that provide contract cheating services to graduate students prey on their desires for academic support and exploit the often-confusing nature of the role of academic advisors.

Theoretical and Research Perspectives on Contract Cheating

Five chapters contribute to theoretical and research perspectives on contract cheating, further strengthening the development of academic integrity as a field of inquiry. In two chapters, Clare and Rundle (2022) and Krásničan et al. (2022) offer critiques of the collection and analysis of self-reported data that have become characteristic of contract cheating research. The authors called for more reliable and robust approaches to contract cheating research that extend beyond self-report methods. In their review of 18 published articles on contract cheating, Krásničan et al. (2022) identified numerous limitations of existing research, including small sample sizes, results from single universities, and a general lack of self-criticality in contract cheating research resulting in no limitations being reported. Clare and Rundle (2022) analysed gaps in current research on the measurement of contract cheating. Clare and Rundle proposed parallels between the measurement of contract cheating and crime, highlighting the ways in which criminologists measure deviance that could be applied to contract cheating. Clare (2022) proposed that research approaches to situational crime prevention (SCP) offer a methodological framework and theoretical underpinnings for research on academic outsourcing, calling for the broadening of the range of interventions (and by extension, research approaches) to contract cheating.

Further contributing to the discussion of theory, Baran and Jonason (2022) and Curtis and Tindall (2022) proposed psychology-based theoretical perspectives on contract cheating, offering possibilities for researchers of contract cheating to be more intentional about the inclusion of theory in future scholarship. Baran and Jonason (2022) explored the theoretical perspective of Dark Triad traits (i.e., narcissism, psychopathy, and Machiavellianism) and the application of this theory to engagement in contract cheating. The authors noted the ways in which contract cheating can be understood as social pathology or pseudopathology. Curtis and Tindall (2022) argued for the use of additional approaches from the field of psychology when researching contract cheating. Specifically, they examined how the theory of planned behaviour (TPB) can provide a framework for understanding what factors, beyond attitudes, are important to consider when predicting contract cheating behaviours.

How We Address Contract Cheating

Chapters in this book demonstrate that multi-pronged approaches are needed to address contract cheating from the classroom, as well as institutional levels. We begin by summarising chapters that address student learning. We then address assessment and identification of possible contract cheating in student work and finally, we summarise key points for institutional level approaches to tackle contract cheating.

There is a throughline between three chapters that propose teaching and learning approaches to contract cheating. We turn first to Stoesz et al. (2022), who discuss the importance of teaching critical thinking skills as one way to promote academic integrity and prevent contract cheating. They argue that underdeveloped critical thinking skills may be one factor that contributes to contract cheating behaviours. Veeran-Colton et al. (2022) demonstrated that financial, academic, and personal factors influence students' choices to engage in contract cheating. Veeran-Colton et al. also posited that raising students' awareness of the risks associated with contract cheating, especially extortion, is important so they can make more informed choices. Then, Lancaster (2022) takes the stance that engaging students as partners is necessary to promote academic integrity. Lancaster presents several ideas for student involvement with an institution's approach to contract cheating, including co-producing research, assessment co-design, events, procedures, and training modules. We then turn our attention to Sutherland-Smith and Dawson (2022). The authors argued that students may be motivated to complete their own work instead of contracting it out if assessments meet students' needs for autonomy, competence, and relatedness.

Other recommendations focus on the detection of contract cheating, such as in specific professional development sessions (Veeran-Colton et al., 2022) or institutional partnerships built upon the academic judgement of faculty (Ellis et al., 2022).

Finally, the administrative level in higher education institutions is the basis of other recommendations, specifically policy built upon a balance of probability model (Crockett, 2022) and quality standards informed by both internal quality monitoring and external auditing measures (Glendinning, 2022). Crockett (2022) showed how information found in multiple levels of student assignments can be used to help identify contract cheating. In a complementary chapter, Ellis et al. (2022) built upon previous work on bibliographic forensics (see Rogerson, 2017) to show how the detection of contract cheating can be improved across an institution.

Two chapters addressed the specific topic of student file-sharing as a behaviour that requires intervention at both classroom and institutional levels. Rogerson (2022) discussed the ongoing confusion around student file-sharing and its probable contribution to incidents of contract cheating. To this end, Rogerson (2022) suggested that institutions openly discuss and clarify what students should be sharing online, how, and with whom. Seeland et al. (2022) framed academic file-sharing as a copyright issue, as well as an academic integrity violation, noting that in countries without legislation that addresses contract cheating specifically, copyright and intellectual property laws may provide a way to address file-sharing from a legal perspective. Seeland et al. (2022) also recommend initiating URL-blocking projects at the institution as another line of defence against contract cheating. Draper (2022) recommends partnering with social media platforms to help combat contract cheating.

Finally, Glendinning (2022) and Lancaster (2022) advocate for institutional academic integrity strategies consisting of fair and consistent policies, where students are partners and all stakeholders receive education on the topic. As their awareness about contract cheating increases, students may feel more empowered to engage in these collaborations with their educational institutions for the betterment of all.

Parnther (2022) and Veeran-Colton et al. (2022) suggested an increase in student awareness related to the many risks associated with engaging in contract cheating. Although this book reveals the abundance of information regarding contract cheating known to those working in higher education institutions around the world, it appears that many students remain unaware of either the existence of or, more commonly, the true nature of this form of academic misconduct.

Combined, these chapters demonstrate that there is no single or "best" way to address contract cheating, rather various and simultaneous approaches are preferred. Although authors may have focused on particular approaches or interventions, none have proposed that their advice excludes or supersedes other perspectives. The chapter authors of this book illustrated that multiple different approaches must be implemented to address contract cheating.

These collective recommendations provide a point of departure to develop institutional or systems-level strategies to take action against contract cheating. One key message to take away from this summary of recommendations is to engage all stakeholders to promote academic integrity and address contract cheating in a variety of ways.

LIMITATIONS AND FUTURE DIRECTIONS

We recognise that although this is the first edited book (to our knowledge) that focuses on contract cheating, the book is not without its limitations. Obviously, the chapters in this book are written in English. We know that contract cheating research is occurring in other languages. As just one example, we acknowledge the work of Rubén Comas Forgas who leads a multi-national group of researchers in the *Red Iberoamericana de Investigación en Integridad Académica* (Iberoamerican Research Network on Academic Integrity), a research network that uses Spanish as their main language of collaboration and investigation. As work on contract cheating and academic integrity continues to develop across the world, it will be important for researchers to transcend geographical and linguistic barriers to further share and mobilise their knowledge. We also recognise the limitation of not having chapters from Asia, Latin America, or Africa.

We acknowledge that this book is focused mostly on higher education contexts, though we know that contract cheating companies also market to children in elementary and secondary school (Better Business Bureau, 2021; Eaton & Dressler, 2019). Children as young as 12 years of age have purchased assignments from contract cheating websites and turned them in for academic credit (Stoesz & Los, 2019). Behaviours practised at a young age become habits that continue through to the high school years and into postsecondary education and/or the workforce. Therefore, it is important to explore at what age, and how, engagement in contract cheating begins in order to determine the most effective way to intervene.

The collection of chapters in this book focuses mainly on the level of students and education institutions, with relatively less focus on the role of teaching staff. As Harper et al. (2019) point out, a large number of university educators are unaware of the scope and methods of the contract cheating industry, and how they can combat these at the level of the classes they teach. Therefore, it is crucial that people teaching at universities receive education and training about academic misconduct generally, and contract cheating specifically.

Finally, we note that although authors who have contributed to this volume have pointed out the need to engage students as partners (Glendinning, 2022; Lancaster, 2022) and some doctoral students or recent graduates have contributed to this book as sole authors or co-authors, we have not included the perspective of students who had used contract cheating services. This remains an area for further exploration and attention.

Drawing from the various chapters across this book, we propose future directions for research, teaching and learning, professional practice, and policy. Educators, professionals, scholars, and others are encouraged to take up and expand upon these ideas in future work on contract cheating:

- Engage students as partners in terms of advocacy and peer education, but also being active partners in research, knowledge mobilisation, and policy-making.
- Take advantage of the multidisciplinary nature of academic integrity by applying methods proven in fields other than education to tackle the complex problem of contract cheating.
- Recognise the value of international cooperation, with an example being the application of QAA and TEQSA works in countries outside of their jurisdictions.
- Build upon the work done on the detection of contract cheating to address the issue institutionally, and in a proactive and educative way.
- Continue to understand the mindset of students and create educational interventions to help prevent contract cheating before it happens.
- Seek opportunities to apply work done on contract cheating specifically to other forms of academic misconduct.

- Pay more attention to contract cheating in elementary and secondary school contexts.
- Be attentive to new advances in technology that continue to shape the educational landscape, such as artificial intelligence, and in particular those that are likely to impact communication, such as Large Language Models (LLMs)/GPT-3.

These recommendations point to the need for large-scale collaborative research to address complexities of contract cheating and other threats to academic integrity.

Call to Action

We conclude with a call to action for more funding and resources to support efforts against contract cheating, at national and even multi-national levels. Although we cannot say for certain what the size of the contract cheating industry is, we have pretty solid indications that this is a global industry that is worth well over US$15 billion (Eaton, 2022). An industry of that size and scope cannot be thwarted by ignoring the problem or simply hoping it will go away. Nor will the efforts of individuals or institutions, however dedicated, be enough. As more than 20 authors from across the world have shown in this book, contract cheating is a global problem. As such, contract cheating requires a global response. We call on educational leaders, politicians, and policy-makers to support efforts against contract cheating in a sustained and sustainable manner.

References

Baran, L., & Jonason, P. K. (2022). Contract cheating and the Dark Triad traits. In S. E. Eaton, G. J. Curtis, B. M. Stoesz, K. Rundle, J. Clare, & J. Seeland (Eds.), *Contract cheating in higher education: Global perspectives on theory, practice, and policy*. Palgrave Macmillan.

Better Business Bureau. (2021, April 2). *BBB Scam Alert: Cheating on homework leads to extortion scam*. Retrieved from https://www.bbb.org/article/news-releases/24032-bbb-scam-alert-students-hire-homework-help-and-end-up-in-extortion-con.

Clare, J. (2022). Applying situational crime prevention techniques to contract cheating. In S. E. Eaton, G. J. Curtis, B. M. Stoesz, K. Rundle, J. Clare, & J. Seeland (Eds.), *Contract cheating in higher education: Global perspectives on theory, practice, and policy*. Palgrave Macmillan.

Clare, J., & Rundle, K. (2022). What can we learn from measuring crime when looking to quantify the prevalence and incidence of contract cheating? In S. E. Eaton, G. J. Curtis, B. M. Stoesz, K. Rundle, J. Clare, & J. Seeland (Eds.), *Contract cheating in higher education: Global perspectives on theory, practice, and policy*. Palgrave Macmillan.

Crockett, R. (2022). Presentation, properties and provenance: The three Ps of identifying evidence of contract-cheating in student assignments. In S. E. Eaton, G. J. Curtis, B. M. Stoesz, K. Rundle, J. Clare, & J. Seeland (Eds.), *Contract cheating in higher education: Global perspectives on theory, practice, and policy*. Palgrave Macmillan.

Curtis, G. J., & Tindall, I. K. (2022). Contract cheating: The influence of attitudes and emotions. In S. E. Eaton, G. J. Curtis, B. M. Stoesz, K. Rundle, J. Clare, & J. Seeland (Eds.), *Contract cheating in higher education: Global perspectives on theory, practice, and policy*. Palgrave Macmillan.

Draper, M. (2022). Essay mills and contract cheating from a legal point of view. In S. E. Eaton, G. J. Curtis, B. M. Stoesz, K. Rundle, J. Clare, & J. Seeland (Eds.), *Contract cheating in higher education: Global perspectives on theory, practice, and policy*. Palgrave Macmillan.

Eaton, S. E. (2022). Contract cheating in Canada: A comprehensive overview. In S. E. Eaton & J. Christensen Hughes (Eds.), *Academic integrity in Canada: An enduring and essential challenge* (pp. 165–187). Springer.

Eaton, S. E., & Dressler, R. (2019). Multilingual essay mills: Implications for second language teaching and learning. *Notos, 14*(2), 4–14. Retrieved from http://hdl.handle.net/1880/110695

Eaton, S. E., Stoesz, B. M., & Seeland, J. (2022). Listening to ghosts: A qualitative study of narratives from contract cheating writers from the 1930s onwards. In S. E. Eaton, G. J. Curtis, B. M. Stoesz, K. Rundle, J. Clare, & J. Seeland (Eds.), *Contract cheating in higher education: Global perspectives on theory, practice, and policy*. Palgrave Macmillan.

Ellis, C., Rogerson, A. M., House, D., & Murdoch, K. (2022). "(Im)possible to prove": Formalising academic judgement evidence in contract cheating cases using bibliographic forensics. In S. E. Eaton, G. J. Curtis, B. M. Stoesz, K. Rundle, J. Clare, & J. Seeland (Eds.), *Contract cheating in higher education: Global perspectives on theory, practice, and policy*. Palgrave Macmillan.

Glendinning, I. (2022). Aligning academic quality and standards with academic integrity. In S. E. Eaton, G. J. Curtis, B. M. Stoesz, K. Rundle, J. Clare, & J. Seeland (Eds.), *Contract cheating in higher education: Global perspectives on theory, practice, and policy*. Palgrave Macmillan.

Harper, R., Bretag, T., Ellis, C., Newton, P., Rozenberg, P., Saddiqui, S., & van Haeringen, K. (2019). Contract cheating: A survey of Australian university staff. *Studies in Higher Education, 44*(11), 1857–1873. https://doi.org/10.1080/03075079.2018.1462789

Krásničan, V., Foltýnek, T., & Dlabolová, D. H. (2022). Limitations of contract cheating research. In S. E. Eaton, G. J. Curtis, B. M. Stoesz, K. Rundle, J. Clare, & J. Seeland (Eds.), *Contract cheating in higher education: Global perspectives on theory, practice, and policy*. Palgrave Macmillan.

Lancaster, T. (2022). Addressing contract cheating through staff-student partnerships. In S. E. Eaton, G. J. Curtis, B. M. Stoesz, K. Rundle, J. Clare, & J. Seeland (Eds.), *Contract cheating in higher education: Global perspectives on theory, practice, and policy*. Palgrave Macmillan.

Parnther, C. (2022). The rise of contract cheating in graduate education. In S. E. Eaton, G. J. Curtis, B. M. Stoesz, K. Rundle, J. Clare, & J. Seeland (Eds.), *Contract cheating in higher education: Global perspectives on theory, practice, and policy*. Palgrave Macmillan.

Rogerson, A. M. (2017). Detecting contract cheating in essay and report submissions: Process, patterns, clues, and conversations. *International Journal for Educational Integrity, 13*(10).

Rogerson, A. M. (2022). The encouragement of file sharing behaviours through technology and social media: Impacts on student cheating behaviours and academic piracy. In S. E. Eaton, G. J. Curtis, B. M. Stoesz, K. Rundle, J. Clare, & J. Seeland (Eds.), *Contract cheating in higher education: Global perspectives on theory, practice, and policy*.

Seeland, J., Eaton, S. E., & Stoesz, B. M. (2022). Leveraging college copyright ownership against file-sharing and contract cheating websites. In S. E. Eaton, G. J. Curtis, B. M. Stoesz, K. Rundle, J. Clare, & J. Seeland (Eds.), *Contract cheating in higher education: Global perspectives on theory, practice, and policy*. Palgrave Macmillan.

Stoesz, B. M., & Los, R. (2019). Evaluation of a tutorial designed to promote academic integrity. *Canadian Perspectives on Academic Integrity, 2*(1), 3–26. https://doi.org/10.11575/cpai.v2i1

Stoesz, B. M., Eaton, S. E., & Seeland, J. (2022). Critical thinking as an antidote to contract cheating. In S. E. Eaton, G. J. Curtis, B. M. Stoesz, K. Rundle, J. Clare, & J. Seeland (Eds.), *Contract cheating in higher education: Global perspectives on theory, practice, and policy*. Palgrave Macmillan.

Sutherland-Smith, W., & Dawson, P. (2022). Higher education assessment design. In S. E. Eaton, G. J. Curtis, B. M. Stoesz, K. Rundle, J. Clare, & J. Seeland (Eds.), *Contract cheating in higher education: Global perspectives on theory, practice, and policy*. Palgrave Macmillan.

Thacker, E. J. (2022). Collaboration and collusion between ghostwriters and students. In S. E. Eaton, G. J. Curtis, B. M. Stoesz, K. Rundle, J. Clare, & J. Seeland (Eds.), *Contract cheating in higher education: Global perspectives on theory, practice, and policy*. Palgrave Macmillan.

Veeran-Colton, T., Sefcik, L., & Yorke, J. (2022). The extortionate cost of contract cheating. In S. E. Eaton, G. J. Curtis, B. M. Stoesz, K. Rundle, J. Clare, & J. Seeland (Eds.), *Contract cheating in higher education: Global perspectives on theory, practice, and policy*. Palgrave Macmillan.

Index[1]

A

Academic integrity, vii, viii, 4, 7, 9, 15, 29, 30, 38, 49, 62–73, 78–82, 84, 85, 110, 112, 114, 148, 149, 153, 157, 186, 187, 196, 199–216, 219–222, 225–229, 233, 240, 242–244, 259, 261, 263, 265, 267, 273, 287, 288, 296, 297, 304–310

Academic judgement, 185–197, 212, 307

Academic misconduct, 9, 16, 45, 62–67, 70–73, 85, 109, 112, 115, 126, 139–142, 144–146, 148, 154, 157, 159, 160, 165, 188, 195, 210, 212–214, 216, 219–222, 229, 239, 243, 251, 254, 255, 264, 267, 274, 280, 281, 287, 288, 291, 295, 297, 303, 308, 309

Accreditation, 96, 200, 201, 205

Advertising, 46, 49, 54, 68, 82, 241, 255, 256, 280
See also Marketing

Africa, 282

Andragogy, 253, 264

Anxiety, 100, 111, 113, 126, 145, 147, 237, 239, 253, 257

Artificial intelligence, 170, 174, 310

Asia, 282

Assessment, 1, 3–6, 8, 17, 20, 25, 31, 44, 45, 52, 53, 62, 65, 66, 69, 70, 77–79, 82, 83, 85, 91–103, 108, 111, 128, 143, 147, 149, 154, 159, 160, 165, 169, 170, 182, 186, 188, 189, 196, 200, 201, 206, 213, 215, 219, 222, 224, 227, 234, 237, 240, 241, 243, 244, 251, 266, 268, 281, 283, 287–297, 306, 307

co-design with students, 224

---

[1] Note: Page numbers followed by 'n' refer to notes.

© The Author(s), under exclusive license to Springer Nature Switzerland AG 2022
S. E. Eaton et al. (eds.), *Contract Cheating in Higher Education*,
https://doi.org/10.1007/978-3-031-12680-2

314   INDEX

Australia, viii, ix, 2, 19, 21, 48–57, 55n3, 201, 203, 204, 207, 208, 241
Awareness, 4, 68, 84, 85, 114, 171, 181, 220, 226–228, 242–244, 306, 307

B
Balance of probability, 196
Bayesian Truth Serum, 17
Bias, 34, 35, 38, 272
Bibliographic forensics, 185–197
Blackmail, 2, 19
  See also Extortion
Bologna Process, 203
Bourdieu, P., 290, 295
Bretag, T., 2–8, 16–18, 30, 31, 37, 62–66, 72, 73, 77–79, 92, 93, 97, 114, 128, 146, 154, 160, 171, 185, 204, 208, 210, 219, 220, 223, 233, 238, 242, 243, 288, 289, 295
Bulgaria, 202, 203, 264
Business, 2, 7, 9, 19, 48, 71, 128, 159, 169, 170, 234, 251, 252, 264, 273, 277, 279, 288, 291

C
Canada, viii, 67, 68, 276, 288, 289, 291, 297
Chatbot, 259, 264
Cheating, vii–ix, 1–10, 15–21, 24–25, 29–39, 43–57, 77–86, 91–100, 102, 103, 107–115, 123–132, 139–149, 153–165, 169–182, 185–197, 199, 200, 203, 204, 206, 208–214, 219–230, 233–244, 251–253, 255–268, 271–283, 287–291, 295–297, 303–310

Chegg, 223
  See also File sharing
Clarke, R., 182
Class, 2, 4, 72, 82, 94, 98, 100, 123, 124, 130, 196, 213, 226, 227, 280, 281, 309
Colleges, 1, 61–73, 99, 140, 199, 200, 210, 265
Collusion, 62, 64, 67, 73, 78, 81, 85, 157, 171, 291
Consequences, 2, 7, 8, 66, 72, 83, 111, 124, 127, 142, 155, 170, 210, 233–242, 244, 262, 264, 265, 267
Copyright, 8, 61–73, 78, 80, 82, 83, 85, 112, 263, 307
Corruption, 200–204, 206, 207, 211, 216, 272
COVID-19, vii, ix, 23, 25, 63, 79–81, 91, 107, 108, 115, 156, 226, 228, 281, 282
Crime, 2, 9, 15–25, 44, 45, 53, 69, 125, 153–165, 242, 272, 305
  criminal justice, 21
  criminal liability, 44
Criminology, 7, 15, 21, 24, 93
Critical thinking, 8, 66, 107–115, 306
Cultural capital, *see* Bourdieu, P.
Customer service, 253, 254, 259–261, 264
Cyprus, 202, 264
Czech Republic, 202, 203

D
Dark Triad, 123–132, 306
Detection, 4, 15, 19, 24, 25, 65, 67, 69, 94, 123, 125, 153–160, 162, 186, 187, 212, 216, 219, 243, 244, 288, 289, 307, 309
Deviance, 21

Digital, 61–63, 70, 81, 82, 86, 91, 254, 289–292, 296, 297
Digital Millennium Copyright Act (DMCA), 68, 70, 83
Discrimination, *see* Bias
Dissertation, 3, 214, 252–267
Diversity, 252, 253, 272

E
Economic, 29, 115, 130, 252, 292, 295
Economic capital, *see* Bourdieu, P.
EduBirdie, 2
England, *see* United Kingdom (UK)
English, 18, 20, 32, 39, 169, 173, 174, 204, 206, 214, 261, 277, 281, 282, 308
Essay, 2, 6, 20, 44, 49, 92, 94, 126, 161, 172, 174, 241, 257, 261, 262, 277–280, 290–292, 294, 295
Essay mill, 43–57, 62, 156, 169, 200, 204, 207, 210, 211, 223, 252
Ethics, 8, 64, 66, 214, 222, 275
Europe, 48, 49, 57, 202, 203
Exam, 1, 3, 5, 16, 29, 34, 54, 62, 69, 72, 93, 94, 97, 125, 126, 128, 129, 143, 157, 200, 234
Examinations, 2, 3, 5, 17, 19, 30, 33, 44, 69, 72, 83, 93, 94, 96, 102, 128, 132, 140–144, 148, 157, 159, 162, 170, 171, 187, 213–215, 240, 241
Exploitation, 83, 125, 279
Expulsion, *see* Consequences
EXtensible Markup Language (XML), 177, 179
Extortion, 240–242
See also Blackmail

F
Fabrication, 195
File sharing, viii, 8, 18, 61–73, 77–79, 82, 83, 85, 108, 113, 223, 225, 307
Fiverr.com, 273
France, 202
Fraud, 25, 44, 46, 56, 57, 202, 204, 242, 263, 267
See also Crime

G
Gender, 35, 38, 276
Ghostwriter, 6, 9, 273, 274, 287–297
Google, 253, 291, 305
Government, 48, 50, 54, 55, 68, 69, 108, 203–205
Grades, 2, 19, 20, 65, 71, 93–95, 97, 98, 100, 101, 111, 126, 128–130, 140, 157, 175, 211, 213, 234, 237, 240, 242, 263, 265, 267
Graduate education, 251–268, 305
Guilt, 80, 81, 127, 128, 148, 237

H
Harper, R., 3, 25, 73, 94, 185–187, 233, 243, 252, 295, 309
Help-seeking, 80–81
Higher education (HE), vii, 1, 3, 4, 6–9, 32, 35, 45, 48–50, 53–56, 64–66, 68, 73, 78, 84, 94, 124, 145, 200–209, 214, 215, 220, 233, 238, 252, 272, 279, 281, 287, 288, 290, 303, 304, 307, 308
massification of, 3
precarious employment, 4
Honour code, 123, 263

I

Identity theft, 267
Impulsivity, 124, 125
India, 205, 276, 291
Intellectual property, 63, 67, 78, 82–84, 86, 264, 266, 307
Internet, 5, 30, 53, 54, 56, 61, 63, 70, 78, 81–83, 180, 223, 282
Ireland, 47–49, 53, 56, 204
Italy, 202, 203

K

Kenya, 272, 273, 276, 279, 291

L

Law, 7, 8, 21, 31, 44–48, 50, 52, 53, 56, 63, 65, 69–73, 82, 108, 129, 239, 261, 307
Learning, 3, 45, 62–64, 66, 73, 79–81, 83, 91, 94–102, 107–115, 127, 130, 147, 161, 172, 173, 188, 189, 199, 210, 213, 215, 219, 220, 223–225, 237, 239–240, 243, 255, 260, 266, 281, 283, 290, 292, 293, 295, 297, 306, 309
Lecture, 77, 81, 83, 112, 226
Legislation, viii, 21, 45, 47–57, 55n3, 69, 84, 204, 307
Library, 252
Loophole, 280

M

Machiavellianism, 8, 124–131, 306
Malaysia, 264
Malta, 202, 203
Marketing, 49, 62, 66, 79, 170, 252, 254, 256, 261, 267, 305
McCabe, D. L., 30, 204

Metadata, 175–177, 179, 180
Modules, educational, 72
Moral disengagement, *see* Morality
Morality, 125, 127, 128, 130
Motivation, 71, 80, 94–103, 108, 129–131, 156, 157, 160, 255, 259, 262, 277, 282, 288, 290, 292, 295, 297
MyMaster, 19, 50, 238

N

Napster, 61, 62
Narcissism, 8, 124–126, 128–131, 306
Narrative, 9, 66, 259, 271–283
New Zealand, 47, 53

O

Online, 5, 19, 23, 31, 32, 52–54, 57, 61–63, 66, 83, 91–93, 108, 109, 112, 113, 126, 128, 156, 159, 162, 169, 174, 180–181, 222, 226–228, 234, 241, 255, 265, 297, 305, 307

P

Pakistan, 264, 273
Paper mills, 6
Paraphrasing, 82, 84
Parents, 35
Pathology, 131
Pedagogy, 110–115
Personality, 8, 9, 124, 125, 129, 131, 157
Philippines, 264
Piracy, 62–65, 68, 77–86
Plagiarism, 4, 6, 48, 65, 67, 68, 77, 126, 140, 144, 146, 148, 157, 172, 200, 221, 226, 238, 255, 260–262

Policy, 9, 21, 25, 53, 63, 65, 67, 69, 71, 72, 81, 84, 98, 108, 155, 201–203, 205–216, 227, 229, 242, 260, 262, 263, 267, 288, 289, 304, 307, 309
Portugal, 202
Pressure, 22, 95, 101, 102, 234, 237, 242, 260, 281, 296
Prevalence, 7, 8, 15–25, 48, 252
Privacy, 78, 263
Procedures, 65, 84, 113, 188, 205, 211–215, 228–229, 306
Proof, 25, 46, 181, 196
Provenance, 169–182
Pseudonym, 271, 275–276
Pseudopathology, 130–132, 306
Psychology, 7, 124, 140, 145, 148, 306
Psychopathy, 8, 124–131, 306

Q
Quality assurance (QA), 9, 48, 54, 65, 200–202, 205–209, 216, 228, 244
Quality Assurance Agency (QAA), 54–57, 55n3, 65, 66, 108, 181, 202, 206–209, 211–213, 215, 288, 309

R
Racism, *see* Discrimination
Rational choice, 155
Referencing, 4, 68, 174, 189, 195, 221, 226–227, 264, 294, 296
Reputation, 2, 45, 48–50, 170, 199, 203, 223, 237–239, 244, 267
Russia, 252

S
Scandal, *see* MyMaster
Sci-Hub, 68
Self-Determination Theory (SDT), 8, 94–96, 98–103
Self-reporting, 16, 17, 29, 31, 32, 36, 37
Sex trade, 277, 278
Sharing, 8, 16, 17, 25, 34, 48, 62, 63, 72, 77–86, 259, 276, 279, 307
Situational crime prevention (SCP), 9, 153–165, 305
Social capital, *see* Bourdieu, P.
Social media, 8, 18, 23, 49, 56, 77–86, 180, 220, 227, 228, 243, 259, 266, 289, 307
  Discord, 256
  Facebook, 2, 23, 256, 264, 272
  Instagram, 85
  Reddit, 256
  Snapchat, 85
  TikTok, 256
  Twitter, 18, 23, 80
  WhatsApp, 85
Social norms, 62, 127, 143
Society, 23, 78, 81, 107, 108, 112, 115, 222
Spain, 202
STEM, 197, 273
Stress, 91, 109, 110, 115, 145, 149, 156, 157, 239, 240, 242, 244, 253, 258
Students, viii, 1, 16, 29, 44, 62, 77, 91, 107, 124, 139, 154, 169, 185, 199, 219, 220, 233, 251, 272, 287, 305
  partnerships with, 220, 221, 227, 229
Student services, *see* Student support
Student support, 252
Survey, 18, 19, 22–25, 30, 34, 35, 38, 142

T

Tertiary Education Quality and Standards Agency (TEQSA), 50, 53, 54, 56, 66, 108, 181, 203, 204, 206, 207, 209, 212, 238, 240–242, 309
Test, *see* Examinations
Text-matching, 4, 67, 108, 126, 159, 234, 288
Theory, 255
Theory of planned behaviour (TPB), 143–145, 148, 149, 306
  See also Theory
Thesis, 252–254, 256, 260–263, 265, 266
  See also Dissertation
Third Space, 290
Training, 47n2, 48, 49, 210–212, 214, 215, 261, 306, 309
Triangulation, 21, 24–25
Turnitin, 182
Tutoring, 221, 255, 256

U

Ukraine, 202

United Kingdom (UK), 21, 43–46, 48, 54–57, 55n3, 65, 73, 206, 207, 220, 221, 225, 226, 263
United States of America (USA), 1, 21, 68, 73, 201, 204–205, 240, 263, 273, 276
Universities, 2, 7, 18, 19, 37, 54, 56, 62–64, 68, 69, 73, 84, 96, 107, 110, 157, 199, 200, 204, 205, 207, 210, 226, 229, 234, 235, 237–240, 242, 244, 251, 258, 263, 267, 275, 277, 281, 305, 309

V

Virtual Learning Environment (VLE), 175
Viva, 3, 92, 93
Viva voce, *see* Examinations

W

Whistle blowing, 161, 163

Y

YouTube, 2